# Information Communication Technologies and Globalization of Retailing Applications

Rajagopal
*Monterrey Institute of Technology and Higher Education, ITESM, Mexico*

Information Science REFERENCE

**INFORMATION SCIENCE REFERENCE**
Hershey · New York

Director of Editorial Content: Kristin Klinger
Senior Managing Editor: Jamie Snavely
Managing Editor: Jeff Ash
Assistant Managing Editor: Carole Coulson
Typesetter: Carole Coulson
Cover Design: Lisa Tosheff
Printed at: Yurchak Printing Inc.

Published in the United States of America by
Information Science Reference (an imprint of IGI Global)
701 E. Chocolate Avenue, Suite 200
Hershey PA 17033
Tel: 717-533-8845
Fax: 717-533-8661
E-mail: cust@igi-global.com
Web site: http://www.igi-global.com/reference

and in the United Kingdom by
Information Science Reference (an imprint of IGI Global)
3 Henrietta Street
Covent Garden
London WC2E 8LU
Tel: 44 20 7240 0856
Fax: 44 20 7379 0609
Web site: http://www.eurospanbookstore.com



Library of Congress Cataloging-in-Publication Data

Information communication technologies and globalization of retailing applications / Rajagopal, editor.

p. cm.

Includes bibliographical references and index.

Summary: "This book critically examines the synergy of technology use and conventional wisdom in retailing and explores contemporary changes determining higher customer value,"--Provided by publisher. ISBN 978-1-60566-248-0 (hardcover) -- ISBN 978-1-60566-249-7 (ebook) 1. Retail trade. 2. Information technology. 3. Marketing. I. Rajagopal, 1957- HF5429.I516 2009

658.8'7--dc22

2008043769

British Cataloguing in Publication Data
A Cataloguing in Publication record for this book is available from the British Library.

# Table of Contents

# Foreword

Globalization has shown significant impact on consumption and technology applications among all levels of consumers. The bottom of the pyramid market segment which is constituted by a large number of small consumers has become the principal target of most of the consumer brands emerging from multinational firms. Large retailing firms penetrated into the bottom line markets using advanced technologies in inventory management, transportation, customer services, on-line buying and through multi-channel retailing. As the use of technology is increasing among retailers, consumer's choices significantly widen to shop among brick-and-mortar stores, catalogues, and e-retailers. Young retailing firms thrive in the global marketplace through a creative use of their resources, people, technologies, brands, suppliers, and effective strategies[1].

There are remarkable changes incorporated into retailing practices in the recent past with the increase of Internet usage among urban and semi-urban shoppers. The prominence of retailing technology is observed with the rise of non-store retailing in reference to direct marketing, catalogues, telephone and the Internet as some of the convenient channels for consumers as well as for the retailers to sell the goods[2]. Retailing firms are giving increasing importance to shifting consumer habits through ingenious market research methods and then using creative communication and sales induction strategies. In this hypercompetitive markets, retailing firms are developing strategies to move into the provision of innovative combinations of products and services as *high-technology integrated solutions* tailored to each customer's needs[3]. Though information and internet based technologies have also promoted new supply chain initiatives in the retailing industry, management research is still to go a long way to conceptualize new strategies and evaluate performance and efficiency impacts of technology on retailing operations.

There is a new retailing concept emerging fast in the multinational firms which is expressed as *rocket science retailing*, a blend of conventional and information and communication technology (ICT) based forecasting systems[4]. This concept is largely based on the strength of the operational efficiency in retailing with the prowess of information technology. Similarly, radio frequency identification (RFID) technologies that use radio waves to automatically identify individual items that carry such identification tags are also being increasingly used by large retailers. As the cost of this new technology falls, the rate of adoption of RFID technology will be significant in the future by the retailing firms[5]. This book addresses the rocket model and RFID applications in retailing and contextualizes these concepts in building customer value. Arguments made by authors in the book critically examine the role of technology in reshaping the conventional wisdom in retailing and delivering value to the customers and identify diverse managerial implications of this stream of innovative ideas.

In this book Dr. Rajagopal and other authors have delineated applied arguments for managers to capitalize on the advantage in retailing through the application of ICT and bridging the customer-technology gap. The *up shot* of the book emerges in redefining the role of technology led retailing strategy frameworks and building synergy towards high performance of retailing firms. The authors develop taxonomy of strategy for integrating technology in the retailing operations which includes communication technology, information systems and diagnostic technologies used in logistics management. They argue that convergence of retailing operations with technology applications is required to enhance not only the business performance of the retailing firms but also to augment the customer value in the competitive marketplace.

In this edited book Dr. Rajagopal has adequately addressed the complex issues of technology and retailing efficiency in the contemporary context. I find a right balance of conceptual and empirical investigation based discussions in the book that determine the pedagogic construct of the book. Dr. Rajagopal must be congratulated for his efforts of bringing two distinct disciplines of technology and retailing under one applied framework and bringing out prolific managerial inputs. I am confident that the contributions made in this volume will serve as a think tank for strategists and researchers to nurture new thoughts towards future research in the area of technological retailing. I hope this book will also be useful to industrial engineers, business managers and students pursuing their studies in the business stream.

*Dr. Luis Herrera Y Marquez*
*Associate Dean*
*Graduate School of Leadership and Management (EGADE)*
*Monterrey Institute of Technology and Higher Education (ITESM)*
*Mexico City Campus, Mexico*

## ENDNOTES


1. Christensen, C. M. & Overdorf, M. (2000). Meeting the challenge of disruptive Change, Harvard Business Review, 78 (2), 66-76.
2. Crittenden, V. L. & Wilson, E. J. (2002). Success factors in non-store retailing: Exploring the great merchants framework, J*ournal of Strategic Marketing, 10*(4), 255 - 272.
3. Rajagopal (2008). Outsourcing salespeople in building arousal towards retail buying. *Journal of Database Marketing and Customer Strategy Management, 15*(2), 106-118.
4. Fisher, Ml. L., Raman, A. & McClelland, A. (2000). Rocket science retailing is almost here: Are you ready? *Harvard Business Review, 78*(4), 115-124.
5. Jones, P., Clarke-Hill, C., Shears, P., Comfort, D., & Hillier, D. (2005). Radio frequency identification in the UK: Opportunities and challenges. *International Journal of Retail & Distribution Management, 32*(3), 164-171.


*__Luis Herrera Y Marquiz__ holds a Bachelor's degree in chemical engineering and obtained his graduate and Doctorate degree in business administration. Dr. Herrera's executive career spanned 15 years during which he held managerial and directive positions in marketing, sales and strategic planning at Coleman de Mexico, Richardson Merrell, Union Carbide and Fabricas de Papel San Rafael, acting afterwards as a General Director in MYRSA, Belco Mexicana and Litografica Cultural, all located in Mexico. Dr.Herrera became an independent consultant in 1993 providing advice in marketing, sales, service quality, strategic planning and reengineering to companies like Wal-Mart, IBM, BBVABancomer, Nestle, Cadbury Schweppes, Cadbury Adams, Frito Lay, Chanel de Mexico, Hasbro de Mexico, Bertelsmann Mexico, Baiersdorf Mexico, DHL Internacional, ICI de Mexico, Pepsico Food System, Institute of Management Resources, Anixter, Janssen Cilag, Schering Plough, Grupo Lala, AstraZeneca, Bayer de Mexico, Sterigenics, Equan, Grace Packaging, Checkpoint de Mexico, Goodyear and Grupo Ilusion, among others. He is currently a member of several boards. Dr. Herrera is serving as Associate Dean in the Mexico City Campus of the Graduate School of Business Administration and Leadership (EGADE) at the Monterrey Institute of Technology and Higher Education (ITESM) with effect from January 2008, where he has been a professor uninterruptedly since 1977. Dr. Herrera is engaged in teaching courses mainly in the marketing field, but also related to strategy, reengineering and business management, and along this period Dr. Herrera has participated intensely in executive training programs in his areas of expertise. He has received several recognitions for his teaching performance both in the graduate and the executive training programs.*

# Preface

Globalization has pushed the use of technology as a necessity in various business and economic functions. Advancing Information and Communication Technology (ICT) has become a key factor in the future development of **services** industry including **banking, transport, logistics, and retailing industries**. Technology applications have significantly contributed to the exponential growth and profits of the retailing institutions worldwide. This evolution had transformed the way retailing firms deliver their services, using technologies such as self service terminals and automated dispensing machines, mobile-marketing, virtual shops, credit card services, point of sales terminals, logistics management using radio frequency identification technology and delivering electronic cash. Whenever a major technology innovation is diffused, a wave of new firms enters the market implementing the innovation for profits and retailing sector has emerged as one of the major hubs of Internet technology.

The technology transfer to retailing industries prompted in mid 70's in developed countries and expanded to developing countries in 90's and has been capitalized by the large retailing companies. Gradually, previous retailing transformations have unfolded to shed light on how retailing may evolve in the Internet era. Application of information and communication technologies in large retail networks spread across countries has established direct relationship with customers and succeeded to the retailing philosophy of "disintermediation," in which service providing company bypasses agents or promoters and connect directly with their customers. New in-store technologies promise managers and customers increased efficiency and more knowledgeable service. However, the performance of retailing technology depends on various organizational factors. Many retailing firms have built websites to disseminate information and attract customers. Financial aggregation presents an opportunity by which they can build stronger relationships with customers. Information technology affects retailing in reducing the costs by replacing physical and paper-based process for buying goods and services and helps to modify the ways in which consumers have access to retail products and services which enhances the contestability of retail firms in the market.

Technology applications in retailing are a recent phenomenon and not many contributions have been made in context to consumer products and services. Along with the internet bubble burst, the technology industry was left facing a host of unrealized opportunities, from e-commerce, retailing, mobile commerce and direct marketing. A large number of customers use the Internet, as a medium of business (electronic-commerce). Self service technologies like automatic vending machines for consumer goods, loyalty cards launched by the retailers, convergence of electronic ordering and physical delivery of goods and services to destination customers, e-banking, mobile shopping and virtual promotions in retailing sector have the ability to function as a secured business medium. Self service technologies offer customers six distinguished benefits to shop goods and services on Internet including perceived convenience and financial benefits, low risk, access to information, self-efficacy, and time management, which play a significant role in the performance of retail operations. Advances in technologies have allowed retailing firms to incorporate many different technologies into the delivery of their services. These technologies have been implemented in the services sector to encourage customers to acquire satisfaction at different levels of buying process.

In the process of enhancing the customer value for the new products, a retailing firm may simultaneously use intensive customer value for technology based retail services and intensive customer relationship management (CRM) strategies to the competitive sales and marketing strategies. The integrated impact of CRM, sales and marketing strategies at different stages of service attractiveness would contribute to the customer value and influence the aggregate returns on the customer value derived at various stages of service attractiveness of the retailing firms. However, a financial institution may need to compute the trend of customer value for all the services in its product line, and measure the variability in the customer values perceived for its new services. The customer values are broadly reflected in the competitive gains, perceived values, and extent of association with the retailing services and level of quintessence with the customer relationship management services of the organization.

Principal thrust of this book is on analyzing the role of ICT in retailing industry in increasing functional performance, customer value and optimizing profit. Retailing technology has emerged as an efficient tool to measure accuracy in forecasting, sales data analysis, and preventing stock outs that will help retailers to determine when to tweak their supply chain processes to get the right products to stores at just the right time. An intriguing map of technology drivers, performance of retailing companies and consumer has been discussed in this book which opens a new window on competitive edge endorsed by proven research studies published by the author in refereed international journals. The discussions in the book critically examine the synergy of technology use and conventional wisdom in retailing and explore contemporary changes determining higher customer value. Discussions in this book also encompass strategy implications for managers to optimize the advantage in retailing through the application of ICT and bridging customer-technology gap. The bottom line of the book is to redefine technology led retailing strategy frameworks and building sustainable customer value for mutual (customer-company) success. Whether it is a physical store, a catalog business, an E-commerce site, or a combination of the three, customers need superior solutions to their needs and ICT retailing connects with them on an emotional level. The complex interplay between consumer and application of self service technology in retailing services determines the success of every product in the competitive environment.

This book carries 15 distinguished chapters contributed by core academics across countries. Discussions in the chapters are based on empirical and conceptual research on the broad theme of convergence of technology and retailing activities. Rajagopal presents a general discussion about contemporary developments in retailing with reference to globalization and technology in **Chapter I**. The growing internationalization of business induces changes in the positioning of competitors and technology led competitive strategies by augmenting customer value. The discussion in the chapter argues that there has been a growing recognition that it is through an effective management of the technology the cost of retailing can be reduced as well as retailing services can be enhanced. Rajagopal and Ananya Rajagopal have emphasized the role of self service technologies in retail banking services in **Chapter II**. The discussion draws conceptual impetus from new technologies in banking services through self service technologies in banking as a tool for optimizing profit **and** analyzes the criteria for successful internet-banking strategy to derive benefits of e-**banking** for banks and their customers.

Customer value and new product retailing dynamics has been discussed in **Chapter III** by Rajagopal, in reference to maximizing total customer value and customer satisfaction which are inter-dependent in the decision making process towards buying new products. This chapter, as a part of emerging literature on customer value management, extends the existing knowledge of the relationship between launch of new products in the market and creating customer value by introducing the framework of a mathematical model. Enrique Portillo along with Rajagopal further carries the discussion on self services technologies and customer value together with focus on measuring customer attitude in **Chapter IV** through a comprehensive empirical research. They argue that customers have more options of buying today and are looking for convenient relationships. Hence self service technologies should be responsive, customer friendly and followed by personal care to the customers. Authors of this chapter suggest that we must think about the importance of the pillars of techno readiness including managerial vision, infrastructure for error free service and testing technology led retailing services.

Variability factors in customer values, technology convergence and profit optimization in a retailing firm has been measured using structural equations by Rajagopal in **Chapter V**. Discussions in the chapter are woven around the framework for measuring the consumer values in reference to establishing the long run relationship by the firm and optimizing its profit levels and arguments endure the core issues of consumer values in retailing the products and services as how to conceptualize consumer values, how to measure it, and how to manage it. Ankush Sharma and Preeta Vyas argue in **Chapter VI** that retailing is in a rapid state of change due to speedy technological developments, changing competitive positions, varying consumer behavior as well as their expectations and liberalized regulatory environment. This chapter discusses the role of Decision Support System (DSS) in managing performance, data and modeling decision in retailing firms. The proposed study aims at understanding DSS, its application in grocery sector and issues arising out of implementation of DSS in Indian retail grocery sector. Dynamics of buyer-supplier co-dependency in optimizing functional efficiency has been discussed in reference to business to business environment by Rajagopal and Amritanshu Rajagopal in reference to Mexico in the following **Chapter VII** of the book. The study analyzes the impact of channel function performance on relationship quality which is moderated by the extent dependence structure of the relationship. In this process, the impact of supplier function performance on different dimensions of relationship quality in reference to satisfaction, trust, commitment and conflict under various dependence structures have also been diagnosed and analyzed. Also, the core areas such as quality management and "interface" disciplines such as networks and buyer-supplier relationships has been the centre of discussion in this chapter.

Rajagopal takes up a new emerging perspective of loyalty cards as tool of acquiring and retaining customers by retailing firms in present global competitive situation, in **Chapter VIII**. This chapter attempts to analyze drivers of compulsive buying behavior induced by store based promotion through empirical investigation in Mexico. The role of point of sales promotions in stimulating arousal and satisfaction among customer and customer relationship management for building store loyalty have been analyzed in the chapter. This study builds arguments towards convergence of attractiveness of point of sales promotions and effectiveness of customer services as a tool for gaining competitive advantage in the retail business environment. Internet, reengineering and technology applications in retailing have been discussed chronologically from the period of its evolution to the present state-of-art experience in **Chapter IX** by Rajagopal. Discussions in this chapter argue that shopping behavior of consumers has shifted with the increasing applications of Internet forcing retailers to redefine their roles to ensure their place in the Internet age and a successful retail store must build upon what the Internet cannot offer and add value to its customer's shopping experience by giving them that 'something extra' to ensure continued patronage. Author also discusses the case of a multinational insurance company which is practicing virtual sales office for increasing client support in Mexico. The discussion on management practices are further methodically carried forward by Amritanshu Rajagopal explaining the role of Six Sigma in enhancing performance of team retailing in **Chapter X**. The team selling approach is followed by many multinational companies for various products and services, which the customer faces as a first-time buy and salespeople need to support such negotiations with comprehensive information needs. The discussion is supported by a shore case analysis of Domino's Pizza towards improving its retailing services.

Ernesto Fierros and Rajagopal present empirical research results on consumer response to high technology mobile phones in emerging markets in reference to Mexico in **Chapter XI**. Authors state that the new information technology is becoming an important factor in the future development of financial **services** industry, and especially **banking** industry. This study suggests developing a high performing customer-centric marketing plan to guide the mobile telecommunication companies to gain competitive advantage in the market. In the following **Chapter XII**, Rajagopal observes that customer centered companies are increasingly engaged in direct marketing activities by outsourcing sales people to enhance the market coverage and augment volume of sales in the competitive business environment. This study attempts to analyze behavioral drivers which influence consumers' leisure shopping behavior and measure customers' value through empirical investigation in Mexico. Also, customer prospecting as direct marketing strategy through outsourced salespeople in swaying the leisure shopping and driving brand loyalty is discussed in the study. Marketing strategy, technology and modes of entry in global retailing are the core issues affecting competitive advantages to retailing firms which are addressed by Rajagopal in **Chapter XIII** delineating the modes of entry of retailing firms in global market place. Contemporary strategy as how a firm would like to involve itself in the international business, may look for its entry into international marketing in many possible ways including exporting, licensing, franchising, or as a production firm with multi-national plant locations have been discussed in the chapter.

Important guidelines that help in improving the planning and management of firms are addressed by Rajagopal and Amritanshu Rajagopal in the **Chapter XIV** meticulously by explaining the Profit Impact of Market Strategy (PIMS) and concepts of brand architecture. Authors argue that each business is a division, product line, or profit centre within its parent company, selling a distinct set of products and/or services to an identifiable group of customers, in competition with a well defined set of competitors, for which meaningful separation can be made of revenue, operating costs, investment, and strategic plans. Finally, challenges ahead in the application of technology in retailing industry have been addressed by Rajagopal in **Chapter XV** which argues that the escalating globalization and competitiveness in the retail environment is thrusting retail firms to meticulously manage store ambiance, inventory, product information, multi-channel retailing opportunities and customer relations through consistent experimentation of new technology. This chapter as concluding remarks to the discussion in the previous chapters delineates that as technology grows sophisticated, the consumer's expectations also swell exponentially and firms should considering converging key technologies with retail management strategies to optimize the win-win situation for both the retailing firms and customers.

Retailing technology is taking over "front office" roles in customer prospecting and relationship management which has brought sparking revolution in how retailing firms prospect, serve and retain customers and compete with rivals. There has been adequate research available on managing technology as well as on developing retailing strategies but these contributions are independent of each other. In particular, there are a few books addressing retailing technology whereas much work has been contributed on e-commerce, mobile commerce and supply chain technologies. This book ponders over specific issues in retailing technology which include self service technologies, point of sales technologies and customer relationship management integrating with the customer value. The contributions made in this volume serve as a think tank for strategists and researchers to hook new thoughts and link to the future business research. Some chapters in this book are based on empirical research which open-up new hypotheses to work in the following course. This book discusses substantially the best practices followed by the companies experiencing win-win strategy with customers in leading competition to achieve success using innovative technologies. Many corporate houses realized that technology sensitive retailing strategies generate customer pull effect which is more powerful than profit driven push approach. This book analyzes the above rationale and puts forth arguments on contribution of technology in retailing.

The book offers enormous potential for developing appropriate strategies to enable collaboration with customers, suppliers, and partners using new technologies. In addition, the readers of the book may acquaint skills to develop effective talent management and customer-relationship building, fast and flexible decision making, and open, credible communications among all partners though discussion portraying various technology-led best retailing practices. Setting the new agenda for managerial success, this insightful book will help managers anticipate and maneuver the technology driven challenges ahead in retailing industry.

*Rajagopal*
*Monterrey Institute of Technology and Higher Education, ITESM, Mexico*
*May 2008*

# Chapter I
# Understanding Retailing Concepts

**Rajagopal**
*Monterrey Institute of Technology and Higher Education, ITESM, Mexico*

Globalization has driven fast changes in the world markets in the world markets resulting into the new emerging markets across the countries. In this century China, India and Latin America and the emerging market based economies in Eastern Europe promise new opportunities for global trade. The Pacific region had shown time-bending leap in the past four decade as significant Asian population participated in the rapid transition in response to the global movement of trade and services. Asia may be portrayed as the fastest growing market for the top brands of western companies and at the same time the Asian companies began penetrating in the western markets at low price-high quality strategy. While the luxury and fashion goods are dominating the Asian and Far-east markets, the specialized product like electronics and automobiles from Asian Markets are trying to capture considerable market share in Europe and North American countries. The emerging markets in the developing countries have shown a strong potential for change in preferences during the late 20$^{th}$ century. In most of the advanced countries the birth rate is declining while it is increasing in the developing countries. It has been observed that the technology has homogenized the world markets for variety of customer and industrial needs. The reduction in the tariff barriers, duties and liberalization process worldwide has further given a stimulus to the international marketing across the regional boundaries.

*Until recently, Honda Motor Co. seemed fast growing. With its sporty Civic compact, stalwart Accord sedan, and a fleet of snazzy sport-utility vehicles and minivans, sales seemed to go nowhere but up. Profits soared, and Honda's U.S. market share rose to 9% in 2003 from 6.7% in 2000. The U.S. problem is twofold: sales of key models are slipping, and the rising yen lowers the value of U.S.-derived profits when they're translated back into the Japanese currency. The company predicts that the strong yen will reduce income by $1.22 billion in the current fiscal year, even worse than the $889 million currency hit in the fiscal year ended Mar. 31, 2005. Today, 80% of the 1.53 million cars Honda sells in North America are made at North American factories, and the parts in Honda's American cars increasingly come from local suppliers[1]. Honda has long been successful because it entered mainstream market segments with offbeat cars. Its high-tech engines offer the best of two worlds: They're zippy and fuel-efficient. The cars handle well, offering a little fun to go with their high quality and utilitarian design. Honda is struggling in newer segments, too. Honda says it would cost too much to revamp its factories to produce all-new platforms and big engines for trucks and luxury cars, so a big shift isn't in the cards soon. Company executives, meanwhile, have high hopes for the new Acura RL sedan. The car will feature all-wheel drive, a first for an Acura sedan, and its V-6 engine will crank out 300 hp. Dick Colliver, executive vice-president for sales and marketing at American Honda Motor Co observes that this is one of the most powerful engines Honda has ever built and that is the kind of excellence rests with the company. However, the problem is that there are a lot of excellent cars on the road these days[2].*

The growing internationalization of business induces changes in the positioning of competitors and appropriate competitive strategies. As the companies attain gradual success in geographically expanding their business and effectively performing international operations, they reach at critical point and would be able to synchronize the proximity to the overseas markets and customer needs. The global companies at this point blue print their successful business systems in the emerging markets by creating relatively decentralized operations in production, marketing and sales.

In a highly competitive global marketplace today pressure on organizations finds new ways to create the pressure on organizations to find new ways to create and deliver value to customers grows ever stronger. The global marketplace has been segmented geographically comprising triad market, pacific- rim, post-communist countries, Latin America, China and India. In the last two decades, technological innovation, logistics and supply chain has moved to the centre stage. There has been a growing recognition that it is through an effective management of the logistics function and the supply chain that the goal of cost reduction and service enhancement can be achieved. The global market place may be described as spatial network of markets across the countries comprising homogenous and customized segments. The multi-domestic and global markets with preferential and standardized products for the marketplace are offered by the multinational companies. A multi-domestic markets is one that is present in many countries but in which the competition occurs on the basis of country by country. In multi-domestic market the companies may experience the competitive advantage from one time transfer of skills and technology from the home markets of various countries. In the global marketplace a company's competitive position is significantly influenced by the companies of other countries. In the view to ease the complexities of the global market place in terms of competition and socio-economic conflicts the international business houses generally cluster the countries by common attributes such as political systems, social structures, economic development and accessibility. The cultural and economic geography that affect the international trade and investment include proximity to the marketplace, common heritage, income levels and ownership of natural resources.

## RETAILING MANAGEMENT

Retailing is a set of activities performed in selling the goods and services directly to the end users. The goods and services sold to the consumers are meant for their personal use and not for resale or business activity. Retailing is the last activity conducted in the chain of product distribution. In principle, retailing is a business activity which involves the sales of goods and services to a large number of consumer spread over a large area. There are different forms of retailing. Many of the forms keep emerging according to the convenience of the buyers and the retailers. In large towns, retailing is organized and mostly performed through stores and automatic vending machines. However, in the rural areas the retailing of goods and services are conducted through the traditional pattern of displaying the goods in the mobile van, carts and on footpaths.

For understanding the types of retailers and their function, we can classify the retailing network into two broad categories (i) store retailing and (ii) non-store retailing. Like the growth cycle of business firms, the retailing activity also passes through 4 stages embryonic, growth, maturity and decline. A retail store observes the period of accelerated growth, reaches the stage of maturity and then starts declining. It has been observed that the old fashioned retail stores took more than five decades to reach the stage of maturity in terms of volume of sales, coverage of consumers and expansion of chain of retail stores. However modern retail store types reach their maturity very fast due to organized retailing management. Some of the major store retailers are briefly described here:

- Departmental store
- Exclusive retail store or specialty store
- Super markets
- Convenience store
- Supermarkets, hyper-store
- Discount store
- Non-franchise or catalogue store

## RETAIL STORE CATEGORIES

A *departmental store* offers a wide range of products in an organized fashion and is easily accessible by the consumer. The product line of departmental stores is substantially long. Departmental stores provide better amenities to consumers for shopping by virtue of having adequate infrastructure for parking, leisure activities and hobbies. Departmental stores provide the consumer services of honoring the product guarantee, warranty, post sale services and the latest technical information. Departmental stores also organize educational program for the benefit of the consumer on the various aspects of products use and other related matters. Exclusive or specialty retail stores are unlike departmental stores and do not have a long product line. These stores are narrow in their product lines and are largely confined to the product line of a specific company. They present a varied assortment within that product line. Examples can be drawn from many consumer goods companies promoting exclusive retail stores like Phillips for a range of electrical, audio and video household gadgets; Raymond's for textiles; Bata for shoes and leather goods, and so on. Exclusive stores can be further classified with a narrow distinction as stated below:

- Single line stores
- Limited line stores
- Super specialty stores

*Single line stores* may be identified as the retail stores selling only one product like textiles. ***Limited line stores*** may be defined as the shops having micro specialization based on goods and services, gender and age, like exclusive Men's wear retail stores, *Kids Shoppe* for garments etc. The retail stores engaged in selling products scientifically designed for a particular purpose may be categorized as ***super specialty stores***, e.g. surgical equipments stores, sports accessories; fashion garments stores and the like. The classification of retail stores and their functions may be well understood through the retail position map plotted in figure 1.1.

*Figure 1.1. Categorical map of retail stores*

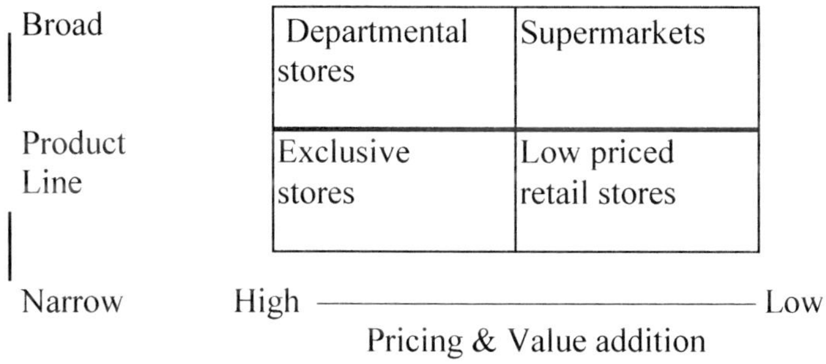


*Super markets* are a type of organized retail stores that handle a relatively large volume of goods and services at a low cost - the high margin principle of retailing. Consumers are provided franchise in the super markets and there are largely organized as self- service outlets. Super markets exhibit a long range of product line of various consumer needs like grocery, household appliances, entertainment, toys, garments etc. It has been observed that super markets earn an operating profit of 1-2% on their sales and 10-15% of their net worth. Super markets also provide consumer conveniences like in-shop entertainment, pantry, home delivery service, opinion survey and consumer education. Super markets have chain retailing in many countries like Woolworth's in the UK and Europe. There is a marginal difference between a super market and a *hyper-store***.** The latter category of stores operates on a larger area (approximately 100-200 thousand square feet) with a wide range of products. These markets have a combination of all retail functions like credit services, discounts, finance and other related services. The basic approach of a hyper-store is exhibiting a wide range of assorted products for all types of consumers and displaying them in bulk. The product handling costs in such stores would be minimal and they also function as the sole distributors to the convenience stores.

The retail self-service stores which largely operate in chain are based on the rationale of *touch, feel and pick* which provides consumers a wide range of options to make buying decisions. The in-stores promotions and *do it yourself* (DIY) opportunities constitute the major motivation for the buyers and also support the in their decision making process. Motivational forces are commonly accepted to have a key influencing role in the explanation of shopping behaviour. Personal shopping motives, values and perceived shopping alternatives are often considered independent inputs into a choice model, we argue that shopping motives influence the perception of retail store attributes as well as the attitude towards retail stores (Morschett *et.al*, 2005). In retail self-service store where consumer exercises in-store brand options, both service and merchandise quality exert significant influence on store performance, measured by sales growth and customer growth, and their impact is mediated by customer satisfaction. The liberal environment of the self-service stores for merchandise decisions, service quality and learning about competitive brands are the major attributes of retail self-service stores (Babakus *et.al*, 2004). The retail self-service stores offer an environment of three distinct dimensions of emotions *e.g.* pleasantness, arousal and dominance. Retail self-service store have broad marketing-mix which helps also the variety seeking customers and few retail self-service store specialize in the certain product categories like *The Home Depot,* which specializes in retailing building construction, interior decoration and gardening equipments. The Home Deport is a US retail self-service chain stores operating in North American and Latin American countries. The retail self-service stores operate on a market size effect and a price cutting effect (Konishi, 1999). As the retail self-service stores display wide range of multi-brand products the consumers enjoy higher chance of finding preferred products (a market size effect). On the other hand, concentration of stores leads to fiercer price competition (a price cutting effect).

*Convenience stores* are small retail outlets located near residential areas for the convenience of the consumers. They are open for long hours and all through the week. This category of stores carries a limited line of consumer products. Convenience stores operate at a high turnover and a relatively higher profit basis compared to any of the other retail stores. The consumer seems to be willing to pay a higher price to the retailers for the convenience provided to them at their door steps. In principle, a discount store should sell all types of merchandise, offering largely reputed brands at lower prices but not inferior goods. Recently, some consumer products manufacturing companies have started owning discount retail stores to sell products earmarked as second grade by their quality control division. Hence, discount retail stores have moved from general stores down to specialty merchandise stores such as discount sporting goods stores, garments, shoes, electronic, book stores and the like.

The catalogue store is a new generation super store which deals with a variety of goods and services of a wide range. Such stores conduct retailing operation for all types of goods including interiors, construction material, mechanical gadgets, electronics, and many more. Consumers buying goods from catalogue shops have to ask for or indent specific goods as per the inventory specification in the catalogue. The consumers wait in the designated place for the delivery of the goods and at times the stores even arrange a home delivery for heavy products. Catalogue stores provide a return facility to consumer within a stipulated period. The goods can be returned to the stores without any reasons if the consumers are not satisfied. Besides on-store retailing the direct selling approach has emerged in the recent past as an effective sales instrument. Direct selling is one of the most popular non-store retailing activities, particularly for consumer goods. The sales representatives of the company / distributors canvass the product on a door to door basis and contribute in augmenting sales. Automatic vending machines for selling consumer products like chilled beverages, etc. are also making use of non-store retailing approaches. The specific non-store retailing types are given below:

- Direct marketing
- Automatic vending machines
- Business by mail orders
- Tele-shopping or Net-shopping
- Mobile retailing

Multi-level retailing stores, chain-retailing stores, cooperatives network and merchandise conglomerates are the new forms of retailing emerged in the recent past.

## TOOLS OF RETAILING

Retailing is considered to be one scientific, grassroots level selling approach in the twentieth century. Hence, a retailer has to make the right decision at the right time to promote his retail business. The specific areas that need to be planned properly are (i) choice of place (ii) choice of products - assorted or exclusive (iii) price level (iv) tools of retailing and (v) consumer services. The decision regarding the choice of place and product are inter-related *e.g.*, in a high income locality, a retailer should plan for high price assorted - product stores and vice versa in a low income consumer locality.

Retail stores play a vital role in product promotion as they are directly associated with consumer. A successful retailer tries to get the consumer involved in the trade by providing a good reception, good facilities and individual attention. However, a retailer follows a variety of approaches to make his retailing a success. Some of the tools used by the retailers for promoting their business are listed below:

i. Retailers dealing with similar products form an association to jointly carry promotional activities such as advertising, pricing and other related matters
ii. Retailers do pre-ticketing by placing price tags on those products indicating all the required information such as the date of manufacture, size, volume, name of the manufacturer, date of expiry , product code of the manufacturer as well as that of the retailer for any complaints or reordering

iii. Retailers also help the consumer in re-indenting the products by sending them reminders and catalogs of the products
iv. Retailers also introduce special prices during the peak seasons for storewide promotion
v. Consumers enjoy the privilege of returning or exchanging damaged goods without paying any additional price and
vi. Distributors and company representatives get the sponsorship of the retailer for demonstrating their products in his store

There are many methods that foreign company adopt to promote the sales of its products. The common approaches may be the cross selling, price discounts, volume packs etc. However there are many advanced ideas, which are used by the multinational companies as described below:

- Coupons – Assuring benefit
- Bonus pack- more product for regular price
- In-pack, On-pack, Near-pack
- Specialty Container – Value added benefits
- Continuity program- rewards system for multiple buying
- Refund- Price draw-back
- Sweepstakes- Random chance of winning
- Contests
- Mail premium – Post-purchase benefits
- Sampling
- Price-off-discounts
- Trade deal- Incentives to retailers
- Cause marketing- social benefit oriented (like soliciting contribution to UNICEF)

Besides these services, retail stores provide many pre- and post-purchase services to satisfy the customers. The *pre-purchase services* include accepting orders via telephone and by mail, in-store and outside store advertising, interior and window display, consumer convenience, fitting rooms, shopping hours, organizing consumer entertainment like the integrated cable TV, fashion shows, recipe contest, baby shows etc. The retailers provide selected *post-purchase* services to consumer such as - home delivery of goods, gift packaging, returns and exchanges, tailoring, installation, demonstrations, accepting credit transactions and cheques. In addition to the services listed large and chain retail stores provide leisure and general amenities to the consumers like rest rooms for consumers, baby sitters, restaurants, etc.

## TEAM RETAILING STRATEGY

The growth of team retailing is changing conventional ideas about sales and customer service. Team selling, also known as cross functional selling, involves the efforts of different people from different areas within an organization working together to sell to and service a customer. This strategy of selling began in early '70s when sales teams were formed in high-technology organizations such as IBM to service the complex needs of their larger customers. It was observed necessary to have, along with a salesperson, technical support people and application specialists involved in *e.g.* inventory control, manufacturing and production planning. Besides IBM, General Motors adapted the team retailing strategy and developed as part of the culture of the company. Executives of the company felt that organizing a sales team is a major task to sell the high technology-high value products. The sales team should necessary have a technical and finance person and likewise others. Interestingly what's happened with team retailing is that over the years it's filtered into less-technology-oriented businesses such as advertising, consumer packaged goods, and financial services. Several issues may emerge before they are formally addressed as the sales teams generally start to form naturally and informally. Communication among team members is difficult to establish, but is one of the keys to the effectiveness of this approach. There are many reasons for a company to choose team retailing because this strategy:

- Provides strategic advantage
- Meets the needs of demanding, global customers more effectively
- Establishes long-term, quality relationships with clients
- Provides competitive advantage through a different kind of customer interface strategy
- Increases flexibility in terms of how customers are served
- Increases sales and potential profitability
- Forces resource allocation decisions at the field level
- Generates better input to new product and services development

Team retailing effectiveness also depends on selection and training. Training to back up the appropriate selection is so important, in fact, that IBM sends their team leaders to a customized executive development program on how to be an effective key account executive. It's a tough, rigorous program and in addition, IBM requires recertification every few years. Also at the organizational level, in order for a team retailing approach to be successful, the supplier organization must have a strong market orientation as part of its organizational culture.

*Roche Diagnostics is a division of F. Hoffmann-La Roche Ltd, Basel, Switzerland. Roche Diagnostics is the world's leading provider of diagnostic systems and decision-oriented health information. Roche is a research, technology and market-driven company, whose unique portfolio of products and services creates superior value for the customers. The company operates in Mexico under the registered name of Roche-Syntex de Mexico SA de CV with its two principal divisions of pharmaceuticals and diagnostic division. The diagnostic division of the company has the research and development and business activities of clinical chemistry, immunology, hematology, coagulation and urinalysis with the centralized diagnostics department. Roche-Syntex Mexico is engaged in selling the diagnostic reagents and equipments to the government and private clinics. The company also provides the diagnostic equipments to these health institutions and hospitals on lease. The diagnostics products and services market in Mexico is largely oriented towards the government health sector and confined to the selected distributors who often do the supply lobbying in the market. The business environment of the diagnostic market in Mexico is highly competitive and distributor oriented. The retail distribution of the company for diagnostics products is based on the strengths of the health care infrastructure and demand for the products and services thereof. The distributors have adopted the policy of reduction in risk and in this context there is no big deal for the company to stress on the distributor oriented sales strategy. The contract tracking is done according to the agreement executed between the company, distributors and the government. The collection of payments is made effective through the shared bank account of the company and distributors. The retail strategy with new structure leads to increase in the market share and expansion of the business into high growth markets. The implementation of such advanced strategy demands value added and secured distribution services, identifying new customers and providing high pre-sales services to the distributors and direct customers.*

The team retailing approach is followed by many multinational companies for the complex product and services, which the customer faces as a first-time buy and salespeople need to support such negotiations with comprehensive information needs. The team retailing would also be advantageous when an account requires special treatment or large number of people are involved in the process of buying decision. In addition, team retailing is more likely to be employed when the potential sale is large for the representative firm and when the product is new to the product line of salespeople.

Technology led retailing has driven also direct marketing strategies which focuses on dissemination of information to customers and offering learning space to buyers in using technology. The Go-to-Market strategy (GTM) encompasses the channels that a company uses to connect with its customers and the organizational processes it develops to guide customer interactions from initial contact through fulfilment. The right go-to-market strategy has a significant impact on a company's ability to cost-effectively deliver its value proposition to each of its target segments. Growth in technology and the proliferation of channel options have certainly played a role as business firms are becoming increasingly focused and sophisticated in the way in which they compete to create superior customer value. GTM strategy may be administered successfully by considering the following process path:

- Understanding customers' needs, expectation and behavior
  Products, Channels, Value Proposition and Markets
- Aggressive use of low cost channels
  Short run market penetration, profit maximization
- Fit between selling approach and selling contents
  Product-Channel Fit, Process Fit, Value Fit
- Trade-off between market coverage and control
  Reaching the range of potential customers
  Exercising control on sales relationship and deliveries
  Market expansion and new channel partners

As companies tailor their value propositions to better address customer needs beyond product specifications and to better align their cost of sales and fulfilment relative to those needs, go-to-market strategy plays a central role. To compensate for less-frequent product launches and a focus on integrated solutions rather than specific products, Microsoft now organizes its marketing efforts around annual GTM campaigns. GTM strategies focus Microsoft and its partners on short-term strategic challenges and provide consistent marketing approaches for most of its business products. GTMs address the lack of new product releases on which to hang marketing campaigns by identifying a strategic issue facing Microsoft and constructing a framework for addressing it with broad-reach advertising, sales tools for partners and the Microsoft field sales force, and customer and partner incentives.

## MARKET UNCERTAINTIES AND ENTRY DECISIONS

In turbulent markets the competitive strategy provides the conceptual magnitude that integrates various functional activities and marketing programs for sustaining the competitive threats. The effective competitive strategies have a direct bearing on possessing the relative market share and growth of the business organization. The strategies are the directional statements and need to be converted into the step-by-step plan of action for effective plan implementation. The strategic directions have four options that can be expressed by 4As - arena, advantage, access and activities. The arena may be defined as serving the targeted market segment through an appropriate scale of operations and scope of activities to be performed for competitive advantage. The advantages in the process consist of positioning the products theme that differentiates the business from competitors. The access may be referred to the communication and distribution channels used to reach the market in the uncertain business conditions. These activities are interdependent and are affected by the change in any of the factors. The arena of the market largely dictates the customers to be served by the company, the competitors to by-passes and the key success factors to be considered upon. Each market has distinctive profile of key success factors developed by the attributes of the market. The recent development of corporate strategies shows that many multi-national companies are considering their choice of the market arena based on the following factors:

- There is an increasing trend of market fragmentation. New segments with specific needs are emerging and are being served by the specialist competitors by offering tailor made goods and services.
- The traditional market boundaries are disappearing as a consequence of the rush of substitutes emerging due to the technological growth.
- The transformation of existing self-contained regional and national markets into global markets.

In the above discussed situations the challenge for the corporate sector management may be observed as to find the right balance of global reach and standardization of the activities versus the traditional strategies or local adaptation. The companies need to find out the competitive advantages within the chosen arena of business. The core issue associated with the competitive advantage is positioning of the theme that sets a business apart from the rivals in the way that is meaningful to target the customers. It is necessary for the companies to move aggressively against the competitors to retain their market territories and build a strong defence. Thus Kodak asserted itself in the film market against the strategies of Fuji in American market. The supply gluts also put pressure on advantages. The markets for the pharmaceuticals, electronics and automobiles suffer chronic global overcapacity to the extent of 15-40 percent. Such problem situation demands the companies to develop the strategies of competitive advantage to hold the key success factors and become the market leader. Such strategies are required as there are too many firms competing and the customers may back integrate by their marketing requirement rather than buying them. This situation reduces the volume of market demand relative to supply and the customers may sell their excess capacity on competition with their one-time supplier.

Need for the competitively advantageous strategies may further be justified as a large number of firms are increasingly productive in reference to the rapid diffusion of the technologies. The customers' bargaining power also works out to be an instrument to either broaden or narrow the differences between the competitors. The companies that use intermediaries are often encountered with balancing the power of distribution and delivery of services. In consumer markets the retail trade is forcing major concessions on the multi-national brands. Such strategies hold the access to the retail network through a long chain of channels. Conventionally the choice of appropriate scale in business and scope thereof were guided by the concepts of *the bigger is better* and *umbrella control of activities.* In the current era of globalization the decentralization of activities and production sharing have become more effective tools in marketing. The profit centre approach (PCA), control circles and total quality management practices has endorsed the success of small integrated units operating in a well defined market. In view to promote the PCA concepts and maintain the control circles, the large companies are increasingly creating the autonomous, small and entrepreneurial units to find responsive solutions to the customer problems in the well defined market niches (Frederick, 1989). Corporate structures are changing in order to accommodate the concept of PCA and control circles and are exploring for the long term advantages by way of heavy investment to develop the core competencies.

*BMW, Honda, and Toyota, among other companies, begin with a strong brand that imparts sales momentum to each model. Brands that are weak—because their products have acquired a reputation for shoddy workmanship, their designs are not evocative, or their models bear little relationship to one another—cannot pursue this top-down approach. But a company stands a good chance of selling more cars and, step by step, of rehabilitating the brand if managers take pains to match each model to the consumer segments most likely to be interested in it, identify and overcome the obstacles that keep browsers from becoming purchasers, and emphasize both the functional and the process and relationship benefits of the model in question. BMW Direct is an initiative of BMW (GB) to help selected company car fleet buyers streamline their service for employees. BMW Direct is a web based, fully personalized, car configuration and ordering system for the purchase of new BMWs. This highly efficient rules based web application delivers a level of information previously unavailable outside of a showroom. The BMW Direct solution provides users with the ability to view details on all eligible cars online and then go on to configure them against a full menu of accessories. BMW Direct is truly 'CRM' compliant, providing two-way communication via automated alerts and e-mails and incorporating a Contact Centre to ensure immediate access to trained product advisors. Users can track online the status of their individual orders whether by web, phone, fax or email. The call centre functionality includes phone and e-campaign generation, customer enquiry handling and profiling to customised promotions*[3]*. Post-sales support is delivered using a thin client solution, (using Citrix) to BMWs contact centre in Croydon and order management centre in Bracknell in UK.*

The technological changes are the main impetus behind new market opportunities. The extent of such change may be explained from super technologies to the appropriate and intermediate technologies. The strategic choices have wide ranging ripple effects through the organization that determine the key success factors and growth performance. Some companies would be making right strategic choices by improving the implementation process of competitive advantages. These companies are guided by the shared strategic vision and are driven by the responsive attitude towards the market requirements. They emphasize the continuous strive to satisfy the customers. A strategic vision in managing markets may be understood as the guiding theme that explains the nature of business and the future projections thereof. These projections or business intentions depend on the collective analysis of the environment that determines the need for the new developments or diversifications. The vision should be commissioned on a concrete understanding of the business and the ability to foresee the impact of market forces on the growth of business. The vision will motivate the organization for collaborative business planning and implementation. The powerful visions are also the statements of intent that create on obsession with winning thorough out the organization (Day, 1990). The business strategy broadly incorporates the following dimensions:

- Customer needs
- Consumer segments
- Technology and resources
- Activities in the value added chain

The strategic thrust has a significant magnitude and direction in sailing the business though the turbulent situation. The factors associated with the competitive advantage and business investments uphold the strategic thrust to achieve the business objectives though the positive channel efforts. The competitive advantage may be assessed in reference to the superior customer value and lowest delivered cost. Such combination of the strategies may be termed as competitive superiority that explains cost effective delivery strategy to enhance the customer value. An overall edge is gained by performing most of the activities at a lower cost than competitors. This would enable the company to optimize its cost of delivery of the new products and simultaneously enhance the value of customer value to up-hold the strategic thrust of the company.

*Canon delivers innovative digital business solutions to ensure that its customers achieve and maintain the information edge. The increasingly competitive global marketplace, and the fact that the organizations must store, process and share immense volumes of information with both speed and accuracy have been the key areas of the company to penetrate in the territorial gateways like Mexico for Latin American market. The company functions with four key areas in Mexican market that include marketing, logistics, sales and services operations. The marketing activities of the company consist of planning and budgeting, pricing, forecasting, purchases, marketing research and developing promotional strategies. The company is also engaged in developing attractive media –mix and advertising campaigns and launches the loyalty programs for its major brands. The virtual shopping network is also a major part of the marketing functions performed by the company in the country. The company feels that the loyal, ongoing customers are the backbone of every business and in the prevailing highly competitive environment, these shoppers cannot be ignored or else they may be won over by competitors. The consumers might have bought such products many times in their life or some might have purchased at least once in life time. There is no single way to segment a market. The most important factors influencing a consumer's involvement level are their perceived risks. The purchase of any product involves a certain amount of risk, which may include product failure, financial, operational, social, personal and psychological. The repeat customers are more apt to buy a full range of merchandise, not merely items that are under promotional programs. This means that the dealers and retailers of the company can reach profit margin goals. The logistics functions of the company is largely international trade oriented as the Canon Mexico is a part of Canon USA and many products of the company are acquired from its USA counterpart as inbound logistics. The import process has been one of the major activities of the company in Mexico. The logistics of the company further involves the key activities of transport, inventory management and developing appropriate overseas trade and information strategies*[4].

There are many critical strategies explored and and given various names by different authors. Often these strategies and tactics are so bold and innovative that they "change the rules of the game." Leaders are increasingly being advised to seek that objective in planning and executing their strategies. The pace of change today is dizzying with new technological breakthroughs occurring at shorter intervals and global competition putting the heat on. Mergers and acquisitions change the competitive landscape unexpectedly, and strategic alliances develop even among the companies that were, or still are, competitors. The concept of "*Hyper-competition* explains the highly aggressive form of competition that characterizes hi-tech industries today. Hyper-competition is said to be increasingly making its way into other industries as well. They speak in terms of surprise, speed and mobility, terms suggestive of the military approach. Not that aggressive action is new in business so much so as the level, intent and severity of business "combat" have changed dramatically. It is necessary to build the strategic business mindset to outwit the competitors and gain competitive advantages over the segmented markets. The following factors need to be considered for achieving the strategic business leadership:

- A clear sense of desired outcomes before acting. Develop a plan capable of delivering outcomes that will add significant value to a state of affairs.
- Explore possibilities outwards to capture the larger context, to see how the pieces fit together.
- Adaptive to realities and flexible in choice of tactics. Recognize that once action begins the "game board" is fluid offering both new threats and new opportunities.
- Wherever possible, attempt to achieve multiple objectives through singular actions.
- Plan a couple of steps ahead of competition.
- Anticipate the actions of business rival and strategically rehearse next responses should those contingencies arise.
- Core discipline to observe the market moves and rival reactions.
- Capitalize on business crises or behavioural change in the markets in order to turn them to advantage.
- Stay future-focused.
- Plan the business strategy implementation in both sequential and parallel direction to accomplish goals and sustain the impact thereof.
- Develop negotiations with the business intermediaries on win-win platform at an acceptable cost.
- Supplement actions with those of others (allies, partners, joint ventures.)
- Be patient, with a good sense of timing.
- Be able to scrap or alter plans when information indicates actions are not attaining their intended results.
- Develop alternate strategies for contingencies
- Use speed and surprise to gain advantage.
- Form alliances with opponents of his opponents in business.
- Learn the strengths and weaknesses of rivals.
- Be aggressive in pursuing goals, cordon the moves and ready to take on to the next.
- Assure that everyone in the company knows one's role and is equipped with the resources to contribute.
- Monitor activities in the operating environment.

- Use "what if" speculation to stretch thinking in the direction of opportunities and possibilities.
- Study the logic of the opponent's tactics with an eye toward determining what their ultimate end purposes may be.

These are some tested aspects of thinking employed by leaders to gain and hold strategic advantage. They can serve as a checklist when responsibilities include thinking strategically. Customers want more of everything they value. If they value low cost they want it lower. If they value convenience they want it easier and faster. If they look for state of the art they want it first and want to push the envelope. If they need expert advice they want more time and dedicated effort and investment. By raising the level of value that customers can expect from everyone, leading companies are driving the market and driving their competitors out of business, or at least into a malaise of mediocrity.

The dynamism of the Competency and Technology (CAT) refers to continuous change for the betterment of the policies and execution of the strategies. The organization must be able to identify the new markets continuously and never be static at any point of time. An organization must have a wide span to discharge their competency without specifying the boundaries of time and area. It is essential for a company to retain its CAT for a longer duration and unrestricted to any areas of change. CAT also varies in their acceptability to the current and future business domains. A competitor cannot always leverage a competence for the new products or services development in changing business domains. The companies must secure that their CAT strategies are not replicated by other firms or used in any distorted manner. Indeed, any CAT of any company should be able to enhance continuously so that it adds to the sustainable advantages. In practice, today's global competition is more dynamic and multidimensional than those models suggest. The mature industry paradox is that leadership demands differentiation, yet differences are quickly copied. Single-factor innovations tap one competency, and capable competitors can usually match it. Multiple competencies strengthen several dimensions and in effect redefine the basis of competition. The "shadow strategy task force" is offered as a method to force managers to relinquish the comfort of the firm's accepted view of itself. This approach begins with the objective of identifying the strategies and competency that, in the hands of competitors, might be used to attack the firm's competitive position successfully. Especially critical on the task force are individuals with insight into how customers, suppliers, and competitors view the firm's products and services. Developing new competency requires constant experimentation. The innovation-imitation-equilibrium cycle suggests that industry leaders teach customers what to demand by defining the current state of the art in performance, price, service, and other dimensions; customers learn to judge competitive offerings against these standards, and the learning effect is cumulative (Werther and Kerr, 1995).

*The LG Electronics India and Samsung in India have entered the electronics market as rivals and are getting along in the business with the same spirit and surviving the market competition. Both the companies are of Korean origin and are into almost identical product segments in the market. Their pricing strategies are similar and they follow largely identical business models to compete with each other in the Indian market. In the marketplace these companies are the most spirited rivals and use throwing punches figuratively on each other's performance to prove their capabilities and build customer loyalty. These two companies fight for each piece of consumer electronic goods in the market. In early July 2000 Samsung came-up with an advertisement proclaiming itself the leader on the 310-litre and above frost-free refrigerators segment, LG responded by challenging both the Samsung and ORG-GFK, which provided the market share data to the advertiser for making it a public claim[5]. Growth in an adjacent market is tougher than it looks; three-quarters of the time, the effort fails. But companies can change those odds dramatically. Results from a five-year study of corporate growth conducted by Bain & Co. reveal that adjacency expansion succeeds only when built around strong core businesses that have the potential to become market leaders. And the best place to look for adjacency opportunities is inside a company's strongest customers. A research study revealed that the most successful companies were able to outgrow their rivals consistently and profitably by developing a formula for pushing out the boundaries of their core businesses in predictable, repeatable ways. Companies use their repeatability formulas to expand into any number of adjacencies. Some companies make repeated geographic moves, whereas others apply a superior business model to new segments. In other cases, companies develop hybrid approaches. The successful repeaters in the study had two common characteristics: they were extraordinarily disciplined, applying rigorous screens before they made an adjacency move, and in almost all cases, they developed their repeatable formulas by carefully studying their customers and their customers' economics[6]. The strategies of Japanese firms have often emphasized its conflicting nature, at least in international markets. It is certainly clear that Japanese firms have more systematic and formal procedures for identifying competitors and analyzing their behavior. It is tempting to conclude that their success is the success of conflict-based strategies. In practice it is almost impossible to come to such judgments. While they are aware of competitors and their weaknesses, they are also keen students of both markets and technology. It is certain that a combination of factors, many of them subtle and difficult to comprehend, leads to the success, in some markets, of Japanese companies. Such success cannot be attributed solely, if at all, to a policy of competitor elimination[7].*

There are many ways to categorize core competency. However, broadly these may distinguish as market-access competency, integrity related competency and functionality related competency. The market access competency includes management of brand development, sales and marketing, distribution and logistics, technical support, etc. All these skills help to put a firm in close proximity to its customers. The attributes associated with competency like quality, cycle time management, just-in-time inventory management and so on which allow a company to do things more quickly, flexibly or with a higher degree of reliability than competitors constitute the integrity related competency of a firm. The functionality related competency lead to the skills which enable the company to invest its services or products with unique functionality, which invest the product with distinctive customer benefits, rather than merely making it incrementally better. The functionality-related competency is becoming more important as a source of competitive differentiation, relative to the other two competence types. In the growing competitive phenomenon, the companies are converging around universally high standards for product and service integrity, and are moving through alliances, acquisitions and industry consolidation to build broadly matching global brand and distribution capabilities. Interestingly, the Japanese concept of quality has shifted from an idea centered on integrity ('zero defects') to one focused on functionality ('quality that surprises' in that the product yields a unique functionality

## SYNERGY OF TECHNOLOGY AND CUSTOMER VALUE

The new information technology is becoming an important factor in the future development of financial **services** industry, and especially **retailing** industry. The developments on information and communication technology have significantly contributed to the exponential growth and profits of the financial institutions worldwide. This evolution had transformed the way banks deliver their services, using technologies such as automated teller machines, phones, the Internet, credit cards, and electronic cash. However, banks face a number of important questions on strategies for deriving full advantage of new technology opportunities and tracking electronic development changes affecting interactions with the customers. In general terms, increasing convenience is a way of raising consumers' surplus provided new technology is adopted by the banks in order to offer convenience to the customers may be through an electronic transaction as a substitute for a trip to the branch. The technology based services imply different combinations of accessibility attributes (time, distance, and search costs), ease of use and price. Another factor in determining the magnitude of the surplus that the bank can seize is the relative importance of cross-selling. The bundle of services provided electronically is usually not the same as the one available at a branch. For this reason new technology based retailing services with high customer value may offer better service conditions to harmonize the flow of information and services across the spatial and temporal dimensions.

The new information technology is becoming an important factor in the future development of financial **services** industry, and especially **retailing** industry. The developments on information and communication technology have significantly contributed to the exponential growth and profits of the financial institutions worldwide. This evolution had transformed the way banks deliver their services, using technologies such as automated teller machines, phones, the Internet, credit cards, and electronic cash. However, banks face a number of important questions on strategies for deriving full advantage of new technology opportunities and tracking electronic development changes affecting interactions with the customers. In general terms, increasing convenience is a way of raising consumers' surplus provided new technology is adopted by the banks in order to offer convenience to the customers may be through an electronic transaction as a substitute for a trip to the branch. The technology based services imply different combinations of accessibility attributes (time, distance, and search costs), ease of use and price. Another factor in determining the magnitude of the surplus that the bank can seize is the relative importance of cross-selling. The bundle of services provided electronically is usually not the same as the one available at a branch. For this reason new technology based retailing services with high customer value may offer better service conditions to harmonize the flow of information and services across the spatial and temporal dimensions.

The role of marketing strategies in fostering controlled consumer empowerment is reflected in the development of information-based consumer-centric marketing strategies that seek to enable and control delegation. In designing such strategies, consumers' familiarity with the use of information and communication technologies are both strengthened and widened, emphasizing the uncontrolled nature of the consumer empowerment process. There is a need to regain control over the marketing process, that is, to either manage the technological empowerment of consumers, or to devise new strategies cognizant of the possibility that such technological empowerment cannot be managed. The valuation of consumer loyalty in this environment rises significantly (Pires *et al*, 2006). Organizations seeking to adopt a more customer-focused strategy will learn from the approach DuPont. It took in grappling with this challenge, based on an extensive program of qualitative and quantitative research with customers around the globe. The customer touch-point analysis of the organization facilitated alignment of functional groups within the organization (product, sales, customer service, etc.) and equipped them to deliver on newly developed, segment-specific value propositions. This major initiative has enabled DuPont to reprioritize internal efforts and business practices and been a catalyst for broader organizational changes notably the dissolution of many functional silos that previously had hindered its ability to deliver against its brand promise (Sena and Petromilli, 2005).

The companies engaged in sales and services of high value-high technology goods like hybrid automobiles need to explore new modes of cooperation among customers, retailers and manufacturers resulting from co-design which leads to a customer-centric business strategy. Co-design activities are performed at dedicated interfaces and allow for the joint development of products and solutions between individual customers and manufacturers (Berger *et al*, 2005). Customer centric research aims at developing pro-customer strategies to focus on better ways of communicating value propositions and delivering the complete experience to real customers. Learning about customers and experimentation with different segmentations, value propositions, and effective delivery of services associate customer in business and help frontline employees acquire and retain customers with increasing satisfaction in sales and services of the firm (Seldon and Macmillan, 2006).

A common observation about self-service retail stores is the *similitude* among in-store ambience and retailing operations. Hence, self service retail stores are increasingly using point of sales promotional activities to drive buying stimulation among consumers through redeemable coupons corresponding to the value of purchase. Such promotional strategy and market dominance have significant implications on the volume of sales and inflow of consumers in retail stores (Parsons and Ballantine, 2004). The prospective customers have objective to buy at the right time so as to minimize the expected price of the acquired item. However, point of sales promotions stimulates compulsive buying behavior among customer which dominates the buying decision despite comparative differences in the prices of alternate channels (Parlar *et al*, 2007). By making the attractive products accessible to customers at point of sales promotion, customers would be driven by the 'me too' feeling and preferential prices. The concept of point of sales promotion to create compulsive buying behavior is based on a brilliant understanding of the human mind and a smart way of increasing volume of store sales. Self service retail stores introduce electronic cash cards (ECC), shopping advantage cards (SAC) and bulk purchase price offers (BPP) as point of sales promotion to acquire new customers and retain existing customers (Rajagopal 2008, Coad, 2006).

Retailing firms build most profitable strategies through services differentiation and competitive advantages offering customers something new they value that other retail outlets don not have. Self service retail stores differentiate at every point of customer services and relationship from the moment customers express store loyalty. Large self service retail stores open up their promotion strategies to stimulate shopping behavior of customers and uncover new opportunities for them to gain long term benefits with the retail stores and stay loyal (MacMillan and Mcgrath, 1997). However, some firms have experienced that point of sales promotion activities can also backfire loudly and put reputations at risk if the tools of promotion such as ECC, SAC and BPP are not effectively managed. Since point of sales promotion has emerged as competitive strategy for retail firms, despite apparent risks managers are exploring the scope of acquiring and retaining customers. This strategy of point of sales promotions has helped large self service retail stores to slash costs on advertising and publicity, increase volume of sales and sharpen their focus on core competencies (Johnson, 2006).

Large self service retail stores or supermarkets are potential outlets where customers experience innovative promotions on variety of products and services which drive the buying decisions. Among various promotional offers price discounts, free samples, bonus packs, and in-store display are associated with product trial. Trial determines repurchase behavior and also mediates in the relationship between sales promotions and repeat buying behavior (Ndubisi and Moi, 2005; Rajagopal, 2005). Among growing competition in retailing consumer products, innovative point of sales promotions offered by super markets are aimed at boosting sales and augmenting the store brand value. Purchase acceleration and product trial are found to be the two most influential variables of retail point of sales promotions. It has been found that there exists significant association between the four consumer promotional approaches including coupons, price discounts, samples and *buy-one-get-one-free* and compulsive buying behavior (Gilbert and Jackaria, 2002). The occurrence and the choice of appropriate retail sales promotion techniques are important decisions for retailers. It is crucial for the retailing firms to apprehend the mechanisms involved at the consumer level regarding these sales promotions. Variables such as variety seeking, perceived financial benefit, brand loyalty and store loyalty towards point of sales promotions have specific influences on the buying behavior and volume of retail sales (Laroche et al, 2003).

Leisure shopping is influenced by time and attractiveness of sales offers which include variables *viz.* hours of work, public holidays, and paid leave entitlements, point of sales promotions and effectiveness of customer relations. These factors vary widely in reference to consumer segments and markets attractiveness and induce compulsive buying behavior among customers, which is judged by the satisfaction in spending and perceiving pleasure of buying occasionally exercising choice and passing time in knowing new products, services, technologies and understanding fellow customers (Watkins and Bond, 2007, Rajagopal 2007a). Retailers using a "store as the brand" strategy invest in creating a specific, unique shopping experience for their target customer and encourage leisure and group buying behavior where delivery of customer satisfaction seems to be an effective source of differentiation (Carpenter *et al*, 2005). Change-of-season sales are most frequently introduced with attractive sales promotions in reference to price discounts or two for one price basis and linked with objectives of moving a volume of stock. Retail promotional sales also include general sales, and these are linked with other promotional objectives and activities such as increasing profit and inventory management (Fam, 2003).

## Smart Cards and Compulsive Buying

Compulsive buying is closely associated with the obsessive behavior of customers who orient to their mind to acquire certain products or services. There exists a close relationship between compulsive buyers and specific types of external stimuli such as sales promotions and bargains offered in the large self service retail stores. Customers who have a higher tendency to buy compulsively are more prone to promotions and are more likely to yield to innovative sales promotions in retail stores. Such customers have a greater likelihood to use promotion tools such as ECC, SAC and BPP offered by retail stores, and subsequently have a greater incidence of compulsive shopping (Vicdan *et al*, 2007). Clinically, compulsive buying is closely related to major depression, obsessive–compulsive disorder, and in particular, compulsive hoarding. Like compulsive hoarding, compulsive buying is thought to be influenced by a range of cognitive domains including deficits in decision-making, emotional attachments to objects and erroneous beliefs about possessions, and other maladaptive beliefs (Kyrios *et al*, 2004).

Point of sales promotion strategy towards prospecting new customers and generating shopping arousal among the existing customers through in-store ECC, SAC and BPP involves impulsive and compulsive buying process. The effects of location convenience, one-stop shopping convenience, reputation of retail stores, in-store ambience, and direct mailings generate shopping arousal among the leisure shoppers. Satisfaction and trust developed by the retail stores during pre-purchase phase help persuading the sales promotions among customers (Liu and Wu, 2007). Consumers respond encouragingly to point of sales campaigns run by the self service retail stores in Mexico, however, customer services associated with point of sales promotions and perceived promotional advantage play a decisive role in the buying process (Rajagopal, 2006; Anselmsson, 2006). Information on the current point of sale promotion and previous experience of customer with the promotional offers of the retail store stimulate consumer feelings and prompt their decision towards experimenting new products on promotional offers (Backstrom, 2006).

Five essential qualities of aesthetic judgment, which include *interest, subjectivity, exclusivity, thoughtfulness, and internality,* need to be nurtured among consumers to develop conviction in buying. The quality of aesthetic judgment driven by in-store aura and arousal on new products, exercised by the customers in association with the sales promoters, determines the extent to which new products and brands promoted enhance quality of life (Dobson, 2007). Convergence of sales promotion, customer's perceptions, value for money and product features drive arousal among customers. The nature of customer-retailer relationship functions as the key in selling and buying process in reference to in-store promotions. However, in this process the perceptional problems with customers can greatly devalue the customer-promoter relationship and brand as a whole (Platz and Temponi, 2007; Rajagopal, 2007b). Consumer appreciation of premium-based promotional offers is more positive when the premium is offered through an easy process and in combination of relatively lower quantity of products to purchase. It has also been found that when value of the premium is mentioned and brand perception is positive compulsive buying tendencies are higher among customer (d'Astous and Jacob, 2002).

The in-store environment variables driving impulsive buying behavior include display of point of sales posters, exhibiting promoting discounts and cheaper prices, while the atmosphere engagement referring to enjoyment, elegance, and attractiveness is conveyed by in-store point of sales posters. Such behavioral drivers may also be referred as in-store promotional effect and atmospheric effect (Zhou and Wong, 2004). It has been observed in some studies that consumers who intend to do shopping in short notice, generally lean towards impulsive or compulsive buying behavior driven by arousal effect in the retail stores. Gender, age, leaning towards unplanned purchases, and tendency to buy products not on shopping lists, serve to predict compulsive tendencies (Shoham and Brencic, 2003). However, there are some common strategies adopted by retailers to overcome the problems of fickle consumers, price-slashing competitors, and mood swings in the economy. Such wishful thinking holds that sales promoters can thrive only if they communicate better with consumers during pre-purchase situations and assist in product demonstrations involving consumers to help their purchase decisions (Berry, 2001).

## Consumers Shopping Behavior

Human personality traits are determined by multi-dimensional factors like the individual's behavior, appearance, attitude and beliefs, and demographic characteristics. Based on the trait theory, researchers have concluded that there are five stable personality dimensions, also called the 'Big Five' human personality dimensions (Batra, Lehmann & Singh, 1993). The Big five factors include extraversion, agreeableness, conscientiousness, neuroticism and openness to experience. Relationship between the point of sales promotions and retail buying decisions is largely governed by the psychographic variables that can be measured broadly by the closeness and farness of the personalities of brand and customer. The type of relationship that customers possess with the point of sales promotions offered by retail stores is largely based on the loyalty levels (Rajagopal 2007a). The new generation marketing approaches include customer focused, market-driven, outside-in, one-to-one marketing, data-driven marketing, relationship marketing, integrated marketing, and integrated marketing communications that emphasize two-way communication through better listening to customers and the idea that communication before, during and after transactions can build or destroy important brand relationships (Duncan and Moriarty, 1998). It has been observed that many consumers are sensitive to the price while making buying decisions and have higher tendency to buy compulsively, are more prone to promotions and are more likely to use online sales promotions (Vicdan *et al*, 2007).

Consumers are found to be attached firmly to the ethnic culture and tend to shop at the same store, especially those stores owned by members of the subculture and stores with Spanish-speaking salespeople (Saegert *et al*, 1985). Marketers reinforce the relationship between consumers and their stores by introducing periodical sales promotions. In general, Hispanic consumers show the tendency of buying products offered in sales promotions (Richins, 1994). In Latin America consumers' diversity is apparent and so is their attitude towards promotions. Consumers considered relative advantages in perceived price and product promotions, and preferred big-bargains offered by the retail stores to buy. Retailers accrued higher benefit from such buying behavior of consumers while defining their promotional strategies, especially emphasizing on every day low prices (EDLP) strategy like Wal-Mart (D'Andrea *et al*, 2006). Practically consumers react favorably to leisure sales campaigns of goods and services. However, customer value plays a decisive role in the shopping process. Sales promoters instill emotions among customers in terms of merchandise choice, visual merchandising, store environment, sales personnel attitude, pricing policies and promotional activities during the pre-purchase stage. These factors are the very foundations of consumer satisfaction and decision drivers towards buying products (Otieno *et al*, 2005).

## Growing Merchandising Trends with Technology

Tendency of compulsive buying in retail stores in response to point of sales promotions among consumers has often been dichotomized in terms of its arousal led compulsive nature and has been found closely associated with the post-buying level of satisfaction leading to determine the customer value and justification to the buying decisions. Such impulsive buying attitude emerging from self reference criterion may lean towards derived cognitions, possibly including compulsive buying, hoarding, and materialism (Doron *et al*, 2007; Wakefield and Inman, 2003).

As new and exciting products are introduced, firms prospect the consumers through inter-personal negotiations managed by the sales promoters and inculcate high arousal among customers towards buying these products. The *visual merchan-*

*dising* and computer aided simulations act as stimuli to consumers who intend to elicit a positive response. This creates shopping arousal among customers in reference to merchandise choice, store ambience, attributes of promotional products, perceived use value, pricing policies and promotional activities. These factors may be considered as foundations of consumer behavior towards point of sales promotions offered in retail stores (Otieno *et al*, 2005). Further, it is predicted that the magnitude of such positive response will be proportional to the value of an option to make buying decision at the available price (Rajagopal, 2006).

isual effects and economic advantage associated with promotional products in the retail stores often stimulate the compulsive buying behavior. Point of sales brochures, catalogues and posters build assumption on perceived use value and motivational relevance of buying decisions of product. Emotional visuals exhibited on contextual factors such as proximity or stimulus size, drive perception and subjective reactions on utility and expected satisfaction of the products (Codispoti and De Cesarei, 2007). Retailers demonstrate higher visual attention and increasing visual stimuli during the point of sales promotions. It reveals that consumers exhibit a muddled search strategy where economic and perceived use value benefits influence the buying decision process among customers (Clement, 2007). In addition, a pleasant store ambience where attractive displays, music, hands-on experience facilities and recreation are integrated helps in maximizing the consumer arousal towards buying. It has been observed that consumers perceive positive effect during interaction with sales promoters if arousal is high (Wirtz *et al*, 2007).

The impact of initial interactions among fellow customers about the point of sales promotions can be measured in reference to the degree of stimulation gained by customers. Interactive tools on product learning provided by the retailers significantly affect the level of arousal and pleasure which contribute towards experience, and thereby influence the buying behavior. As higher stimulation or interactive learning provided by the sales promoters focuses on gaining initial experience on the product use, consumers tend to engage in higher arousing activities and adhere to the sale promotions offered by the retail stores (Rajagopal, 2008; Menon and Kahn, 2002; Mulhern and Williams, 1994). Retailers use point of sales promotions to build shopping arousal, gain satisfaction and stay loyal to the stores (Deshpande *et al*, 1986). The magnitude of consumer response to clearance sales is weighed in two ways- evaluative and behavioral. Firstly, consumer satisfaction with the decision process leading to the expected level of *satisfaction* is measured, which may be expressed as one of a number of cognitive and affective responses. Satisfaction is the customer's perception of the value received in a transaction or relationship and it helps in making re-patronage decisions on the basis of their predictions concerning the value of a future product. Hence, many retailers develop innovative approaches to prospect new customers for new products by strengthening customer relationship and value management strategies (Ganesh, *et al*, 2000).

## REFERENCES

Anselmsson Johan (2006). Sources of customer satisfaction with shopping malls: A comprehensive study of different customer segments. *The International Review of Retail, Distribution and Consumer Research, 16*(1), 115-138.

Backstrom, Kristina (2006). Understanding recreational shopping. *The International Review of Retail, Distribution and Consumer Research,* 16 (2), 143-158.

Batra, R., Lehmann D. and Singh, D. (1993), The brand personality component of brand goodwill: Some antecedents and consequences, in Aaker & Bie. *Brand Equity and Advertising : Advertising's Role in Building Strong Brands,* (pp. 83-95). Hillsdale, NJ : Lawrence Erlbaum Associate Publishers.

Berger, C., Möslein, K., Piller, F., & Reichwald, R. (2005). Co-designing modes of cooperation at the customer interface: learning from exploratory research. *European Management Review, 2*(1), 70-87.

Berry, L. L. (2001). The old pillars of new retailing. *Harvard Business Review, 79*(4), 131-137.

Carpenter, J .M., Moore, M. & Fairhurst, A. E. (2005). Consumer shopping value for retail brands. *Journal of Fashion Marketing and Management, 9*(1), 45-53.

Clement, J. (2007). Visual influence on in-store buying decisions: An eye-track experiment on the visual influence of packaging design. *Journal of Marketing Management, 23*(9-10), 917-928.

Coad, T. (2006). The future for `do-it-yourself' customer service. *Journal of Database Marketing & Customer Strategy Management, 13*(4), 324-330.

Codispoti, Maurizio & De Cesarei, Andrea (2007). Arousal and attention: Picture size and emotional reactions. *Psychophysiology, 44*(5), 680-686.

d'Andrea, G., Schleicher, M., & Lunardini, F. (2006). The role of promotions and other factors affecting overall store price image in Latin America. *International Journal of Retail & Distribution Management, 34*(9), 688-700.

d'Astous, A. & Jacob, I. (2002). Understanding consumer reactions to premium-based promotional offers. *European Journal of Marketing, 36(*11), 1270-1286.

Dawson-Saunders, Beth K. (1982). Correcting for BIAS in the canonical redundancy statistic. *Educational and Psychological Measurement, 42*(1), 131-143.

Day, George S. (1990). *Market driven strategy: Process for creating value,* (pp. 10-18). New York: The Free Press.

Deshpande, R., Hoyer, W. D. & Donthu, N. (1986). The intensity of ethnic affiliation: A study of the sociology of Hispanic consumption. *Journal of Consumer Research, 13*, 214-220.

Dobson, J. (2007). Aesthetics as a foundation for business activity. *Journal of Business Ethics, 72*(1), 41-46.

Doron, G., Kyrios, M. & Moulding, R. (2007). Sensitive domains of self-concept in obsessive–compulsive disorder (OCD): Further evidence for a multidimensional model of OCD. *Journal of Anxiety Disorders, 21*(3), 433-444.

Duncan, T. & Moriarty, S. E. (1998). A Communication based marketing model for managing relationships. *Journal of Marketing, 62*, 1-13.

Dunlap, William P., Silver, Clayton N., & Phelps, Glenn R. (1987). A Monte Carlo study of using the first Eigenvalue for averaging intercorrelations. *Educational and Psychological Measurement, 47*(4), 917-923.

Fam, K. S. (2003). Managing an effective promotion campaign: Lessons from retail advertisers in New Zealand, Portugal and Hungary. *Marketing Intelligence & Planning, 21*(5), 282-291.

Gilbert, D. C. & Jackaria, N. (2002). The efficacy of sales promotions in UK supermarkets: a consumer view. *International Journal of Retail & Distribution Management, 30*(6), 315-322.

Ganesh, J., Arnold, M.J., & Reynolds, K.E. (2000). "Understanding the customer base of service providers: An examination of the difference between switchers and stayers". *Journal of Marketing, 64*, 65-87.

Hunt, S. D. & Morgan, R. M. (1995). The comparative advantage theory of competition. *Journal of Marketing, 59*(2), 1-15.

Jaccard, J., Turrisi, R. & Wan, C.K. (1990). *International effects in multiple regression.* Thousand Oaks, CA: Sage University Press.

Johnson, L. K. (2006). Successful business process outsourcing. *Sloan Management Review, 47*(2), 5-6.

Kyrios, M., Frost, R. O. & Steketee, G. (2004). Cognitions in compulsive buying and acquisition. *Cognitive Therapy and Research, 28*(2), 241-258.

Laroche, M., Pons, F., Zgolli, N., Cervellon, M. C. & Kim, C. (2003). A model of consumer response to two retail sales promotion techniques. *Journal of Business Research, 56*(7), 513-522.

Liu, T. C. & Wu, L. W. (2007). Customer retention and cross-buying in the banking industry: An integration of service attributes, satisfaction and trust. *Journal of Financial Services Marketing, 12*(2), 132-145.

MacMillan, I. C. & McGrath, R. G. (1997). Discovering new points of differentiation. *Harvard Business Review, 75*(4), 133-145.

Menon, S. & Kahn, B. (2002). Cross-category effects of induced arousal and pleasure on the internet shopping experience. *Journal of Retailing, 78*(1), 31-40.

Mulhern F J and Williams J D (1994), A comparative analysis of shopping behavior in Hispanic and non-Hispanic market areas, *Journal of Retailing*, 70, 231–251

Narver, J. C. & Slater, S. F. (1990). The effect of market orientation on business profitability. *Journal of Marketing, 54*(4), 20-35.

Ndubisi, N. O. & Moi, C. T. (2005). Customers behavioral responses to sales promotion: the role of fear of losing face. *Asia Pacific Journal of Marketing and Logistics, 17*(1), 32-49.

Otieno, Rose, Harrow, Chris, & Lea-Greenwood, Gaynor (2005). The unhappy shopper, a retail experience: Exploring fashion, fit and affordability. *International Journal of Retail & Distribution Management, 33*(4), 298-309.

Otieno, R., Harrow, C. & Lea-Greenwood, G. (2005). The unhappy shopper, a retail experience: exploring fashion, fit and affordability. *International Journal of Retail & Distribution Management, 33*(4), 298-309.

Parlar, M., Perry, D. & Stadje, W. (2007). Optimal shopping when the sales are on - A markovian full-information best-choice problem. *Stochastic Models, 23*(3), 351-371.

Parsons, A. G. & Ballantine, P. W. (2004). Market dominance, promotions, and shopping mall group performance. *International Journal of Retail & Distribution Management, 32*(10), 458-463.

Parasuraman, A., Zeithaml, V. & Berry, L. (1988). SERVQUAL: A multiple-item scale for measuring consumer perceptions in services quality. *Journal of Retailing, 64*(1), 12-40.

Pires, G. D., Stanton, J. & Rita, P. (2006). The internet, consumer empowerment and marketing strategies. *European Journal of Marketing, 40*(9-10), 936-949.

Platz, L. A. & Temponi, C. (2007). Defining the most desirable outsourcing contract between customer and vendor. *Management Decision*, *45*(10), 1656-1666.

Rajagopal (2005). Buying decisions towards organic products: Analysis of customer value and brand drivers. *International Journal of Emerging Markets*, *2*(3), 236-251.

Rajagopal (2007a). Influence of brand name in variety seeking behavior of consumers: An empirical study. *International Journal of Management Practice*, *2*(4), 306-323.

Rajagopal (2007b). Stimulating retail sales and upholding customer value. *Journal of Retail and Leisure Property*, *6*(2), 117-135.

Rajagopal (2008). Outsourcing salespeople in building arousal towards retail buying. *Journal of Database Marketing and Customer Strategy Management*, *15*(2), 106-118.

Richins, M. L. (1994). Valuing things: The public and private meanings of possessions. *Journal of Consumer Research*, *21*, 504–521.

Ruekert, R. W. (1992). Developing a market orientation: An organizational strategy perspective. *International Journal of Research in Marketing*, *9*(3), 225-245.

Saegert, J., Hoover, R. J. & Hilger, M. T. (1985). Characteristics of Mexican American consumers. *Journal of Consumer Research*, *12*, 104–109.

Selden, L. & MacMillan, I. C. (2006). Manage customer-centric innovation systematically. *Harvard Business Review*, *84*(4), 108-116.

Sena, K. & Petromilli, M. (2005). How DuPont used insights from needs-based research to redefine brand, business. *Handbook of Business Strategy*, *6*(1), 73-79.

Shoham, A. & Brencis, M. M. (2003). Compulsive buying behavior. *Journal of Consumer Marketing*, *20*(2), 127-138.

Vicdan, H., Chapa, S. & de Los Santos, G. (2007). Understanding compulsive buyers' online shopping incidence: A closer look at the effects of sales promotions and bargains on Hispanic Americans. *Journal of Customer Behaviour*, I(1), 57-74.

Watkins, M. & Bond, C. (2007). Ways of experiencing leisure. *Leisure Sciences*, *29*(3), 287-307.

Webster Jr., Frederick E. (1989). *It's 1990- Do you know where your marketing is?* Cambridge:Mass Marketing Science Institute.

Werther, William B. & Kerr, Jaffrey L. (1995). The shifting sands of competitive advantage. *Business Horizons*, May, 1995.

Wirtz, J., Mattila, A. S. & Tan, R. L. P. (2007). The role of arousal congruency in influencing consumers' satisfaction evaluations and in-store behaviors. *International Journal of Service Industry Management, 18*(1), 6-24.

Zhou, L. & Wong, A. (2004). Consumer impulse buying and in-store stimuli in Chinese supermarkets. *Journal of International Consumer Marketing, 16*(2), 37-53.

## ENDNOTES

1. David Welch, Ian Rowley and Michael Eidam : How Honda is Stalling in US, Business Week Online, May 24, 2004
2. Annual report of American Honda Motor Company 2003
3. Rajagopal (2003), *Building Customer Loyalty Through Relationship Networking : A Case of BMW Mexico,* Discussion Case, ITESM, Mexico City Campus, 1-16
4. Rajagopal (2003), *Striving with Competition in Global Imaging Market : Canon in Mexican Business Environment,* Discussion Case, ITESM, Mexico City Campus, 1-22
5. Business Today, September 21, 2000 p 22
6. Zook Chirs and Allen James: Growth Outside the Core, *Harvard Business Review*, December, 2003
7. For details on the competitive behavior of Japanese companies see Easton G *et.al., Managers and Competition*, Blackwell, Oxford, UK, 1993, 246-281

# Chapter II
# Self Service Technologies in Retail Financial Sector

**Rajagopal**
*Monterrey Institute of Technology and Higher Education, ITESM, Mexico*

**Ananya Rajagopal**
*HSBC, Mexico*

## INTRODUCTION

It has been recognized that enhancing the role of technology in a service organization would serve to reduce costs and improve service reliability. The new information technology is becoming an important factor in the future development of financial **services** industry, and especially **banking** industry. However, it is argued that there remains an important role for customized relationships in the delivery of any service proposition (Durkin *et al*, 2008). The developments information and communication technology have significantly contributed to the exponential growth and profits of the financial institutions worldwide. This evolution had transformed the way banks deliver their services, using technologies such as automated teller machines, phones, the Internet, credit cards, and electronic cash. For this reason and as the Internet becomes yet more pervasive in retail banking and the importance of self services perspectives through innovative technology in serving customers effectively is increasingly important for e-banking (Durkin *et al*, 2007). However, banks face a number of important questions on strategies for deriving full advantage of new technology opportunities and tracking electronic development changes affecting interactions with the customers.

In general terms, increasing convenience is a way of raising consumers' surplus provided new technology is adopted by the banks in order to offer convenience to the customers may be through an electronic transaction as a substitute for a trip to the branch. The technology based services imply different combinations of accessibility attributes (time, distance, and search costs), ease of use and price. Another factor in determining the magnitude of the surplus that the bank can seize is the relative importance of cross-selling. The bundle of services provided electronically is usually not the same as the one available at a branch. For this reason new technology based banking services with high customer value may offer better service conditions to harmonize the flow of information and services across the spatial and temporal dimensions. The growth in online or e-banking has resulted in customers interacting with their banks through remote technological channels to a greater extent. However, there is much variation in online banking registration and adoption levels and little is understood about actual customer motivators and perceived barriers to registration for online banking services. It has been observed that convenience offering 24-hour banking access and reassurance about security are the most important considerations for customers in registering for e-banking (Durkin, 2007).

Self service technologies introduced in retail banking have the ability to function as a secured business medium. A large number of customers use the Internet, as a medium of business (electronic-commerce). Association of self service technologies with customers indicate that six attributes common to the diffusion model including perceived convenience and financial benefits, risk, previous use of the telephone for a similar purpose, self-efficacy, and Internet use, play a significant role in the performance of retail banking operations (Eastin, 2002). It can be state that banks adopting information technology based capital-intensive techniques are more efficient as both cost and profit frontier gain competitive advantage in the financial markets (Casolaro and Gobby, 2007).

The following sections of the paper will critically examine the available recent literature on this subject and present strategies for enhancing contribution of various attributes related to technology and customer value in banking services. The common services enhanced through new technology include brokerage and asset management services, personal banking services, checking accounts, and services bills collections, which are standardized and homogenized across branches of the banks. The rationale of shifting conventional practices to technology based operations, its implications on customer value and performance of banking institutions are also argued in the paper. This paper also discusses managerial implications on converging self service technologies with the customer value and business performance in retail banking.

## ELECTRONIC BANKING VS. CONVENTIONAL WISDOM

The maxims of technology spread in the operations of financial institutes may have relational effect with the size and volume of operations of the organization. Whenever the innovation is initially introduced, large banks have an advantage to adopt it first and enjoy further growth of size. Over time, as the innovation diffuses into smaller banks, the aggregate bank size distribution increases stochastically towards a new steady state. Applying the theory to a panel study of internet banking diffusion across 50 US states, it has been observed that technological, economic and institutional factors largely govern the transaction process supported with technology. Conventional baking system has established problems in the use of product-market segmentation methods and offering customized services. Internet banking that focuses on the extent to which retail-bank customers can be clustered according to an adapted decision-making framework and it is found that high levels of Internet use at work positively influence e-banking operations (Durkin, 2004). However, in some developing countries accessibility to Internet, awareness of e-banking, and customers' reluctance to change are the factors have significantly affected the usage of e-banking while there are no significant differences between the age and educational qualifications of the electronic and conventional banking users (Sadiqu and Shanmugham, 2003). An empirical study suggests that many traditional banks tend to be larger, have smaller net interest margins, have relatively fewer core deposits, and exhibit less risk. Such operations have intuitive appeal and conform to conventional wisdom while larger banks have fewer core deposits and face more competitive interest rate conditions, resulting in narrow spreads from traditional intermediation. Such financial institutions have more diverse sources of revenue and greater access to financial markets, which reduces risk (Rogers and Sinkey, 1999).

The empirical findings disentangle the interrelationship between internet banking adoption and growth of average bank size, and explain the variation of diffusion rates across geographic regions (Sullivan and Wang, 2005). Technology in banking industry also has cost implications which lead to slow down the adaptation process in many countries. The effect of technical change on the costs of banking firms operating in Central and Eastern European countries has been studied using Fourier - flexible cost function specification for the period 1995–2002. A common cost frontier with country-specific variables is employed in order to take into account the macro-economic and regulatory conditions that vary over country and time. The findings of the study reveal that the rate of reduction in costs resulting from technical change increased during the sample period. Banks operating in Hungary, Czech Republic and Poland benefited more from technical change than their counterparts. In terms of cost reduction, large banks benefited more from technical progress which underpins that large banks are more able to change their optimal input mix in response to changes in technology (Adnan and Saadet, 2006).

Non-conventional banking practices have been largely supported with the self service technologies and Internet banking options to customers. Branchless banking using information and communication technologies and retail channels to reduce the costs of delivering financial services holds great promise for clients beyond the reach of traditional banks. Much of the current drone involves mobile phone banking and retail agents serving as *banking correspondents* equipped with point-of-sale terminals (Prochaska and Brix, 2008). Conventional wisdom in banking industry led customers towards safety perspectives but limited the flow of information due to time, distance and information search cost. In view of growing financial needs there appears to be an overwhelming customer need for more product information and more involvement with banks. This has major implications for the banks in formulating and implementing relationship management strategies through self service technologies (Howcroft *et al*, 2007). The rationale of shift form conventional wisdom to electronic banking using varied self services technologies has been illustrated in Figure 1.

*Figure 1. Customer-Banker relationship and performance paradigm*

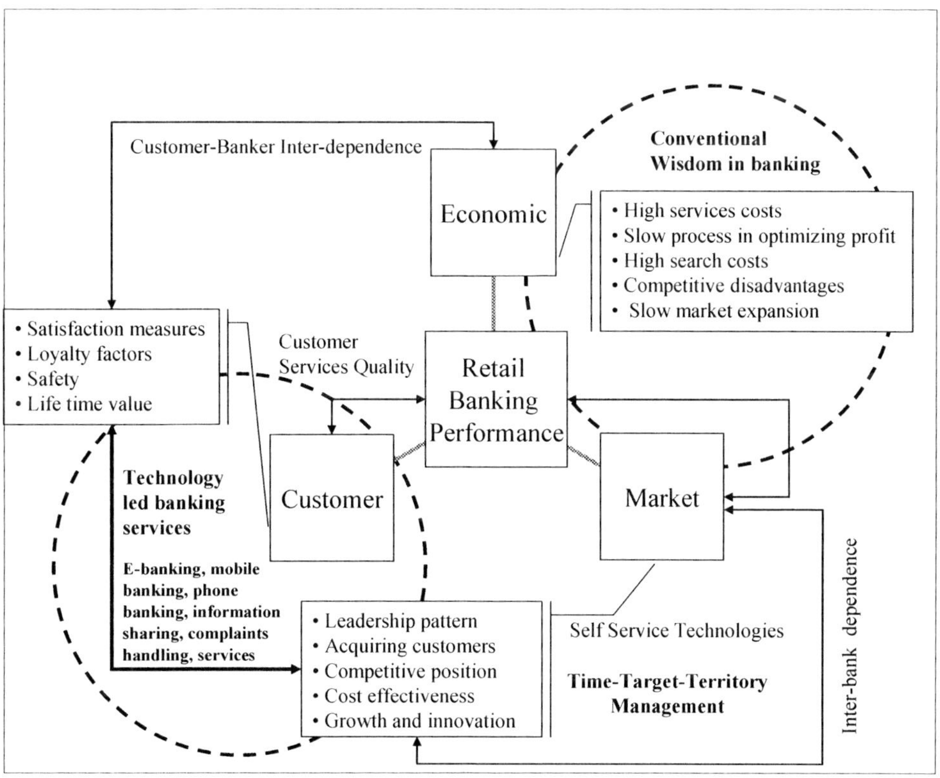

It may be seen from the above exhibit that though conventional wisdom in banking had personal touch in delivering services and developing emotional loyalty towards the institution, it had he major problems of integrating time, target (categorical customers with products) and territories. The self services technology has boosted the concept of branchless banking and networking the customers on global platforms.

The recent dotcom boom/bust cycle, as equilibrium industry dynamics triggered by technology innovation, has been analyzed in various studies. When a major technology innovation arrives, a wave of new firms enters the market implementing the innovation for profits. However, if the innovation complements existing technology, some new entrants will later be forced out as more and more incumbent firms succeed in adopting the innovation. Such situation has revealed that the diffusion of Internet technology among traditional brick-and-mortar firms is indeed the driving force behind the rise and fall of dotcoms as well as the sustained growth of e-commerce (Wang, 2005). However in reference to banking reforms in India, technology has been found to be the major input in driving competition which has been evidenced in a study revealing a positive relationship between the level of competition and banking efficiency. However, a negative relationship between the presence of foreign banks and banking efficiency is found, which attributes to a short-run increase in costs due to the introduction of new banking technology by foreign banks (Ali and Hang, 2006). Availability of computers in the selected developing countries and rate of penetration of internet services are exhibited in the Table 1.

*Table 1. Computer and Internet Penetration Rates (2004)*

| Country/Group | Computers per 100 | Internet Users per 100 |
|---|---|---|
| China | 4.08 | 7.23 |
| India | 1.21 | 3.24 |
| Brazil | 10.71 | 12.18 |
| Mexico | 10.68 | 13.68 |
| Thailand | 6.00 | 11.25 |
| Malaysia | 19.16 | 38.68 |
| Developing Countries | 3.68 | 5.95 |
| Transition Countries | 11.89 | 13.98 |
| Developed Countries | 56.64 | 51.83 |
| World | 12.24 | 13.65 |

*Adapted from Source: Chinn and Fairlie (2006)*

Many financial institutions have built websites to inform and attract customers. Financial aggregation presents an opportunity by which they can build stronger relationships with customers. Information technology affects banking in two main ways. First, it may reduce costs by replacing paper based, labor intensive methods with automated processes. Second, it may modify the ways in which consumers have access to banks' services and products and, hence, may enhance the contestability of markets, especially in retail banking. Due to deregulation and technological advances, new opportunities become available, but the skill needed to exploit them effectively may be unknown. Early entry of financial institutions into the technology expanding activities may have learning benefits that are manifested in discovery of the skill needed to operate effectively. E-banking products and services are getting more and more advanced and increasing in variety by providing information at the early stage to providing transactional activities. The average e-banking penetration for developing countries by the end of 1999 was close to 5 percent. In Brazil, the number of e-banking users reached 8 million in 2000 while in Mexico, the number of e-banking users reached 1.25 million in 2000.

There are many socio-cultural factors associated with adaptation of technology in services industry which should have the compatibility to the customer culture. However, as a concept, self service technology (SST) has been generally limited to technical or functional factors and with regard to value compatibility among the SST providing organization and customers. Cultural disparities among the customers also affect the performance of self service technology offered by the banking industry (Bunker et al, 2007). Retail banking increasingly relies on SST applications to augment efficiency in rendering financial services to their customers and in such information and communication technology environment, customers serve themselves at the convenience of these service options more than ever before. Banks in retailing their products try to create and sustain a competitive advantage by offering customer value based on the utilization of SST options, while customers try to receive the best value for their participation in service production and delivery (Anitsal and Flint, 2006). It is found that self service technologies which can be customized by the users build higher sense of belongingness and safety with the banking industry. The association with the self service technologies in a financial operations lead to three forms of positive attachment, based on three different foundations, which include the credibility of the organization, compatibility between the values of the organization and those of the consumer, and interpersonal or relational considerations (Aldlaigan and Buttle *et al*, 2005).

The e-banking services include e-remittances, e-payments, e-trades, and e-credit. However, many e-banking businesses have been forced out of market due to the low customer perception such as e-procurements supporting the banking transactions of large work tenders. Internet-based transactions require their own security measures for which private solutions may not be sufficient. For example, government actions are needed to set up a framework for digital signatures and to designate agencies or processes to authenticate public keys associated with transactions. Consequently, internet-only banks have been substantially less profitable. They generate lower business volumes and any savings generated by lower physical overheads appear to be offset by other types of non-interest expenditures, notably marketing to attract new customers (de Young 2001). However, e-banking develops automated credit authorization system by developing appropriate credit scoring system and cash-flow scoring system to reduce operating costs, improve asset quality, and increase client profitability. One of the major benefits of credit scoring system is that lenders can make credit decisions without necessarily obtaining financial statement, credit reports, or other time-consuming and hard-to-get information.

There have been strings of research studies exploring the economic and relational issues on internet and advanced technology diffusion in the banking industry. The model developed for estimating the internet banking adoption at the early stages when there is considerable uncertainty about consumers' demand argues that relative bank size and demographic information predictive of future demand positively influence the process of internet banking adaptation (Courchane et al, 2002). Similarly, the Logit model estimates the determinants of internet banking adaptation, which reveals that larger banks are more likely to adapt to internet banking when they are younger, better performing, located in urban areas, and members of a bank holding company (Furst et al, 2001). However, other studies analyze the reverse effect of technology on bank performance but obtain mixed results in reference to characteristics, including costs and profitability, of early adopters of internet banking and find little difference from non-adopters (Sullivan, 2000) though many banks enjoyed rising profits during the 1990s, and attribute this to banks' increasing market power gained by adopting new technologies (Berger and Mester, 2003).

Advances in technologies have allowed service providers to incorporate many different technologies into the delivery of their services. These technologies have been implemented in the service encounter for the customer to use with varying degrees of success. The factors influencing consumer attitudes towards and adoption of self-service technologies (SSTs) across three different technologies used in the banking industry reveals that service attributes related to trust, quality and time are major attributes influence attitudes toward each of these technologies and offers an explanation of the varying degrees of acceptance found among consumers (Curren and Mueter, 2005). Further, on the issue of technology adaptation Lassar *et al* examine the relationships between consumer innovativeness, self-efficacy on the internet, internet attitudes and online banking adoption, while controlling for personal characteristics. While results confirm the positive relationship between internet related innovativeness and online banking they also surprisingly show that general innovativeness is negatively related to online banking (Lassar *et al*, 2005). Bank characteristics such as asset size, number of employees, number of full service locations, areas of lending, and return on assets largely influence the technology diffusion process and adaptation at the customer levels. It has been observed in a study that a number of bank composition and operations variables behaved statistically independent between size variables (assets, number of employees, and number of branches) and wide area network access. The survey data also indicate that return on assets and network system variables are independent. Therefore, networks systems have not had a direct impact on the bottom line (Zhu *et al*, 2004).

## CUSTOMER VALUE MANAGEMENT

The customer values for banking services are shaped more by habits, reinforcement effects, and situational influences than strongly-held attitudes. However, the aggregate returns on the customer value towards the new product from the perspective financial institution may be manifesting in enhancing the market share, services coverage and augmenting profit in a competitive environment. The academics, consultants and business people speculated that marketing in the new century would be very different from the time when much of the pioneering work on customer loyalty was undertaken (Churchill 1942; Brown 1953; Cunningham, 1961; Tucker 1964; Frank 1967). Yet there exists the scope for improving the applied concepts as there have been many changes over conventional ideologies. It has been observed in one of the studies that the customer values are created through individual perceptions, and organizational and relational competence (Johanson *et.al.*, 2001). Management of business relationships is a key strategic success factor to fully utilize the market potential. The goal of relationship development has been defined as the ability to attract, maintain, and enhance new customer relations (Berry 1983). Contributions to this area have developed a number of models for relationship management (Zeithaml, Berry and Parasuraman 1988) and a common denominator of these models is that firms need to adjust to market conditions. This involves, for instance, narrowing perceptional gaps, to adjust workflows in the organization, or to activate the customer as a relationship partner.

The value concept in the above relationship governs the customer portfolio decision in terms of formulation of recursive utility over time. It shows that the optimal portfolio demand for products under competition varies strongly with the values associated with the brand, industry attractiveness, knowledge management and ethical issues of the organization. The extent of business values determines the relative risk aversion in terms of functional and logistical efficiency between the organization and supplier while the switching attitude may influence the customers if the organizational values are not strong and sustainable in the given competitive environment (Rajagopal, 2006[a]).

A study examines the success of product pricing practices and the conditions upon which success is contingent discussing three different pricing practices that refer to the use of information on customer value, competition, and costs respectively. The study argues that the success of these practices is contingent on relative product advantage and competitive intensity. The study reveals that there are no general "best" or "bad" practices, but that a contingency approach is appropriate (Ingenbleek *et.al.*, 2003). Value and pricing models have been developed for many different products, services and assets. Some of these are extensions and refinements of convention models value driven pricing theories (Gamrowski & Rachev, 1999; Pedersen, 2000). Also there have been some models that are developed and calibrated addressing specific issues such as model for household assets demand (Perraudin & Sorensen, 2000). The key marketing variables such as price, brand name, and product attributes affect customers' judgment processes and derive inference on its quality dimensions leading to customer satisfaction. The experimental study conducted indicates that customers use price and brand name differently to judge the quality dimensions and measure the degree of satisfaction (Brucks *et.al.*, 2000).

The value of corporate brand endorsement across different products and product lines, and at lower levels of the brand hierarchy also needs to be assessed as a customer value driver. Use of corporate brand endorsement either as a name identifier or logo identifies the product with the company, and provides reassurance for the customer (Rajagopal and Sanchez, 2004). A perspective from resource-advantage theory (Hunt and Morgan, 1995) is used to formulate expectations on the degree to which the use of information on customer value, competition, and costs contribute to the success of a price decision. It is argued that the success of these practices is contingent on the relative customer value the firm has created and the degree to which this position of relative value is sustainable in the competitive market place. These expectations are empirically tested on pricing decisions with respect to the introduction of new industrial capital goods.

The studies that advocate the models of building customer value through traditional relationship marketing discuss the long term value concepts to loyal customers. Most importantly, these are expected to raise their spending and association with the products and services of the company with increasing levels of satisfactions that attribute to values of customers (Reichheld and Sasser, 1990). In the most optimistic settings, such value creation is observed to generate new customers for new products in view of the customer relationship and value management strategies of the firm (Ganesh, *et.al.*, 2000). In the high customer value framework, the firm ensures diminished costs to serve (Knox, 1998) and exhibits reduced customer price sensitivities. A database-driven approach, customer tenure in reference to the length of a customer's relationship and values retention with a company has often been used to approximate the loyalty construct (Ganesh *et.al.*, 2000; Reinartz and Kumar, 2000; 2002). Hence the relationship marketing with a customer value orientation thrives on the concept that raises the length of the customer-company relationship which contributes in optimizing the profit for the firm (Reichheld and Sasser, 1990). However, the contributions of long-life customers were generally declining and in a non-contractual setting short-life but high-revenue customers accounted for a sizeable amount of profits (Reinartz and Kumar, 2000).

The role of customer value has been largely recognized over time by the financial institutions as an instrument towards stimulating market share and profit optimization. The customer values for a new product of financial institution in competitive markets are shaped more by habits, reinforcement effects, and situational influences than strongly-held attitudes. A strong and sustainable customer value associated with a new product launched by a financial institution may also lead to build the customer loyalty in the long run. An analysis of the new product-market structuring based on customer value may be developed well within the microeconomic framework of financial institutions. The aggregate returns on the customer value towards the baking services from the perspective of financial institution may be observed manifesting in enhancing the market share, services coverage and augmenting brand in a given market. The value of a customer may be defined in reference to a firm as the expected performance measures are based on key assumptions concerning retention rate and profit margin and the customer value also tracks market value of these firms over time. The value of all customers is determined by the acquisition rate and cost of acquiring new customers (Gupta *et al*, 2003).

In the process of enhancing the customer value for the new products, a financial institution may simultaneously use intensive customer value for technology based banking services and intensive customer relationship management (CRM) strategies to the competitive sales and marketing strategies. The integrated impact of CRM, sales and marketing strategies at different stages of service attractiveness would contribute to the customer value and influence the aggregate returns on the customer value derived at various stages of service attractiveness of the financial institutions. However, a financial institution may need to compute the trend of customer value for all the services in its product line, and measure the variability in the customer values perceived for its new services. The customer values are broadly reflected in the competitive gains, perceived values, and extent of association with the financial services and level of quintessence with the customer relationship management services of the organization.

## GENERAL DISCUSSION AND MANAGERIAL IMPLICATIONS

Few contributions address the measurement of the customer value as an intangible asset of the financial institutions, though substantial literature is available discussing the customer relations and loyalty building perspectives. In view of growing customer demand for innovative technology with quality banking services to accelerate the information and transaction process, it may be observed that greater household access to the Internet drives a higher website adoption rate. There are many information and transaction access outlets in developed western countries and developing countries of Latin America and Caribbean which include phone banking, mobile services and internet banking portals. However, greater household access to the Internet and mobile devices in banking operations may be negatively related to local average bank assets. A possible explanation is that once the customers have access to the information and transactions on internet and mobile devices, they would form a relationship with bank outside of their region/country, which may have a negative impact on the size of banks in their region.

Over time, due to internal and external changes in the organizational environment in reference to customer demand, technology progress and improvements in banking regulation, the innovation diffuses into smaller banks. The major factors affecting technology adoption and augmenting include mean bank size, per capita income, household access to internet, average bank age, bank loan specialization, competitive advantages in banking products, product-mix of banks, self-service technologies, cost of adoption, level of customer satisfaction and customer density in the region availing banking services. The costs of accessing electronic banking services need to be reduced for wider coverage of customers on e-banking bay. Comprehensive knowledge dissemination and trust play pivotal role in creating customer value, in absence of which knowledge barriers may limit the size of the market to a subset of bank customers in the short term. Therefore, once a bank has taken the decision of adopting new technology for improving its services and optimizing profit, the bank will lean to depend on market-specific demand characteristics.

The common services such as brokerage and asset management services, personal banking services, checking accounts and services bills collections are standardized and homogeneous, hence self-service technologies can be considered as a substitute to a branch transaction regardless the issue of complementarity of the entire bundle of banking services. Exploring the synergy between online and offline channels in general reveals that a bank typically delivers standardized, low-value-added transactions such as bill payments, balance inquiries, account transfers and credit card lending through the inexpensive Internet channel, while delivering specialized, high-value-added transactions such as small business lending, personal trust services and investment banking through the more expensive branch channel. By providing more service options to its customers, an improved technology adoption will enable the bank to retain its most profitable customers and generate more revenue from cross-selling. Some banks, which operate on branchless concepts and depend only on internet, have lower asset returns than incumbent branching banks as well as new branching entrants. This is primarily due to their lower interest margins and fee income, lower levels of loan and deposit generation, fewer business loans, and higher non-interest expense for equipment and skilled labor. The financials of such banks turn robust after implementing stick surveillance measure to sustain future competition.

An augmented and sustainable customer value builds the loyalty towards the product and brand implying that bank managers should develop customer driven strategies so that relationship augmentations can be achieved. This is not simply a matter of segmenting customers, but also signals the need to manage the reciprocities of relationship. It has been argued that relationships are constituted by value creating transformations in which the customer may contribute in different ways. It is necessary for retail banking firms to understanding Market Requirement (MR) for Enabling Innovations (EI) which would lead to enhanced Business Opportunities (BO) in the region. These opportunities, *when realized*, spur growth through Business Performance (BP) that further makes possible the creation of customer value (CV). The above relationship of functional factors may be expressed as: Relationship development is to improve these processes by capitalizing on an increasing customer involvement in adaptation of new technology used in the bank. However, acquiring new customers is the easiest way to develop enhanced customer-technology relations favoring the growth of the bank. Self-service technologies are large customer centric but their performance is based on adaptation of services and intensity of usage of applications. Phone banking has many advantages in delivering financial services; however there are many security issues which emerge despite a well knit key public infrastructure assured by the banks. The pattern of processing technology let banking services in reference to enhancing customer values has been exhibited in Figure 2.

Systematically explored concepts in the field of customer value, and market driven approach towards new products would be beneficial for a company to derive long term profit optimization strategy over the period. Hence, a comprehensive framework for estimating both the value of a **customer** and profit optimization need to be developed. The self-service technology is distinguished by consumer participation in service production and delivery which is independent of service personnel and marginal interpersonal interaction between consumers and service organization. In view of this intrinsic attribute of SST, it fails to perform as promised, some major challenges arise for managers including lack of security or reassurance of service personnel to assist them, customer are unable to voice their dissatisfaction and lack

*Figure 2. Technology enabled Business Performance Cycle*

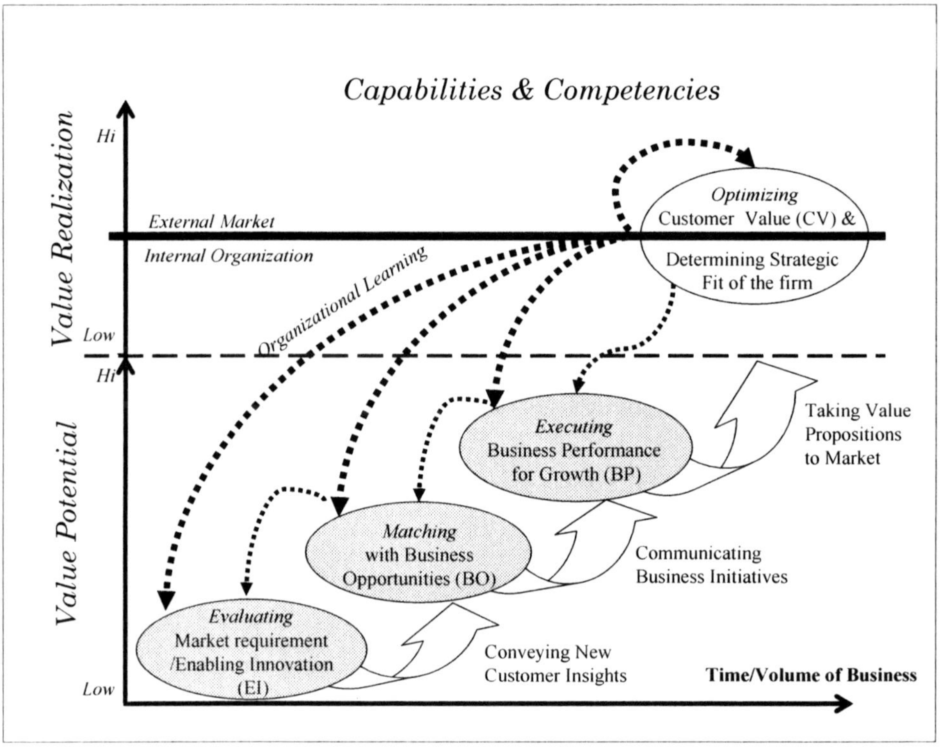


of responsiveness to the resolve customer complaints. As reports of consumer dissatisfaction with SSTs become increasingly common, it is important, therefore, to investigate how organizations with SST-based offerings can encourage consumers to voice their dissatisfaction directly to the organization. Although the antecedents of consumer voice are well documented in the interpersonal services context, in the context of SSTs they have been subject to very little conceptual or empirical examination. However, on a tactical level, managers need to consider the optimum spread of customers on a matrix of product attractiveness and market coverage. This needs careful attention and the application of managerial judgment and experience to measure the value driven performance of the product of the firm. It is necessary for the managers to understand that customer value is context dependent and there exists a whole value network to measure, not just a value chain. This value network will contain important entities far beyond the ones commonly taken into consideration in financial projections and business analyses.

## REFERENCES


Aldlaigan, A. & Buttle, F (2005). Beyond satisfaction: customer attachment to retail banks. *The International Journal of Bank Marketing*, *23*(4), 349-359.

Ataullah, Ali & Le, Hang (2006). Economic reforms and bank efficiency in developing countries: The case of the Indian banking industry. *Applied Financial Economics*, *16*(9), 653-663.

Anitsal, Ismet & Flint, Daniel J. (2006). Exploring customers' perceptions in creating and delivering value technology-based self-service as an illustration. *Services Marketing Quarterly*, *27*(1), 57-72.

Berger, Allen & Mester, Loretta (2003). Explaining the dramatic changes of performance of U.S. banks: Technological change, deregulation and dynamic changes in competition. *Journal of Financial Intermediation*, *12*(1), 57-95.

Berry, L (1983). Relationship marketing. In L. Berry, L. Shostack & G. Upah (Eds.), *Emerging perspectives on services marketing*, (pp. 25-28). Chicago:American Marketing Association.

Brown, George H. (1953). Brand loyalty - Fact or fiction. *Advertising Age*, *24*. Reprinted in A.S.C. Ehrenberg & F.G. Pratt, *Customer Behaviour*, Middlesex, UK: Penguin, 1971, 28-35

Brucks, Merrie, Zeithaml, Valarie A. & Naylorm Gilian (2000). Price and brand name as indicators of quality dimensions of customer durables. *Journal of Academy of Marketing Science*, *28*(3), 359-374.

Bunker, Deborah, Kautz, Karl-Heinz, Nguyen, Anne Luu Thanh (2007). Role of value compatibility in IT adoption. *Journal of Information Technology*, *22*(1-2), 69-78.

Casolaro, L. & Gobbi, G. (2007). Information technology and productivity changes in the banking industry. *Economic Notes*, *36*(1), 43-76.

Chinn, M. D., & Fairlie, R.W. (2006). *ICT uses in the developing world: An analysis of differences in computer and internet penetration*. National Bureau of Economic Research, NBER Working Paper # 12382.

Churchill, H. (1942). How to measure brand loyalty. *Advertising and Selling*, *35*, 24.

Cunningham, R.M. (1956). Brand loyalty - What, where, how much? *Harvard Business Review*, *34*, 116-128.

Courchane, Marsha, David Nickerson & Richard J. Sullivan, (2002). Investment in Internet banking as a real option: Theory and tests. *The Journal of Multinational Financial Management*, 12(4-5), 347-63

Cunningham, R. M. (1961). Customer loyalty to store and brand. *Harvard Business Review, November-December,* 127-137.

Curran, James M. & Meuter, Matthew L. (2005).Self-service technology adoption: comparing three technologies. *Journal of Services Marketing, 19*(2), 103-113.

de Young, Robert (2001). *The financial progress of pure-play internet banks.* BIS Papers, No. 7, November.

Durkin, M. (2004). In search of the Internet-banking customer: Exploring the use of decision styles. *The International Journal of Bank Marketing, 22(7*), 484-503.

Durkin, M. (2007). Understanding registration influences for electronic banking. *The International Review of Retail, Distribution and Consumer Research, 17*(3), 219-231.

Durkin, M., O'Donnell, A., & Crowe, J. (2008). Relationship disconnect in retail banking. *Journal of Financial Services Marketing, 12*(4), 260-271.

Durkin, M., O'Donnell, A., Mullholland, G. & Crowe, J. (2007). On e-banking adoption: from banker perception to customer reality. *Journal of Strategic Marketing, 15*(2-3), 237-252.

Eastin, M. S. (2002). Diffusion of e-commerce: An analysis of the adoption of four e-commerce activities. *Telematics and Informatics, 19*(3), 251-267.

Frank, Ronald E. (1967). Is brand loyalty a useful basis for market segmentation? *Journal of Advertising Research, 7*(2), 27-33.

Furst, Karen, Lang, William & Nolle, Daniel (2001). Internet banking in the U.S.: Landscape, prospects, and industry implications." *Journal of Financial Transformation, 2*, 45-52

Ganesh, J., Arnold, M.J. & Reynolds, K. E. (2000). Understanding the customer base of service providers: An rxamination of the fifference between switchers and stayers. *Journal of Marketing, 64*, July, 65-87.

Gamrowski, B. & Rachev, S. (1999). A testable version of the Pareto-Stable CAPM. *Mathematical and Computer Modeling, 29*, 61-81.

Gupta, S., Lehmann, D. R. & Stuart, J. A. (2003). *Valuing customers.* HBS Marketing Research Paper, No. 03-08.

Howcroft, B., Hamilton, R., & Hewer, P. (2007). Customer involvement and interaction in retail banking: an examination of risk and confidence in the purchase of financial products. *Journal of Services Marketing, 21*(7), 481-491.

Hunt, S. D. & Morgan, R. M. (1995). The comparative advantage theory of competition. *Journal of Marketing, 59,* April, 1-15.

Ingenbleek ,Paul, Debruyn,e Marion, Frambach, Ruud T. & Verhallen, Theo (2003). Successful new product pricing practices: A contingency approach. *Marketing letters, 14*(4), December, 289-305.

Johnson, Ulf, Martensson, Maria & Skoog, Matti (2001), Measuring to understand intangible performance drivers. *European Accounting Review, 10*(3), 407-437.

Kasman, Adnan & Kasman, Saadet Kirbas (2006). Technical change in banking: Evidence from transition countries. *International Journal of the Economics of Business, 13*(1), 129-144.

Knox, S. (1998). Loyalty brand segmentation and the customer development process. *European Management Journal, 16*(6), 729-737.

Lassar, Walfried M., Manolis, Chris, & Lassar, Sharon S. (2005). The relationship between consumer innovativeness, personal characteristics, and online banking adoption. *The International Journal of Bank Marketing, 23*(2), 176-199

Ofek, Elie (2002). *Customer profitability and lifetime value.* Harvard Business School, Note, August, 1-9 (Publication reference 9-503-019).

Pederson, Christian S. (2000). Sparsing risk and return in CAPM: A general utility based model. *European Journal of Operational Research, 123*(3), 628-639.

Perraudin, William R. M. & Sorensen, B. E. (2000). The demand of risky assets: Sample selection and household portfolios. *Journal of Econometrics, 97,* 117-144

Prochaska, K . & Brix, L. (2008). Regulating transformational branchless banking: Dispatches from the policy frontlines. *Enterprise Development and Microfinance, 19*(1), 31-45.

Rajagopal (2005). Measuring variability factors in consumer values for profit optimization in a Firm – A Framework for analysis. *Journal of Economics and Management, 1*(1), 85-103.

Rajagopal (2006a). Measuring customer value gaps: An empirical analysis in the Mexican retail market. *Economic Issue, 10*(1), 19-40.

Rajagopal (2006b). Measuring customer value and market dynamics for new products of a firm: An analytical construct for gaining competitive advantage. *Global Business and Economics Review, 8*(3-4), 187-205.

Rajagopal and Sanchez, R. (2004). Conceptual analysis of brand architecture and relations within product categories. *The Journal of Brand Management, 11*(3), 233-247.

Reichheld, F. F. & Sasser, W. E. (1990). Zero defections: Quality comes to services. *Harvard Business Review, 68*, 105-111.

Reinartz, W. J. & Kumar, V. (2000). On the profitability of long-life customers in a non-contractual setting: An empirical investigation and implementation for marketing. *Journal of Marketing, 64*(4), 17-35.

Reinartz, W. J. & Kumar, V. (2002). The mismanagement of customer loyalty. *Harvard Business Review*, July, 4-12.

Rogers, K. & Sinkey, J. F. (1999). An analysis of nontraditional activities at U.S. commercial banks - evidence of market discipline. *Review of Financial Economics, 8*(1), 25-39.

Sadiq, SI M. & Shanmugham, B. (2003). E-banking and customer preferences in Malaysia: An empirical investigation. *Information Sciences, 150*(3), 207-217.

Sullivan, Richard J. (2000). *How has the adoption of Internet banking affected performance and risk in banks? A look at Internet banking in the Tenth Federal Reserve District.* Financial Industry Perspective, Federal Reserve Bank of Kansas City, Occasional Papers.

Sullivan, Richard J. & Wang, Zhu (2005), *Internet banking: An exploration in technology diffusion and impact.* Federal Reserve Bank of Kansas City, Payments System Research Working Paper # PSR-WP-05-05, (pp. 1-45).

Tucker, William T. (1964). The development of brand loyalty. *Journal of Marketing Research, 1*(3), pp 32-35.

Wang, Zhu (2005). *Technology innovation and market turbulence: A dot com example.* Federal Reserve Bank of Kansas City, Payments System Research Working Paper # PSR-WP-05-02, (pp. 1-49).

Zeithaml, V., Berry, L., & Parasuraman, A. (1988). Communication and control process the delivery of services quality. *Journal of Marketing*, 52, 35-48

Zhu Zhiwei, Scheuermann, Larry & Babineaux Jr., Billy J. (2004). Information network technology in the banking industry. *Industrial Management & Data Systems, 104(*5), 409-417.

# Chapter III
# Customer Value and New Product Retailing Dynamics:
## An Analytical Construct for Gaining Competitive Advantage

**Rajagopal**
*Monterrey Institute of Technology and Higher Education, ITESM, Mexico*

The customer value concept is utilized to assess product performance and to determine the competitive structure of the new products. The analytical approach to the new product-market structuring based on customer value may be fitted well within the microeconomic framework. The measure of customer value as the product efficiency may be viewed from the customer's perspective towards a ratio of outputs (e.g., perceived use value, resale value, reliability, safety, comfort) that customers obtain from a product relative to inputs (price, running costs) that customers have to deliver in exchange. The efficiency value derived can be understood as the return on the customer's investment. Products offering a maximum customer value relative to all other alternatives in the market are characterized as efficient. Different efficient products may create value in different ways using different strategies (output-input combinations). Each efficient product can be viewed as a benchmark for a distinct sub-market. Jointly, these products form the efficient frontier, which serves as a reference function for the inefficient products (Bauer *et.al*, 2004). Thus, customer value of new products is defined as a relative concept. Market partitioning is achieved endogenously by clustering products in one segment that are benchmarked by the same efficient peer(s). This ensures that only products with a similar output-input structure are partitioned into the same sub-market. As a result, a sub-market consists of highly substitutable products. The individual values of the customer may be estimated as base values and changes in such values are affected by the corresponding measures of the specific value drivers. The base value ties to the most important of all complements that may be determined as customers' need. Estimating value drivers for a new product can be tricky because there is no direct historical data. However, we can assume that the impact from changes in price or availability of complements will be similar to what other markets have experienced.

In recognizing the need to contribute research in the area of customer value measurement and the concept of customer satisfaction leading towards creating the customer value, the study aims at developing a methodological construct to measure the customer value for new products introduced by a firm. The following discussion attempts to critically examine the available literature on the subject, discuss a model that provides a framework for analyzing the variables associated with customer value and to identify potential research areas. A basic premise of the arguments in this chapter are that the focus should be on maximizing total customer value and customer satisfaction which are inter-dependent in the decision making process towards buying new products. This chapter, being a part of emerging literature on customer value management, extends the existing knowledge of the relationship between launch of new products in the market and creating customer value by introducing the framework of a mathematical model. The framework of the construct is based on a proposed model which integrates all aspects so as to maximize the potential of the organization and all its subsystems to create and sustain satisfied customers. The approach begins with a conceptualization phase in which the concept of customer satisfaction is explored. Attributes are then classified into services and this is then extended to integrate the internal customer into a total service model; applying gap-analysis to this model. Enterprise satisfaction provides the basis for extending the total service model; positioning is applied to the customer satisfaction strategy; and operationalizing this strategy is proposed through an implementation model.

## PREVIOUS CONTRIBUTIONS

It has been observed that there is increasing number of customer goods and services offered in recent years suggest that product-line extensions have become a favored strategy of product managers. A larger assortment, it is often argued, keeps customers loyal and allows firms to charge higher prices. There also exists a disagreement about the extent to which a longer product line translates into higher profits keeping the customer value higher. The academics, consultants and business people speculated that marketing in the new century would be very different from the time when much of the pioneering work on customer loyalty was undertaken (Churchill 1942; Brown 1953; Cunningham 1956, 1961; Tucker 1964; Frank 1967). Yet there exists the scope for improving the applied concepts as there have been many changes over conventional ideologies. A study using market-level data for the yogurt category developed an econometric model derived from a game-theoretic perspective explicitly considers firms' use of product-line length as a competitive tool (Dragnska and Jain, 2005). On the demand side, the study analytically establishes the link between customer choice and the length of the product line and includes a measure of line length in the utility function to investigate customer preference for variety using a brand-level discrete-choice model. The study reveals that the supply side is characterized by price and line length competition between oligopolistic firms.

Another study explores qualitatively the understanding of the importance of intangibles as performance drivers in reference to Swedish organizations using a combination of evolutionary theory, knowledge-based theory and organizational learning. The study reveals that the customer values are created towards the new products through individual perceptions, and organizational and relational competence (Johanson *et.al.*, 2001). The firms need to ascertain a continuous organizational learning process with respect to the value creation chain and measure performance of the new products introduced in the market. In the growing competitive markets the large and reputed firms are developing strategies to move into the provision of innovative combinations of products and services as 'high-value integrated solutions' tailored to each customer's needs than simply 'moving downstream' into services. Such firms are developing innovative combinations of service capabilities such as operations, business consultancy and finance required to provide complete solutions to each customer's needs in order to augment the customer value towards the innovative or new products. It has been argued that the provision of integrated solutions is attracting firms traditionally based in manufacturing and services to occupy a new base in the value stream centered on 'systems integration' using internal or external sources of product designing, supply and customer focused promotion (Davies,2004). Besides the organizational perspectives of enhancing the customer value, the functional variables like pricing play a significant role in developing the customer perceptions towards the new products.

A study examines the success of new product pricing practices and the conditions upon which success is contingent discussing three different pricing practices that refer to the use of information on customer value, competition, and costs respectively. The study argues that the success of these practices is contingent on relative product advantage and competitive intensity. The study reveals that there are no general "best" or "bad" practices, but that a contingency approach is appropriate

(Ingenbleek *et.al.*, 2003). Value and pricing models have been developed for many different products, services and assets. Some of them are extensions and refinements of convention models value driven pricing theories (Gamrowski & Rachev, 1999; Pedersen, 2000). Also there have been some models that are developed and calibrated addressing specific issues such as model for household assets demand (Perraudin & Sorensen, 2000). The key marketing variables such as price, brand name, and product attributes affect customers' judgment processes and derive inference on its quality dimensions leading to customer satisfaction. The experimental study conducted indicates that customers use price and brand name differently to judge the quality dimensions and measure the degree of satisfaction (Brucks *et.al.*, 2000). The value of corporate brand endorsement across different products and product lines, and at lower levels of the brand hierarchy also needs to be assessed as a customer value driver. Use of corporate brand endorsement either as a name identifier or logo identifies the product with the company, and provides reassurance for the customer (Rajagopal and Sanchez, 2004). A perspective from resource-advantage theory (Hunt and Morgan, 1995) is used to formulate expectations on the degree to which the use of information on customer value, competition, and costs contribute to the success of a price decision. It is argued that the success of these practices is contingent on the relative customer value the firm has created and the degree to which this position of relative value is sustainable in the competitive market place. These expectations are empirically tested on pricing decisions with respect to the introduction of new industrial capital goods.

Research on consumer reaction to price has been largely confined to examining consumers' price information search, evaluation of price alternatives, and individual purchase behaviors without regard to situational influences. At the same time, consumption has often been dichotomized in terms of its functional-hedonic nature and closely associated with the level of satisfaction leading to determine the customer value influence (Wakefield and Inman, 2003). As the new products are introduced, a firm may routinely pass these costs on to consumers resulting into high prices. However a less obvious strategy in a competitive situation may be to maintain price, in order to drive the new product in the market with more emphasis on quality, brand name, post-sales services and customer relations management as non-price factors. In many ways, such strategies of a firm with the new products may drive the consumer behavior towards being sensitive to the price increase when it comes to making a buying decision. Some of the marketplace and experimental studies show that consumers are more sensitive to changes in price than to innovation and new products introduced by the firm (Gourville and Koehler, 2004). There are some critical issues associated to the price sensitive consumer behavior, whether customers are equally price-sensitive while purchasing products for functional (*e.g.* purchasing frozen vegetables, toiletries or paper towels) versus hedonic (*e.g.* purchasing a high technology computer or a video camera) consumption situations and whether perceived value derived during consuming the product influences price sensitivity. It may also be stated that higher price volatility makes consumers more sensitive to gains and less sensitive to losses, while intense price promotion by competing brands makes consumers more sensitive to losses but does not influence consumers' sensitivity to gains (Han *et.al*, 2001).

The studies that advocate the models of building customer value through traditional relationship marketing discuss the long term value concepts to loyal customers. Most importantly, these are expected to raise their spending and association with the products and services of the company with increasing levels of satisfactions that attribute to values of customers (Reichheld and Sasser, 1990). In the most optimistic settings, such value creation is observed to generate new customers for new products in view of the customer relationship and value management strategies of the firm (Ganesh, *et.al.*, 2000). In the high customer value framework, the firm ensures diminished costs to serve (Knox, 1998) and exhibits reduced customer price sensitivities. A database-driven approach, customer tenure in reference to the length of a customer's relationship and values retention with a company has often been used to approximate the loyalty construct (Ganesh *et.al.*, 2000; Reinartz and Kumar, 2000; 2002). Hence the relationship marketing with a customer value orientation thrives on the concept that raises the length of the customer-company relationship which contributes in optimizing the profit for the firm (Reichheld and Sasser, 1990). However, the contributions of long-life customers were generally declining and in a non-contractual setting short-life but high-revenue customers accounted for a sizeable amount of profits (Reinartz and Kumar, 2000).

The analysis of the perceived values of customers towards new products is a complex issue. Despite considerable research in the field of measuring customer values in the recent past, it is still not clear how value interacts with marketing related constructs. However there exists the need for evolving a comprehensive application models determining the interrelationship between customer satisfaction and customer value, which may help in reducing the ambiguities surrounding both concepts. One of the studies in this regard discusses the two alternative models yielding empirically tested results in a cross-sectional survey with purchasing managers in Germany. The first model suggests a direct impact of perceived value on the purchasing managers' intentions. In the second model, perceived value is mediated by satisfaction. This research suggests that value and satisfaction can be conceptualized and measured as two distinct, yet complementary constructs (Eggert and Ulaga, 2002).

Improving customer value through faster response times for new products is a significant way to gain competitive advantage. In the globalization process many approaches to new product development emerge, which exhibit an internal focus and view the new product development process as terminating with product launch. However, it is process output that really counts, such as customer availability. A study proposes that with shortening product life cycles it should pay to get the product into the market as quickly as possible, and indicates that these markets should be defined on an international basis. The results of the study reveals that greater new product commercial success is significantly associated with a more ambitious and speedier launch into overseas markets as the process of innovation is only complete when potential customers on a world scale are introduced effectively to the new product (Oakley, 1996). The retail sales performance and the **customer** value approach are conceptually and methodically analogous. Both concepts calculate the value of a particular decision unit by analytical attributes forecast and the risk-adjusted value parameters. However, virtually no scholarly attention has been devoted to the question if any of these components of the shareholder value could be determined in a more market oriented way using individual **customer** lifetime **values (Rajagopal, 2005)**. The value of a customer may be defined in reference to a firm as the expected performance measures are based on key assumptions concerning retention rate and profit margin and the customer value also tracks market value of these firms over time. The value of all customers is determined by the acquisition rate and cost of acquiring new customers (Gupta, Lehmann and Stuart, 2003).

## FRAMEWORK FOR ANALYSIS

A retail chain is modeled as a dummy control center (CC) that helps in evolving strategies, marketing designs and building corporate image. The CC is an integrated part of the corporate headquarters that is instrumental in making most of the business decisions. Let us assume that there are L networks and $D_m$ spatially spread markets. $\Delta_j \subseteq \{1,2,...,D_m\}$ denotes the set of markets served by chains j and $\varphi_h \subseteq \{1,2,...,L\}$ denotes the set of chains serving markets h, the operations of chain in j$^{th}$ store in market h in period $t$ are fully described by an N-dimensional vector, $Z^{j,h}(t) \equiv \left(Z_1^{j,h}(t),...,Z_N^{j,h}(t)\right) \in \{1,...,R\}^N$, where $Z_K^{j,h}(t)$ is the practice for the k$^{th}$ dimensions of the store operations. There are then R feasible practices for each dimension. The store operations of chain $j$ is represented by an element of $\{1,2,...,R\}^{N|\Delta_j|}$.

### Measuring the Customer Value

The customer values for goods and services are largely associated with the retail stores brands and customer services offered therein. The beginning of customer preferences is the basic discrete time that helps the customers in making a buying decision and maximizing the value of product. Ofek Elie (2002) discussed that the value of product and service are not always the same and are subject to value life cycle that governs the customer preferences in the long-run. If customers prefer the product and service for N periods with Q as value perceived by the customer, the value may be determined as Q>N, where Q and N both are exogenous variables. If every customer receives higher perceived values for each of his buying, the value added product $q \geq Q$, where 'q' refers to the change in the quality brought by innovation or up-graded technology. The customer may refrain from buying the products if $q \leq Q$, that does not influence his buying decisions. However, a strong referral 'R' may lead to influence the customer values, with an advantage factor β that may be explained by price or quality factor. In view of the above discussion it may be assumed that customer preferences have high variability that grows the value factors in retail buyers' decisions:

$$D_{bn} = \sum_{t=1}^{N} \beta^{t} \mu \left(C_t, \hat{Z}\right) + \beta^{N+1} Q_t \qquad \text{(i)}$$

Where, $D_{bn}$ is expressed as initial buying decision of the customers, $C_t$ represents consumption, $\hat{Z}$ is a vector of customer attributes (*viz.* preferential variables) and $Q_t$ is the value perceived by the customer.

A customer value is a dynamic attribute that plays a key role in buying and is an intangible factor to be considered in all marketing and selling functions. The value equation for customer satisfaction may be expressed as a function of all value drivers wherein each driver contains the parameters that directly or indirectly offer competitive advantages to the customers and enhance the customer value.

$$V' = K_s, K_m, K_d, K_c \left[\prod \left\{V\left(x, t, q, p\right)\right\}\right] \qquad \text{(ii)}$$

In the above equation $V'$ is a specific customer value driver, $K$ are constants for supplies($K_s$),margins ($K_m$), distribution ($K_d$), and cost to customers ($K_c$); $x$ is volume, $t$ is time, $q$ is quality and $p$ denotes price. The perceived customer value ($V$) is a function of price ($p$) and non-price factors including quality ($q$) and volume ($x$) in a given time $t$. Hence $\prod$ has been used as a multiplication operator in the above equation. The quality of the product and volume are closely associated with the customer values. The total utility for the conventional products goes up due to economy of scale as the quality is also increased simultaneously ($\partial_v/\partial_x$>0). The $\partial$ customer value is enhanced by offering larger volume of product at a competitive price in a given time ($\partial_v/\partial_p$>0) and ($\partial_v/\partial_t$>0). The conventional products create lower values to the customers ($\partial_v/\partial_x$<0) while the innovative products irrespective of price advantages, enhance the customer value ($\partial_v/\partial_x$>0). The value addition in the conventional products provides lesser enhancement in customer satisfaction as shift in the technology may be expressed as:

$$V'_{hj} = a\left[\sum \frac{T_p}{(1+V_p)^{(1+j+i)}}\right] + b(X_j) \tag{iii}$$

In this equation $V'_{hj}$ represents enhancements in customer value over the transition from conventional to innovative products, *a* and *b* are constants, $T_p$ denotes high-tech and high-value products, $V_p$ represents value of product performance that leads to enhance the customer value, the volume is denoted by *X* and j is the period during which customer value is measured.

Besides the high-tech and high-value products the customers and companies may also find scope of enhancing values with appropriate promotional strategies. The customer values often get enhanced by offering better buying opportunities that reflect on short- and long- term gains. Let us assume that the competitive advantage in existing products over time is $G_x$ that offers $j^{th}$ level of satisfaction through various sales promotion approaches adopted by the company. Such market situation may be explained as:

$$G_x = \left[r_1m_1; r_2m_2; r_3m_3; ......; r_jm_j\right] \tag{iv}$$

Where $r_j$ denotes the $j^{th}$ level of satisfaction (j = 1,2,3,....,n) and $m_j$ is the number of customers attracted towards buying the product. It may be stated that competitive advantage for the existing products of a firm over time is determined by the level of satisfaction derived by the customers and number of customers favoring the buying decisions for the products in a given market. The parameters of customer satisfaction may include product innovativeness, perceived use value, sales promotion, influence of referrals, price and non-price factors. The competitive advantage of a firm is also measurable from the perspective of product attractiveness to generate new customers. Given the scope of retail networks, a feasible value structure for customers may be reflected in repeat buying behavior ($\hat{R}$) that explains the relationship of the customer value with the product and associated marketing strategies. The impact of such customer value attributes in a given situation may be described as:

$$\sum_{j=1}^{n} r_j m_j = \hat{R} \tag{v}$$

The repeat buying behavior of customers is largely determined by the values acquired on the product. The attributes, awareness, trial, availability and repeat (AATAR) factors influence the customers towards making re-buying decisions in reference to the marketing strategies of the firm. The decision of customers on repeat buying is also affected by the level of satisfaction derived on the products and number of customers attracted towards buying the same product, as a behavioral determinant.

## MARKET COVERAGE AND CUSTOMER VALUE ENHANCEMENT

The fast moving consumer goods (FMCG) may be of the nature which has a quick shelf turnover, at relatively low cost and quick buying decisions of consumers. The rate of change within the FMCG market sectors continues apace, particularly in the area of innovation and value additions. A firm may combine innovation and technologies in the new products to create customer value and competitive gains. New and modem players have moved rapidly into the growing fast moving consumer goods retail market. The FMCG sector in the retail market segments are largely attracted by the innovations in product attributes and packaging besides the price sensitivity. It has been observed that the effects of the consumers' decision on their probability to try the new product are systematically moderated by elements of the marketing strategy associated with the new product and by FMCG characteristics (Steenkamp and Gielens, 2003). Most of the new products in the FMCG category, like processed food products, cosmetics, etc face competition in the market and the firms penetrate into the oligopolistic market conditions. Under such market conditions the customer value is also driven by the satisfaction that is offered by the substitutes. Often, the firms face competition within their product line due to implementation of product overlap strategy, which generates conflicting customer values. When a firm introduces a high value product derived out of the research and development efforts, it prescribes the use value for it, however the perceived use value for the product may not match with the prescribed use value tagged to the product by the firm. Such uncertainty may cause low performance of product in terms of buying preferences.

A firm may introduce the new product with the high investment $M_t^{(i_1+i_2+i_3+\dots i_n)j}$ in terms of product attributes ($i_1$), distribution ($i_2$), promotion ($i_3$) and other related factors ($\dots i_n$) related with gaining competitive advantage in a given time (t) in the $j^{th}$ market. Let us assume that $s$ is the estimated market coverage for the new product, the customer value ($V_{np}$) may be initially positive and high, resulting into deeper market penetration (with $s$ increasing). This may be described as:

$$M_t^{(i_1+i_2+i_3+\ldots)j} = \frac{\partial s}{\partial t} = k \qquad \text{(vi)}$$

However, $V_{np} \leq \frac{\partial v}{\partial t}$ may become negative following product competition within the product line due to the product overlap strategy of the firm. In the above equation, volume of buying is represented by $\partial v$ in a given time $t$. To augment the customer value and enhance market coverage for the new products in the potential markets the firm may optimize the product line $[s]_{pt}^{j,h}$ by pruning the slow moving products in the $j^{th}$ chain in h market in order to reposition them in new market. The opportunity cost in moving the slow performance products may be derived by inputting the values of V′ from equation (ii) as:

$$[s]_{Pt}^{j,h} = \left[\frac{\partial v}{\partial t}\right]^{j,h} + \Pi\{V(x,t,q,p)\} \qquad \text{(vii)}$$

Hence to enhance the market coverage for the new product with enhancing the customer value for the new product of the firm, the strategy may be described as:

$$s = \iint \left[k + \{s\}_{Pt}^{j,h}\right] \partial t + \beta' R \qquad \text{(viii)}$$

Where in $s$ is the market coverage of the new product, $k$ is the investment on market functions derived in a given time [equation (vi)] and R is the referral factor influencing the customer values with an advantage factor coefficient $\beta$ in time $t$. The products constituting the optimal product line of the firm in a given time is represented by $P_t$ in the above equation. The firm may measure the customer value shocks accordingly and shield the uncertainties occurring to the estimated market coverage due to declining customer values for the new products. As is common the new products are susceptible to such value shocks in view of the companies' own product line strategy.

## SPEED OF MARKET PENETRATION AND CUSTOMER VALUE

It is also possible for a firm to penetrate in the market faster and outperform the close competing products that exist, if the ex-factory market dynamics is comparatively faster. We may determine such dynamics as escape velocity for the new products, which manifests in increasing customer value, market coverage, just-in-time supply management, augmenting product performance through in-store and point of-sales demonstrations. It is observed that faster the market penetration of new products, higher is the opportunity of market coverage over the competing product in a given time and territory. The new product attractiveness may comprise the product features including improved attributes, use of advance technology, innovativeness, extended product applications, brand augmentation, perceived use value, competitive advantages, corporate image, product advertisements, sales and services policies associated therewith which contribute in building sustainable customer values towards making buying decisions on the new products. The introduction of new technological products makes it important for marketers to understand how innovators or first adopters respond to persuasion cues. It has been observed in a study that the innovativeness and perceived product newness which are one of the constituents of new product attractiveness were independent constructs that had independent effects on customer's attitude toward the brand and purchase intent for the new product (Lafferty and Goldsmith, 2004). The attractiveness of new products is one of the key factors affecting the decision making of customers and in turn is related to market growth and sales. The higher the positive reactions of the customers towards the new products in view of their attractiveness, higher the growth in sales and so in market.

Let us assume that the new product attractiveness is $F_x$ and initial product market investment is $M_t^{(i_1+i_2+i_3+...i_n)j}$, perceived customer value of the new product is $V_{np}$ and competitive advantage driver for the customer is $C_{at}$ at a given time.

$$F_x = \sum_t^{jh} \left[ M_t^{(i_1+i_2+...i_n)j} \right] \left( V_{np} \right) \left( C_{at} \right) \qquad \text{(ix)}$$

Hence

$$F_x = M_t^{i_n,j} \frac{\partial v'}{\partial t} = M_t^{in,j} \frac{\partial b'}{\partial s} \frac{\partial s}{\partial t} = M_t^{in,j} \frac{\partial v}{\partial s} \left( V_{np} \right) \left( C_{at} \right)$$

Where in $M_t^{i_n,j}$ denotes the initial investment made by the firm for introducing $t$ the new products, $V'$ represents the volume of penetration of new product in a given market in time $t$ with estimated market coverage $s$. In the equation $b'$ expresses the volume of repeat buying during the period, the new product has been penetrated in the market by the firm. The total quality for new products goes up due to economy of scale as the quality is also increased simultaneously $\left( \partial_v / \partial_s > 0 \right)$ and $\left( \partial_{b'} / \partial_s > 0 \right)$. In reference to the new products $x$, the competitive products create lower values to the customers $\left( \partial_v / \partial_x < 0 \right)$ while the innovative products irrespective of price advantages, enhance the customer value $\left( \partial_v / \partial_x > 0 \right)$. The value addition in the competitive products provides lesser enhancement in customer satisfaction as compared to the innovative products if the new products have faster penetration, re-buying attributes and market coverage.

Therefore $\int s\partial s = \int V_{np} + C_{at}$ (x)

In the above equation $V_{np}$ denotes the customer value for the new product and $C_{at}$ represents for the competitive advantage at a given time.

The prospect theory laid by Tversky and Khanman (1981) proposes that the intensity of gains plays strategic role in value enhancement as $G_{xt} = g_{pt}\left(\partial_x / \partial_p\right)$. In this situation $t$ represents the period wherein the promotional strategies were implemented to enhance the customer values in reference to product specific gains ( $g_{pt}$ ). However, in order to measure relationship/variability between the repeat buying behavior and customer value, it would be appropriate to determine the cumulative decision weights ($w$) and substituting it in the equation (i), (iv) and (v), that may reveal as:

$$G_{xt} = w\sum_{k=1}^{jh}\left[g_{pt}\left(r_j m_j\right) + \beta^{n+1} Q_t\right] \quad \text{(xi)}$$

The customer value however may be the driver function of gains on buying decision on new products and the influencing variables such as perceived use value and referrals.

## AGGREGATE RETURNS ON CUSTOMER VALUE

Measuring the overall value acquired by the customer for the new products over time, in competitive products market is a complex issue. However, the customer value may be measured in phases of the new products movement in the given market at the given time. It is necessary to define the product attractiveness stage in the market for new product overtime in reference to volume of buying and market coverage$\left(\partial v' / \partial s\right)$, which determines the stages of product attractiveness ($x_0, x_1, x_2, \ldots x_{n-1}, x_n$) with reference to the derived advantage from the competing product in a given market at a given time (t). In the process of enhancing the customer value for the new products a firm may use intensive customer value for new products; a firm may use intensive customer relationship management (CRM) strategies simultaneously to the competitive sales and marketing strategies. The integrated impact of CRM, sales and marketing strategies at different stages of product attractiveness would contribute to the customer value. Such an aggregated customer value represented by $R_n$ is exhibited in figure 1 can be measured by a firm. Hence the $R_n$ can be calculated with the following operation:

$$A(R_n) = f(x_0)\Delta x + f(x_1)\Delta x + f(x_2)\Delta x + .... + f(x_{n-1})\Delta x \qquad \text{(xii)}$$

Further simplifying this equation, we get,

$$A(R) = A(R_n)_{\lim n \to \infty} + \sum_{km}^{jm} \left[ (\Delta v' + \Delta b')(\Delta s) \right]^{t} \qquad \text{(xiii)}$$

In the above equation A(R) represents the aggregate returns on the customer value derived at various stages of product attractiveness and quantitative changes in the volume of goods positioned by the firm, repeat buying, and market coverage in terms of changes in the market shares of the firms. The aggregate returns on the customer values may be measured by a firm for not only the existing products in the market but also for the new products in the potential markets $A(R_n)_{\lim n \to \infty}$. The number of customers attracted towards the new product promotion, influence of referrals and augmented perceived use values derived by the customers may be the major factors contributing in determining the potential markets for the new products. However a firm may identify the potential markets in reference to its new products and market expansion policies. Besides, a firm may need to compute the trend of customer value for all the products in its product line, and measure the variability in the customer values perceived for its new products. The customer value trend for a given product line $(p_l)$ may be derived through the following equation substituting the equations (xiii) and (ix).

$$V_{p_l}^{t_0 - \infty} = \sum_{kn}^{jm} \left[ A(R + F_x) \right] \frac{\partial s}{\partial t} \qquad \text{(xiv)}$$

In the above equation the customers' value spread across the time frame $V^{(t_0 - \infty)}$ which represents the value spread from the time of introduction of the new product $(t_0)$ till the project period $(t^{\infty})$. It may be possible that the new product of a firm may acquire a higher market share but relative performance in reference to the products within the given product line may be comparatively lower. Under such conditions the profit contributed by the new product of the firm may be described as

$$Y_t = f\left[F_x, v', b'\right] \frac{\partial s}{\partial t} \qquad \text{(xv)}$$

Wherein $Y_t$ represents the profit contribution by the new product in time *t*.

The model explains that the value based customer portfolios would enhance the **customer value** as the product efficiency viewed from the **customer's** perspective, i.e., as a ratio of outputs (*e.g.* resale **value**, reliability, safety, comfort) that the customers obtain from a product relative to inputs (price, running costs) that the customers have to deliver in exchange. The derived efficiency **value** can be understood as the return on the customer's investment. Products offering a maximum **customer value** relative to all other alternatives in the market are characterized as efficient. Market partitioning is achieved endogenously by clustering products in one segment that are benchmarked by the same efficient peer(s). This ensures that only the products with a similar output-input structure are partitioned into the same sub-market. As a result, a sub-market consists of highly substitutable products. The customer values are reflected in their competitive gains, perceived use values, volume of buying and level of quintessence with the customer relationship management services of the organization. If these variables do not measure significantly, there emerges the development of switching attitude among the customers. If the organizational values are low, the supplier relationship may be risk averse due to weak dissemination of values from organization to the suppliers.

## MEASURING CUSTOMER VALUE GAPS

Customer lifetime value (CLV) is a key-metric within customer relationship management. Although, a large number of marketing scientists and practitioners argue in favor of this metric, there are only a few studies that consider the predictive modeling of CLV. Customer lifetime value also represents the net present value of profits, coming from the individual customer, which creates a flow of transactions over time. Finns look at their investments in terms of cost per sale, rate of customer retention, and also conversion of prospects. CLV is, then, used as a convenient yardstick of performance. The concept of the lifetime value of a customer is well established in the theory and practice of database marketing. The lifetime value of a customer, defined to be the expected present value of the net cash flows from the firm's relationship with the customer over his or her lifetime, is often used as an upper limit on spending to acquire the customer (Pfeifer, 1999). Many firms agree that their efforts should be focused on growing the lifetime value of their customers. However, few have come to terms with the implications of that idea for their marketing management with focus on decision making and accountability of customer values (Rust *et.al*, 2004). The customers' lifetime value is constituted by three components- customer's value over time, length of customers association and the services offered to the customer. The satisfaction is the customer's perception of the value received in a transaction or relationship and it helps in making re-patronage decisions on the basis of their predictions concerning the value of a future product. It may be thus be stated that the customer value paradigm is contemporary, which includes many elements of the customer satisfaction paradigm and is being more widely adopted and deployed by the firms (Hallowell,1996, Gale,1997)

Some studies focus on the prediction of CLV in customer goods manufacturing and marketing firms. In these industries, customer behavior is rather complex, because customers can purchase more than one service, and these purchases are often not independent from each other (Donkers *et.al.*, 2003). However, it has been observed that low perceived use value; comparative advantages over physical attributes and economic gains of the product make significant impact on determining the customer value for the relatively new products. The customer value gap, may be defined as the negative driver, that lowers the returns on the aggregate customer value. This is an important variable, which need to be carefully examined by a firm and measure its impact on the profitability of the firm in reference to spatial (coverage of the market) and temporal (over time) market dimension (*e.g.* Marjolein and Verspagen, 1999).

In view of maximizing the lifetime value of customers, a firm must manage customer relationships for the long term. In a disagreement to this notion a study demonstrates that firm profits in competitive environments are maximized when managers focus on the short term with respect to their customers (Villanueva *et. al.,* 2004). Intuitively, while a long term focus yields more loyal customers, it sharpens short term competition to gain and keep customers to such an extent that overall firm profits are lower than when managers focus on the short term. Further, a short term focus continues to deliver higher profits even when customer loyalty yields a higher share-of-wallet or reduced costs of service from the perspective of the firm. Such revenue enhancement or cost reduction effects lead to even more intense competition to gain and keep customers in the short term. The findings of the study suggest that the competitive implications of a switch to a long term customer focus must be carefully examined before such a switch is advocated or implemented. Paradoxically, customer lifetime value may be maximized when managers focus on the short term.

There have been limited studies that have discussed the impact of convergence of product services offered by a firm to the new products towards generating customer value over time. However, some of the studies find no evidence of absolute convergence, while a few find evidence of conditional convergence, *i.e.* convergence having controlled for differences in technological and behavioral parameters (Kenny and Marshall, 2000). The lack of evidence of absolute convergence leads to the lowering of perceived use value of the new products and further results into the lowering the returns on the aggregate customer value in terms of repeat buying ($b'$) and market coverage ($s$) for a firm in a given time. However, most of the convergence studies are aimed at proving or disproving the neoclassical growth model and hence there is need to take the 'product' as the unit of measurement of customer value. The customer value gap (CVG) model has been exhibited in Figure 1.

The customer values are reflected in their competitive gains, perceived use values, volume of buying and level of quintessence with the customer relationship management services of the organization. If these variables do not measure significantly, there emerges the development of switching attitude among the customers. If the organizational values are low, the supplier relationship may be risk averse due to weak dissemination of values from organization to the suppliers. The CVG-1 as exhibited in the Figure 1 may exist for the new products due to the negative difference between the customer value for the product assessed by the firm and the perceived value acquired by the customers upon its buying. If the customer receives the higher degree of perceived value ($q^t_p$) for the new product in each buying with increasing product attractiveness, the firm may be able to enhance its market share of the new product over time and territory. On the contrary the customer value may

*Figure 1. Customer Value Gaps Model*

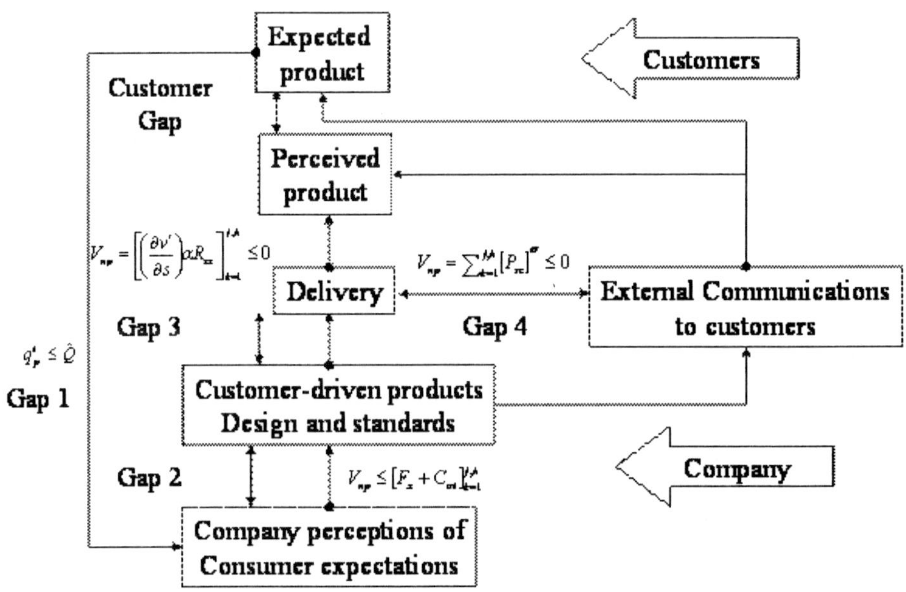

deteriorate and fall if $q_p^t \leq \hat{Q}$, where $\hat{Q}$ refers to the value estimated for the product by the firm. Such gap may emerge due to inadequate market research, lack of focus on the product quality, poor communications within the firm, lack of appropriate market segmentation and weak customer relationship management. The customer value may also be negative or low if the attributes are not built into the new product to maximize the customer value as per the estimation of the firm. The attributes lead to the satisfaction to the customers and is reflected through the product attractiveness ($F_x$). This is explained as CVG-2 as $V_{np} \leq [F_x + C_{at}]_{k=1}^{j,h}$ wherein $V_{np}$ represents the customer value for the new products, $F_x$ is product attractiveness and $C_{at}$ is competitive advantage for buying the new product in a given time. There are many factors that contribute to the CVG-2 situation such as unsystematic, vague and undefined product designs, lack of customer product defined standards and setting the quality control goals by the firm.

The customer value gap for the new products is also generated due to lack of proper product delivery at the retail stores or outlets where customer has an easy access to the product as exhibited in CVG-3. In delivering the product ($p$) to the customers the major considerations that a firm should make is towards the volume of product to be penetrated ($v'$) in a given time in the predetermined market coverage ($s$). The just-in-time product management and services offered to the customers in the retail outlets ($R_{sx}$) through which the new products are sold, largely affects the customer preferences and the values. The customer value may enhance if there is a positive relationship of all these factors. However, it may have a negative or low impact if

$$V_{np} = \left[ \left( \frac{\partial v'}{\partial s} \right) \alpha R_{sx} \right]_{k=1}^{j,h} \leq 0 \qquad \text{(xvi)}$$

Where, $\alpha$ is a constant used for measuring the customer services provided by the retails stores. The external communications such as advertisements, referrals and word of mouth play significant role in building the customer value at the point of purchase. If the communication spread for the new products in terms of the above discussed variables is positive, its integrated impact would develop strong self reference criterion among the customers and help in enhancing the returns on the aggregate customer value. On the contrary the CVG-4 may be described as

$$V_{np} = \left[ \beta_0 + \beta_1 (P_{sw}) \mu_t + \beta_2 (P_{sr}) \mu_t + \beta_3 (P_{sa}) \mu_t + \varepsilon_t \right]_{k=1}^{j,h} \qquad \text{(xvii)}$$

Wherein, $\beta$ is the constant used for the score of word-of-mouth ($P_{sw}$), opinion score of referrals ($P_{sr}$) and perceptions derived through the commercials on the product inserted in the media ($P_{sa}$). In the equation $\varepsilon_t$ has been used as the random error and $\mu_t$ denotes the mean time of obtaining the perceptional scores on new product communication. Upon simplifying, this equation may be represented as:

$$V_{np} = \sum_{k=1}^{j,h} \left[P_{sc}\right]^{\sigma} \leq 0 \qquad \text{(xviii)}$$

In the above equation ($P_{sc}$) denotes the integrated effect on perceptions derived by the customers on new products. If this value goes negative across the markets in a given time, it will pull down the customer value lowering the volume of buying and shrinking market coverage estimates of the firm.

This framework analyzes optimal portfolio choice and consumption with values management in the firm-supplier-customer triadic relationship. The value concept in the above relationship governs the customer portfolio decision in terms of formulation of recursive utility over time. It shows that the optimal portfolio demand for products under competition varies strongly with the values associated with the brand, industry attractiveness, knowledge management and ethical issues of the organization. The extent of business values determines the relative risk aversion in terms of functional and logistical efficiency between the organization and supplier while the switching attitude may influence the customers if the organizational values are not strong and sustainable in the given competitive environment. The model assumes that a high functional value integrated with the triadic entities would raise the market power of organization, sustain decisions of customer portfolios and develop long-run relationships thereof. The **customer value** concept is utilized to assess product performance and eventually to determine the competitive market structure and the product-market boundaries.

## APPLICATION PROSPECTS IN MANAGEMENT

One of the challenges for the marketing manager of a firm is to incorporate the preferences of the customer into the design of new products and services in order to maximize the customer value. An augmented and sustainable customer value builds the loyalty towards the product and brand. Systematically explored concepts in the field of customer value and market driven approach towards new products would be beneficial for a company to derive long term profit optimization strategy over the period. Hence, a comprehensive framework for estimating both the value of a **customer** and profit optimization need to be developed. On a tactical level, managers need to consider as what is the optimum spread of customers on a matrix of product attractiveness and market coverage. This needs careful attention and the application of managerial judgment and experience to measure the value driven performance of the product of the firm. It is necessary for the managers to understand that customer value is context dependent and there exists a whole value network to measure, not just a value chain. This value network will contain important entities far beyond the ones commonly taken into consideration in financial projections and business analyses.

The model discussed in this paper provides a holistic view of the customer value by proposing ways to measure the different variable associated with it *viz.* product attractiveness, market coverage, communication and point-of-purchase services offered to the customers. The analysis of these variables would help the managers develop appropriate strategies to enhance the customer value for the new products and optimize the profit of the firm. Managers of a firm may consider the measurement of customer value with the advent of one-to-one marketing media, *e.g.* targeted direct mail or internet marketing; the opportunities to develop **customer** relationship management campaigns are enhanced in such a way that it is now both organizationally and economically feasible to profitably support a substantially larger number of marketing segments. The discussion in the paper on the customer value gaps in the process of marketing new products explores the possible situations that may lead to lower the customer value. An appropriate preventive strategy may be developed by the managers upon measuring the extent of such gaps to protect the deterioration in the customer values and optimize the profit of the firm.

## CONCLUSION

The customer value in terms of satisfaction is one of the indicators for building profit oriented strategies in a firm. The customer value concepts may be applied by the firms to evaluate the product performance in the given market and determine the approach for competitive advantage. In order to gain the returns on the aggregate customer value, firms need to methodically estimate the profitability associated thereof in terms of product attractiveness, volume of buying and market share thereof. The ultimate goal of the firms may be to generate continual revenue streams by maintaining the customer value. There appears to be a need for exploring the gaps that may occur in the marketing process that lowers the customer satisfaction and aggregate customer value. The existing theoretical and methodological issues are reviewed in this study and a new framework has been proposed for future research in measuring the customer value in specific reference to the new products as launching innovative and high technology products is a continuous process for the firms in the present competitive markets. The framework for measuring the customer values discussed in this paper provides analytical dimensions for establishing the long run customer relationship by the firm and to optimize its profit levels.

## REFERENCES

Bauer, H. H., Hammerschmidt, M., & Staat, M. (2004). *Analyzing product efficiency: A customer oriented approach.* University of Mannheim, February.

Brown, G. H. (1953). Brand loyalty - Fact or fiction. *Advertising Age. 24.* Reprinted in A.S.C. Ehrenberg and F.G. Pratt (Eds.), *Customer behavior* (pp. 28-35). Middlesex, UK: Penguin.

Brucks, M., Zeithaml, V. A., & Naylor, G. (2000). Price and brand name as indicators of quality dimensions of customer durables. *Journal of Academy of Marketing Science, 28*(3), 359-374.

Churchill, H. (1942). How to measure brand loyalty. *Advertising and Selling, 35,* 24.

Cunningham, R. M. (1956). Brand loyalty - What, where, how much? *Harvard Business Review, 34,* 116-128.

Cunningham, R. M. (1961). Customer loyalty to store and brand. *Harvard Business Review, November-December,* 127-137.

Davies, A. (2004). Moving base into high-value integrated solutions: A value stream approach, *Industrial and Corporate Change, 13*(5), October, 727-756.

Donkers, B., Verhoef, P. C., & Jong M. D. (2003). *Predicting customer lifetime value in multi-service industries.* ERIM Report Series, April, (Ref ETS-2003-038-MKT), Rotterdam School of Management, Erasmus University, Rotterdam.

Draganska, M., & Jain, D. C. (2005). Product line length as a competitive tool. *Journal of Economics and Management Strategy, 14*(1), 1-28.

Eggert, A., & Ulga, W. (2002). Customer perceived value- A substitute for satisfaction in the business markets. *The Journal of Business and Industrial Marketing, 17*(2), 107-118.

Frank, R. E. (1967). Is brand loyalty a useful basis for market segmentation? *Journal of Advertising Research, 7*(2), 27-33.

Gale, B. T. (1997). Satisfaction is not enough. *Marketing News, 32*(21), 18.

Ganesh, J., Arnold, M. J., & Reynolds, K. E. (2000, July). Understanding the customer base of service providers: An examination of the difference between switchers and stayers. *Journal of Marketing, 64,* 65-87.

Gourville, J. T., & Koehler, J. J. (2004, January). *Downsizing price increases: A greater sensitivity to price than quantity in consumer markets*. HBS Marketing Research Paper No. 04-01.

Gramrowski, B., & Rachev, S. (1999). A testable version of the Pareto-Stable CAPM. *Mathematical and Computer Modeling, 29*, 61-81.

Gupta, S., Lehmann, D. R., & Stuart, J. A. (2003). *Valuing customers*. HBS Marketing Research Paper, No. 03-08.

Hunt, S. D., & Morgan, R. M. (1995, April). The comparative advantage theory of competition. *Journal of Marketing, 59*, 1-15.

Hallowell, R. (1996). The relationships of customer satisfaction, customer loyalty, and profitability: An empirical study. *International Journal of Service Industry Management*, *7*(4), 27-42.

Han, S., Gupta, S., & Lehmann, D. R. (2001). Consumer price sensitivity and price thresholds. *Journal of Retailing, 77*(4), 435-456.

Ingenbleek, P., Debruyne, M., Frambach, R. T., & Verhallen, T. (2003). Successful new product pricing practices: A contingency approach. *Marketing letters, 14*(4), 289-305.

Johnson, U., Martensson, M., & Skoog, M. (2001, September). Measuring to understand intangible performance drivers. *European Accounting Review, 10*(3), 407-437.

Kenny, D., & Marshall, J. F. (2000). Contextual marketing. *Harvard Business Review*, 119-125.

Knox, S. (1998). Loyalty brand segmentation and the customer development process. *European Management Journal, 16*(6), 729-737.

Lafferty, B. A., & Goldsmith, R. E. (2004). How influential are corporate credibility and endorser attractiveness when innovators react to advertisement for a new high technology product? *Corporate Reputation Review, 7*(1), 24-26.

Marjolein, C., & Verspagen, B. (1999). *Spatial distance in a technology gap model*. Maastricht Economic Research Institute on Innovation and Technology (MERIT), Working Paper No. 021.

Oakley, P. (1996). High tech NPD success through faster overseas launch. *European Journal of Marketing, 30*(8), 75-91.

Ofek, E. (2002). *Customer profitability and lifetime value*. Harvard Business School, Note, August, (pp. 1-9) (Publication reference 9-503-019).

Pederson, C. S. (2000). Sparsing risk and return in CAPM: A general utility based model. *European Journal of Operational Research, 123*(3), 628-639.

Perraudin, W. R. M., & Sorensen, B. E. (2000). The demand of risky assets: Sample selection and household portfolios. *Journal of Econometrics, 97*, 117-144.

Pfeifer, P. E. (1999). On the use of customer lifetime value as a limit on acquisition spending. *Journal of Database Marketing, 7*(1), 81-86.

Rajagopal (2005). Measuring variability factors in customer values for profit optimization in a firm- A framework for analysis. *Journal of Economics and Management, 1*(1), 85-103.

Rajagopal & Sanchez, R. (2004). Conceptual analysis of brand architecture and relations within product categories. *The Journal of Brand Management, 11*(3), 233-247.

Reichheld, F. F., & Sasser, W. E. (1990). Zero defections: Quality comes to services. *Harvard Business Review, Sep-Oct*, 105-111.

Reinartz, W. J., & Kumar, V. (2000). On the profitability of long-life customers in a non-contractual setting: An empirical investigation and implementation for Marketing. *Journal of Marketing, 64*(4), 17-35.

Reinartz, W. J., & Kumar, V. (2002, July). The mismanagement of customer loyalty. *Harvard Business Review*, 4-12.

Rust, R. T., Zeithaml, V. A., & Lemon, K. N. (2004, September). Customer centered brand management. *Harvard Business Review.*

Steenkamp Jan-Benedict, E. M., & Gielens, K. (2003). Consumers and market drivers of trial probability of new consumer packaged goods. *Journal of Consumer Research, 30*(3), 368-384.

Tucker, W. T. (1964). The development of brand loyalty. *Journal of Marketing Research, 1*(3), 32-35.

Tversky, A., & Kahnman, D. (1981). The framing decisions and psychology of choice. *Science, 211*, 453-458.

Villanueva, J., Bharadwaj, P., Chen, Y., & Balasubramanian, S. (2004). *Managing customer relationships- Should managers really focus on long term*. IESE Business School, Working Paper # D/560, May, (pp. 1-37).

Wakefield, K. L., & Inman, J. J. (2003). Situational price sensitivity: The role of consumption occasion, social context and income. *Journal of Retailing, 79*(4), 199-212.

# Chapter IV
# Measuring Consumer Attitudes Towards Self-Service Technologies

**Jesús Enrique Portillo Pizaña**
*Monterrey Institute of Technology and Higher Education, Juárez City Campus, Mexico*

## INTRODUCTION AND MOTIVATION

In the midst of many trends taking place at this historic moment – such as deregulation of industries, privatization of state-owned enterprises, geographical diversification of powerful companies and massive destruction of small ones – "there are two forces that are shaping today's economic landscape: information technology and globalization" (Kotler 1999). By "shaping", we mean that we are learning to harness them, to learn from them and to channel them. They are taking form, and we are trying to contribute in a small way forming them. Today, the marketplace concept has changed. Customers no longer need to move to where products are sold. They are now making the rules from the intimacy of their computers. Jeffrey F. Rayport and John J. Sviokla, in their article "*Managing in the Market Space*" (1994), describe the market-space concept as a "virtual realm where products and services exist as digital information and can be delivered through information based channels". We need to understand that even as this historic moment challenges our generation with the task of defining the Information Technology Revolution, we are not merely dealing with just another management theory or strategic proposition. The Information Technology Revolution is an extensive process of "informalization" of markets which constitutes the technological transition from standardized manufacturing to mass individualized relationships.

Marketers know that customer time is very valuable and that they spend a lot of time trying to figure out what their best buying option is. Customer decisions are now made more cautiously, examining more information about product quality, price, and convenience. They feel the need to trust people they buy from and to establish a connection with them. In the near future, and thanks to the e-market, most customers will have a broader array of products and suppliers from all over the world, and increasingly user-friendly and fast electronic formats. "Technological developments in information technology on the one hand, and increasing labor costs on the other, are leading to a period of considerable change in the design of service" (Karmarkar, Uday S. and Richard Pittbaldo 1995).In terms of customer perspective, what Patricia B. Seybold proposes makes total sense: "Loyal customers have become the most precious commodity. Today the hardest thing for a company to acquire is not investment capital, products, employees, or even a brand, its customer loyalty. Customer relationships are the fundamental source of value in the new customer economy". Of course we are not saying that we must forget about Information Technology and concentrate only on customer relationships, but rather that there is a strong need to adapt and transform the information overflow into strategies that build customer loyalty.

*The pace of change is so rapid that the ability to change has now become a competitive advantage*
Richard Love of Hewlett Packard

Efficiency and quick adaptation to change appear to be the answers for today's consumer needs. As company characteristics, they create loyalty. Whether we are talking about personal relationships or technological contact, satisfied customers represent more profits, a positive word of mouth, and a successful "caring" image. It is important then to understand the crossing line between the need and acceptance of Self Service Technologies and Personal Encounters. Selnes and Hansen (2001), propose two models to understand these relationships. In the first model (the replacement model) they propose the idea that if people need less personal service and instead they look for self service, they will not create social bonds and as a result, customer loyalty will be lessened. The second model (the hybrid model) proposes the idea that self service removes operational service activities allowing service personnel to concentrate on consultative service activities. This is based

*Figure 1. Service-Quality Model*

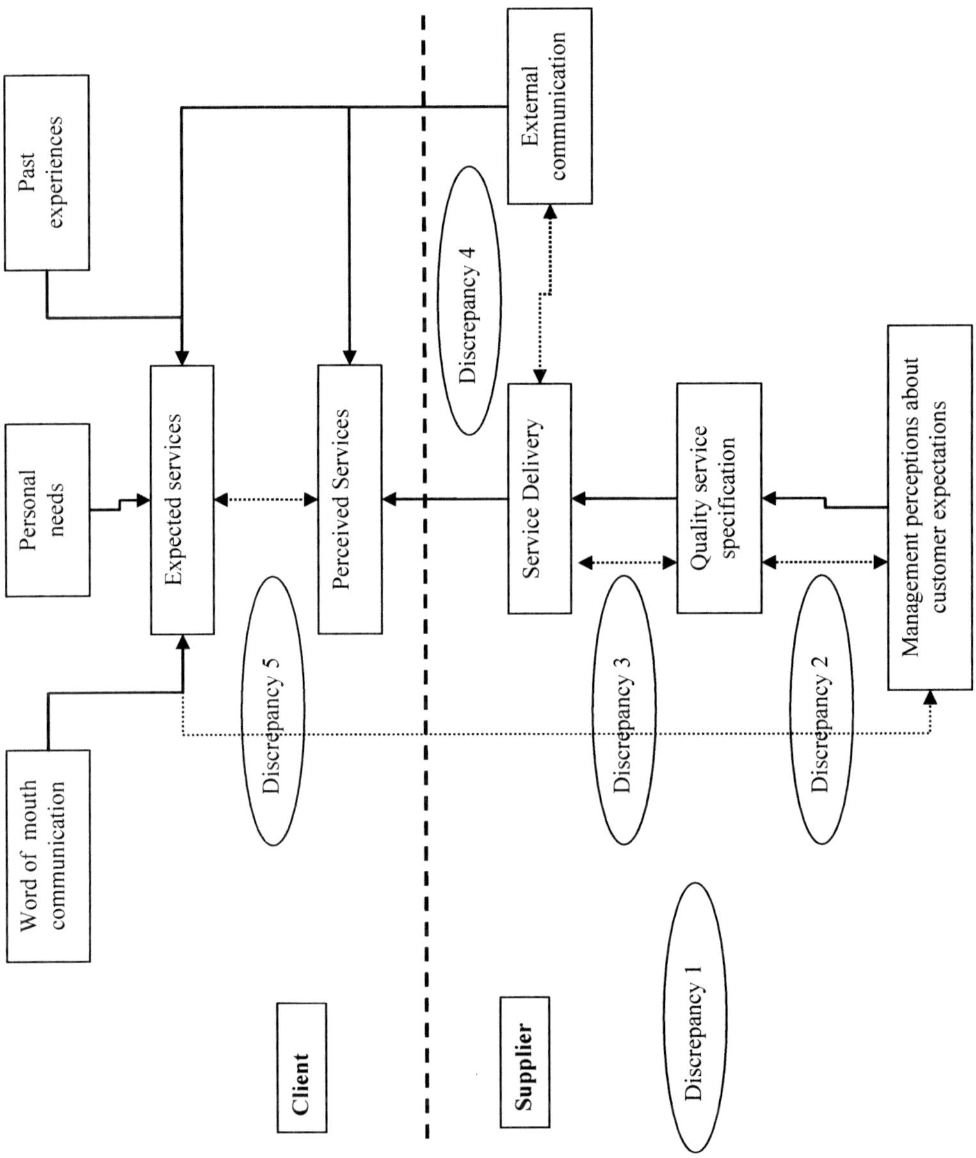

on Christopher Lovelock's idea (1983) that there are two kinds of service interactions, operative and consultative. Operative is for the service employee repetitive in nature and consultative interaction requires a high degree of individual judgment. Operative procedures are well suited for automation whereas consultative activities are not.

Efficiency and quick adaptation also stimulate product adoption. "If a company markets its technology in an appropriate way, this will represent an acceleration of the product adoption process. This, in turn, makes it easier for customers to do business with the company" (Seybold 1999). It is extremely important for companies to maintain product quality and price leadership, but it is more important to inform appropriately about it (using the advantages of self service technologies) and to gain customer confidence (through personal customer contact with company product experts who can assist them an solve their problems). A better understanding of this technological construct will lead to a better definition of market strategies. If we have the ability to understand the rationale governing preferences for self service technologies or for personal service, we can adapt and adopt in order to create customer loyalty. The opportunity to create lasting relationships with customers through consumer education and attention programs will always be there. How can self service and personal service be integrated? That's the question we must re-frame (Selnes and Hansen, 2001).

## PROBLEM DEFINITION

The preceding examples lead us to a couple of relatively old but still present problems: what should the balance between expected service and perceived service be? (As illustrated in Fig 1), and what is the size of a tolerance zone? (Zeithaml, Parasuraman, Berry, 1990) (Zeithaml and Bitner, 2000).

Taking these concepts as a background for our problem definition, we can consider that there might be a difference between the perceived level of satisfaction received through self service technologies, and the level of satisfaction through personal service. In fact, there is an increasing interest in this topic. There are a few articles - Parasuraman (2001), Bitner et al (2001), Dabholkar and Bagozzi (2002), Selnes and Hansen (2001) - that show the importance of knowing the difference between virtual service and personal service. Equally important is to know the factors that influence consumer preferences regarding these two options. Nowadays we know the personal service dimensions (Zeithaml, Parasuraman, Berry, 1990), but we are not sure about the one's affecting self service technologies. For the purposes of this project, we'll define self service technologies as: "technological interfaces that enable customers to produce a service independent of direct service employee involvement" (Meuter et. all, 2000).

## Customer Economy vs. Information Economy

These days, there's an increasing discussion about the pros and cons of self service technologies. These concepts have a huge market potential in business strategy, especially if we consider the "cocooning" trend, that is, the impulse to stay inside when the outside gets too tough and scary, Popcorn (1992). However, we are still in the first stages in using self service technology, and we cannot be certain that people will always prefer this option. Although customers are looking for some positive attributes of self service, if they don't get them, if they don't work properly for them, or if they didn't find any assistance in using them, they will find another option; of course, this option will always be personal assistance, and here is were our discussion starts, we need to discover how to integrate both concepts, self service technologies and customer focus.

### Why Customer Economy?

Customers are now in control, and they are tired of fighting with companies that don't care and don't want to attend their needs. Today, customers have more options and are looking for convenient relationships. They can say "if you don't want my money, somebody else will". Customers are "no longer willing to be locked in. They want great service, fair prices and innovative offerings. If they don't get these, they'll go elsewhere and they'll tell the world" Patricia B. Seybold (2001). "The paradigm has shifted. Products come and go. The unit of value today is customer relationship" Bob Wayland (Kotler 1999). But, if (according to this kind of marketing strategy), we need to focus primarily in customer relationships, How can we build a virtual relationship? Well, we can, we need toll free lines, 24 hour lines, we need computers with video cameras, we need internet connections with all kind of assistance buttons, but more important, we need to make things clear and easy for consumers. If we can do this, we are going to create mass individualized digital relationships with any customer in the world. If we can do this and have the prices and products customer are looking for, we are going to win the e-commerce battle by "possessing" more loyal customers in our databases.

### Why Information Economy?

In the other hand, thanks to Internet and to all different kind of wireless devices and self service technologies, customers have now control regarding search, evaluation and buying decisions. They are better armed for the market battle, and ironically as it sounds, companies are giving them the weapons. Besides those weapons, there are peaceful keys that open companies' doors. Every company wanting to succeed in the future marketspace should give its key to every single customer; again, to understand the divergence between customer and technology focus, we need to understand the basis for each approach; customer economy focus on customer needs, while information economy focus in technological development (not necessarily what customer know he need, but what technology can build for them).

### Learn to Assist

The statement above may apply for some personal, social or even political relationships, but it is absolutely wrong for business management and strategic planning. We need to understand the how and the why of things. We need to know about their dynamics, their dimensions, and their interactions. In order to master the use of the information economy process, and to increase customer share, we need to know how it works. But if we are trying to understand only the ups and downs of the information economy, we are going to miss the real and meaningful transformation taking place right now: customers are now in control over the market space. Customers "now expect us to harness information technology to make life more convenient to them" (Seybold, 2001). In addition, "companies are beginning to realize that people like to browse online and shop around" "More people are doing product evaluation and research, and often want to go to the site to make a purchase. In terms of e-commerce, the whole idea is to make the shopping experience as easy as possible" Reg Baker, COO of Market Strategies Inc. (Vence, 2002).

However, the purpose of adaptation is evolution. Human customer service is costly. A call handled from start to finish by an IVR system costs, on average, 45 cents, according to a research conducted in 2001 by the Garner Group. "When we let a human into the act the cost jumps to $7.60" (Ashbrook, 2001). We need to teach and support customers shoulder to shoulder in this learning process, but we don't want to be in the "learning process forever". As Jeff Bezos said "we'll stay on the phone and teach a customer how to place an order online, but we don't want them to get in the habit of calling us" (Lardner, 2001). People still want to touch, smell and feel the products, still want to have expert assistance on complicated decisions; they still need to trust on honest company's representatives, they still need to have social encounters!

## THEORETICAL FOUNDATIONS

In the past, a vast majority of services research work was made focusing on relationships between service employees and customers, and the kind of outcomes generated on those interactions. Today, this approach is no longer appropriate. Even when there is a lot of research based on the idea that an interaction between a service employee and a customer is needed for the delivery of the service to be completed, this is not necessarily true. Services "can be very well provided by hard technologies" (Thomas 1978). A good example of this is customer service over the telephone. At one time it required a company representative to talk to, and now the service in many cases is automated. We don't know how this may influence the interaction. Moreover, we don't have the service dimensions for this new type of encounter. At the beginning there were only the ATM machines, but now, "there are three main forms of self service interactions: automated response telephone lines, internet based interactions and self service machines or kiosks" (Bitner 2001).

A central purpose of any academic and scientific investigation is to propose new ways and definitions to better understand constructs and variable relationships. Today, due to the increasing amount of service delivered through self service technologies, it is crucial to understand self service technologies dimensions that influence the service encounter. In this investigation we assume that there are some variables affecting consumer selection of automated services and we also assume we can measure it. There are many theories handling the service construct, and they all start from the existing relationship between customers and a company's service employee. There have been different attempts to integrate the idea of customer-employee interactions in several business areas. Two of the most interesting are marketing and operations management - based on the general idea that efficient operations will lead to satisfied and loyal clients. Consequently, to understand self service dimensions, we need to start thinking about the service encounter, in other words, the "period of interaction between customer and service provider" (Gutek et al 1999). This comes straight from Customer Contact Theory.

## CUSTOMER CONTACT THEORY

Customer Contact Theory has gained renewed interest nowadays; basically because it is the departure point for understanding what consumers want from a service interaction. The customer contact concept appeared in 1977 when Chase and Aquilano proposed a differentiation of service systems from manufacturing systems. They put forward the idea of three levels of services, from pure services to quasi-manufacturing services. Later Chase (1978) suggested the idea of classifying services along a continuum, from high to low contact, where customer contact refers to the length of time the customer is in contact with a company's service. Service delivery process will require certain specific characteristics depending of the required level of customer contact, like operational design, prepared staff, infrastructure support, efficiency and so on. Continued work by Richard Chase on customer contact theory lead to the formal introduction of the construct idea and the first operational definition: "the time in the system relative to the total time of service creation" (Chase 1981); also Chase and Tansik (1983) presented the Customer Contact Model to introduce several dimensions of service production and comparing advantages and disadvantages for the different levels of service categories. But it was Weemmerlöv (1990) the one who designated it Customer Contact Theory; although he proposed a taxonomy for service processes, based primarily in Chase proposal of a continuum of customer contact and also based on an extended literature review in service design and operations management, he recognized that there is still a lot of research needed to understand the Customer Contact Theory.

Kellog and Chase (1995) identified however that "there are some essential dimensions or variables to be considered when defining Customer Contact. These dimensions can be grouped under three broad theories: Coupling, Interdependence and Information Richness". But in the same article, Kellog suggest the idea that Customer Contact is defined primarily by three factors: communication time, intimacy level and information richness. More recently, Silvestro, Fitzgerald, Johnston and Voss (1992) proposed one of the first attempts to categorize service processes considering several classifications and also based on Chase (1978) customer contact continuum. In his work, these authors proposed what could be a first movement to service categorizations:

Equipment/ people focus
Customer contact time per transaction
Degree of customization
Degree of discretion
Value added back office/ front office
Product/ process focus

## SERVICE QUALITY THEORY

Delivering Quality Service (Zeithaml, Parasuraman and Berry, 1990) is a research work that discovered the dimensions that consumers seek on personal service relationships and also discovered the relative importance of each factor. One of the first important contributions of this "Research Journey", as the authors described it, is the general idea that there were service quality dimensions. As we can see, there was a first approach to understand Customer Assessment of Service Quality; the authors suggested the possibility of 10 dimensions (or variables) affecting the perceived Service Quality. After an exploratory research, there was a quantitative phase involving customer surveys in different sectors from where it appear the

*Figure 2. Customer assessment of service quality model*

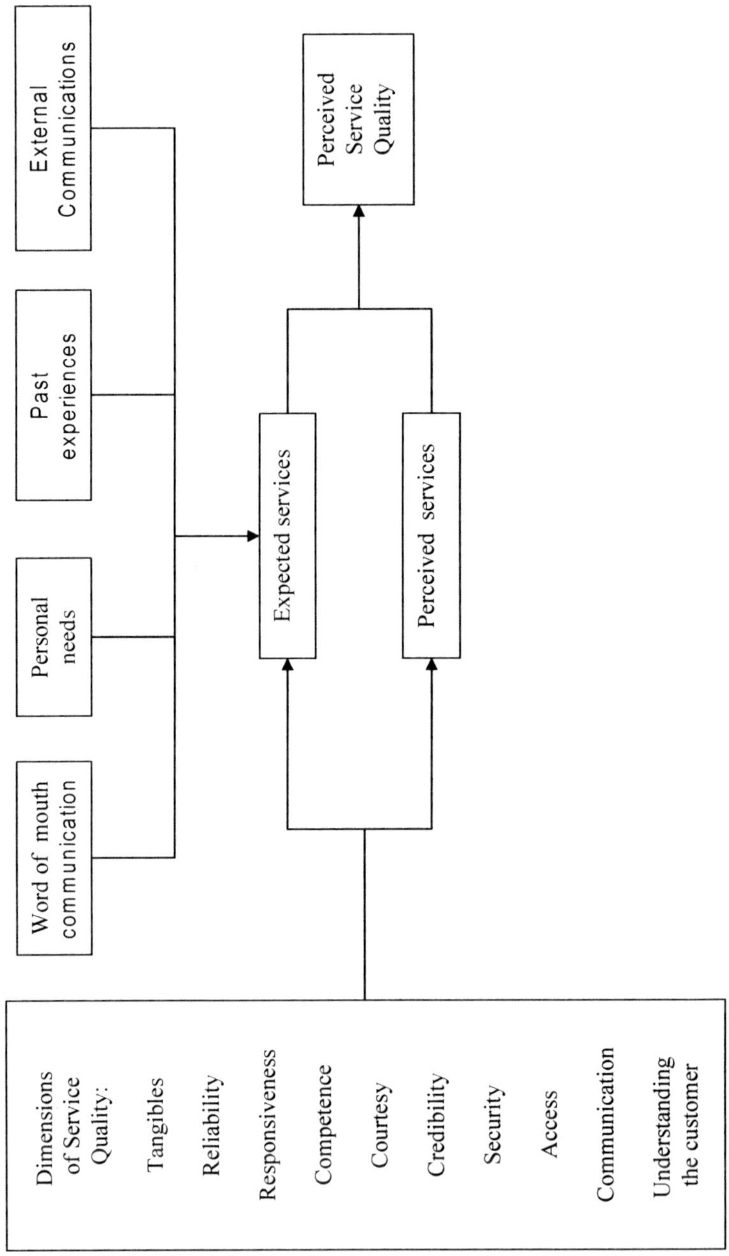

SERVQUAL's five dimensions (SERVQUAL is the authors proposed instrument for measuring customers' perceptions of service quality).

When trying to identify the relative importance of the final five dimensions, the authors find that the most important one was reliability, which means consumers expect companies to do what they are supposed to do and offer.

In self service technologies interactions, it is highly probable that this factor could have the same importance, but the meaning of reliability could be very different. In self service technologies, reliability means performance or technological systems operation. In a different way, interpersonal interactions mean a person's ability to perform a service. This may sound similar, but the difference is the possibility of standardization of the outcome. Self service technologies may offer a more standardized product. On the other hand, they might have other limitations *e.g.* lack of personal assistance to complete a task and the lack of customization.

It is important then to understand the mix of strategy, self service and personal service in order to better serve both customer and company needs. In some cases, consumers' don't have options. If you want to check your personal bank account, you first have to wait until the printed version arrives through postal service (late in many cases) or call to the bank and interact with an automated telephone system. This leads you through different dialling numbers without giving you the chance to interact with a person if you want (or need). When this happens for the first time, consumers do not react negatively to that interaction, why should they? At the end it is an effort of the companies to give you another option to serve you (through self service technologies) or not? But, what happens when this turns to be a common experience? Do customers tolerate the service failure? Do they prefer to switch to personal assistance and for how long? How do these accumulated experiences affect the Service Quality Model? Zeithaml, Parasuraman and Berry (1990) demonstrated

*Table 1. Service dimensions*

| | |
|---|---|
| Reliability (32%) | The ability to perform the promised service dependably and accurately |
| Tangibles (11%) | The appearance of physical facilities, equipment, personnel, and communications |
| Responsiveness (22%) | The willingness to help customers and to provide prompt service |
| Assurance (19%) | The knowledge and courtesy of employees and their ability to convey trust and confidence |
| Empathy (16%) | The provision of caring, individualized attention to customers |

that in many cases consumers "accept" a lower level of achievement in first time service due to lower expectations and expect a higher level when companies offer the service for a second or third time.

Many managers understand that self service technologies are a very important tool for information, image and sales; the problem here is that in many cases, they don't understand what consumers are looking. This of course is reflected in the way they interpret the "market opportunity", they know that self service technologies give them a chance to interact with consumers in a different level (when they needed it) and at lower cost. This lack of technology knowledge gives us the opportunity to realize the need for understanding the different dimensions of self service technologies (if there is any) based on Quality Service Theory. At this point, and considering both the Customer Contact and Quality Service theories, we need to jump to another important theory to understand and propose a Self Service Technology Operation Paradigm. Despite the time and quality of an interaction a company thinks a customer is involved in, it is the customers' perception of that interaction which might influence his attitudes about the service encounter, not the "objective" measurements of the company's performance in each factor. So, even when appropriate measures are valuable for managers, in the marketing arena, "there is a battle of perceptions, not products" Ries and Trout (1993). Therefore, this investigation will focus on customers' perceptions and feelings about using Self Service Technologies - while gaining a more complete understanding of technology design and automated service quality encounters.

## THEORY OF REASONED ACTION

For many years, investigators from different areas have been seduced by behavioral models from social psychology as an attractive theoretical and practical option to understand and predict an individual's behavior. The Theory of Reasoned Action is one of the most adopted models to explain human behavior for a simple reason: it is "designed to explain virtually any human behavior", Ajzen and Fishbein (1980). Managers have a very limited ability to control customer beliefs and attitudes. At best, they can only hope to appropriately design the service so that the customer will form beliefs that lead to a positive attitude (like satisfaction), making them more likely to engage in future contact and repeat business (loyalty).Fishbein (1965) (as cited by Cohen, Fishbein and Ahtola, 1972) stated that:

*Essentially, the theory may be stated as follows: (1) an individual holds many beliefs about any given object, that is, many different characteristics, attributes, values, goals, and concepts are positively or negatively associated with any given object; (2) associated with each of these 'related objects' is a mediating evaluative response- an attitude; (3) these evaluative responses summate; (4) through the mediation process, the summated evaluative response is associated with the attitude object; and thus (5) on future occasions the attitude object will elicit this summated evaluative response- this attitude...According to the theory, then, an individuals attitude toward any object is a function of (1) the strength of his beliefs about the object and (2) the evaluative aspect of those beliefs."*

In addition, a Behavioral Intention is conceptualized as a measure of the strength of one's intention to perform a specified behavior. An Attitude is defined as an individual's positive or negative feelings about performing a specific behavior. Fishbein's Model also proposed the existence of Subjective Norms influencing behavioral intentions. A Subjective Norm is defined as: "a person's perception that most people who are important to him think he should or should not perform the behavior in question" (Fishbein and Ajzen 1975)

The implication of this model is that there are certain beliefs associated with a specific group of characteristics (dimensions) offered in a contact experience that may lead to an attitude towards the entity offering that experience (an automated service for the purpose of this research). In addition, an evaluation of those dimensions will be correlated with customers intentions to use automated service. In summary, we can argue that there are many beliefs associated with any particular object and that a combination of this beliefs leads to an attitude towards that object in the minds of consumers. Attitudes and norms don't directly predict behavior, they predict intentions - and intentions predict behaviors. Any other variable that may influence behavioral intentions could do so only indirectly, trough Attitudes or Norms. This means that any perceived and evaluated aspect will fall under the

*Figure 3. Reasoned action model*

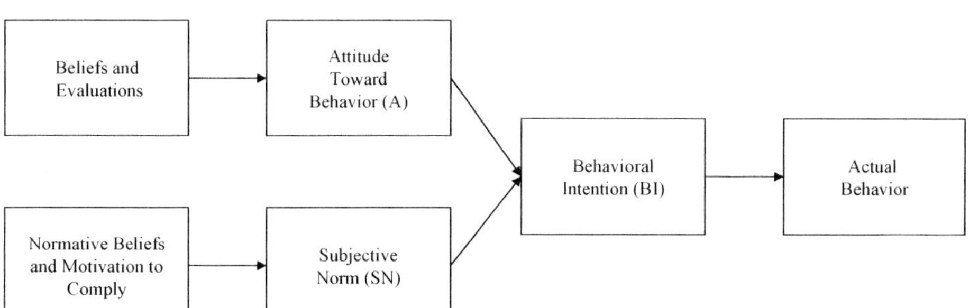

classification of "external variable" (Fishbein and Ajzen 1975). If this is the case, then we must consider attitude as a moderating factor between any internal (psychological) or external (environmental) variable and behavior.

## TECHNOLOGY ACCEPTANCE MODEL

A derivation of the Fishbein Model is the Technology Acceptance Model (Davis 1986). This model included and tested two specific beliefs: perceived Usefulness and perceived Ease of Use. Perceived Usefulness is defined as "the prospective user's subjective probability that using a specific application system will increase his or her job performance within an organizational context". Perceived Ease of Use, "refers to the degree to which the prospective user expects the target system to be free of effort" (Davis et al 1989)

What's interesting from this proposal is that it suggests two possible variables affecting attitudes towards technology acceptance (in this case for computer systems). The extracted general idea from Perceived Usefulness is that users (or consumers in general) will benefit from the continuous usage of technology, and that there will be a certain kind of reward or value generated through the use of automated systems. On the other hand, Ease of Use means that if consumers feel there are complications in using a certain technology, chances are high that they will stop using it or change to another variation of that technology. Thus, the easier it is to interact with an automated system the more positive attitude towards the intention to use it. These two factors account for about 40% of the variance in intention to use and actual usage behavior.

The main contribution of the Technology Acceptance Model is the recognition of what may well be the first two variables affecting people's choice of automated systems. This sets a precedent for identifying the names of the "external variables" recognized by the Theory of Reasoned Action (Fishbein and Ajzen 1975). The

*Figure 4. Technology Acceptance Model*

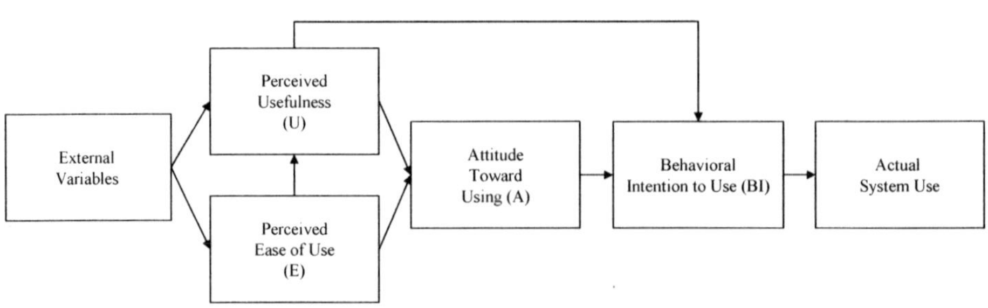

Technology Acceptance Model also shows that there is some kind of relationship between each dimension. A perceived ease of use could lead to a sense of efficacy and usefulness. Recently, other authors are trying to propose other factors. One is "perceived risk" (Featherman and Fuller 2002). This approach suggests the idea that consumers may be influenced during the buying decision process by feelings like uncertainty, discomfort, anxiety, conflict, concern, and cognitive dissonance.

## TECHNO-READY MARKETING

To build reliability in marketing services (Quality Service Theory), we must consider several elements to be successful. Berry and Parasuraman (1991), propose the "Three Pillars of support for service reliability". Here, the authors emphasize the appropriate management vision (customer focused), the specific need for adequate infrastructure, and the need for testing the "product". It is important to offer the customer new ways to approach our companies, but it is equally important to understand how they feel about us and how they interact with us.

Four recent outstanding articles deal with the influence of technology in consumer behavior: "Technology readiness index (TRI): a multiple item scale to measure readiness to embrace new technologies" by A. Parasuraman (2001); "Self Service Technologies: Understanding customer satisfaction with technology-based service encounters" by Meuter et al (2001); "Paradoxes of Technology: customer

*Figure 5. Three pillars of support for service reliability*

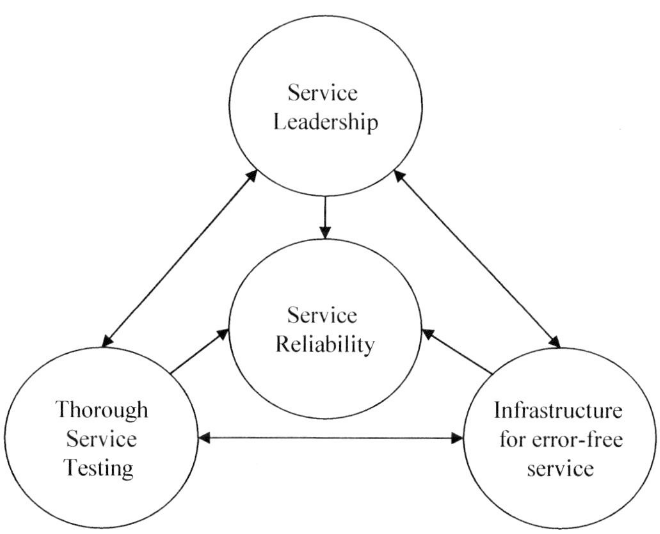

cognizance, emotions and coping strategies" by Mick and Fournier (1998); and "An attitudinal model of Technology-based self service technologies: moderating effects of consumer traits and situational factors by Dabholkar and Bagozzi (2002). These articles show different approaches to understand the influence of technology in our daily lives, especially in service encounters. In addition to the theories presented before, there are some other important factors considered as a base to identify an empirical definition of what could be the dimensions of self service technologies interactions: fulfilment of needs, efficiency, performance, safety, convenience, design, human touch, and novelty. These concepts are important in measuring the level of satisfaction for individuals using this kind of virtual service, as well as their level of willingness and disposition to interact with automated systems.

We also have the following forces, called the Digital Dozen, Seybold (2001).

How many cases do we know of managers who were so impatient to implement new technologies that they did it before they were ready, before having the appropriate infrastructure or before enough testing with consumers? How did this lack of information and this misguided process affect consumers' decisions? Here is where the concept of Techno-Ready Marketing (Parasuraman and Colby, 2001) comes into play. It introduces the idea of taking personal care in consumer support. Clients trust the specialist, and they need this specialist at the beginning of a process when they don't know how to use the "new products". Clients need education and support during the initial moments of fear and frustration. In the next years, "we are going to see the need to invest in consumer education programs; not because they are more stupid, but because they are more intelligent due to the information age" (Honevbein, 1996).

Self Service Technologies do not require interpersonal contact to complete a transaction. In many cases, the flexibility, adaptability, availability and profitability of technology may compete with the company's customer service employees and sellers. In other cases, technology may not be the appropriate answer or may not be able to directly an immediately address customers needs.

There are basically three types of interfaces for self service technologies known: Telephone/Interactive Voice Recognition Systems (IVR's), Internet and Interactive

*Table 2. The digital dozen forces*

| | | |
|---|---|---|
| Open, equal access | Convenient access | Pricing transparency |
| Control over their information | Information portability | Choice of distribution channels |
| Real time information | Process transparency | The ability to set prices |
| Specialist information | Logistics transparency | Fair, global pricing |

*Figure 6. Techno Ready Marketing Model*

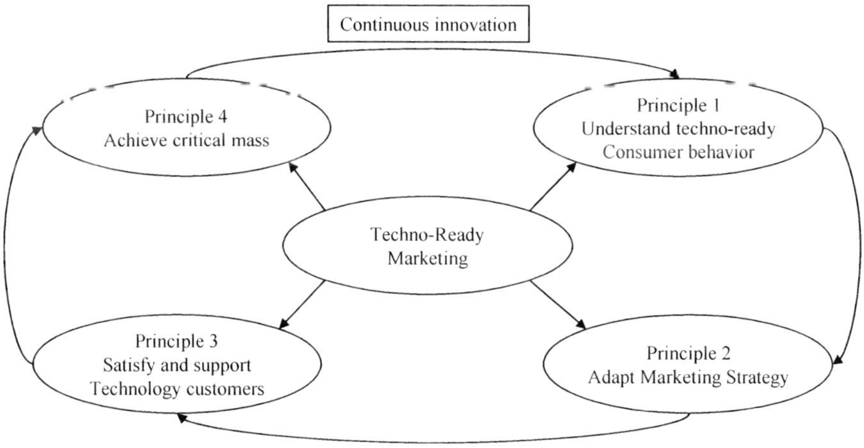


Kiosks/ATM's (IK's) (Meuter et. all, 2000). We exclude the video/CD alternative proposed by Meuter, because it includes any of the other three alternatives.

## SATISFACTION THEORY

Trying to propose a new definition of consumer satisfaction could result in time wasting and is not a meaningful activity for the purpose of this research. There are several researchers attempting to offer a definition of what could be the construct of consumer satisfaction and they also distinguish different characteristics, from "attitude-like post consumption evaluative judgment" where "satisfaction is not an emotion itself, but has been suggested to be the evaluation of an emotion" (Hunt 1977), to a "continuum evaluative process" (Oliver, 1989; Westbrook and Oliver 1991). There's also a Differential Emotions Scale (Izard 1977) that contains 10 subscales representing the intensity with which subjects experience the 10 fundamental emotions of Izard's Theory. Researchers also distinguish between the influence of emotions and evaluations on satisfaction (Cohen and Areni, 1991). Some try to distinguish between the individual level of satisfaction and the market level satisfaction (Johnson, Anderson and Fornell, 1995). Others look for satisfaction as an individual transaction-specific measure or evaluation of a particular product or service experience (Cronin and Taylor 1992). There's even an apparent disagreement as "to whether perceived service quality is an antecedent to transaction-specific satisfaction (Parasuraman, Zeithaml, and Berry 1988) or transaction –specific satisfaction is an antecedent to perceived service quality (Bitner 1990; Bolton and Drew, 1991)" as cited by Johnson, Anderson and Fornell (1995). In the same article (Johnson, Anderson and Fornell 1995) the authors present a different approach to the customer satisfaction definition. They argue that "satisfaction is an abstract construct that describes customers total consumption experience with a product or service... (because) directly affects customer loyalty and subsequent profitability, it serves as a common denominator for describing differences across firms and industries". There is also an excellent early "Critical Review of Consumer Satisfaction" by Youjae Yi (1990) that presents the Consumer Satisfaction construct from different perspectives: definitions, measurements, antecedents, determinants and consequences. For simplification reasons, we will consider a definition of satisfaction based on Westbrook's (1987) idea of satisfaction as the result of two possible effect states after a specific transaction based on positive or negative effects (emotions). Moreover, we are considering the One Factor Theory "postulating that satisfaction and dissatisfaction are opposites on a single, bipolar continuum", Yi (1990).

## EXPECTATION-DISCONFIRMATION PARADIGM

The outcome of a product or service interaction-evaluation process gives us the same level of ambiguity and abstraction as the satisfaction construct. There have been some attempts to understand consumer satisfaction consequences. Again, one of the most complete compilations is the one made by Youjae Yi (1990) "Critical Review of Consumer Satisfaction". In this work, the author presents some key variables and definitions to understand Consumer Satisfaction. The Expectation-Disconfirmation Paradigm is a modification of the Adaptation-Level Theory (Helson 1964). This paradigm is used in several research papers (Oliver, 1977, 1980, 1981, 1989), and tells us that we need to recognize that the outcome of Consumer Satisfaction could be summarized in three forms: Positive disconfirmation (performance exceeds expectations), confirmation (performance equals expectations), and negative disconfirmation (performance is below expectations). It is important to also recognize the proposed deficiency of this paradigm by La tour and Peat (1979): they argued that the Expectation-Disconfirmation Paradigm did not consider the consumer past experiences and other consumer experiences as sources of expectations in consumer's minds. Some authors proposed a modification of the Comparison Level Theory (Thibaut and Kelley, 1959), considering basically three factors: (1) Consumer's prior experiences with similar products, (2) situational product expectations and (3) the experience of other consumers who serve as referent persons. For the purpose of this research, we are going to work on the basis of consumer's ability to form expectations and perceptions no matter what sources are involved in their evaluations.

Disconfirmation is the disparity between expectations and performance. There are two types of disconfirmation: objective disconfirmation (real product/service performance) and subjective disconfirmation (consumer's perceived performance). Again, for the purpose of this research, it is important to consider only the idea that a discrepancy may exist between expectations and perceptions met, and that as a result of this evaluation process an emotion could emerge in every consumer's mind. That emotion influences a consumers' decision to stay with product/service or step aside from it. For further clarification of the expectation-consumer satisfaction sequence see Yi (1990), Figure 2 p. 81.

# CONCEPTUAL MODEL AND FORMAL HYPOTHESES

## Conceptual Model

After reviewing several different theories and literature related to Self Service Technology Adoption and considering the Service Quality Theory, the Theory of Reasoned Action and the Technology Acceptance Model as a basis for this investigation, a conceptual model came up. First of all, taking the customer assessment of Service Quality, we can argue that there might be different variables (Dimensions) influencing expectations (or attitudes) and this attitudes will have moderating effects on behavioral intentions which may in turn have an influence on actual behavior and Perceived Service Quality. Subsequently - and including the first two tested variables in the model, Usefulness and Ease of use (Davis 1986) -, we are hypothesizing about the rest of the external variables and their relationships. We assume that even when Davis (1986) stated that all other variables would affect usefulness and ease of use, there might be some other factors equally influencing the attitude towards behavior. We should say at this time that there could be some similarity between some of our proposed variables (efficiency and convenience) and the first two. They may even be the same. In addition, we are considering the Expectation-Disconfirmation Paradigm as an outcome of actual behavior (perceived service quality). As a result, our suggested first model will be:

## Operational Definitions and Formal Hypotheses

To understand the "relationship between the different factors influencing satisfaction" (Meuter et al 2000) or attitude towards the "interaction with a self service technology" (Dabholkar and Bagozzi 2002), we read different articles and books and found similarities that helped us to build a general summary from which this

*Figure 7. Initial Conceptual Model*

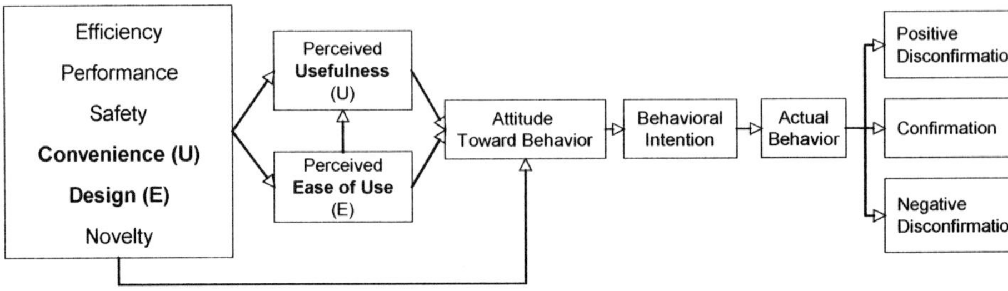


research can advance. After this first step, we then generated the following service dimensions to be tested.

## Efficiency

From a consumers' perspective, efficiency means that technology could help reach the goals he/she sets with less effort. Self Service Technologies can facilitate or reduce the time and effort spent in certain activities, but technology can also lead to more effort or time in performing certain activities. Self Service Technologies can make you more efficient in your occupations, giving you alternatives to handle your time better. In addition, you can be confident that the output of your interaction with technology will be what you wanted and what you expected. Here, it is important to consider the apparently strong relationship with the Perceived Ease of Use construct proposed by Davis (1986).

**H1:** *The more positive the consumer's beliefs about efficiency of a self service technology encounter, the more positive his/her intention to use that service and the higher the level of satisfaction will be.*

## Performance

A positive perception about the performance of Self Service Technologies means that the outcome of interacting with it is reliable and accurate. Satisfaction results from "the mere fascination with the capabilities of various SSTs and a sense of ¡Wow it really works! "(Meuter et al, 2000). If the technology does not work as intended, the consumer may face a disillusion. Consequently, in order to generate a good and positive perception of an automated service, technologies must complete the task for which they have been created. In other words, they should do their job as intended, work continuously in an appropriate manner, and generate a reliable outcome.

**H2:** *The more positive the consumer's beliefs about the performance of a self service technology encounter, the more positive his/her intention to use that service and the higher the level of satisfaction will be.*

## Safety

In many cases, Self Service Technologies are not so secure or safe to work with. It is common to find people who make comments about bad experiences and risks they faced using credit cards or paying trough the Internet. It is a sense of insecurity, discomfort and fragility: a lack of personal protection. A "distrust of technology and skepticism about its ability to work properly is defined as Insecurity", (Parasuraman 2000). Therefore, we need to understand that every time that a consumer faces a possible interaction with a Self Service Technology, he must feel secure about it, he must perceive an atmosphere of protection against third parties (or technology itself), and he must recognize an environment of privacy where he's the only one involved in making a purchase (usage) decision.

**H3:** *The more positive the consumer's beliefs about safety of a self service technology encounter, the more positive his/her intention to use that service and the higher the level of satisfaction will be.*

## Convenience

This construct deals with the general idea of "a positive view of technology and a belief that it offers people increased control, flexibility and efficiency in their lives" (Parasuraman 2000). Consumers may perceive some type of benefit if they use a Self Service Technology. The belief that SST's offers people variety, increased task control, accessibility, money savings, permanent availability, independence, place availability, diversity and time availability, would represent a general perception of convenience. It is important again to consider the similarity with the "Perceived Usefulness" proposed construct (Davis 1986).

**H4:** *The more positive the consumer's beliefs about convenience of using a self service technology, the more positive his/her intention to use that service and the higher the level of satisfaction will be.*

## Design

Although Design has a lot in common with expected Performance (they could be interrelated), the distinction is based on system features and how they perform trough each step of a single process, and how properly the expected outcome is achieved. Design is planning step by step the desired interaction with a customer, even at the required stage of post-purchase. It's about considering the different obstacles they may face, and the different options they want to find through the complete process. Design also means technical adaptation to consumer's capabilities. It may be expressed in reference to following issues:

- Planned compensation when technology fails,
- An adequate and logical (from consumer's perspective) progression of tasks with unnecessary repetitions,
- Simplified operations,
- Task clarity and adaptability to consumers needs,
- Including enough and clear information to proceed trough the complete process,
- Service assistance at any time in case of failure, and finally,
- It means giving customers a tangible evidence of company's achievements to handle complaints.

**H5:** *The more positive the consumer's beliefs about design of a self service technology, the more positive his/her intention to use that service and the higher the level of satisfaction will be.*

## Novelty

There are many definitions and constructs related with Novelty. Technology innovativeness (Parasuraman, 2000) or inherent novelty seeking (Dabholkar and Bagozzi, 2002) are two of them. For the purposes of this research, we need to address a single general definition for the Novelty construct. Novelty can be stated as the level of desire to seek out new and challenging stimuli prior to other members in a society. There are two known groups of consumers (innovators and early adopters) (Rogers 1983) willing to test and try new products or services prior to anyone else. They are pioneers enthusiastic enough to venture into new journeys. These kinds of customers look for unique products or services, trying to discover what the products can offer them. They are just curious. These customers will try to do things first in almost any occasion. For them, it is a challenge to demonstrate that they can deal with new tasks. These customers seek complete access to products and to have an information control advantage. They want to know before anybody else how a product works so they can pass on the knowledge.

**H6:** *The more positive the consumer's beliefs about novelty of a self service technology, the more positive his/her intention to use that service and the higher the level of satisfaction will be.*

## METHODOLOGY

The article "*A Paradigm for Developing Better Measures of Marketing Constructs*" (Churchill 1979) is one of the most recognized articles dealing with scale development. In this article, the author suggested a specific procedure to build better measurement instruments. The problem with scale development is that we need to appeal

*Figure 8. A paradigm for developing better measures of marketing constructs*

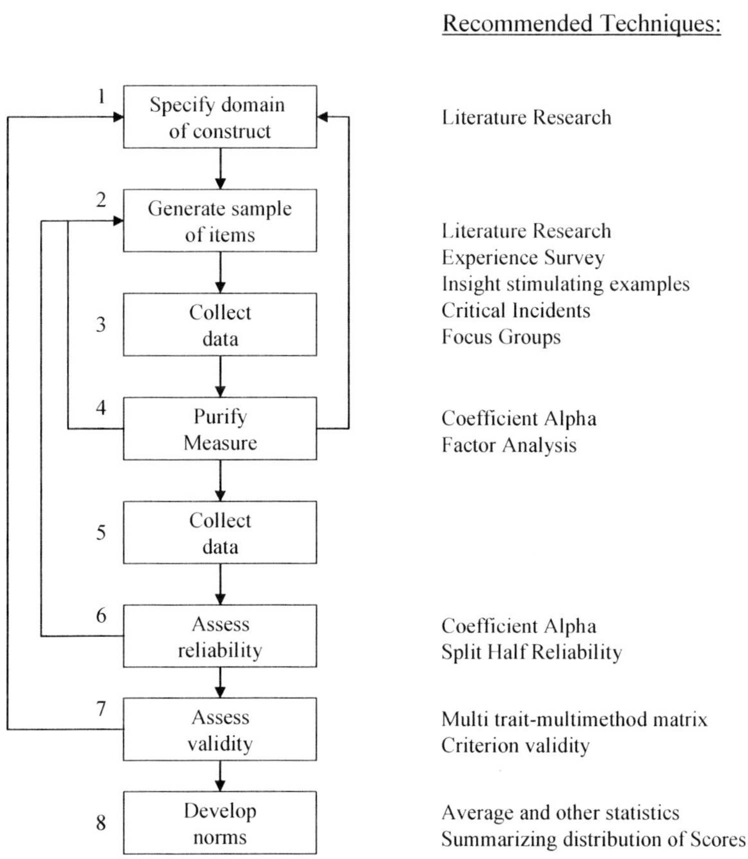

to people's perceptions and thoughts and assign numbers to their attitudes towards the constructs we are trying to measure. They usually offer only partial answers to what we are trying to measure. Churchill proposed a step by step methodology to assess reliability and validity. For the purpose of this research, we consider this methodology as the most appropriate to follow.

## RESULTS AND DISCUSSION

### Factor Analysis and Regression model

After reviewing and testing all attitude variables, the next step in this automated services research was to conduct factor, ANOVA and regression analysis. For factor analysis we followed three different approaches to test all possibilities while eliminating the appropriate variables. The best option we found to develop factor analysis was through the elimination of variables with low factor loadings. So, we started to eliminate those variables with factor loadings lower that .500, which indicates not appropriate or unclear loadings. The applied procedure was:

- Check KMO Sampling Adequacy Measure. In all steps, the measure was always appropriate for factor analysis.
- Verify Bartlett's Test of Sphericity
- Conduct Rotated Factor Analysis
- Check for vague variable factor loadings
- Eliminate the variable with the most unclear loading
- Start the process from step one until there where no more variables with imprecise factor loadings
- Perform the Scale Reliability Analysis until there are no chances to increase reliability.

In conclusion, this approach shows a Total Explained Variance of 57.915 and reveals a more consistent and clear factor structure. So, we finally have the following components with their respective grouping variables.With the following suggested categorization of components:

- **Ubiquity:** You can be sure that you might buy your products whenever you need them, wherever you want them, and at the time and price you want.
- **Failure Response:** An appropriate response (personal or mechanical) in case of technological failures.

- **Control:** Provides users a sense of situational and operational control.
- **Technological dependence:** It gives a sense of technological dependence/in-dependence while using automated services.
- **Human Interaction:** A person's need to be assisted by a human being when technology doesn't work. People may want to negotiate with people to find appropriate solutions; automated services are limited when it comes to finding appropriate answers
- **Convenience:** A sense of technological profitability through time and money savings.
- **Safe Design:** People's need to operate in a reliable and appropriate automated service.
- **Novelty:** People's readiness to interact with technology.

## The Regression Model

At this point, the following step was to run a regression analysis trying to find any influence between the extracted components and people's intention to use SST's. The objective of multiple regression analysis is to examine the relationship between a single dependent variable and a set of independent variables. The main purpose on this research is to distinguish a clear and reliable relationship between both kinds of variables in case it exists. We need to understand if there is a multivariate effect of the extracted independent variables on the selected dependent variable, we need to know if any of the extracted independent variables affect intention to use automated services. After factor analysis, we need to modify the initial model and consider the new extracted components to test any statistical relationship with consumer's intentions to use SST's:

*Figure 9. Modified Conceptual Model*

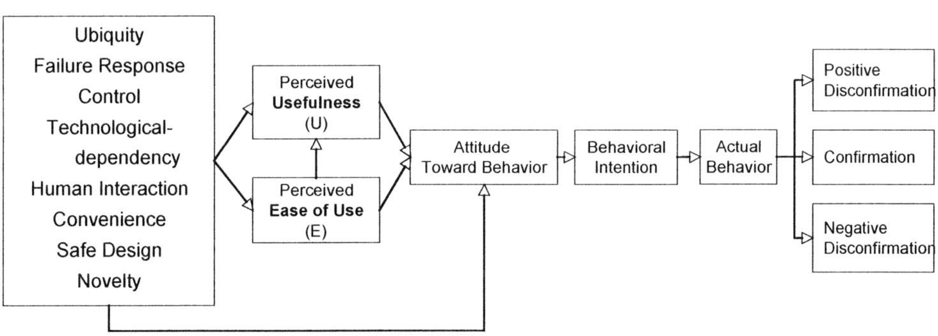

To explain the following propositions, we will follow the analogy of a rocket launch. Accordingly, three basic and important questions must be answered: 1) why do we need to launch a rocket? 2) How should we build the rocket? and 3) how should we launch the rocket?

## Discussion

**Why do we need to launch a rocket?** Because we trying to create the paths, rather than follow them. We needed to find statistical evidence to encourage companies to focus on SST's as soon as possible. Here are some of the managerial implications considered:

- SST's help companies reduce operative costs through repetitive task automation, and also let customer service representatives focus on specialized assistance.
- SST's increase customer satisfaction and loyalty if customers perceive appropriate automated solutions or professional interpersonal attention.
- The inclusion of automated technologies will lead companies to reach new market segments that they were previously unaware of, or which were not accessible.
- Automated Services will improve customer service, allowing service personnel to focus on finding answers to complex customer's demands.
- SST's will enable a-synchronic, direct, and permanent transactions considering ubiquity.
- SST's will allow customer learning and feedback to improve automated processes.

The research provides some insights about customers behavior towards Self Service Technologies. At this moment, even when there is not much penalty for failure – given that everybody is equally bad - we should keep in mind that SST's might be the differentiation tool we were looking for. We now have evidence that customers avoid automated services 1) when they fail; 2) when they are poorly designed; 3) when they are not safe; 4) when they do not perform better than the personal alternative, and 5) when there is no one available to attend failures. We have also tested the possible impact of perceived de-personalization while using SST's. We should keep in mind that no matter how focused companies are in customer service, if a client perceives any form of inattention (particularly in the introductory stage) this will negatively affect his/her buying intentions. It may also influence or even destroy brand loyalty. We have found empirical evidence of this behavior.

It is extremely important to look at de-personalization as a factor, not as a limitation. We need to remember that even when SST's provides convenience and comfort, we always have to rely on a person to assist us when technology fails. We need to create effective social bonds to sustain us when the latter happens. SST's allow company employees to separate and perform two different activities: operation and consultation. People's use of SST's will basically depend on two important issues: technological life cycle and degree of task specialization. If an automated service is recently introduced and customers don't know how it works, it is important to educate them until they don't need any additional assistance. If a service is highly repetitive and consumers already know how to use it, they will not require personal assistance to get what they want - unless it fails). On the other hand, if a service is highly specialized they will not seek rigid automated services.

## Theoretical Implications

**How should we build the rocket?** We should consider three basic elements: Initial Propulsion (propellers), Rocket Body (differentiators) and Main Cabin (value added). From the research findings, we can get some interesting ideas:

Brand positioning is a continuum of product evaluations. Customer perceptions of the brand interactions are more likely to influence his/her attitudes towards a brand or service than the "real or objective" product performance. Three main elements should be continuously evaluated: technological performance, customer's ability to interact with technology, and personnel's ability and mood to interact with customers when required.

Interaction with SST's (as opposed to personnel attention) requires not only consumers' disposition to buy, but also their cognitive effort to interact. In many cases consumers accept lower levels of achievement in first time service due to lower expectations and expect higher levels when they interact with services for the second or third time. This is why SST's interaction creates stress at the beginning when customers do not know the device or procedure. After a period of experience customers establish their self services technologies standards, and take decisions based in these standards. This means that we need to make a strong effort in the INFORMATION PROCESS, through consumer education and attention programs.

However, we need to consider another important fact, customers now search for information through SST's, compare prices, receive product information, novelties, technical information, nearest stores to buy and so on. Nonetheless, often times they prefer go buy their products on retail stores to try the product, to see it, to feel it, to smell it, and to eliminate any error caused by imagination. Through the entire research we were trying to find the main factors affecting people's intentions to use SST's.

After Factor Analysis we found statistical evidence for 8 extracted components. However, ANOVA and the regression model have found statistical support for:

| | |
|---|---|
| Novelty | Safe Design |
| Control | Technological Dependency |

Additionally, we found two other statistically supported components while performing literature research:

Ease of use

Usefulness-Convenience

To achieve a summary of the recollected information and strive to present it in a friendly and practical way, our proposal is:

**Propellers:**
Convenience (Usefulness): SST's should encourage a sense of technological profitability through time and money savings, especially to young people.
Technological Dependence/Independence: SST's must permit the customization of services allowing independency while using automated services.

**Differentiators:**
Control: SST's should maintain people updated regarding the processes they follow, providing users a sense of situational and operational control.
Ease of use (Design): adequate, safe and friendly designs.

**Value added:**
Novelty: Even when the SST's processes are simple, companies should seek to entice the customer. They must be prepared for people's readiness to interact with technology.

So, that's how we build the Rocket Model:

*Figure 10. The Rocket Model*

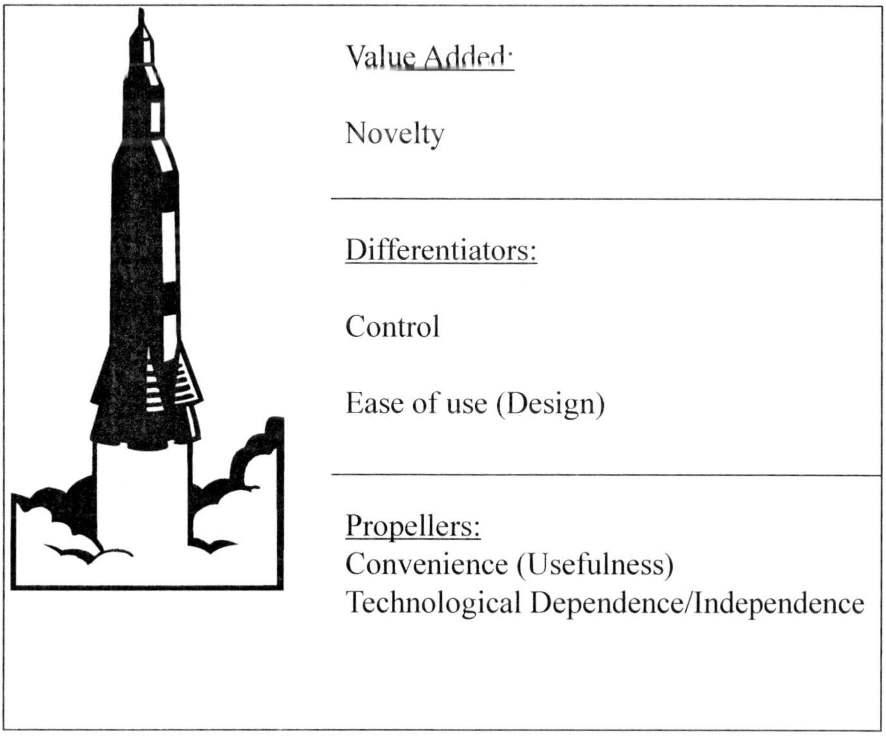


## MANAGERIAL IMPLICATIONS

*We can launch the rocket in the following way:*

**Identify internal and external service needs:** Ask what consumers are expecting from you and what employees need to do to differentiate through service. We must think about the importance of the pillars of techno readiness (managerial vision, infrastructure for error free service and service testing). To test your SST's you must think as a customer, feel like them, live like them, behave like them, and specially ask the kind of questions they ask when interacting with SST's. The success of self-services is tied to the success customers have finding what they are looking for.

We should always consider and evaluate three important elements: technological performance, customer's ability and motivation to interact with self service technologies, and employee's ability and mood to interact with customers and technology. We propose an adaptation from Kotler's Triangle Model (1994) and Parasuraman

*Figure 11. Fundamentals of Technological Marketing Strategy*

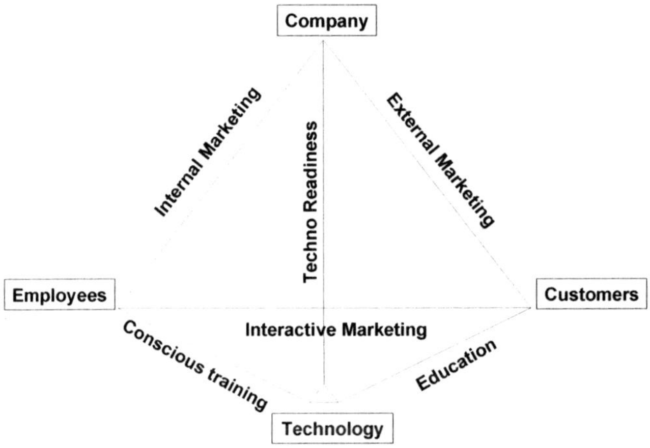


Pyramid Model (1996). This idea suggests the importance of a three-dimensional triangle, considering also the importance of the linkage between:

- Company and technology, based on management vision, commitment, allocated resources and performance metrics.
- Customers and technology, considering user adoption, security concerns, change resistance, educational programs, recovery systems and feedback methodologies.
- Employees and technology, developing motivational, training, supervising and support programs.

Research shows evidence that young people interact heavily with automated services (especially the Internet). This means that there is a clear need to concentrate immediately on this kind of services to reach them in the near future.

**Concentrate on automated service value added.** Do not offer anything if you have nothing to offer. We need to adapt our marketing strategy to technological needs - focusing on each of the traditional 4 P's of the marketing mix.

- **Price:** Development of new technology has a cost but we should keep in mind that customers have the personal alternative (they can always go to stores to buy products). There is no reason to increase cost if we automate operations (this means cost reduction).
- **Product:** Thousands of retail kiosks are being installed nowadays, unfortunately, many of these will fail because we are in many cases improvising

automated services. We should keep in mind all of the investigated components and elements while considering, designing and installing SST's. We should consider security, privacy, colors, materials, speed connection, and so on, because they affect customer usability. We should also consider staff acceptance based in friendly, comfortable, efficient, operational and convenient designs. Study suggests that SST's need to be faster, accurate and supported. We definitely should not think about SST's without a back up team. They must be always there. When implementing SST's, service delivered through human contact will shift from tedious, routine and high opportunity cost to an assistance of important customer issues and desires. While SST's must be used in routine operations, human assistance must be used when there are high value added tasks. Additionally, this form of splitting tasks would let consumer interact with service representatives just when they need it, rather than be forced to interact with tired employees.

- **Place:** This is what all is about!!! We should benefit from reaching new market segments through permanent open transaction possibilities. We can have automated representatives doing business 24 hours a day, 365 days a year. We should consider and evaluate channel interaction efficiency while aligning channels and service models.
- **Promotion:** We should keep in mind an important strategy: Through the entire research we have mentioned the importance of this process. We should start communicating benefits to attract customers. Then, we should guarantee the existence of the Propeller and Differentiator components of the Rocket Model.

*Figure 12. Marketing Strategy Focus*

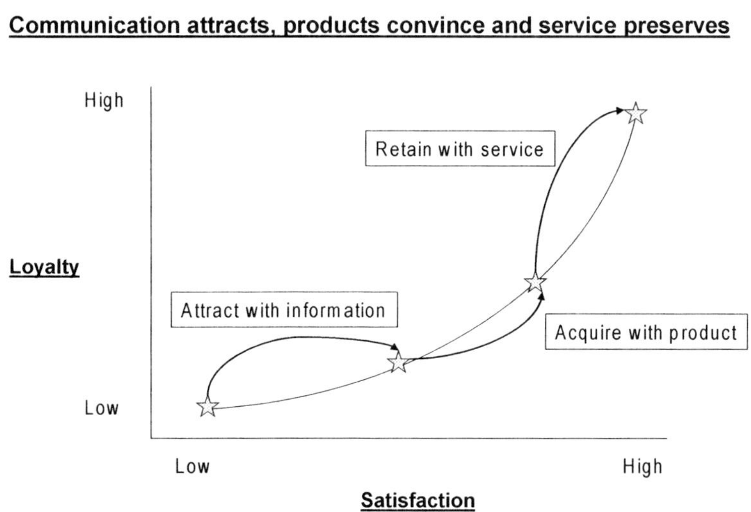

Finally, to retain customers we should focus on value added service (the value added components).

Often companies develop self service technologies in isolated research departments, rather than involving the entire organization. The result can be a mixture of inconsistent messages and methods of customer service representative interaction. Successful companies understand that self service has to be flawlessly integrated with other contact channels, through the entire organization. It is important to help internal and external customers help themselves, understand technology, benefit from it, tend to their evolving needs, guarantee support when SST's fail. We need to establish information programs - to educate and support internal and external customers. The idea of focusing on service should also be based on staff ability, commitment and motivation to create social bonds through customer's confidence, faith and trust.

**Formalize the service strategy through internal and external customers.**

**Step I.**

Find the right internal champion for self service proposals, considering the elements of the proposed adapted triangle: Company Vision, Technological Infrastructure, Prepared Employees and Delighted Customers. An SST Champion is a person motivated enough to move an entire organization to invest in a refundable dream. He/she is the one in charge of creating a plan considering business objectives, he/she must manage the budget, develop the required infrastructure, motivate and train employees, help employees help themselves, and develop the communication and marketing program.

**Step II.**

Develop an SST introductory plan. Our recommendation is to INCLUDE employees in this plan development, based on the idea of motivating involvement. Motivated employees will perform better if they create the rules. The introductory marketing plan should be discussed internally at first. Companies should remember that customers (like employees) need to learn the process, so every effort must be done to educate and guide them in order to reduce technological stress.

**Step III.**

Implement external communication plan. Clients trust the specialist. INFORMATION means <u>education and support</u> during the initial moments of fear and frustration. We need to invest in communication and education programs, not because customers are ever more stupid, but because they are ever more intelligent as access to information increases.

**Generate customer's confidence:** Don't panic. Panic communicates insecurity, which translates into uncertainty. Instead, find correct answers, keep alert and pay attention to technological opportunities. This of course should include customers' involvement to turn disappointments into opportunities for creating alternative solutions. Develop a corporate risk tolerance and create a service recovery strategy .Grow in knowledge and confidence trough small steps, don't try to run before you can walk. Properly designed self service applications can truly enhance the buyer-seller relationship. Customers who try to solve their own problems before calling customer service (and there are many who do so) appreciate that companies offer them an alternative. But companies that design systems that "trap" customers in the self service loop, are condemned to fail.

**Don't give up**, if you do so then you will start to accept failure, and that's not an option. Ask again: What self service resources are offered today? What do customers find most effective? What are the key metrics and benchmarks used to measure self service effectiveness? What strategies and best practices are required to increase success and deflection rates for self service? How do you increase customer use and adoption of self services? How do you pick applications, functions and users that are ready for self service? How do you create a plan, and get everyone on board? How do you identify and "sell" the benefits of self service to users and management? Deploying successful self service applications is as much about meeting user needs and creating effective processes, as it is about deploying the right technology.

## REFERENCES

Agarwal, R., & Prasad, J. (1999). Are individual differences germane to the acceptance of new information technologies? *Decision Sciences, 30*(2).

Ajzen, I., Fishbein, M. (1980). *Understanding attitudes and predicting social behavior.* Englewood Cliffs, NJ: Prentice Hall.

American Management Association (2000). *American Management Association Survey: E-business in the year 2000.* New York.

American Marketing Association (2002, March). Marketing news: Random sampling..

Ashbrook, J. (2001, July). To voice mail hell and back. *Business 2.0.*

Baron, R. M., & Kenny, D. A. (1986). The moderator-mediator variable distinction in social psychological research: Conceptual, strategic, and situational considerations. *Journal of Personality and Social Psychology,* American Psychological Association.

Berry, L., & Parasuraman, A. (1991). *Marketing services, competing through quality.* The Free Press.

Briody, D. (2000, February). Holiday numbers are in. *Info World.*

Business Week (1999).

Chase, R. B., & Aquilano, N. J. (1977). *Production and operations management: A life cycle approach* (First Edition). Homewood, IL: Richard D Irwin, Inc..

Chase, R. B. (1978). Where does the customer fit in a service operation? *Harvard Business Review, 56*(4).

Chase, R. B. (1981). The customer contact approach to services: Theoretical bases and practical extensions. *Oper. Res., 29.*

Chase, R. B., & Tansik, D. A. (1983). The customer contact model for organizational design. *Management Science,* Linthicum, *29.*

Churchill Jr., G. A. (1979, February). A paradigm for developing better measures of marketing constructs. *Journal of Marketing Research, XVI.*

Cohen, J. B., & Charles, S. A. (1991). Affect and consumer behavior. In T. S. Robertson & H. J. Kassarjian (Eds.), *Handbook of consumer behavior.* Englewood Cliffs, NJ: Prentice Hall.

Cohen, J. B., Fishbein, M., Ahtola, O. T. (1972, November). The nature and uses of expectancy-value models in consumer attitude research. *Journal of Marketing Research, 9.*

Cronin Jr., J. J., & Taylor, S. A. (1992). Measuring service quality: A reexamination and extension. *Journal of Marketing.*

Dabholkar, P. A., & Bagozzi R. P. (2002). An attitudinal model of technology-based self service technologies: Moderating effects of consumer traits and situational factors. *Journal of the academy of marketing science.*

Davis, F. D. (1986). *A technology acceptance model for empirically testing new end-user information systems: Theory and results.* Doctoral Dissertation, Sloan School of Management, Massachusetts Institute of Technology.

Davis, F. D. (1989, August). User acceptance of computer technology: A comparison of two theoretical models. *Management Science, 35*(8).

Donkers, B., Verhoef, P. C., & Martin de J. (2003, April). *Predicting customer lifetime value in multi-service industries.* ERIM Report Series Research Management.

Featherman, M., & Fuller, M. (2002). Applying TAM to e-Services adoption: The moderating role of perceived risk. In *Proceedings of the 36$^{th}$ Hawaii International conference on System Sciences.*

Fishbein, M. (1965). A consideration of beliefs, attitudes, and their relationships. I. D. Steiner & Martin Fishbein (Eds.), *Current studies in social psychology.* New York: Holt, Rinehart and Winston.

Fishbein, M., & Ajzen, I.(1975). *Belief, attitude, intention and behavior: An introduction to theory and research.* Reading, MA: Addison-Wesley.

Ganesh, J., Arnold, M. J., & Reynolds, K. E. (2000, July). Understanding the customer base of service providers: An examination of the differences between switchers and stayers. *Journal of Marketing, 64.*

Gutek, B. A., Bhappu, A. D., Liao, T., Mathew, A., & Bennett, C. (1999). Distinguishing between service relationships and encounters. *Journal of Applied Psychology.*

Helson, H. (1964). *Adaptation-level theory.* New York: Harper & Row.

Honevbein, P. (1996, October). *Strategies for effective customer education.* NTC Business Books.

Hunt, H. K. (1977). CS/D- Overview and future research directions. In H. Keith Hunt (Eds.), *Conceptualization and measurement of consumer satisfaction and dissatisfaction.* Cambdridge, MA: Marketing Science Institute..

Izzard, C. E. (1977). *Human emotions.* New York: Plenum.

Jarvis, S. (2002). Yes I would like some help thank you. *Marketing News.* American Marketing Association.

Johnson, M. D., Anderson, E. W., & Fornell, C. (1995). Rational and adaptive performance expectations in consumer satisfaction framework. *Journal of Consumer Research.* The University of Chicago Press.

Karmarkar, U. S., & Pittbaldo, R. (1995, December). Service markets competition. *Journal of Operations Management.*

Kellogg, D. L., & Chase, R. B. (1995, November). Constructing an empirically derived measure for customer contact. *Management Science. 41*(11).

Kotler, P. (1999). *Kotler on marketing; How to create, win and dominate markets.* Free Press.

Kotler, P., & Armstrong, G. (1994). *Principles of marketing 6/E.* Prentice Hall.

Lamb, C. Hair, J., & McDaniel, C. (1999). *Marketing 4/E.* South Western College Publishing.

Lardner, J. (2001, July). Building a customer centric company. *Business 2.0.*

Lovelock, C. H. (1983). Classifying services to gain strategic marketing insights. *Journal of Marketing.*

Mason, J. B., & Himes Jr., S. H. (1973). An exploratory behavioral and socioeconomic profile of consumer action about dissatisfaction with selected household appliances. *Journal of Consumer Affairs.*

Malhotra, N. K. (1996). *Marketing research: An applied orientation.* 2nd Edition. Prentice Hall.

Mick, D. G., & Fournier S. (1998). Paradoxes of technology: Customer cognizance, emotions and coping strategies. *Journal of consumer research, 25.*

Meuter M. L., Ostrom, A. L., Roundtree, R. I., & Bitner M. J. (2000). Self service technologies: Understanding customer satisfaction with technology-based service encounters. *Journal of Marketing, 64.*

Oliver, R. L. (1989). Processing of satisfaction response in consumption: A suggested framework and research propositions. *Journal of Consumer Satisfaction, Dissatisfaction and Complaining Behavior.*

Parasuraman, A. (2000). Technology readiness index (TRI): A multiple-item scale to measure readiness to embrace new technologies. *Journal of Service Research, 2*(4).

Parasuraman, A., & Colby, C. (2001). *Techno ready marketing: How and why your customers adopt technology.* The Free Press.

Pescovitz, D. (2000). Hello, may I help you? *The industry Standard.*

Pickle, H. B., & Bruce, R. (1972, September). Consumerism, product satisfaction/dissatisfaction: An empirical investigation. *Southern Journal of Business.*

Popcorn, F. (1992). The popcorn report. *Harper Business.* New York.

Rayport, J. F., & Sviokla, J. J. (1994). Managing in the marketspace. *Harvard Business Review, 72.*

Ries, A., & Trout, J. (1993). *The immutable laws of marketing.* Harper Collins Publishers, Inc.

Rogers, E. M. (1983). *Diffusion of innovations.* New York: Free Press.

Roth, A. V. (2000). *Service strategy and the technological revolution: The 7 myths of e-services.*

Selnes, F., & Hansen, H. (2001, November). The potential hazard of self-service in developing customer loyalty. *Journal of Service Research, 4*(2).

Seybold, P. B. (1999). Customers.com, How to create a profitable business strategy for the internet and beyond. *Crown Business.*

Seybold, P. B. (2001). The customer revolution. *Crown Business.*

Silvestro, R., Fitzgerald, L., Johnston, R., & Voss, C. (1992). Towards a classification of service processes. *International Journal of Service Industry Management, 3*(3).

The Wall Street Journal (2000).

Thibaut, J. W., & Kelley, H. H. (1959). *The social psychology of groups.* New York: John Wiley & Sons, Inc.

Thomas, D. R. E. (1978). Strategy is different in service business. *Harvard Business Review.*

Vence, D. L. (2002). How one co. listened its way to success. *Marketing News.* American Marketing Association.

Westbrook, R. A. (1987, August). Product/consumption-based affective responses and post purchase processes. *Journal of Marketing Research.*

Westbrook, R. A., & Oliver, R. L. (1991). The dimensionality of consumption emotion patterns and consumer satisfaction. *Journal of Consumer Research.*

Wyner, G. (2000). Customer experience on the Web. *Marketing Management, 9*(4).

Yi, Y. (199). A Critical Review of Consumer Satisfaction. In V. A. Zeithaml (Ed.), *Review of Marketing 1990.* Chicago: American Marketing Association.

Wemmerlöv, U. (1990). A taxonomy for service processes and its implications for system desgin. *International Journal of Service Industry Management.*

Zeithaml, V., & Bitner, M. J. (2000). *Services marketing, integrating customer focus across the firm,* (2nd Ed). McGraw Hill.

Zeithaml, V., Parasuraman, A., & Berry, L. (1990). *Delivering quality service, balancing customer perceptions and expectations*. The Free Press.

Zeithaml, V., Parasuraman, A., & Berry, L. (1991). Understanding customer expectations of service. *Sloan Management Review.*

# Chapter V
# Measuring Variability Factors in Customer Values, Technology Convergence and Profit Optimization in a Retailing Firm:
## A Framework for Analysis

**Rajagopal**
*Monterrey Institute of Technology and Higher Education, ITESM, Mexico*

Developing consumer value through retailing lies at the heart of the marketing concept. The pursuit of this goal implies that the company is not only interested in making the sale or achieving trial purchase at any cost, but is also aiming on developing the strategies to achieve long-term profitability through repeat buying and consumer retention. Such approach builds the loyalty on one hand and enriches the consumer values on products, services and related factors on the other. The consumer products companies attempt to build and maintain consumer value, wherein the brand managers supplement their mass-media advertising with more direct communications through direct and interactive methods, internet communications, and other innovative channels of distribution (Pearson 1996; Peppers and Rogers 1997; Barwise and Hammond 1998).

Consumer value may be defined as a tool to measure the prolonged satisfaction and an on-going propensity to buy the products and services. While there are continuing discussions on the consumer value, it may be argued that the consumer value is of strategic importance to management as it highlights the *manifest* nature of consumer satisfaction in providing a revenue stream to the company with high involvement and repeat purchase behavior. The individual values of the consumer may be estimated as base values and changes in such values are affected by the corresponding measures of the specific value drivers. The base value ties to the most important of all complements that may be determined as a *consumer need*. The base value may be estimated in reference to the price that a consumer is already paying for obtaining a similar utility or from the size of the savings that the product brings. It is challenging to estimate the base value far out in the future because unexpected new applications are often discovered over a very long period of time.

Estimating value drivers for a new product can be tricky because there is no direct historical data. However, we can assume that the impact from changes in price or availability of complements will be similar to what other markets have experienced. Following discussion in the chapter develops the framework for measuring the consumer values in reference to establishing the long run relationship by the firm and optimizing its profit levels. The discussions in the chapter attempt to endure the core issues of consumer values in retailing the products and services as how to conceptualize consumer values, how to measure it, and how to manage it.

## REVIEW OF LITERATURE

The concept of consumer satisfaction has a long history in marketing thoughts. Studies of consumer behavior emphasize consumer satisfaction as the core of the post-purchase period. Because consumer satisfaction presumably leads to repeat purchases and favorable word-of-mouth publicity, the concept is essential to marketers. In saturated markets consumer satisfaction is thought to be one of the most valuable assets of a firm. Consumer satisfaction serves as an exit barrier, thereby helping the firm to retain its consumers. The impact of loyal consumers is considerable; for many industries, the profitability of a firm increases proportionally with the number of loyal consumers and high sales to new consumers can be attributed to word-of-month referrals. Several contributions have been made in relation to various mechanisms for improving and using consumer satisfaction. Barsky and Labagh (1992) proposed a consumer-satisfaction matrix as a tool for evaluating guest information and attitudes, and for identifying related strengths and weaknesses. Dube et al. (1994) described how consumer satisfaction data can be used for positioning strategies that will help the business carve a niche, whereas Morgan

(1993) investigated consumers' value of benefits offered in mid-scale restaurant chains. Some contributions in the marketing literature suggest that there are very high expectations for these loyalty-building initiatives (Reichheld and Sasser 1990; Nalebuff and Brandenburger 1996; Reichheld 1996). The academics, consultants and business people speculated that marketing in the new century would be very different from the time when much of the pioneering work on consumer loyalty was undertaken (e.g. by Churchill 1942; Brown 1953; Cunningham 1956, 1961; Tucker 1964; Frank 1967). Yet there exists the scope for improving the applied concepts as there have been many changes over conventional ideologies.

The well-known disconfirmation of expectations model of satisfaction suggests that consumer satisfaction is a result of a comparison between company performance and consumer expectations (Oliver, 1980; 1981). Disconfirmation models are usually focused on performance of specific attributes and expectations (Bearden and Teel, 1983; Churchill and Surprenant, 1982; Tse and Wilton, 1988; Oliver, 1993). However, there is a gap in our current understanding of satisfaction in a channel's context where relationship-building rather than transactional exchange assumes importance. The comparison process between actual performance and expectations may be moderated by the presence of firm and environmental variables such as consumer power, consumer size, rivalry, channel configuration, product line growth rate, supplier flexibility and consumer service. The relationship between consumer service and satisfaction has been investigated to a limited extent in the logistics literature (Mentzer *et al.,* 1989; Emerson and Grimm, 1996). Mentzer *et al.* (1989) call for a formal analysis of logistics and marketing consumer service items in order to establish certain general dimensions of consumer service and to investigate their impact on consumer satisfaction. Further, Mentzer *et.al.* (1989) and Emerson and Grimm (1996) found that the performance on certain logistics and marketing consumer service dimensions directly contributes to consumer satisfaction in a channels setting.

The key marketing variables such as price, brand name, and product attributes affect consumers' judgment processes and derive inference on its quality dimensions leading to consumer satisfaction. The experimental study conducted by Brucks *et.al.* (2000) indicates that consumers use price and brand name differently to judge the quality dimensions and measure the degree of satisfaction. Zeithaml (2000) synthesizes contemporary evidence and identifies relationships between service quality and profits reviewing the direct effects of service quality on profits. He also discusses the link between perceived service quality and purchase intentions, customer and segment profitability, and among key service drivers of service quality, customer retention, and profitability. Lam Shun *et.al.* (2004) discuss the interrelationships between customer value, satisfaction, loyalty and switching costs by developing a conceptual framework linking all these constructs in a business-to-business service setting. On the basis of the cognition-affect-behavior model, the authors hypothesize that customer satisfaction mediates the relationship between customer value and customer loyalty, and that customer satisfaction and loyalty have significant reciprocal effects on each other.

The consumer value concept is utilized to assess product performance and eventually to determine the competitive market structure and the product-market boundaries. The consumer value may be measured as the product efficiency viewed from the consumer's perspective, i.e., as a ratio of outputs (e.g., resale value, reliability, safety, comfort) that consumers obtain from a product relative to inputs (price, running costs) that consumers have to deliver in exchange. The efficiency value derived can be understood as the return on the consumer's investment. Products offering a maximum consumer value relative to all other alternatives in the market are characterized as efficient. Different efficient products may create value in different ways using different strategies (output-input- combinations). Each efficient product can be viewed as a benchmark for a distinct sub-market. Jointly, these products form the efficient frontier, which serves as a reference function for the inefficient products. This ensures that only the products with a similar output-input structure are partitioned into the same sub-market. As a result, a sub-market consists of highly substitutable products. In addition, value-creating strategies (i.e., indications of how to vary inputs and outputs) to improve product performance in order to offer maximum consumer value are provided. The impact of each performance parameter on consumer value may be determined that is identified along with the value drivers among them. Based on the interplay between potential **value** and realized **value**, managers can devise **consumer** specific strategies. Christopher(1988) after surveying existing models of retailing, discusses on the idea that the retailer saves its consumers costs by assembling goods in one place. This introduces an essential non-convexity and importantly affects the conditions under which shops compete with each other and the constraints on their value attributes. The value of a consumer may be defined in reference to a firm as the expected performance measures are based on key assumptions concerning retention rate and profit margin and the consumer value also tracks market value of these firms over time. The value of all consumers is determined by the acquisition rate and cost of acquiring new consumers as discussed by Gupta, Lehmann and Stuart (2003).

It is necessary to develop a strong approach for measuring the consumer value, which is a key factor that influencing the process of profit optimization in a firm. The previous research contributions as discussed in the pretext, largely argue towards building consumer value by measuring the levels of satisfaction. There exists the scope for deriving the consumer value by measuring the intangible factors in the retail transactions, transitional movements in the value for non-conventional products, promotional appeals and dynamics of retail and technology convergence.

The framework for measuring consumer value discussed in this paper would help in determining the exit-voice-loyalty, based on the interplay between the potential value and realized value, which may lead the managers to develop appropriate strategies to augment the consumer satisfaction. Hirschman (1970) had initiated this concept to measure the value among the marketing channels. The analytical framework in the following text is discussed also in reference to the prospect theory developed by Tversky and Kahnman (1981) towards framing decisions and understanding the dynamics of choices that consumers may exercise in order to optimize their satisfaction and ultimate value.

## FRAMEWORK FOR ANALYSIS

A retail chain is modeled as a dummy control center (CC) that helps in evolving strategies, marketing designs and building corporate image. The CC is an integrated part of the corporate headquarters that is instrumental in making most of the business decisions. Let us assume that there are L networks and $D_m$ spatially spread markets. $\Delta_j \subseteq \{1,2,...,D_m\}$ denotes the set of markets served by chains j and $\varphi_h \subseteq \{1,2,...,L\}$ denotes the set of chains serving markets h, the operations of chain is $j^{th}$ store in market h in period $t$ are fully described by an N-dimensional vector, $Z^{j,h}(t) \equiv \left(Z_1^{j,h}(t),...,Z_N^{j,h}(t)\right) \in \{1,...,R\}^N$, where $Z_K^{j,h}(t)$ is the practice for the $k^{th}$ dimensions of the store operations. There are then R feasible practices for each dimension. The store operations of chain $j$ is represented by an element of $\{1,2,...,R\}^{N|\Delta_j|}$.

### Measuring the Consumer Value

The consumer values for goods and services are largely associated with the retail stores brands and consumer services offered therein. The beginning of consumer preferences is the basic discrete time that helps the consumers in making a buying decision and maximizing the value of product. Ofek Elie (2002) discussed that the value of product and service are not always the same and are subject to value life cycle that governs the consumer preferences in the long-run. If consumers prefer the product and service for N periods with Q as value perceived by the consumer, the value may be determined as Q>N, where Q and N both are exogenous/ variables. If every consumer receives higher perceived values for each of his buying , the value added product $q \geq Q$, where 'q' refers to the change in the quality brought by innovation or up-graded technology. The consumer may refrain from buying the products if $q \leq Q$, that does not influence his buying decisions. However, a strong referral 'R' may lead to influence the consumer values, with an advantage factor β that may be explained by price or quality factor. In view of the above discussion it may be assumed that consumer preferences have high variability that grows the value factors in retail buyers' decisions:

$$E\left[\sum_{t=1}^{N}\beta'\mu\left(C_t,\tilde{Z}\right)+\beta^{N+1}Q_{N+1}\left(V_{N+1}\right)\right] \qquad \text{(i)}$$

Where $C_t$ represents consumption and technology convergence $\tilde{Z}$ is a vector of consumer attributes (*viz.* preferential variables), $Q_t$ is the value perceived by the consumer and $V_{N+1}$ denotes the value perceived by the consumer maximizes his value $Q_t$ in a given time and also enhances his values for future buying as the influence of referrals is not negative $V_{N+1} \geq 0$.

A consumer value is a dynamic attribute that plays key role in buying and is an intangible factor to be considered in all marketing and selling functions. The value equation for consumer satisfaction may be expressed as a function of all value drivers wherein each driver contains the parameters that directly or indirectly offer competitive advantages to the consumers and enhance the consumer value.

$$V' = K_s, K_m, K_d, K_c\left[\prod\left\{V\left(x,t,q,p\right)\right\}\right] \qquad \text{(ii)}$$

In the above equation $V'$ is a specific consumer value driver, $K$ are constants for supplies(s),margins (m), distribution (d), and cost to customers (c); $x$ is volume, $t$ is time, $q$ is quality and $p$ denotes price. The total utility for the conventional products goes up due to economy of scale as the quality is also increased simultaneously ($\delta_v/\delta_x$>0). The consumer value is enhanced by offering larger volume of product at a competitive price in a given time ($\delta_v/\delta_p$>0) and ($\delta_v/\delta_t$>0). The conventional products create lower values to the consumers ($\delta_v/\delta_x$<0) while the innovative products irrespective of price advantages, enhance the consumer value ($\delta_v/\delta_x$>0). The value addition in the conventional products provides lesser enhancement in consumer satisfaction as compared to the innovative products. Such transition in the consumer value, due to shift in the production product may be expressed as

$$V'_{hj} = a\left[\sum\frac{T_p}{\left(1+V_p\right)^{(1+j+i)}}\right]+b\left(X_j\right) \qquad \text{(iii)}$$

In this equation $V'_{hj}$ represents enhancements in consumer value over the transition from conventional to innovative products, $a$ and $b$ are constants, $T_p$ denotes high-tech and high-value products, $V_p$ represents value of product performance that leads to enhance the consumer value, the volume is denoted by x and j is the period during which consumer value is measured.

Besides the high-tech and high-value products the consumers and companies may also find scope of enhancing values with appropriate promotional strategies. The consumer values often get enhanced by offering better buying opportunities that reflect on short- and long- term gains. Let us assume that the competitive advantage in existing products over time is $G_x$ that offers $j^{th}$ level of satisfaction through various sales promotion approaches adopted by the company. Such market situation may be explained as:

$$G_x = \left[ r_1 m_1 ; r_2 m_2 ; r_3 m_3 ; ......; r_j m_j \right] \tag{iv}$$

Where $r_j$ denotes the $j^{th}$ level of satisfaction ($j = 1,2,3,....,n$) and $m_j$ is the number of consumers attracted towards buying the product. Given the scope of retail networks, a feasible value structure for consumers may be reflected in repeat buying behavior ($\tilde{R}$) that explains the relationship of the consumer value with the product and associated marketing strategies. The impact of such consumer value attributes in a given situation may be described as:

$$\sum_{j=1}^{n} r_j m_j = \widehat{R} \tag{v}$$

The prospect theory laid by Tversky and Kahnman (1981) proposes that the intensity of gains plays strategic role in value enhancement as $G_{xt} = g_{pt} (\delta_x / \delta_p)$. In this situation't' represents the period wherein the promotional strategies were implemented to enhance the consumer values in reference to product specific gains ($g_{pt}$). However, in order to measure relationship/variability between the repeat buying behavior and consumer value, it would be appropriate to determine the cumulative decision weights (*w*) and substituting it in the equation (i), (iv) and (v), that may reveal as :

$$G_{xt} = w \sum_{k=1}^{jm} \left[ g_{pt} \left( r_j m_j \right) + \beta^{n+1} Q_{N+1} \left( V_{n+1} \right) \right]$$

The consumer value however may be the driver function of gains on buying decisions and the influencing variables such as perceived use value and referrals.

The value measurements have been used as one of the principal tools to assess the trend of consumer behavior for the non-conventional products. The value syndrome influences the individual and group decisions in retail and bulk deals, and conditionalizes the decision process of consumers. The conditional consumption behavior suggests that the consumption depends heavily on the utility function and on the source of uncertainty (Carroll and Kimball, 1996 and Deaton 1992).

The dynamics of retail consumption and technology convergence behavior may be expressed as:

$$c_t = \alpha_0 + \alpha_1 y_t + \alpha_2 w_t + u_t \qquad \text{(vi)}$$

Where $c_t$ is a log of real per capita total consumption, $y_t$ is the log of real per capita disposal income, $w_t$ is the per capita expenditure on buying and $u$ denotes the random error term. Under this assumption $c_t$, $y_t$, and $w_t$ are co-integrated, $u_t$ is $\leq 0$ in the process of measuring the consumer behavior in reference to preference variables leading to price and non-price determinants, the dependent factor is the rate of change in the consumption ($\Delta_{ct}$) and change in technology $(\Delta_{ta})$. In view of the above discussion the dynamic consumption function that reflects the retail consumer behavior for particular products may be estimated as [deriving from equation (vi)]:

$$\Delta_{ct} = \beta_0 + \beta_1 (L) u_{t-1} + \beta_2 (L) \Delta_{yt} + \beta_3 (L) \Delta_{wt} + \beta_4 (L) \Delta_{rt} + \beta_5 (L) \Delta_{ta} + \varepsilon_t \qquad \text{(vii)}$$

Where $\Delta$ is the change factor, r is the concentration ratio of retail stores in a given location and $\varepsilon_t$ is a random error term. The test of this model requires time series data to be analyzed for trend values, taking (L) as polynomial log operator. It has been observed in previous studies that value to expenditure ratios increase consumer sensitivity in volume of buying and driving repeat buying decisions for the regular and high-tech products (Carroll and Dunn 1997). Belessiotis (1996) had explained in one of his studies that consumer confidence index derived of value factors, forecasts more than changing expectations.

## Rationale of Consumer Preference and Market Demand

Each market operates in a predetermined consumer segment being defined by a vector of ideal store practices which is referred to as a consumer's type. A consumer's type is a random draw from a distribution which is parameterized by his core benefit value which is an element of a proper subset of {1,…..,R}. If a consumer's core benefit value is *s* then his type is a random draw from $\{s\text{-}E, \ldots, s+E\}^N \subset \{1,\ldots,R\}^N$ according to a uniform distribution where E is a parameter. The seeds for the consumers in market *h* are distributed according to a triangular density function over $\{S_h\text{-}G,\ldots,S_h+G\} \subset \{1,\ldots,R\}$. This construction of the distribution of consumer types is performed independently for each market. By this specification, markets differ according to the single parameter $S_h$ and the heterogeneity between markets $h'$ and $h''$ can be measured $|S_{h'}\text{-}S_{h''}|$.

E controls the degree of correlation in a consumer's preference; that is, the degree to which preferring particular values for one dimension implies that similar values tend to be preferred for other dimensions. If E = 0 then a consumer's ideal vector of store practices is an element of {(1,..,1),...., (R,...,R)} so that consumers assign the same correlation ideal value to all dimensions. More generally, the lower the E, the greater is the correlation across dimensions. A reason for such a correlation is the presence of a few consumer traits – such as income, parents' traits, and education – which influence preferences over a large set of dimensions. For example, people with higher income may not incur greater search costs (due to their higher value of time) so they would prefer everyday low prices with fewer sales. Form the retailer's perspective fewer product lines and larger inventories reduce the chances of being out-of-stock of a product and thus creating the need for another trip of consumer to the store.

Consumer decision making with respect to 'which store to buy from' and 'how much to buy from that store' is assumed to depend only on the distance between the consumer's ideal store practices and the actual practices of stores. We use Euclidean distance which takes the form $\sqrt{\sum_{k=1}^{N}(z_k - w_k)^2}$ for a consumer of type $\underline{w} \equiv (w_1,\ldots,w_N)$ and a store with practices $\underline{z} \equiv (z_1,\ldots,z_N)$. A consumer ranks stores according to this metric. Furthermore, it is assumed that the number of units demanded by a consumer equals

$$\left[A - \sqrt{\sum_{k=1}^{N}(z_k - w_k)^2}\right]^{\sigma} \quad \text{(viii)}$$

and such decisions are largely governed by the convenience factor associated with buying the products and services; where $\sigma > 1$ and $A \geq \sqrt{N(R-1)^2} + 1$ so that $\left[A - \sqrt{\sum_{k=1}^{N}(z_k - w_k)^2}\right] > 1$ for all $(\underline{w}, \underline{z})$.

## Consumer Positioning

If a Market $h$ is served by the chains in $\Phi_h$, each consumer has $|\Phi_h|$ stores from which to chose. In any time period, a consumer shops from exactly one store but, as will be described below, he can change stores over time. As started above, consumers rank buying points according to the convenience between his preferences and accessibility. Thus, a consumer of type $\underline{w}$ prefers a store with practices $\underline{z}'$ to a store with practices $\underline{z}''$ if and only if:

$$\sqrt{\sum_{k=1}^{N}\left(z_k' - w_k\right)^2} < \sqrt{\sum_{k=1}^{N}\left(z_k'' - w_k\right)^2} \qquad \text{(ix)}$$

A consumer enters each period with a "favorite buying place" that is the place he currently prefers most. Associated with a favorite store is the consumer's perception of the distance between the store and the consumer. Suppose chain *j*'s store in market *h* is the favorite store of a consumer in market *h*. Furthermore, suppose the consumer last visited that store in period $t'$ (why it might not have been the previous period will be made clear momentarily). The consumer's perception of the distance between the store and the consumer is specified to be $\sqrt{\sum_{k=1}^{N}\left(z_k^{j,h}(t') - w_k\right)^2}$ where $\underline{z}^{j,h}(t)$ is this store's set of practices as of period *t*.

Search proceeds as follows. In each period, a consumer buys from his favorite store with probability 1-Q. In that event, his favorite store remains unchanged though the perceived distance from that store is updated to reflect the current practices of the store. With probability Q, he engages in search which involves randomly selecting a store from the rest of the stores in his market (excluding his favorite store) and then buying from that store. At the end of the period, the consumer compares the distance for the store just visited with the distance assigned to his favorite store. If the former is larger then the consumer does not change his favorite store (nor the distance assigned to it). If the former is smaller then the consumer changes his favorite store to the store just visited and assigns to that store a distance based on the store's current practices. The random variable determining whether a consumer positioning is appropriate or not is assumed across strength of existing consumers and time interval during the search and realizing the purchase. If $Q = \frac{|\Phi_h| - 1}{|\Phi_h|}$, a consumer has no loyalty as the *ex ante* probability of buying from a predetermined place is the same, it may be assumed that $Q \in \left[0, \frac{|\Phi_h| - 1}{|\Phi_h|}\right]$ where Q = 0 is absolute loyalty as no experimentation occurs.

This framework analyzes optimal portfolio choice, consumption and convergence of technology with values management in the firm-supplier-consumer triadic relationship. The value concept in the above relationship governs the consumer portfolio decision in terms of formulation of recursive utility over time. It shows that the optimal portfolio demand for products under competition varies strongly with the values associated with the brand, industry attractiveness, knowledge management and ethical issues of the organization. The extent of business values determines the relative risk aversion in terms of functional and logistical efficiency between the organization and supplier while the switching attitude may influence the consumers if the organizational values are not strong and sustainable in the given competitive environment. The model assumes that a high functional value integrated with the triadic entities would raise the market power of organization, sustain decisions of consumer portfolios and develop long-run relationships thereof. The **consumer value** concept is utilized to assess product performance and eventually to determine the competitive market structure and the product-market boundaries.

The model explains that the value based consumer portfolios would enhance the **consumer value** as the product efficiency viewed from the **consumer's** perspective, i.e., as a ratio of outputs (e.g., resale **value**, reliability, safety, comfort) that the consumers obtain from a product relative to inputs (price, running costs) that the consumers have to deliver in exchange. The derived efficiency **value** can be understood as the return on the consumer's investment. Products offering a maximum **consumer value** relative to all other alternatives in the market are characterized as efficient. Market partitioning is achieved endogenously by clustering products in one segment that are benchmarked by the same efficient peer(s). This ensures that only the products with a similar output-input structure are partitioned into the same sub-market. As a result, a sub-market consists of highly substitutable products.

The consumer values are reflected in their competitive gains, perceived use values, volume of buying and level of quintessence with the consumer relationship management services of the organization. If these variables do not measure significantly, there emerges the development of switching attitude among the consumers. If the organizational values are low, the supplier relationship may be risk averse due to weak dissemination of values from organization to the suppliers.

## APPLICATION PROSPECTS IN MANAGEMENT

The retail sales performance and the **consumer** value approach are conceptually and methodically analogous. Both concepts calculate the value of a particular decision unit by analytical attributes forecast and the risk-adjusted value parameters. However, virtually no scholarly attention has been devoted to the question if any of these components of the shareholder value could be determined in a more market oriented way using individual **consumer** lifetime **values**. Systematically explored concepts in the field of consumer value and market driven approach would be beneficial for a company to derive long term profit optimization strategy over the period. Hence, a comprehensive framework for estimating both the value of a **con-**

**sumer** and profit optimization need to be developed. On a tactical level, managers need to consider as what is the optimum spread of consumers on a matrix. This needs careful attention and the application of managerial judgment and experience to measure the value driven performance of the firm. It cannot be prescribed by a text. They should also be prepared to vary their management style in response to the analysis they prepare. For example, a different style may well be needed to deal with consumers who do not yield much profit and present high costs to serve. All of these have postulated that portfolio theory is a useful theoretical approach to the analysis, categorization and management of supplier-consumer relationships. The following applied portfolios may be developed by the companies in order to gain the high consumer value –high profit matrix:

- **High-profitability:** Consumers who have high actual and potential value, coupled with relatively low cost to service.
- **High-potential:** Consumers who have high potential value, medium actual value, and low cost to service.
- **Underperforming:** Consumers who are currently unprofitable.

The consumer portfolio management process should then lead to plan and create strategies to maximize return on consumer relationships, either by portfolio or individual accounts.

## CONCLUSION

The consumer value in terms of satisfaction is one of the indicators for building profit oriented strategies in a firm. The consumer value concepts may be applied by the firms to evaluate the product performance in the given market and determine the approach for competitive advantage. In order to gain the benefits of comprehensive consumer value, firms need to systematically estimate the profitability associated thereof. The ultimate goal of the firms may be to generate continual revenue streams by maintaining the customer value. There appears to be a need for new research that will advance consumer satisfaction and value measurement methodologies. The existing theoretical and methodological issues are reviewed in this study and a new framework has been proposed in this paper for future research in measuring the consumer value. The framework for measuring the consumer values discussed in this paper provides analytical dimensions for establishing the long run consumer relationship by the firm and to optimize its profit levels.

## REFERENCES

Barsky, J. D., & Labagh, R. (1992). A strategy for consumer satisfaction. *The Cornell Hotel and Restaurant Administration Quarterly, 33*, 32-37.

Barwise, P., & Hammond, K. (1998). *Predictions: Media.* London: Phoenix Paperback.

Bearden, W. O., & Teel, J. E. (1993). Some determinants of consumer satisfaction and complaint reports. *Journal of Marketing Research, 20.*

Belessiotis (1996). *Consumer confidence and consumer spending in France.* Economic Paper #116, European Commission, September.

Brown, G. H. (1953). Brand loyalty - Fact or fiction, *Advertising Age,* 24. Reprinted in A.S.C. Ehrenberg & F.G. Pratt (Eds.), *Consumer behaviour,* (pp. 28-35). Middlesex, UK: Penguin.

Brucks, M., Zeithaml, V. A., & Naylor, G. (2000). Price and brand name as indicators of quality dimensions for consumer durables. *Journal of Academy of Marketing Science, 28*(3), 359-374.

Carroll, C. D., & Kimball, M. S. (1996). On the concavity of the consumption function. *Econometrics, 64*(4), 981-992.

Carroll, D., & Dunn, W. E. (1997). *Unemployment expectations.* Working paper, 6081, NBER.

Christopher, B. (1988). A theory of retail pricing. *Journal of Industrial Economics, 36*(4), 375-391.

Churchill, H. (1942). How to measure brand loyalty. *Advertising and Selling, 35*(24).

Churchill, G. A., & Surprenant, C. (1982, November). An investigation into the determinants of consumer satisfaction. *Journal of Marketing Research, 19*, 491-504.

Cunningham, R. M. (1956). Brand loyalty - What, where, how much? *Harvard Business Review, 34*, 116-128.

Cunningham, R. M. (1961). Consumer loyalty to store and brand. *Harvard Business Review*, (pp. 127-137).

Deaton, A. (1992). *Understanding competition.* Oxford: Oxford University Press.

Dube, L., Renaghan, L. M., & Miller, J. M. (1994). Measuring consumer satisfaction for strategic management. *Cornell Hotel and Restaurant Administration*

*Quaerterly, 35*, 39-47.

Emerson, C. J., & Grimm, C. M. (1996). Logistics and marketing consumer service: An empirical test of the Mentzer, Gomes, and Krapfel model. *International Journal of Physical Distribution & Logistics Management, 26*(9), 29-42.

Emerson, C. J., & Grimm, C. M. (1998). The relative importance of logistics and marketing consumer service: A strategic perspective. *Journal of Business Logistics, 19*(1), 17-32.

Frank, R. E. (1967). Is brand loyalty a useful basis for market segmentation? *Journal of Advertising Research, 7*(2), 27-33.

Gupta, S., Lehmann, D. R., & Stuart J. A.(2003). Valuing consumers. *HBS Marketing Research Paper* # 03-08.

Hirschman, A. O. (1970). *Exit, voice and loyalty: Responses to decline in firms, organizations and states.* Cambridge, MA: Harvard University Press.

Lam, Y. S., Venkatesh, S., Erramilli K. M., & Murthy, B. (2004). Customer value, satisfaction, loyalty and switching costs: An illustration from a business-to-business service context. *Journal of Academy of Marketing Science, 32*(3), 293-311.

Mentzer, J. T., Gomes, R., & Krapfel Jr., R. E. (1989). Physical distribution service: A fundamental marketing concept? *Journal of the Academy of Marketing Science, 17*(1), 53-62.

Morgan, M. S. (1993). Benefit dimensions of mid-scale restaurant chains. *Cornell Hotel and Restaurant Administration Quarterly, 34*, 40-45.

Nalebuff, B. J., & Brandenburger, A. M. (1996). *Co-opetition*. London: Harper-Collins Business.

Ofek, E. (2002). Customer profitability and life time value. *HBS Marketing Research* Paper, 1-9.

Oliver, R. (1980, November). A cognitive model of the antecedents and consequences of satisfaction decisions. *Journal of Marketing Research, 17*, 460-469.

Oliver, R. (1981). Measurement and evaluation of satisfaction processes in retail settings. *Journal of Retailing, 57*, 25-48.

Oliver, R. (1993). Cognitive, affective, and attribute bases of the satisfaction response. *Journal of Consumer Research, 20*, 418-30.

Pearson, S. (1996). *Building brands directly.* London: Macmillan Business.

Peppers, D., & Rogers, M. (1997). *Enterprise one to one: Tools for competing in the interactive age.* New York: Currency Doubleday.

Reichheld, F. F., & Sasser, W. E. (1990). Zero defections: Quality comes to services. *Harvard Business Review, 68* (September-October), 105-111.

Reichheld, F. F. (1996). *The Loyalty Effect: The hidden force behind growth, profits and lasting value.* Boston: Harvard Business School Press.

Tse, D. K., & Wilton, P. C. (1988, May). Models of consumer satisfaction formation: an extension. *Journal of Marketing Research, 25*, 204-12.

Tucker, W. T. (1964). The development of brand loyalty. *Journal of Marketing Research, 1*(3), 32-35.

Tversky, A., & Kahnman, D. (1981). The framing decisions and psychology of choice. *Science, 211*, 453-458.

Zeithaml, V. A. (2000). Services quality, profitability and the economic worth of customers: What we know and what we need to learn. *Journal of Academy of Marketing Science, 28*(1), 67-85.

# Chapter VI
# Decision Support Systems in Indian Organised Retail Sector

**Ankush Sharma**
*Institute of Technology and Management, Navi Mumbai, India*

**Preeta Vyas**
*Indian Institute of Management, India*

## INTRODUCTION

Retailing as simply defined is the end process of supply chain management where there is a direct interaction with the end-user or the customer. Hence forth availability, assortment, display, proper handling of product plays a vital role in a competitive world.

Organised retail stores are characterized by large professionally managed format stores. They provide goods and services that appeal to customers, in an excellent ambience that is conducive for shopping, created based on consumer preference analysis, and offer good value as some of the benefits of large-scale purchases are passed on to consumers. In India, retail has its deep root since long back –and that is why India is being known as "Nation of Shopkeepers" with about 12 million retailers by 2003[1]. Organised retailing contributes 2 percent to the total Indian retail sector and expected to increase to 5 percent , by 2010. Retail sector forms 10-11 percent of GDP[2]. It is attractive in terms of investment, employment opportunity, and usage of technology. Indian organised retail industry was worth Rs. 13,000 crore in the year 2000 and was expected to grow by 30 per cent in the next five years touching Rs. 45,000 crore in 2005. [3] Food and personal care amounted to Rs. 1000 crore in 2000. Retailing is in a rapid state of change due to speedy technological developments, changing competitive positions, varying consumer behaviour as well as their expectations and liberalized regulatory environment. In such a scenario, information is crucial to plan and control profitable retail businesses and it can be an important source of competitive advantage so long as it is affordable and readily available. DSS (Decision Support Systems) which provide timely and accurate information can be viewed as an integrated entity providing management with the tools and information to assist their decision making.

In west, retail businesses have been the early adopters of Information Technology (IT). As there is a need to capture accurate information and make it available not only within the store but send it to warehouse, distributors and manufacturers in real time to manage the short shelf life of some goods in grocery sector and costs of inventory, varied DSS tools have been adopted by organised retailers. VMIs- vendor managed inventory systems, Scanner at the counters- point of sales systems, RFID- radio frequency identification, OLAP (online analytical processing), supply chain management systems, forecasting systems, CRM- customer relationship management systems, ERP- enterprise resource performance system etc. are the tools used by organized retailers in developed nations.

Most retailers collect and have access to huge amount of data, collected from day to day operations e.g. customer loyalty data, retail store sales and merchandise data, demographic projection data etc. Currently retailers are data rich but information poor. There is a great potential to develop systems that enable analysts and decision makers to manage, explore, analyze, synthesize and present data in a meaningful manner for decisions. Retail managers are in a constant need for right kind of information for making effective decisions. Modern advancements in ITES (Information Technology Enabled Services) and communication has permitted deployment of DSS (Decision Support Systems). DSS can be defined as computer based systems that help decision makers to confront ill structured problems through direct interaction with data and analysis models.[4]

DSS are basically characterized by three capabilities; dialogues, data and modeling- the emphasis of each varies from organization to organization. DSS includes a wide variety of systems, tools and technology that support decision making. EIS(electronic information system),ESS( Electronic support system),GIS(geographic information system),OLAP (online analytical processing),software agents, knowledge discovery system and group DSS – all can be considered as DSS .Broadly two major categories[5] of DSS namely enterprise wide DSS and desktop DSS exist . Enterprise wide DSS are linked to large data warehouses and serve several decision makers in a company whereas desktop single user DSS are small systems residing on individual manager's personal computer. Thus it is an interactive computerized system that gathers and presents data from a wide range of sources, typically for business purposes. The organization needs to pool in both internal and external data, software, customer data, models and trained people to appreciate and use the systems for decision making which will help build sustainable competitive advantage. This can be depicted in the following Figure-1[6].

As seen from the above, external data and software alone would not provide competitive advantage, but organization's own customer and business data, models which convert data into useful information and people, who will operate the systems, analyze outputs and make decisions based on the information provided-all these would be required for competitive edge. Companies need to make decisions faster, across more channels and product lines, leverage more data, under greater regulatory demands and competitive pressures, and with more complicated constraints and trade-offs. DSS entails development of approaches for applying information systems, technology to increase the effectiveness of decision makers. Each sector with unique characteristics poses very different challenges to an organization; hence in-depth understanding of one sector would provide deeper insight into the requirement of DSS to enable managers in that sector to take effective decisions. The proposed study aims at understanding DSS, its application in grocery sector and issues arising out of implementation of DSS in Indian retail grocery sector.

*Figure 1. Managing Decision Support System in Retailing*

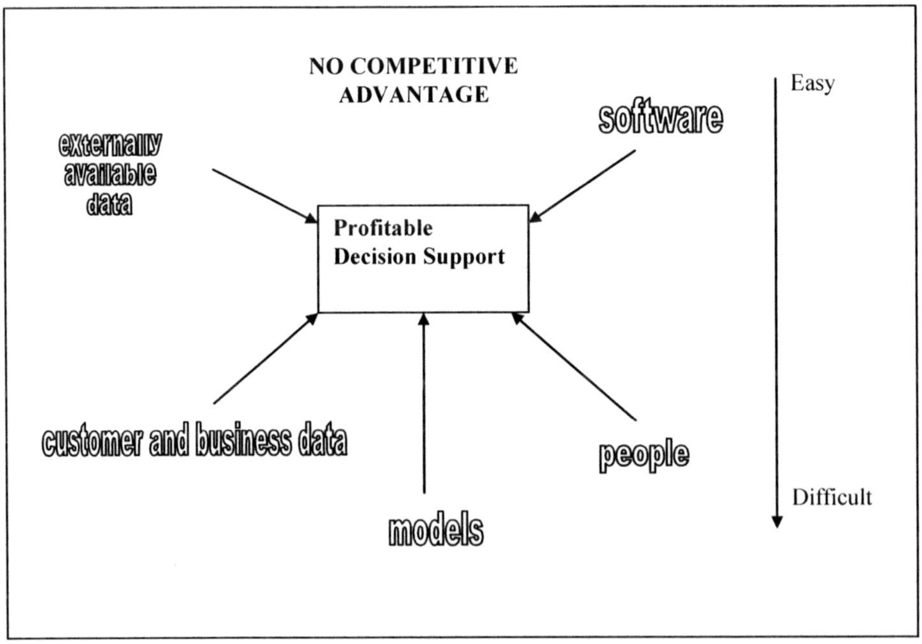

## OBJECTIVES

The study being exploratory in nature adopted a case study approach to understand practices of organized retailers regarding applications of various DSS tools. An in-depth study would enable to understand current nature of DSS tools being applied to arrive at operational decisions, benefits realized thereof, to understand the problems arising out of using DSS and future outlook. Hence, the objectives of the research study are:

- To provide a conceptual overview of DSS, possible applications of organized retail formats in grocery sector,
- To understand practices and usage of DSS for operational decisions in grocery sector
- To discuss managerial issues in design and implementation of DSS.

The focus is on store level operational decision-making assuming strategic decisions would be centralized and taken by the head office of an organised retail chain. In this age of information explosion, a plethora of operational level solutions have emerged that support transactions. Competitive strategy however requires linking information with intelligence. Hence nature of tools deployed impact on the processes and perceptions of users about its benefits and issues were explored.

## METHODOLOGY

In order to address the aforesaid objectives, we first reviewed available current literature on DSS in organized retail. This would help us in understanding-

- What is DSS and How DSS has been applied in organized retailing?
- How DSS is applied in developed world?
- What varied tools are being employed?

On the basis of the literature review, conceptual understanding about DSS was developed. Practices in Indian context were studied by looking at DSS applications in organized grocery retailing. Convenience purposive sampling was taken up. Two national players and two local players in Ahmedabad were selected. Store managers in charge of operations of these retail outlets were interviewed to understand current deployment of DSS tools in their operational decisions viz. inventory management, sales forecasting, supply chain management, CRM(Customer relationship management), category/ assortment management, campaign and promotion management. An in-depth interview guide (lead questions) was used for personal interviews (appendix-1) with store managers. Perceptions about usefulness of the tools in operations were tapped and problems encountered were probed. Websites of the suppliers of DSS tools to organized retailers were visited (surfed) to understand availability of various tools and perspectives /observations of IT suppliers were compiled.

## LITERATURE REVIEW

Scanning the relevant literature on DSS applications in organized retailing; brief overview is presented in the following section. Gallegos, Frederick(1999) describes applicability of DSS in a wide variety of applications of semi-structured and unstructured problems confronting managers and offers categorization of DSS into model-oriented and database oriented DSS. Decision support systems allow people at many levels to systematically analyze problems before making a decision. In the process, these systems extend the range and capability of the decision-making process, increasing its effectiveness. Eom, S B, Lee, S M, Kim, E B, Somarajan, C( 1998) report 271 published applications of DSS in organizations in a survey of DSS applications between period 1988-1994. It was found that there appears to be more creative applications of optimization and suggestion models and a decrease of representation models. Moreover, group decision support systems, executive support systems, and knowledge-based systems applications are becoming more prevalent in many organizations. There are non-MS/OR tools including graphics, artificial intelligence, and visual interactive modelling are emerging as powerful DSS tools. In their subsequent study, an extension of previous study for the period 1995-2001, they identified two hundred ten published applications. To examine the development pattern of a specific DSS over time, they proposed a framework to classify the articles/applications into various categories according to: (1) the area of application; (2) the year of publication in each area of application; (3) the distribution of underlying tools in DSSs; (4) a classification based on Alter's taxonomy; and (5) the management level (operational, tactical, or strategic) for which the DSS was designed.

Adam, Frederic, Fahy, Martin, Murphy, Ciaran(1998) provides a framework of classification of DSS usage across organizations. They have classified the organizations studied, based on the extent to which they used DSS for different decision situations using two specific measurements: DSS spread and DSS complexity. The results obtained suggest that the framework which was developed by the authors is useful for categorizing the degree of maturity of organizations regarding their usage and development of actual DSS applications. Alan Montgomery (2005) has discussed implementation challenges of Decision Support Systems in Pricing for retail managers. With the evolution/explosion of quality data and computing ability, retail managers have desired to implement demand based management. Demand based management uses statistical models to predict consumer price response using historical information. Many firms are offering software to perform price optimization. The article discusses contribution of academic research to implementation of these systems and raises likely concerns of developers and users. It also raises practical and research challenges for using transaction data for developing pricing DSS for retailers.

Nikitas et. al.(2000) suggest that any DSS for strategic, tactical or operational planning is based on interaction of information systems and decision models and progressive transformation of data into information and knowledge. They have illustrated a DSS for supply chain planning (SCP) decisions. The SCP system has an embedded decision engine that uses a two-stage stochastic program as a paradigm for optimization under uncertainty. The system has been used for decision making in diverse domains, including automotive manufacturing and consumer products. The role of model-based decision making is gaining increasing acceptance as organizations try to gain a competitive advantage. The progress in information systems development has led to a natural coupling between the data modeling, symbolic modeling and "What-if" analysis phases of a decision support system (DSS). DSS tools help companies automate an enterprise-wide assessment of cause and effect. The software monitors "soft" factors, which indicate whether a certain strategy has been successful, as opposed to operational measures. These tools can help in creating a culture of management based common views and goals.

Leonard Lodish (1982) describes components of marketing strategy development through DSS for retailing. The goal of the DSS system is to improve marketing strategy and marketing resource allocation for a large multi store, multi department retailer. However he warns that effectiveness of the system will depend on willingness on the part of managers to adapt. DSS evolves constantly as its users and developers interface, generate problems, questions and desires. Little (1989) suggest that DSS must be simple, robust, easy to control, adaptive, as complete as possible and easy to communicate with.

## DSS IN RETAILING

Decision support "represents one of the key enabling technologies allowing corporations to unlock useful information hidden away in databases." Decision support queries need to be executed against large databases which often grow into the "hundreds of gigabytes" range. The technology is prohibitively expensive, except for the largest retailers such as Walmart, it is difficult to implement. Walmart uses a three

- terabyte database using a competing parallel processing product from Teradata, a unit of AT&T Global Information Solutions, formerly NCR. It is expected that technology - based competition and innovation is escalating because of competitive pressures in retail industry. Technology is viewed as one way of competing but needs to become more affordable. According to Sheldon Leitch, a principal at Toronto - based Ernst & Young, who tracks the retail industry[7],"there are three things retailers need to do well: build in a front end at the point - of - sale, segment the market by demographics and build so - called merchandise allocation systems".

Thus DSS range from what if spread sheet and simulation analyses to "expert system"- applications of artificial intelligence. While developing the DSS in the organization, it is very essential that views of different stakeholders are taken into consideration. For example; executives and professionals are the users, MIS managers are the developers managing the process of development and installation, Information specialists build and develop systems, system designers who create and assemble technology on which DSS are based and researchers who study DSS and its process. Thus following are the key characteristic requirements[8] of DSS: As managerial decisions are always made with organisation's own culture, routine and operating procedures, DSS should have **adaptabiity**. System must allow **integration** of organisation's routine, procedures and policies. System should **facilitate** communication among decision makers and **provide mechanism** for conflict resolution. System must **allow** and **support** both **analytic** and **holistic** perspectives viewing overall problem, focusing on few assumptions, issues or implications. System must help **solve** unprogrammed, unstructured problems. It should **possess** easy **interactive querry facility.** It should **support** rather than **replace** managerial judgment.

Advantages of DSS are: faster data accessibility, stock availability resulting into no lost sales due to stock outs, better choice of assortments, timely distribution, tracking buying patterns of consumers and quick decisions. Having seen the DSS applications in marketing and organized retail in western context, this paper now outlines findings of DSS applications in Indian organized retail Grocery sector.

## FINDINGS AND DISCUSSION

Profile of the sample retail outlets: Convenience store[9] as the name signifies, are stores that provide a high level of convenience to their customers in terms of convenient location and extended operating hours. They mostly deal in food and other essential items. Small self-service formats located in crowded urban areas. Department stores are very large stores which are usually multi-tiered and stock a vast range of products in separate departments. The variety of merchandise stocked is very wide with broad variety and deep assortment and high service level and organized into separate departments for displaying the merchandise. It provides a one stop shop catering to varied consumer needs. In our sample, three of the stores were departmental store and one was a convenience store as seen in the table given below.

| Retail Outlet | AMPM | STAR BAZAR | BIG BAZAR | ADANI |
|---|---|---|---|---|
| Retail Format | Convenience | Departmental | Departmental | Departmental |

**Big bazaar**[10] of Pantaloon Group had entered with four 'Big Bazar' discount stores, introducing the concept of hyper market - discount stores - for the first time in India in 2004. Big Bazar stores, modeled on the lines of overseas retail stores such as Wal-Mart, sell around 1,30,000 branded and non-branded goods at discounts ranging from 6 to 60 percent. **Star Bazaar**[11]: The Star India Bazaar resembles big bazaar in size and spread of its merchandising basket. The economies of scale available to it, is translated into low prices for customers, who can pick from a wide selection of staples, fresh goods, consumer durables, household products, apparel, luggage and much more. "We aim to be the cheapest in the market," according to company spokesperson. Each product category has several choices on offer. For example, rice is available in 10-12 varieties. Considering the options and the discounts, it tries to create the mass-market appeal. The aim is to target middle and the upper-middle classes with low prices. Besides offering a 5-7 per cent discount over the 'maximum retail price' (MRP) for most of the brands that it stocks, the store also makes available its own private line of products, where prices are way below the discounted prices of its branded products.

**AMPM** is a local store operating in a basement located in a catchments area of upper middle class families representing cosmopolitan culture. It is a convenience store and facing competition from national players like star bazaar and big bazaar and Adani, a local chain of stores in the same catchments area .The approximate floor area is 800-1000 Sq ft. **Adani's chain**[12]: Adani Retail Limited is the largest supermarket chain of the Western India. Quality, Service, Convenience, Satisfaction and Assured Benefits are the backbone of the Adani Retail Limited. ARL currently have 15000+ SKUs, with the major categories of FMCG, Household goods and Appliances, Apparels, Gifts & Articles, Luggage & related items and catering 2,50,000+ families across the state of Gujarat. At present Adani Retail operates in 9 Cities across the State of Gujarat with the chain of 47 stores. ARL is having 27 stores in Ahmedabad, 10 stores in Baroda, 3 in Surat, 2 in Rajkot, one each in Anand, Gandhinagar, Mundra, Nadiad & Navsari. ARL operates through the format of Neighbourhood Store, Supermarket Store, and Hypermarket Store. ARL plans to continue its journey to reach total 19 cities with the store strength of

60+ in the state of Gujarat. ARL also plans to expand its operation in the neighbouring states of Rajasthan, Madhya Pradesh, Maharashtra and Chhattisgarh. The following Table-1 gives information about the sample stores.

All the stores visited are in proximity to each other in a radius of 5 kilometres. They are catering to same catchments area on western part of the city and three being located in a posh residential area and one on a highway but in a close proximity of residential areas. Following discussion emphasizes the DSS operations of sample retails stores.

*Table 1. Retail Stores Infrastructure Profile*

| **Store/Profile** | **ANPM** | **STAR BAZAR** | **BIG BAZAR** | **ADANI** |
|---|---|---|---|---|
| When opened? | 2001 | 2004 | 2004 | 1998 |
| Store Size(Area): | 800-1000 Sq Ft | 55,000 Sq ft(Grocery) | 100,000-1,60,000 Sq ft(Entire floor area) | 2000-5000 Sq ft (Average Store Size) |
| Averagefootfall(day, week, month): | NA | Variation across weekdays and weekend | Variation across weekdays and weekend | NA |
| Average billing amount (grocery) | 100 Rs/day approx | 450 Rs/day | 450-500 Rs/day | 250-300 Rs/day |
| # of categories: | NA | 150 approx | 150-200 | NA |
| # of SKUs | NA | 6000 | 8000 | NA |
| # of vendors: | 10-15 | 30-40 | 60-80 | 30-40 |
| Location Catchment area | Judges Bunglow Road | Satelite Area | On a highway near Hare Rama Hare Krishna Temple | Judges Bunglow Road |
| Contribution of private label brand | NA | 85%(staple foods) | 80-85%(staple foods) | NA |

## AMPM

| Functional area | Sales forecasting | Inventory management | Visual Merchandizing | Addition of new SKUs | Campaign management | Inbound logistics |
|---|---|---|---|---|---|---|
| Type of DSS used | spread sheet | one store so spread sheet is used for managing inventory | margins provided by specific player but as store is not big so there is no DSS system in used | on the basis of sales and turnover | promotional offer given by company | spread sheets |
| IT /SW Tools | customized package for item listing and bar code reader for billing | | | | | |
| Time taken to implement DSS | As DSS used in AMPM are very need specific so there is no specific time limit set up for this | | | | | |

## STAR BAZAR

| Functional area | Sales forecasting | Inventory management | Visual Merchandizing | Addition of new SKUs | Campaign management | Inbound logistics |
|---|---|---|---|---|---|---|
| Type of DSS used | ERP package | PoS / ERP package | decision taken on top selling agents and margins | through their own customised software | Managed by head office | Packages by PoS(point of sale) Pune and now shifting to erp |

*continued on following page*

| | |
|---|---|
| IT /SW Tools | Bar code reader ,Visual Basic (VB) based programme, special WiFi enabled swiping introduced recently ,<br>pos software (customized software ) , special surveillance tag for avoiding theft from the store |
| Time taken to implement DSS | ERP package implementation takes two three years ,whereas software catering to specific requirement takes 3-6 months |

## BIG BAZAR

| Functional area | Sales forecasting | Inventory management | Visual Merchandizing | Addition of new SKUs | Campaign management | Inbound logistics | Other |
|---|---|---|---|---|---|---|---|
| Type of DSS used | in-house software /recently shifting to ERP gradually | EOQ level managed through item replenishment | gondolas placed on the basis of negotiation done with the manufacturer | requirement of the store /demand supply mechanism used | In- house package | shifting to ERP | |
| IT /SW Tools | special surveillance system in place ,VB based packages ,proper ERP mechanism environment is being developed | | | | | | |
| Time taken to implement DSS | ERP implementation takes longer time then normal in-house software | | | | | | |

## ADANI

| Functional area | Sales forecasting | Inventory management | Visual Merchandizing/ Display | Addition of new SKUs | Campaign management | Inbound logistics |
|---|---|---|---|---|---|---|
| Type of DSS used | In-house package RoQ level (return on quantity level) maintained | stock replenishment check is being done at the end of the day | margins and top selling items are most important criteria and stock replenishment DSS tools are used for this purpose | promotion and selling pitch provided by the company | company based promotions | stock replenishment packages |
| IT /SW Tools | VB as front based and SQL as backend in-house software packages are taken into consideration while pursuing specific decision | | | | | |
| Time taken to implement DSS | three to six months | | | | | |

ERP (Enterprise resource planning) provides seamless integration of all functions such as sales forecasting, merchandising, point of sale, distribution, logistics, pay roll, accounting front and back office store systems and merchandising etc. of a retail operation. The success of ERP solution depends on synergy between technology and management. Factors to consider while choosing the right system for ERP are; magnitude of retail operations, number of locations and expectations from the system. Benefits of erp are customer profiling and analysis, targeted communications, loyalty programmes and other customer relationship initiatives, merchandise management and store localization. An integrated supply chain helps the retailer in maintaining his stocks, getting his supplies on time, preventing stock-outs and thus reducing his costs, while servicing the customer better.

It was found that varied customized DSS tools ranging from spread sheet to in-house software packages were used for operational decisions .Even though national players had implemented ERP package ,there was a tendency to use in house packages like POS (point of sale) or VB (visual basics) based packages. For campaign management decisions intuitive judgement was used or decision from head office was followed. It was observed that national players were willing to invest in IT tool for 1) Surveillance to avoid losses due to shop lifting and 2) To reduce the waiting time for billing by introducing WIFI enabled swipe equipments.

The typical decisions involved in adopting decision support systems/ERP generally are: Type of software platforms, Networking , Operating system ,Retail applications- applications to what decisions?, Type of hardware- point of sale systems, bar coding system, main computer system ,Server and Nodes . Benefits of DSS were realized by the sample respondents. It was found that even though they generally agreed on the benefits, they were unable to prioritize and quantify the benefits: Superior coordination, higher profitability, diagnostic help in identifying problem areas, high morale of employees, help for maintaining relationship with stakeholders , streamlining of operations, productivity enhancement , reduction in stock out situations, systematic planning of inventory resources due to accurate forecasting and enhancement of impulse purchase due to application of DSSto merchandising and display. There seemed a general agreement on realization of benefits but no system was in place to measure the benefits at present (or it was not shared).

## ISSUES OF DSS

Following key issues were faced by respondent's include two national chains, which had implemented ERP partially, faced similar type of problems with respect to ERP implementation- system integration problems and need for proper training for the operational staff as well as motivation to adopt change. A major challenge faced by a local chain retailer was that of implementing ERP. Because of the differences in systems followed by different suppliers and manufacturers, integration between suppliers and manufacturer and the outlet was a major challenge. Also in ERP implementation phase, as few modules were implemented, that also created problems with the existing system of data. Man power at the operational level is always reluctant to change for ERP environment because there is always a fear of downsizing in ERP implementation. Low level of computer education of persons in charge of floor operations results in poor service to the customer and inaccurate data handling. It is feared that training costs would increase. Inaccurate data handling results in improper data management which becomes a major bottleneck in stock replenishment. Collaboration and co-ordination problems: Problem faced in coordinating with different vendors using DSS tool on different platform (like visual basic, fox pro, oracle etc) Local chain having their own systems- either developed in house or sourced from domestic supplier also faced problems because of the high employee attrition rate - resulting in frequent training to new employees. DSS system ideally should provide counter checks in terms of warning or pop ups so that wrong entry /mistake can be identified instantly.(such a provision exist in ERP as experienced by a sample respondents.)

## PERSPECTIVES OF SUPPLIERS OF DSS

It was found that in the short term, IT needs of the organised retailer would revolve around his ability to service the customers in a better manner by using CRM and OLAP tools, and to reduce costs by using Web-based systems of vendor management and CPFR(collaborative planning and forecasting) tools. It was observed that retailers need to understand how information technology would support the efficient implementation of the revised systems and procedures in terms of computer systems, hardware, software and networking. Retailers also need to understand how the IT systems would be integrated and networked across the country's stores and the head office of the retailer. With the projected growth of organised retailing in India, large to mid-sized retailers will have to upgrade their IT systems and take into consideration the technology trends — some of which are currently nascent, but which will evolve to become important assets for the future.

The Indian experience in implementing Retail ERPs has been difficult due to the lack of trained ERP package implementers in India. Hence, the cost of implementation has gone up, as package experts have to be brought in from abroad. But this is true for all ERP implementation in India, whether in the retail sector or in the manufacturing sector. In the past, manufacturing industries also faced difficulties in implementing ERP packages specifically meant for the industry, but over time, with expertise in the packages and in their implementation building up within India, the success rates of such implementations have increased. Hence, over the next two to three years, Retail ERP expertise will grow and will be able to support the needs of Indian retailers, who in that timeframe would have progressed up the learning curve on the benefits of information technology.

Future outlook of DSS :

- **Proper exhaustive implementation of all the modules of ERP packages:** As implementation costs are very high, user tends to implement in phases which results in system integration and coordination problems. Once that is in place, many of the issues would automatically get resolved.
- **Need for data warehousing and Data mining:** Indian retail sector is lagging behind their western counterparts in investments in information technology. Respondents were not even willing to share the investments made so far. This may inhibit the proper usage of the rich data available at point of sale. If harnessed properly, it can be used as a competitive advantage.
- **WIFI environment in retail outlets:** At least one of the national retail chain had plans to invest in WIFI technology which would enable less time spent on queues for billing . Once foreign participation and FDI is allowed, many will adopt this technology.
- **Wide spread use of CRM application:** With the growing use of plastic money retailers will use various loyalty programme to grab the larger share of consumer wallet .
- **DSS tools for visual merchandising ,pricing and campaign management:** In west such tools are in use. Indian retail sector is likely to follow suit.

## CONCLUSION

Decision Support System plays a vital role for organized retailers. There is a tremendous change in the type of DSS in retail outlet, as growth in technology results in more sophisticated DSS tools. Our study shows that even the local to national level retail outlet give at most importance to high end DSS tools, and if ROI is high companies are willing to invest heavily on support tools. Study also shows that reluctance to change and not aware about how to use specific technology also acts as stumbling block in implementation of DSS. ERP implementation is also helping companies to enhance there productivity. There is an avenue for conducting research for the study of high end DSS tools and impact assessment of usage of DSS on retail operations.

## REFERENCES

Achabal, D. B., et.al. (n/d). A decision support system for vendor management inventory. *Jorunal of Retailing, 76*(4), 407-413.

Angehm, A. A., & Jelassi, T. (1994, November). *DSS research and practice in perspective decision support system. Amsterdam, 12*(4,5), 267-276.

Beaumont, J. R. (1988). An overview of decision report system for retail management. *Journal of Retailing, 64*(4), 361-373.

Eom, S. B., et. al. (1998, February). A survey of decision support system applications (1988-1994). *The Journal of the Operational Research Society, 49*(2), 109-121. Oxford.

Gallegos, F. (1999). Decision support systems: An overview. *Information Technology, 15*(2), 42-46.

Green, P. E., Vijay, M., et. al. (1984). A decision support system for developing retail promotional strategy. *Journal of Retailing, 39*(3), 116-143.

Hernandez, T. (2005, May). Visual decisions: Geovisualisation techniques within retail decision support. *Journal Of Targeting, Measurement and Analysis for Marketing, 13*(3), ABI/INFORM Global (pp. 209-219).

Li, S., Russell, K., Yanging, D., Edwards, J. S. (2000). Computer –based support for marketing strategy development. *European Journal of Marketing.*

Little, J. D. C. (1979). DSS for marketing managers. *Journal of Marketing, 43*(3), 9-26.

Lodish, M. (1982). A marketing decision support system for retailers. *Marketing Science*, (1), 31-56.

Montgomery, A. (2005). The implementation challenge of pricing decision support systems for retailer managers: Applied stochastic models. *Business and industry, 21*, 367-378. Published online in Wiely, Interscience, (www.interscience.wiley.com).

Power, D. J. (1997). *DSS glossary.* http://dss.cba.uni.edu/glossary/dssglossary.html.

Thompsan, T., & Walker, J. (2005, May). Retail network planning –Achieving competitive advantage through geographical analysis. *Journal Of Targeting, Measurement, & Analysis for Marketing, 13*(3), ABI/INFORM Global 252-257.

## Web Bibliography

http://www.indiainbusiness.nic.in/

http://www.decisioncraft.com/dss/index.htm

http://www.etretailbiz.com/apr2003/news2.html(accessed on 8/6/06)

http://www.expresscomputeronline.com/20030113/indtrend1.shtml

http://www.pantaloon.com/html/bigbazaar.htm, accessed on 16/06/2006.

http://www.tata.com/trent/articles/20050127_trent.htm, accessed on 16/06/2006

http://www.adanigroup.com/comp_b2c.html, accessed on 12/06/2006

## ENDNOTES

1 Euromonitor.com,2004

2 Retail Management-An Asian Perspective Draft Monograph,2006

3 http://www.indiainbusiness.nic.in/india-profile/ser-retail.html

4 John R Beaumont,"An Overview of Decision Support System for Retail Management",Journal of Retailing Vol 64 No 4 Winter 1988 pp361-373

5 http://dss.cba.uni.edu/glossary/dssglossary.html

6 Andy Thompson & Jonathan Walker," Retail Network Planning- Achieving Competitive Advantage through Geographical analysis" Journal of Targeting, Measurement and Analysis for Marketing, May, 2005;13,3;ABI/INFORM Global,Pg. 250.

7 Slofstra, Martin," Tandem takes DSS to retailers," *Willowdale*: Mar 30, 1994. Vol.20, Iss. 7; pg. 1, 2 .

8 Little, John D. C.," Decision Support Systems for Marketing Managwers" *Journal Of Marketing*, 1979,43(summer):9-26.

9 A J Lambha" The Art of Retailing" 2003, Tata Mcgraw Hill , 476p.

10 http://www.pantaloon.com/html/bigbazaar.htm, accessed on 16/06/2006.

11 http://www.tata.com/trent/articles/20050127_trent.htm, accessed on 16/06/2006

12 http://www.adanigroup.com/comp_b2c.html, accessed on 12/06/2006.

# Chapter VII
# Dynamics of Buyer–Supplier Co–Dependency in Optimizing Functional Efficiency

**Rajagopal**
*Monterrey Institute of Technology and Higher Education, ITESM, Mexico*

**Amritanshu Rajagopal**
*Dentalia, Mexico*

The role of sales network is fundamental within the value creation chain of the firm, as creating shareholder value is strictly linked with creating buyer value. As supplier networks are the main point of contact with buyers, choosing the best possible supply structure is vital. Firms are increasingly implementing electronic distribution strategies to augment existing physical infrastructure for product and service delivery. The study analyzes the impact of channel function performance on relationship quality which is moderated by the extent dependence structure of the relationship. In this process, the impact of supplier function performance on different dimensions of relationship quality in reference to satisfaction, trust, commitment and conflict under various dependence structures have also been diagnosed and analyzed. This discussion also aims to contribute to and link the areas of quality management and buyer-supplier relationships. Indeed, Voss (1995) points out that the relationship between core areas such as quality management and "interface" disciplines such as networks and buyer-supplier relationships provide significant scope for further empirical research.

## REVIEW OF LITERATURE

Over time, the horizontal consolidation of product delivering process and growth of automation in marketing activities have driven the manufacturers towards a convenient approach, bypassing the supply channels and to go for direct marketing. It has been observed that conventional suppliers have responded to this situation or other destructive acts in a number of different ways. Some had shown inclination for the exit, in the belief that a better quality of service and relationship advantages could be found elsewhere. Others are moved by loyalty to voice complaint, protest or anger, with a view to eliciting an improvement in the quality of service. It is contended that enhanced understanding of this important aspect of business-to-business relationships leads to the development of more closely aligned strategic plans which may improve return on relational investment. This has important implications for the development of theory as well as the behavioral stances adopted by individuals engaged in relational development through the process of face-to-face negotiation (Harwood, 2006).

Suppliers also adapt frequently the developing countervailing power through dependence-balancing actions. These actions are designed to strengthen transactional bonds that are explained through the buyer-seller relationships. Such bonds often manifest themselves in anticipation of improved channel services to buyers. Managers responsible for procuring services build relationship based on co-dependency and collaboration between the supplier and purchaser of services. The burden of transaction cost economics encourages aggregation of the services supply chain which in turn, when managed carefully, facilitates an improved working/partnering opportunity with a few select suppliers. The suppliers benefit in turn by increasing volumes, allowing them to protect margins and the purchasers benefit through overall lower total cost of service, more attentive suppliers and potentially a much enhanced working relationship (Rogers, 2006).

The effect of functional performance on relationship quality in situations characterized by high relative dependence of the supplier on the buyer is largely governed by the effective channel functions. Buyer supplier collaboration may have significant effects on the focal firm's in reference to the flexibility, responsiveness and modularization capabilities which would help building capability of supplier firms towards increasing competitive advantage and gaining high customer value (Squire et al, 2005). A study on buyer-seller relationships is commissioned in some well-established frameworks such as transaction cost theory, political economy theory, social exchange theory and resource dependence theory (Robicheaux and Oleman, 1994). In addition, empirical models, drawing on a variety of management disciplines, have been proposed and tested in the literature. Optimal performance of relational contracts in partnerships such as joint ventures or buyer-seller alliances appears to be a continuing process but may require termination of the relationship after bad outcomes. Payments between the partners depend on their relative performance. In the case of bilateral trade with specific investments, optimal relational contracting results in a price that varies with cost and demand conditions but is more stable than under spot market bargaining (Doornik, 2006).

A four-way classification of quality definitions that incorporates excellence, value, conformance to specifications, and meeting exceeding buyer requirements has been set to argue that the diversity inherent in these definitions implies that the complexity and multiple perspectives historically associated with the concept have made theoretical and research advances difficult (Reeves and Bednar, 1994). Empirical studies identify core quality practices that included top management support, quality information, process management, product design, workforce management, supplier involvement and buyer orientation (Flynn *et al.*, 1994; Black and Porter, 1996). There have been very few empirical studies of the effects of contingency variables on the relationship between quality practices and quality performance. High levels of front-line employee performance and inter-departmental buyer orientation have a positive effect on distribution center service and supply chain performance (Voss et al, 2005).

The buyer-supplier relations concerning logistics and supplies are subject to both controllable and non-controllable forces of change, which may not always have a positive effect on the logistics performance or the relationship itself. Inter-organizational dynamics not only relate to learning, competence development, or adaptation, as suggested by other studies, but also to how such dyadic relationships are governed. As the dyad accumulates experience over time, changes will occur in the balance between the two parties in terms of goal congruence and risk preferences, which has a strong influence on the nature of contracts and other safeguards governing the relationship (Halldórsson and Skjøtt-Larsen, 2006). Such developments in the business may also prompt the switching costs in a dynamic buyer-seller relationship where quality is not contractible and the sellers retain private information about their quality-relevant abilities. Consequently, the channel switching costs increase the bargaining power of the manufacturer or service provider in negotiations for the second contract and to preempt improved transactional relationship in a given business environment (Mehmet, 2000). Although communication, trust and satisfaction are always important as determinants of elements, their importance is higher when "core" products are considered.

The transactional relationship can be broadly referred to two major marketing channels for both goods and services - the independent and the exclusive agency systems. Independent agents place business with several companies, while exclusive agents function for only one company. Some of the studies found that the independent agency system is less efficient than the exclusive agency system with a view to develop buyer-seller relationship (Cummins and Van Derhei, 1979). It has been found that the market orientation is positively associated with measures of channel performance such as service quality and overall buyer relationship level. Market orientation also has a positive influence on measures of cost efficiency, such as productivity and sales per employee. In addition, profitability measures are highly associated with operating effectiveness and cost efficiency (Chang *et.al.*, 1999). The adoption of a market orientation can help supply channels to design and offer a service mix that is perceived by core buyers as of superior quality, while making a profit and building competitive advantage. Owing to the nature of the dyadic exchange process, the effect of a market orientation for the supply channels may be more evident because customization may be observed directly by the buyers.

Trust has been defined as the firm's belief that another company will perform actions that will result in positive actions for the firm, as well as not take unexpected actions that would result in negative outcomes for the firm (Anderson and Narus, 1990). *Trust* is widely recognized as an essential dimension of relationship quality (Morgan and Hunt 1994; Garbarino and Johnson 1999; Geyskens *et al*, 1998)Some of the researchers define trust as the most frequently used dimension in buyer-supplier relationship built on the performance parameters (Wilson and Kristan Moller, 1991) This is because the presence of trust can reduce the specification and monitoring of contracts, provide material incentives for co-operation, and reduce uncertainty (Hill, 1990). Satisfaction plays an important role in relationships, is instrumental in increasing cooperation between channel partners, and leads to fewer terminations of relationships (Ganesan 1994). Commitment, similar to trust, is also viewed as an essential indicator of relationship quality that may be defined as a desire to develop a stable relationship, a willingness to make short-term sacrifices to maintain and sustain the relationship (Rajagopal, 2005). Relationship value is an antecedent to relationship quality and behavioral outcomes and displays a stronger impact on satisfaction than on commitment and trust. Value also directly impacts a customer's intention to expand business with a supplier. In turn, its impact on the propensity to leave a relationship is mediated by relationship quality (Ulaga and Eggert, 2006).

Buyer-supplier relationship gets closer and stronger through the information management at both the ends. Supplier information sharing helps to develop higher quality supplier relationships. Interestingly, even if the initial level of trust in the retailer is low, the relationship quality substantially improves. In a more competitive situation, the suppliers respond more favorably to the retailer's information-sharing initiative (Smith *et al*, 2002). Besides, above studies many research studies on relationship quality in the marketing channels literature have focused on the impact of the interdependence structure of the relationship (Anderson and Narus 1990; Brown *et al*, 1995; Kumar *et al*, 1995) on relationship quality. Although the interdependence structure has been found to affect the quality of the relationship, its effect is relatively small (Kumar *et al*, 1995). On the contrary, firms pursuing focused commitment strategy (FCS) may be subject to risks that offset transactional and scale-related benefits. Detriments from too much focused commitment erode the firm's manufacturing-based competitive performance. In addition, the evidence indicates that profitability and market share growth also suffer (Swink and Zsidisin, 2006). An FCS involves committing long-term investments with a limited number of suppliers to achieve superior performance.

## HYPOTHESES

Some studies on relationship marketing describe that buyer-supplier transactions are of short duration referring to previous agreements (Dwyer *et al*, 1987; Noordewier *et al*, 1990). On the contrary, a high likelihood of future interactions exists with relational orientation (Ganesan 1994). It has been observed that long-term and high-quality relationships, characterized by frequent interactions between different members of a supply channel offer advantages for both sellers and buyers. The quality of performance of supply services is positively related to relationship quality. The extent of satisfaction of the organizational buyers depends on the good financial conditions, a convenient assortment, good location features, clear information, and buyer friendly personnel. Hence,

**H1 (a):** *The level of performance of the marketing functions shown by the supplier is directly proportional to the level of satisfaction of the organizational buyers (large accounts).*

**H1 (b):** *The consequence of such direct relationship between the supplier and buyers will lead to decrease in the channel conflict.*

The interdependence structure of a dyadic relationship refers to the extent of relative dependence that exists to stimulate the transactions mutually between the two parties (Emerson 1962; Kumar *et a*l, 1995). The measure of dependence may be categorized as total interdependence and asymmetry or relative dependence.

Total interdependence is the sum of both parties' dependencies on each other while interdependence asymmetry refers to the difference between each party's dependence on the other. This difference has also been referred to as the more dependent party's relative dependence (Anderson and Narus 1990) or the less dependent party's relative power (Frazier and Rody 1991). Relational contracts and informal agreements between the manufacturers-suppliers and buyers is sustained by the value of length of relationships. It has been found that the integration affects the parties' temptations to renege on a given relational contract, and hence affects the best relational contract the parties can sustain. Therefore, the hypotheses are framed as:

**H2 (a):** *There is an inverse relationship between the relative dependence of the supplier on the organizational clients and the extent of buyer satisfaction, trust and commitment to the supplier.*

**H2 (b):** *Such inverse relationship tendency between the supplier and organizational buyer results into increase in the channel conflicts.*

Supplier can protect buyers from dysfunctional behavior and distrust by improving the relationship quality. Under situations with high total interdependence, both parties are motivated to develop, maintain, and improve the relationship. Hence, the performance of marketing functions by the supplier will have a stronger impact on relationship quality in a high interdependence situation. Thus,

**H3:** *The impact of the supplier's performance of various functions on the organizational buyer's satisfaction, trust, commitment and the extent of channel conflict will be stronger when the total dependence between the supplier and buyer is higher.*

Trust is a collective behavior which emerges over a period through the personality traits of individuals in a business community. When trust is damaged community as a whole suffers in dealing with any matter-distribution, buyer value or corporate reputation. However, in general trust is a situational feature (Rajagopal, 2006[a]). When trust is low in a cultural setting it affects the confidence of the people and so depletes their responsiveness to the given situation. If a buyer relies on trust and it is not reciprocated, he will suffer from substantial harm (Butler, 1991). Empirical advances in the area initially focused on the identification of core quality practices that include top management support, quality information, process management, product design, workforce management, supplier involvement and buyer orientation (Flynn *et al.*, 1994; Black and Porter, 1996). Subsequent empirical studies switched their focus to the quality practices-quality performance relationship and quality performance-business performance relationship with significant support for the former but only mixed support for the latter (Ittner and Larcker, 1996). Significantly, efficient quality management further up the supply chain was one of the most significant contributors to explaining variation in supplier quality performance, which underlines the importance of managing quality throughout the value chain (Forker, 1997). While there is mixed empirical support for this hypothesis, it is of particular significance to management given the effort and resources dedicated to quality improvement programs. Hence, hypotheses have been framed as:

**H4(a):** *Quality practices of supply channels have a positive effect on buyer satisfaction and conformance quality.*

**H4(b):** *Relationship strength endorses the co-dependence between quality practices of suppliers, degree of conformance and buyer satisfaction.*

Quality practices initially have a direct effect on both internal quality performances such as design quality and conformance quality, which has indirect impact on external quality comprising quality-in-use and buyer satisfaction over long run (Hanson et al 1996, Peck, 2006). The process approach to supply chain integration presents a mechanism that can be applied to any industry. It represents a systematic methodological business renovation approach involving cost cuts, quality improvements and lead-time improvements. The novel combination of business process and demand/supply simulation enables an estimation of changes in lead-times, process execution costs, quality of the process and inventory costs (Trkman *et al*, 2007). These empirical studies reviewed all support the relationship between quality practices and conformance quality.

With the exception of Forker's (1997) study, there has been no major empirical study of the interaction between quality practices, quality performances and the strength of buyer-supplier relationships. However, one of the major weaknesses of existing studies is their limited conceptualization of the nature of buyer-supplier relationships. As a result, the relationship strength as a comprehensive construct that captured the critical dimensions of relationships has been hypothesized. Hence, the hypothesis that the relationships between quality practices and design quality, and quality practices and conformance quality are moderated by relationship strength. The rationale for this hypothesis is the strong partnership-type relationships, which score positively across all dimensions of a buyer-supplier relationship in the market.

## THEORETICAL CONSTRUCT

The research model broadly consists of three sets of constructs. These concern (a) supplier channel function performance, (b) (inter-) dependence, and (c) relationship quality. The hypotheses of the study are tested by performing regression analysis as below:

$$\omega = \beta_0 + \beta_1 + \beta_2 + \beta_3 + \beta_4 + \beta_5 + \varepsilon \qquad (1)$$

Where, $(\omega)$ represents buyer satisfaction/quality relationship, $\beta_1$ denotes levels of performance of suppliers, $\beta_2$ indicates relative dependence, $\beta_3$, $\beta_4$ and $\beta_5$ represent total dependence, functional conflicts and overall business performance respectively.

In the process of measuring the buyer-supplier co-dependence in reference to preference variables leading to cost and quality determinants, the dependent factor is the rate of supplier performance $\left(P_{st}^{m}\right)$ in a given market $m$ at time $t$. Accordingly, the dynamic consumption function that reflects the retail supplier behavior for particular products may be estimated as:

$$P_{st}^{m} = \Delta_{ct}\left\{\beta_0 + \beta_1(L)u_{t-1} + \beta_2(L)\Delta_{yt} + \beta_3(L)\Delta_{wt} + \beta_4(L)\Delta_{rt} + \beta_5(L)\Delta_{sq} + \beta_6(L)\Delta_{bz} + \varepsilon_t\right\} \qquad (2)$$

In the above equation, $\Delta$ is the change factor, r is the concentration ratio of suppliers in a given location, $c_t$ is a log of real per capita total consumption, $y_t$ is the log of real per capita demand, $w_t$ is the available supplies, $s_q$ denotes quality of supplies, $b_z$ represents total cost incurring to buyers and $\varepsilon_t$ denotes the random error term. Under this assumption $c_t$, $y_t$, and $w_t$ are co-integrated, $\varepsilon_t$ is $\leq 0$ (Rajagopal, 2007). The test of this model requires time series data to be analyzed for trend values, taking (L) as polynomial log operator. It has been observed in previous studies that value to expenditure ratios increase consumer sensitivity in volume of buying and driving repeat buying decisions for the regular and high-tech products (Carroll and Dunn 1997).

If the performance of the suppliers is positive to the buyer satisfaction, its integrated impact would develop strong self reference criterion among the buyers and help in enhancing the returns on the relationship value of suppliers. Such attributes to the performance and conformance of suppliers would lead to augment their market coverage and volume of operation (Rajagopal, 2006[b]). Accordingly, the following equation may be derived as:

$$C_{st}^{m} = \omega\left[k_0 + k_1(P_{sw})\mu_t + k_2(P_{sr})\mu_t + k_3(P_{sa})\mu_t + \varepsilon_t\right] \qquad (3)$$

Wherein, $\left(C_{st}^{m}\right)$ denotes conformance of suppliers in a given market $m$ at time $t$, $k$ is the constant used for the quality of supplies pertaining to available products ($P_{sw}$ ), supplier benefits over competitors($P_{sr}$ ) and satisfaction derived through the conformance of quality supplies in a new supply area($P_{sa}$ ). In the above equation $\varepsilon_t$ has been used as the random error while $\mu_t$ denotes the market specific performance score of the supplier. Upon simplifying the equations 1, 2 and 3, we get:

$$P_{st}^{m} = \Pi\left(\omega, C_{st}^{m}\right) + \left[\left(P_{sc}\right)^{\sigma} \leq 0\right] \tag{4}$$

It may be observed from the above equation that supplier performance $\left(P_{st}^{m}\right)$ is a result of buyer satisfaction and quality relationship $(\omega)$ and conformance of suppliers $\left(C_{st}^{m}\right)$. Hence $\Pi$ has been used as a multiplication operator in the above equation. Further, in the above equation ($P_{sc}$ ) denotes the integrated effect on perceptions derived by the buyers on products and services. If this value goes negative across the markets in a given time, it will pull down the buyer value lowering the volume of buying and shrinking market coverage estimates of the firm.

This framework analyzes optimal portfolio choice and consumption with values management in the firm-supplier-buyer triadic relationship. The value concept in the above relationship governs the buyer portfolio decision in terms of formulation of recursive utility over time. It shows that the optimal portfolio demand for products under competition varies strongly with the values associated with the brand, industry attractiveness, knowledge management and ethical issues of the organization. The extent of business values determines the relative risk aversion in terms of functional and logistical efficiency between the organization and supplier while the switching attitude may influence the buyers if the organizational values are not strong and sustainable in the given competitive environment. The model assumes that a high functional value integrated with the triadic entities would raise the market power of organization, sustain decisions of buyer portfolios and develop long-run relationships thereof. The **buyer value** concept is utilized to assess product performance and eventually to determine the competitive market structure and the product-market boundaries.

## RESEARCH DESIGN

The samples selected for this study were companies supplying the office equipments to the large accounts in Mexico. This sector was selected due to heterogenity in terms of sub-sectors, relationship tiers and product/process complexity (Dicken, 1998). A total of 214 supply agencies were selected for the study. From the initial frame of 236 suppliers, 22 were removed from the sample, as they were inappropriate. The instrument used to test the stated hypotheses was a survey questionnaire based on measurement scales suitable to the research constructs. The construct of the research is laid on inter-relationship of the factors as exhibited in Figure1.

The data was collected initially on 54 variables closely related towards influencing the buyer-supplier co-dependence. Information pertaining to these variables was subjected to decision filters at various levels of buyers' decision making process in reference to supplier performance and 43 major variables were chosen for data analysis as shown in Table 1.

*Table 1. Variables chosen for the study*

| **Customer Centric Variables** | | **Quality Function Variables** | | | |
|---|---|---|---|---|---|
| Product based | Comparative performance | Process Control | Technology application | Supply design | Brand functions |
| *CCV1* | *CCV2* | *QFV1* | *QFV2* | *QFV3* | *QFV4* |

*Figure 1. Research Design: Hypothesis mapping*

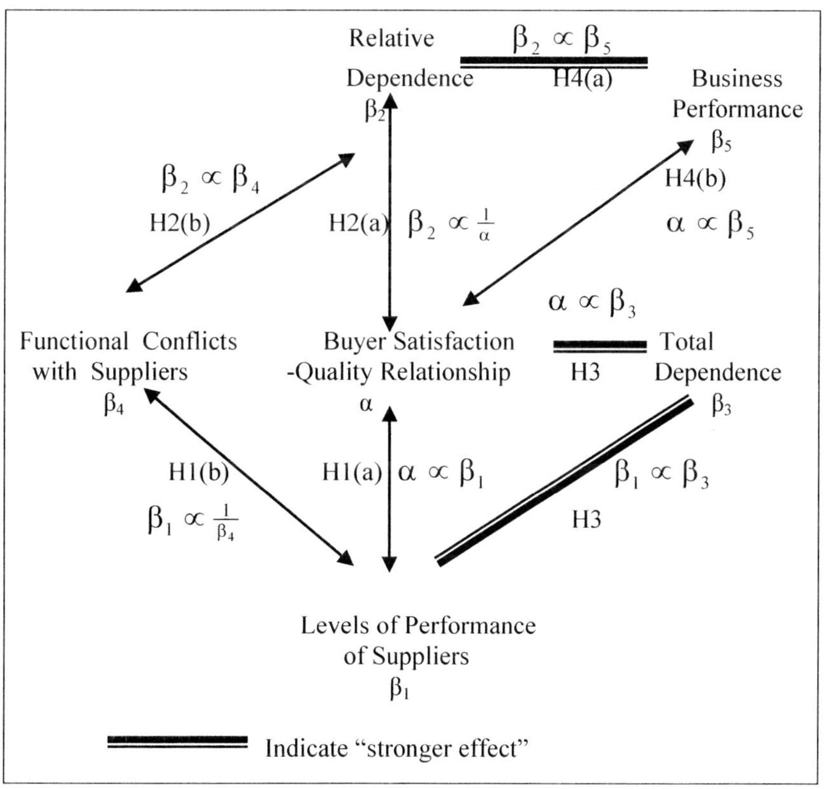

| | | | | | |
|---|---|---|---|---|---|
| Demand<br>Preferences<br>Services<br>Availability<br>Product information<br>Delivery cost | Value for money<br>Price sensitivity<br>Buying cost<br>Services cost<br>Guarantee<br>Cross promotion<br>Value additions<br>Competitiveness<br>Buyer support | Quality functions deployment<br>Routing supplies<br>Inventory management<br>Order generation<br>Order compliance<br>Stock transfers<br>Time management<br>Team work<br>Conformance quality | Innovative<br>High technology (RFID)<br>Customization<br>Compatibility<br>Serviceability<br>Value based | Display<br>PoS support<br>Availability<br>Delivery<br>Responsiveness<br>Prospecting<br>Negotiation<br>Supplier involvement | Reputation<br>New brand<br>Extensions<br>Loyalty<br>Social status<br>Strong referral |

*CCV= Customer Centric Variables*

*QFV= Quality Function Variables*

*RFID= Radio frequency identification*

*PoS = Point of Sales*

These variables include various perspectives of buyer satisfaction and supplier practices applied in providing products and services to the buyers for gaining optimal market share and aggregate returns on consumptions. The descriptive statistics of the data sets for the variable segments used in the analysis of the study is exhibited in Table 2.

*Table 2. Descriptive Statistics and Reliability Scores for the Selected Variable Segments for the Study*

*n= 241*

| Variable Segment | CCV1 | CCV2 | QFV1 | QFV2 | QFV3 | QFV4 |
|---|---|---|---|---|---|---|
| Mean | 5.920 | 4.621 | 5.769 | 4.563 | 6.765 | 6.651 |
| Standard Deviation | 1.033 | 0.785 | 0.810 | 0.892 | 1.256 | 1.381 |
| Standard Error | 0.074 | 0.054 | 0.094 | 0.061 | 0.064 | 0.076 |
| Skewness | -0.946 | -1.485 | -1.150 | -0.773 | -0.693 | 0.285 |
| Sample Variance | 1.261 | 0.940 | 0.657 | 0.793 | 1.604 | 1.399 |
| Data reliability test-Cronbach (α) scores | 0.74 | 0.76 | 0.86 | 0.82 | 0.70 | 0.72 |

Respondents were asked, on a five-point Likert scale (anchored by strongly agree=1/strongly disagree=5), the extent to which quality management practices were implemented. Measuring relationship strength is further confounded by the fact that many suppliers frequently supply their buyers with different types of product, and these relationships differ according to product type. The chi-square and comparative-fit index for the factor loadings have been analyzed for the model. Measures have been validated and the suppliers' performance construct was developed for the scores that emerged out the data analysis. Regression analysis was performed in order to ensure that the results on these constructs become non-correlated with the mutual interaction terms (Jaccard *et.al.*, 1990).

## FINDINGS AND DISCUSSION

The perceived buyer satisfaction in reference to the supplier performance $\left(P_{st}^{m}\right)$ has been estimated as discussed in the paper in reference to the gaps model. The result has been exhibited in Table 3. The estimations represent for all the observations of the study and standard error has been calculated accordingly.

In Table 3, first column displays the results when the initial robust weighting matrix is employed and the second column presents the results from optimal weighting matrix. The standard error (*SE*) has been estimated with the adjusting parameters for $c_t, y_t, w_t, s_q$ and $b_z$ as discussed in the paper. The results showed that *SE* typically increases once the adjusted and calibrated parameters $\gamma_0$ and $\gamma_1$ have accounted for measuring the gap between the expectations of the buyers and performance of suppliers in reference to existing market conditions.

*Table 3. Structural estimation results*

*n*=241

| Parameters | Robust Weighting | Optimal Weighting |
|---|---|---|
| $\hat{\beta}$ | 0.91932 | 0.93643 |
| *SE* | 0.0159 | 0.0144 |
| $\partial$ | 4.156 | 4.667 |
| $p$ | 0.5236 | 1.3266 |
| $\gamma_0$ | 1.0215 | 5.6231 |
| $\gamma_1$ | 0.0716 | 0.0613 |
| Chi-square | 121.06 | 137.11 |

*Table 4. Non-parametric test of the research constructs*

*n=241*

| Construct | Chi-square ($\chi^2$) | Comparative Fit Index |
|---|---|---|
| Distribution channel function performance | 338.76 | 0.92* |
| Dependence structure | 52.47 | 0.94* |
| Relationship Quality | 175.36 | 0.96* |

* *p-values significant at 1 percent level*

Supplier performance has been measured in terms of the longevity of the channel in the selected business, location for supplies to client accounts, store assortment, promotional strategies and client services. The average value of factor loading was found to be 0.72 and the chi-square for this construct has been 338.76 ($p<0.001$). The dependence structure in the relationship between the supplier and the organizational client was measured in reference to relative dependence and the total interdependence. The chi-square for the dependency structure construct was 52.47 ($p<0.001$). The average factor loading for the variable representing the dependence of suppliers was 0.83 and 0.79 for the buyer dependence construct. The Table exhibits the validation measures of the constructs of the study.

The quality of relationship between the suppliers and an organizational buyer is a function of satisfaction, commitment, trust and the level of conflict encountered in the relationship. The satisfaction measured in this construct referred to the overall satisfaction derived from the supplier (Sirohi *et al*, 1998). Trust was measured in reference to the honesty and reliability of the supply channel. The repeat purchase and retention of buyer was considered as the commitment, while the conflict was determined as the amount of antagonism in the relationship between the buyer and supplier. The chi-square for this construct was 221.42 ($p<0.001$). The average factor loading for the variables of satisfaction, commitment, trust and conflict were 0.69, 0.77, 0.88 and 0.81 respectively. The comparative fit index for all the constructs were above the acceptance level of 0.90 in general.

The results of the study between the supplier relationship with buyer and their interdependence are exhibited in Table 5. The results reveal that the organizational buyers perceive better quality of the relationship in a given frame of functions that are performed effectively by the supplier lowering the extent of conflicts thereof. The increasing satisfaction, trust and commitment were acting against the increase of the functional conflicts between the buyer and suppliers. Such situation also contributed to augment the channel performance. This finding establishes the hypotheses H1 (a) and H1 (b).

*Table 5. Performance attributes analysis: Regression coefficients*
*n=241*

| Relationship Attributes | Buyer based performance analysis variables | | | |
|---|---|---|---|---|
| | Satisfaction | Trust | Commitment | Conflict |
| Performance of channel functions | 0.532* | 0.514* | 0.297* | -0.286* |
| Relative dependence | -0.351* | -0.253* | -0.198* | 0.201 |
| Total (inter-) dependence | -0.092 | 0.176 | 0.126 | 0.177* |
| Functional conflicts | 0.093 | 0.058 | 0.076 | -0.011 |
| Business performance | 0.365 | 0.342 | 0.441 | -0.138 |
| $R^2$ | 0.427 | 0.316 | 0.179 | 0.144 |
| F ratio | 45.121* | 31.428* | 21.772* | 14.446* |

* *p-values significant at 1 percent level*

The relationship that explains the dependence of buyer on the supplier has been perceived less favorable by the buyers compared to the situation in which the supplier is less dependent on the buyer. This finding confirms H2 (a) while H2 (b) is further confirmed by the results showing that the supplier dependence leads to power satisfaction, trust and commitment posing a higher level of channel conflict. The results of the study revealed that co-dependence of the buyer-supplier is frequent though a few dyads become dysfunctional occasionally. The behavioral issues obstruct the process of achieving the goal when both the parties are closely interdependent that causes dissatisfaction among them leading to increasing level of conflicts. However, such conflicts may not have long-run negativity in continuing the relationship and can also become functional. Accordingly, the hypothesis H3 is also established endorsing that the supplier and buyer relationship is highly interdependent characterized by higher buyer trust and commitment and their higher co-dependence will also lead to the increasing conflicts. However, the conditions of high interdependence often lead into a protected relationship. In such situations, buyers and suppliers are more tolerant of opportunistic behavior by each other (Wathne and Heide 2000) and accept consequent higher levels of conflict. The study revealed that quality performance of suppliers is critical for high-quality relationships between buyers and sellers and emphasizes the importance of channel function performance for buyer-seller relationships.

It has been observed that quality supply design coupled with effective buyer services leads to higher buyer satisfaction. This determines high conformance of suppliers and quality relationship to offer high customer satisfaction. Accordingly, the study evidenced to support the hypothesis that improved quality performance is positively related to improve overall supplier performance. This confirms the hypotheses H4 (a) and H4 (b). This may seem to be intuitive in the context of previous research such as the profit impact on market strategy studies that provide support for the relationship between product quality and firm performance of business (Buzzel and Weirsema, 1981). Table 6 exhibits the descriptive statistical and correlation results of the relationship variables.

With the sole exception of the association between satisfaction and interdependence, all correlation coefficients are significant at the 1 percent level. This supports the argument that the relationship strength construct incorporates the various relationship dimensions that have appeared in the literature. Sub-group analysis was used to test the moderating effect of buyer-supplier relationship strength. A moderator effect implies that the moderator variable (relationship strength) modifies the form of the relationship (i.e. the slope of the regression line as represented by the regression coefficient) between the independent variable (buyer satisfaction) and the major dependent variable (quality performance of the suppliers). Accordingly, the sample was sorted in ascending order of the hypothesized moderator (relationship strength).

## MANAGERIAL IMPLICATIONS

Supplier firms may need to delineate the significance of undertaking actions that facilitate dependence-balancing. The enforcement of any business related pressures

*Table 6. Correlation of relationship and performance attributes*
*n=241*

| *Attributes* | $A_1$ | $A_2$ | $A_3$ | $A_4$ | $A_5$ | $A_6$ | $A_7$ | $A_8$ | $A_9$ |
|---|---|---|---|---|---|---|---|---|---|
| Supplier function ($A_1$) | 1.000 | | | | | | | | |
| Supplier dependence ($A_2$) | -.259* | 1.000 | | | | | | | |
| Buyer dependence ($A_3$) | .735* | .441 | 1.000 | | | | | | |
| Buyer Satisfaction ($A_4$) | .771* | -.522 | .251 | 1.000 | | | | | |
| Buyer Trust ($A_5$) | .534* | -.092 | .437 | .638* | 1.000 | | | | |
| Commitment ($A_6$) | .458 | -.063 | .556* | .516 | .594 | 1.000 | | | |
| Supplier Conflicts ($A_7$) | -.369 | .467 | .170 | -.618 | -.588 | -.431 | 1.000 | | |
| Supplier performance ($A_8$) | .624* | -.341 | .231 | .731* | .527* | .313 | -.661 | 1.000 | |
| Conformance on quality ($A_9$) | .492 | .416 | .369 | .649* | .637* | .422 | -.521 | .782* | 1.000 |
| Means<br>σ | 8.924<br>1.003 | 3.885<br>1.214 | 3.621<br>1.046 | 5.642<br>0.764 | 5.655<br>0.752 | 6.982<br>1.018 | 3.825<br>0.301 | 6.240<br>0.962 | 7.221<br>0.322 |

* *p-values significant at 1 percent level*

by the manufacturers on the suppliers would not largely affect the buyer relationship provided the performance quality is maintained. It is necessary for the suppliers to build buyer relationship on performance quality attributes. The suppliers need to focus on performing functions effectively in order to strengthen relationships, which can balance the dependence structure in buyer-supplier relationships. The managerial decision may be taken towards expanding the size of supply operations in order to maximize the quality of channel services delivered and be competitive in the market environment. Another managerial implication that emerged from the study is the need to comprehensively address the various dimensions of quality performance with a view to build the buyer-supplier relationship. It is contended that enhanced understanding of this important aspect of business to business relationships leads to the development of more closely aligned strategic plans which may improve return on relational investment.

One of the challenges for the supplier firms is to incorporate the preferences of the buyer into the supply design and services in order to maximize the buyer value. An augmented and sustainable customer value builds the loyalty towards the product and the brand. Systematically explored concepts in the field of buyer value and market driven approach towards improve supply designs would be beneficial for a company to derive long term profit optimization strategy over the period. On a tactical level, managers need to consider the optimum spread of buyers and supply designs on a matrix for determining higher conformance to the buyer satisfaction and enhance market coverage. This needs careful attention and the application of managerial judgment and experience to measure the value driven performance of supply design of the firm.

The relationship between quality performance and business performance also needs to be considered from a theoretical perspective. The results suggest that one way the suppliers can improve service quality and related measures of quality performance is by developing trust and commitment, adapting to each other's needs and improving communication and co-operation. Future research could examine issues related to the buyer perceptions of quality and supplier performance. The impact of environmental variables on the quality perceived -quality performance relationship may also be considered given the findings of this study. Identifying the variables that have an intervening effect on the quality-performance relationship may provide both the academics and managers with potentially compelling answers to the question of why supplier oriented quality improvement programs sometimes do not succeed.

## CONCLUSION

The buyer-supplier relations are subject to both controllable and non-controllable forces of change, which may have varying effect on the logistics performance. However, effective co-dependence would help sustainable length of relationships and optimize the performance of suppliers through higher degree of conformance to buyers' satisfaction on the services offered. The effect of functional performance on relationship quality in situations characterized by high relative dependence of the supplier on the buyer is largely governed by the effective supply functions. The model discussed in this paper provides a holistic view of the buyer-supplier co-dependence by proposing ways to measure the different variables associated with it *viz.* supply design, market coverage, conformance to buyers' satisfaction and point-of-sales services. The analysis of these variables would help the managers develop appropriate strategies to enhance the supply designs and augment buyer value to optimize profit of the firm.

## LIMITATIONS OF THE STUDY

Like many other empirical studies, this research might also have some limitations in reference to sampling, data collection and generalization of the findings. The samples drawn for the study may not be enough to generalize the study results. The questionnaires were translated in Spanish for the respondents in Mexico which might have conveyed varied conceptual sense to some extent. The open ended questions were answered by the Mexican respondents in Spanish and some issues might have overlooked during transcription of the audio. The study does not indicate as how behavior control, price differentiation, and promotion design efficiency cause changes in the consequences leading to managing buyer satisfaction. However to ensure that the data cover a wider spatial and temporal dimensions in the study region, data should be cleansed and filtered with many variability factors affecting the buyer behavior and supplier performance.

## REFERENCES

Anderson, J. C., & Narus, J. A. (1990). A model of supplier firm and manufacture firm working partnership. *Journal of Marketing, 54*, 42-58.

Black, S. A., & Porter, L. J. (1996). Identification of critical factors of TQM. *Decision Sciences, 27*(1), 1-27.

Brown, J. R., Lusch, R. F., & Nicholson, C. Y. (1995). Power and relationship commitment: Their impact on marketing channel member performance. *Journal of Retailing, 71*(4), 363-392.

Butler, J. K. (1991). Towards understanding and measuring conditions of trust: Evolution of trust inventory. *Journal of Management, 17*, 643-663.

Buzzel, R. D., & Weirsema, F. D. (1981). Model changes in market share: A cross sectional analysis. *Strategic Management Journal, 2*(1), 27-42.

Carroll, C. D., & Kimball, M. S. (1996). On the concavity of the consumption function. *Econometrics, 64*(4), 981-992.

Chang, T. Z., Mehta, R., Chen S-J., Polsa, P., Mazur, J. (1999). The effects of market orientation on effectiveness and efficiency: The case of automotive distribution channels in Finland and Poland. *Journal of Services Marketing, 13*(4-5), 407-418.

Cummins, D. J., & Van Derhie, J. (1979). A note on relative efficiency of perperty-liability insurance distribution system. *Bell Journal of Economics, 10*(2), 709-719.

Dicken, P. (1998). *Global shift-transforming the world economy.* London: Paul Chapman.

Doornik, K. (2006). Relational contracting in partnerships. *Journal of Economics and Management Strategies, 15*(2), 517-548.

Dwyer, F. R., Schurr, P. H., & Oh, S. (1987, April). Developing buyer-seller relationships. *Journal of Marketing, 51*, 11-27.

Emerson, R. M. (1962, February). Power-dependence relationship. *American Sociological Review, 27*, 31-41.

Flynn, B. B., Schroeder, R. G., & Sakaibara, S. (1994). A framework for quality management research and an associated measurement instrument. *Journal of Operations Management, 11*(4), 339-366.

Forker, L. B. (1997). Factors affecting supplier quality performance. *Journal of Operations Management, 15*(4), 243-269.

Frazier, G. L., & Raymond, C. R. (1991). The use of influence strategies in inter-firm relationships in industrial product channels. *Journal of Marketing, 55*, 52-69.

Ganeshan, S. (1994, April). Determinants of long term orientation in buyer-seller relationships. *Journal of Marketing, 58*, 1-19.

Garbarino, E., & Johnson, M. S. (1999, April). The different roles of satisfaction, trust and commitment in buyer relationships. *Journal of Marketing, 63*, 70-87.

Geyskens, I., Jan-Benedict, E. M. S., & Nimalya, K. (1998). Generalization about trust in marketing channel relationships using meta-analysis. *International Journal of Research in Marketing*, *15*, 223-248.

Halldórsson, Á., & Skjøtt-Larsen, T. (2006). Dynamics of relationship governance in TPL arrangements – A dyadic perspective. *International Journal of Physical Distribution & Logistics Management*, *36*(7), 490-506.

Harwood, T. G. (2006). Developing buyer-seller relationships through face-to-face negotiations. *Journal of Relationship Marketing*, *4*(3-4), 105-122.

Hibbard, J. D., Nirmalya, K., & Stern, L. W. (2001). Examining the impact of destructive acts in marketing channel relationships. *Journal of Marketing Research*, *38*, 45-61.

Hill, C. (1990). Cooperation opportunism and invisible hand: Implication for transaction cost theory. *Academy of Management Journal*, *15*(3), 500-514.

Hirschman, A. O. (1970). *Exit, voice and loyalty: Responses to decline in firms. organizations and states*. Cambridge, MA: Harvard University Press.

Ittner, C. D., & Larcker, D. F. (1996). Financial impact of quality initiatives. *Advances in the Management of Organization Quality*, *1*, 1-37.

Jaccard, J., Turrisi, R., & Wan, C. K. (1990). *International effects in multiple regression*. Thousand Oaks, CA: Sage University Press.

Kumar, N., Scheer. L. K., & Jan-Benedict, E. M. S. (1995, August). The effects of perceived interdependence on dealer attitudes. *Journal of Marketing Research*, *32*, 348-356.

Mehmet, B. (2000, November). Switching costs and screening efficiency of incomplete contracts. *Canadian Journal of Economics*, *33*(4), 1034-1048.

Morgan, R. M., & Hunt, S. D. (1994, July). The commitment –Trust theory of relationship marketing. *Journal of Marketing*, *58*, 20-38.

Noordewier, T. G., George, J., & Nevin, J. R. (1990, October). Performance outcomes of purchasing arrangements in industrial buyer-vendor relationships. *Journal of Marketing*, *54*, 80-93.

Peck, H. (2006). Reconciling supply chain vulnerability, risk and supply chain management. *International Journal of Logistics*, *9*(2), 127-142.

Rajagopal (2005). Measuring variability factors in consumer values for profit optimization in a firm – A framework for analysis. *Journal of Economics and Management, 1(1), 85-103.*

Rajagopal (2006a). Trust and cross-cultural dissimilarities in corporate environment. *Team Performance Management-An International Journal, 12*(7-8), 237-252.

Rajagopal (2006b). Measuring customer value gaps: An empirical study in Mexican retail markets. *Economic Issues, 11*(1), 19-40.

Rajagopal (2007). Influence of brand name in variety seeking behavior of consumers: An empirical study. *International Journal of Management Practice, 2*(4), 306-323.

Reeves, C. A., & Bedner, D. A. (1994). Defining quality: Alternatives and implications. *Academy of Management Review, 19*(3), 419-445.

Robicheaux, R. A., & Colman, J. E. (1994). The structure of marketing channel relationships. *Journal of Academy of Marketing Science, 22*(1), 38-51.

Rogers, P. A. (2006). Optimizing supplier management and why co-dependency equals mutual success. *Journal of Facilities Management, 4*(1), 40-50.

Sirohi, N., Mclaughlin, E. W., & Wittink, D. R. (1998). A model of consumer perceptions and store loyalty intentions for a supermarket retailer. *Journal of Retailing, 74*(2), 223-245.

Smith, W., van Bruggen, G. H., & Wierenga, B. (2002). *Building stronger channel relationship though information sharing* (pp. 1-62). Discussion Paper, 235, Erasmus Research Institute of Management.

Squire, B., Cousins, P. D., & Brown, S. (2005). Collaborating for customization: An extended resource-based view of the firm. *International Journal of Productivity and Quality Management, 1*(1-2), 8-25.

Swink, M., & Zsidisin, G. (2006). On the benefits and risks of focused commitment to suppliers. *International Journal of Production Research, 44*(20), 4223-4240.

Trkman, P., Štemberger, M. I., Jaklic, J., & Ales, G. (2007). Process approach to supply chain integration. *Supply Chain Management: An International Journal, 12*(2), 116-128.

Ulaga, W., & Eggert, A. (2006). Relationship value and relationship quality: Broadening the nomological network of business-to-business relationships. *European Journal of Marketing, 40* (3-4), 311-327.

Voss, M. D., Calantone, R. J., & Keller, S. B. (2005). Internal service quality: Determinants of distribution center performance. *International Journal of Physical Distribution & Logistics Management, 35*(3), 161-176.

Wathne, K. H., & Jan, B. H. (2000, October). Opportunism in inter-firm relationships: Forms, outcomes and solutions. *Journal of Marketing, 64*, 36-51.

Wilson, D. T., & Moller, K. E. (1991). Buyer-seller relationship: Alternative conceptualization. In S. J. Poliwoda (Ed.), *New perspectives on international marketing* (pp. 87-107). London: Routledge.

# Chapter VIII
# Loyalty Cards in Retailing Industry:
## Technology Application in Customer Relations

**Rajagopal**
*Monterrey Institute of Technology and Higher Education, ITESM, Mexico*

## INTRODUCTION

A common observation about self-service retail stores is the *similitude* among in-store ambience and retailing operations. Hence, self service retail stores are increasingly using point of sales promotional activities to drive buying stimulation among consumers through redeemable coupons corresponding to the value of purchase. Such promotional strategy and market dominance have significant implications on the volume of sales and inflow of consumers in retail stores (Parsons and Ballantine, 2004). The prospective customers have objective to buy at the right time so as to minimize the expected price of the acquired item. However, point of sales promotions stimulates compulsive buying behavior among customer which dominates the buying decision despite comparative differences in the prices of alternate channels (Parlar *et al*, 2007). By making the attractive products accessible to customers at point of sales promotion, customers would be driven by the 'me too' feeling and preferential prices. The concept of point of sales promotion to create compulsive buying behavior is based on a brilliant understanding of the human mind and a smart way of increasing volume of store sales. Self service retail stores introduce electronic cash cards (ECC), shopping advantage cards (SAC) and bulk purchase price offers (BPP) as point of sales promotion to acquire new customers and retain existing customers (Rajagopal 2008, Coad, 2006).

Retailing firms build most profitable strategies through services differentiation and competitive advantages offering customers something new they value that other retail outlets don not have. Self service retail stores differentiate at every point of customer services and relationship from the moment customers express store loyalty. Large self service retail stores open up their promotion strategies to stimulate shopping behavior of customers and uncover new opportunities for them to gain long term benefits with the retail stores and stay loyal (MacMillan and Mcgrath, 1997). However, some firms have experienced that point of sales promotion activities can also backfire loudly and put reputations at risk if the tools of promotion such as ECC, SAC and BPP are not effectively managed. Since point of sales promotion has emerged as competitive strategy for retail firms, despite apparent risks managers are exploring the scope of acquiring and retaining customers. This strategy of point of sales promotions has helped large self service retail stores to slash costs on advertising and publicity, increase volume of sales and sharpen their focus on core competencies (Johnson, 2006).

This chapter attempts to analyze drivers of compulsive buying behavior induced by store based promotion through empirical investigation in Mexico. The role of point of sales promotions in stimulating arousal and satisfaction among customer and customer relationship management for building store loyalty have been analyzed in the chapter. Also, acquiring new customers through innovative in-store promotions towards driving the compulsive shopping tendency and swaying store-brand loyalty through point of sales promotions in chain self service stores are discussed in the following text. This study builds arguments towards convergence of attractiveness of point of sales promotions and effectiveness of customer services as a tool for gaining competitive advantage in the retail business environment.

## REVIEW OF LITERATURE

### Point of Sales Promotions

Large self service retail stores or supermarkets are potential outlets where customers experience innovative promotions on variety of products and services which drive the buying decisions. Among various promotional offers price discounts, free samples, bonus packs, and in-store display are associated with product trial. Trial determines repurchase behavior and also mediates in the relationship between sales promotions and repeat buying behavior (Ndubisi and Moi, 2005). Repeat buying behavior of customers is largely determined by the values acquired on the product.

The attributes, awareness, trial, availability and repeat (AATAR) factors influence the customers towards making re-buying decisions in reference to the marketing strategies of the firm. The decision of customers on repeat buying is also affected by the level of satisfaction derived on the products and number of customers attracted towards buying the same product, as a behavioral determinant (Rajagopal, 2005). Among growing competition in retailing consumer products, innovative point of sales promotions offered by super markets are aimed at boosting sales and augmenting the store brand value. Purchase acceleration and product trial are found to be the two most influential variables of retail point of sales promotions. It has been found that there exists significant association between the four consumer promotional approaches including coupons, price discounts, samples and *buy-one-get-one-free* and compulsive buying behavior (Gilbert and Jackaria, 2002). The occurrence and the choice of appropriate retail sales promotion techniques are important decisions for retailers. It is crucial for the retailing firms to apprehend the mechanisms involved at the consumer level regarding these sales promotions. Variables such as variety seeking, perceived financial benefit, brand loyalty and store loyalty towards point of sales promotions have specific influences on the buying behavior and volume of retail sales (Laroche et al, 2003).

Leisure shopping is influenced by time and attractiveness of sales offers which include variables *viz.* hours of work, public holidays, and paid leave entitlements, point of sales promotions and effectiveness of customer relations. These factors vary widely in reference to consumer segments and markets attractiveness and induce compulsive buying behavior among customers, which is judged by the satisfaction in spending and perceiving pleasure of buying occasionally exercising choice and passing time in knowing new products, services, technologies and understanding fellow customers (Watkins and Bond, 2007, Rajagopal 2007a). Retailers using a "store as the brand" strategy invest in creating a specific, unique shopping experience for their target customer and encourage leisure and group buying behavior where delivery of customer satisfaction seems to be an effective source of differentiation (Carpenter *et al*, 2005). Change-of-season sales are most frequently introduced with attractive sales promotions in reference to price discounts or two for one price basis and linked with objectives of moving a volume of stock. Retail promotional sales also include general sales, and these are linked with other promotional objectives and activities such as increasing profit and inventory management (Fam, 2003).

## Compulsive Buying

Compulsive buying is closely associated with the obsessive behavior of customers who orient to their mind to acquire certain products or services. There exists a close relationship between compulsive buyers and specific types of external stimuli such as sales promotions and bargains offered in the large self service retail stores. Customers who have a higher tendency to buy compulsively are more prone to promotions and are more likely to yield to innovative sales promotions in retail stores. Such customers have a greater likelihood to use promotion tools such as ECC, SAC and BPP offered by retail stores, and subsequently have a greater incidence of compulsive shopping (Vicdan *et al*, 2007). Clinically, compulsive buying is closely related to major depression, obsessive–compulsive disorder, and in particular, compulsive hoarding. Like compulsive hoarding, compulsive buying is thought to be influenced by a range of cognitive domains including deficits in decision-making, emotional attachments to objects and erroneous beliefs about possessions, and other maladaptive beliefs (Kyrios *et al*, 2004).

Five essential qualities of aesthetic judgment, which include *interest, subjectivity, exclusivity, thoughtfulness, and internality,* need to be nurtured among consumers to develop conviction in buying. The quality of aesthetic judgment driven by in-store aura and arousal on new products, exercised by the customers in association with the sales promoters, determines the extent to which new products and brands promoted enhance quality of life (Dobson, 2007). Convergence of sales promotion, customer's perceptions, value for money and product features drive arousal among customers. The nature of customer-retailer relationship functions as the key in selling and buying process in reference to in-store promotions. However, in this process the perceptional problems with customers can greatly devalue the customer-promoter relationship and brand as a whole (Platz and Temponi, 2007; Rajagopal, 2007b). Consumer appreciation of premium-based promotional offers is more positive when the premium is offered through an easy process and in combination of relatively lower quantity of products to purchase. It has also been found that when value of the premium is mentioned and brand perception is positive compulsive buying tendencies are higher among customer (d'Astous and Jacob, 2002).

The in-store environment variables driving impulsive buying behavior include display of point of sales posters, exhibiting promoting discounts and cheaper prices, while the atmosphere engagement referring to enjoyment, elegance, and attractiveness is conveyed by in-store point of sales posters. Such behavioral drivers may also be referred as in-store promotional effect and atmospheric effect (Zhou and Wong, 2004). It has been observed in some studies that consumers who intend to do shopping in short notice, generally lean towards impulsive or compulsive buying behavior driven by arousal effect in the retail stores. Gender, age, leaning towards unplanned purchases, and tendency to buy products not on shopping lists, serve to predict compulsive tendencies (Shoham and Brencic, 2003). However, there are some common strategies adopted by retailers to overcome the problems of fickle consumers, price-slashing competitors, and mood swings in the economy. Such wishful thinking holds that sales promoters can thrive only if they communicate better with consumers during pre-purchase situations and assist in product demonstrations involving consumers to help their purchase decisions (Berry, 2001).

## Hispanic Consumers Shopping Behavior

Human personality traits are determined by multi-dimensional factors like the individual's behavior, appearance, attitude and beliefs, and demographic characteristics. Based on the trait theory, researchers have concluded that there are five stable personality dimensions, also called the 'Big Five' human personality dimensions (Batra, Lehmann & Singh, 1993). The Big five factors include extraversion, agreeableness, conscientiousness, neuroticism and openness to experience. Relationship between the point of sales promotions and retail buying decisions is largely governed by the psychographic variables that can be measured broadly by the closeness and farness of the personalities of brand and customer. The type of relationship that customers possess with the point of sales promotions offered by retail stores is largely based on the loyalty levels (Rajagopal 2007a). The new generation marketing approaches include customer focused, market-driven, outside-in, one-to-one marketing, data-driven marketing, relationship marketing, integrated marketing, and integrated marketing communications that emphasize two-way communication through better listening to customers and the idea that communication before, during and after transactions can build or destroy important brand relationships (Duncan and Moriarty, 1998). It has been observed that Hispanic consumers are sensitive to the price while making buying decisions and have higher tendency to buy compulsively, are more prone to promotions and are more likely to use online sales promotions (Vicdan *et al*, 2007).

Hispanic consumers are found to be attached firmly to the ethnic culture and tend to shop at the same store, especially those stores owned by members of the subculture and stores with Spanish-speaking salespeople (Saegert *et al*, 1985). Marketers reinforce the relationship between consumers and their stores by introducing periodical sales promotions. In general, Hispanic consumers show the tendency of buying products offered in sales promotions (Richins, 1994). In Latin America consumers' diversity is apparent and so is their attitude towards promotions. Consumers considered relative advantages in perceived price and product promotions, and preferred big-bargains offered by the retail stores to buy. Retailers accrued higher benefit from such buying behavior of consumers while defining their promotional strategies, especially emphasizing on every day low prices (EDLP) strategy like Wal-Mart (D'Andrea *et al*, 2006). Practically consumers react favorably to leisure sales campaigns of goods and services. However, customer value plays a decisive role in the shopping process. Sales promoters instill emotions among customers in terms of merchandise choice, visual merchandising, store environment, sales personnel attitude, pricing policies and promotional activities during the pre-purchase stage. These factors are the very foundations of consumer satisfaction and decision drivers towards buying products (Otieno *et al*, 2005).

## CONCEPTUAL MOTIVATION

Point of sales promotion strategy towards prospecting new customers and generating shopping arousal among the existing customers through in-store ECC, SAC and BPP involves impulsive and compulsive buying process. The effects of location convenience, one-stop shopping convenience, reputation of retail stores, in-store ambience, and direct mailings generate shopping arousal among the leisure shoppers. Satisfaction and trust developed by the retail stores during pre-purchase phase help persuading the sales promotions among customers (Liu and Wu, 2007). Consumers respond encouragingly to point of sales campaigns run by the self service retail stores in Mexico, however, customer services associated with point of sales

*Figure 1. Interactive sales strategies in customer prospecting and developing shopping arousal*

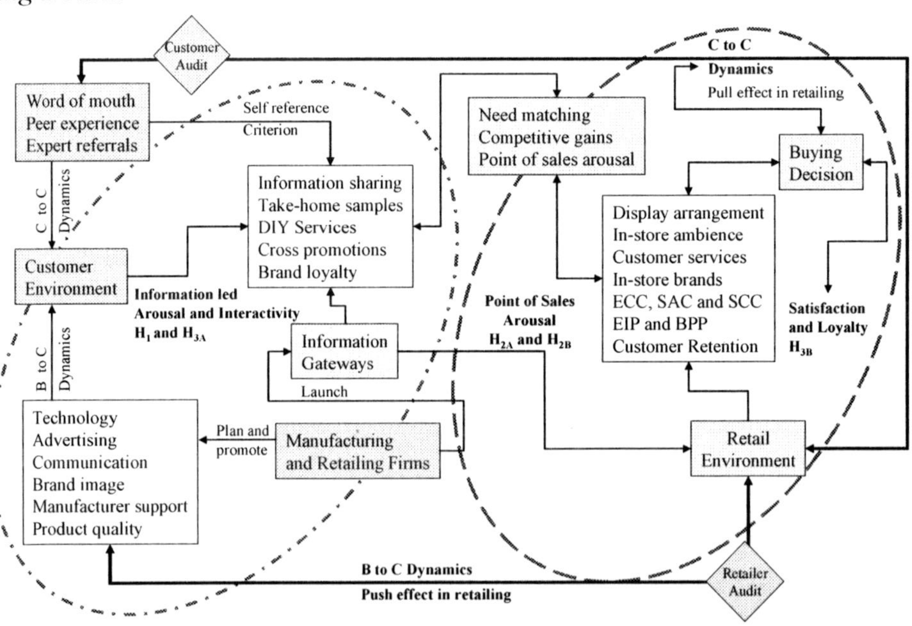

promotions and perceived promotional advantage play a decisive role in the buying process (Rajagopal, 2006; Anselmsson, 2006). Information on the current point of sale promotion and previous experience of customer with the promotional offers of the retail store stimulate consumer feelings and prompt their decision towards experimenting new products on promotional offers (Backstrom, 2006). The strategy of point of sales promotion in acquiring new customers, retaining existing customer and increase the volume of sales by shopping arousal has been derived from the previous research studies reviewed in the pretext and exhibited in Figure 1.

Figure 1 illustrates that shopping arousal and compulsive buying behavior are developed by the retailing firms through point of sales promotions engaging innovative promotional offers. Such promotional attractions to oversell products drive business-to-consumer (B-to-C) marketing approaches. Retailing firms develop the point of sales satisfaction and post-sales satisfaction which prompts consumer-to-consumer (C-to-C) interactions and help in building store loyalty. The hypotheses H1 and H2(a) and H2(b) have been framed considering point of sales shopping dynamics and the construct of hypotheses H3 (a) and H3 (b) are based on post-sales satisfaction leading to store loyalty as an impact of promotional offers.

## RESEARCH DESIGN

### Framework of Hypotheses

Tendency of compulsive buying in retail stores in response to point of sales promotions among consumers has often been dichotomized in terms of its arousal led compulsive nature and has been found closely associated with the post-buying level of satisfaction leading to determine the customer value and justification to the buying decisions. Such impulsive buying attitude emerging from self reference criterion may lean towards derived cognitions, possibly including compulsive buying, hoarding, and materialism (Doron *et al*, 2007; Wakefield and Inman, 2003).

As new and exciting products are introduced, firms prospect the consumers through inter-personal negotiations managed by the sales promoters and inculcate high arousal among customers towards buying these products. The *visual merchandising* and computer aided simulations act as stimuli to consumers who intend to elicit a positive response. This creates shopping arousal among customers in reference to merchandise choice, store ambience, attributes of promotional products, perceived use value, pricing policies and promotional activities. These factors may be considered as foundations of consumer behavior towards point of sales promotions offered in retail stores (Otieno *et al*, 2005). Further, it is predicted that the magnitude of such positive response will be proportional to the value of an option to make buying decision at the available price (Rajagopal, 2006). Accordingly, hypothesis may be framed as:

**H1:** *Consumers are influenced in making buying decisions by the product attractiveness and in-store shopping arousal generated by the point of sales promotions introduced by the retail stores.*

Visual effects and economic advantage associated with promotional products in the retail stores often stimulate the compulsive buying behavior. Point of sales brochures, catalogues and posters build assumption on perceived use value and motivational relevance of buying decisions of product. Emotional visuals exhibited on contextual factors such as proximity or stimulus size, drive perception and subjective reactions on utility and expected satisfaction of the products (Codispoti and De Cesarei, 2007). Retailers demonstrate higher visual attention and increasing visual stimuli during the point of sales promotions. It reveals that consumers exhibit a muddled search strategy where economic and perceived use value benefits influence the buying decision process among customers (Clement, 2007). In addition, a pleasant store ambience where attractive displays, music, hands-on experience facilities and recreation are integrated helps in maximizing the consumer arousal towards buying. It has been observed that consumers perceive positive effect during interaction with sales promoters if arousal is high (Wirtz *et al*, 2007). Hence, it may be hypothesized as:

**H2 (a):** *Consumers develop compulsive buying behavior and higher store loyalty while responding to the point of sales promotions.*

**H2 (b):** *During the point of sales promotions retailers boost up higher shopping arousal leading to conformity towards buying decision.*

The impact of initial interactions among fellow customers about the point of sales promotions can be measured in reference to the degree of stimulation gained by customers. Interactive tools on product learning provided by the retailers significantly affect the level of arousal and pleasure which contribute towards experience, and thereby influence the buying behavior. As higher stimulation or interactive learning provided by the sales promoters focuses on gaining initial experience on the product use, consumers tend to engage in higher arousing activities and adhere to the sale promotions offered by the retail stores (Rajagopal, 2008; Menon and Kahn, 2002).

It has been demonstrated in some researches using store-level data that shoppers in predominantly Hispanic communities actually buy fewer name brands and more store brands (Mulhern and Williams, 1994). Marketers reinforce this perception between consumers and their stores by consistently offering them loyalty offers as Hispanic consumers are more loyal than non-Hispanic consumers. Hence retailers use point of sales promotions to build shopping arousal, gain satisfaction and stay loyal to the stores (Deshpande *et al*, 1986). In view of such consumer arousal led compulsive behavior in retail buying; the hypothesis may be delineated as:

**H3 (a):** *Shopping arousal generated through interpersonal communication and product experience offered to the customers during the point of sales promotions, increase randomness of variety-seeking behavior and impulsive buying.*

**H3 (b):** *In response to the sales promotion offers loyal customers purchase more store brands than non-store brands.*

The magnitude of consumer response to clearance sales is weighed in two ways-evaluative and behavioral. Firstly, consumer satisfaction with the decision process leading to the expected level of *satisfaction* is measured, which may be expressed as one of a number of cognitive and affective responses. Satisfaction is the customer's perception of the value received in a transaction or relationship and it helps in making re-patronage decisions on the basis of their predictions concerning the value of a future product. Hence, many retailers develop innovative approaches to prospect new customers for new products by strengthening customer relationship and value management strategies (Ganesh, *et al*, 2000).

## Sampling

This study has been conducted in 16 branches of the 4 chain self service retail stores of Mexico-Commercial Mexicana, Chedraui, Gigante-Soriana and Wal-Mart de Mexico located in Mexico City (Federal District of Mexico). The samples respondents were selected for this study who regularly shops in the above self service stores in Mexico City and suburbs. These respondents showed homogeneity in shopping behavior in reference to store loyalty, point of sales promotions, promotional brands, product categories, point of sales arousal on store promotions and post-promotion satisfaction on buying. Data was collected administering pre-coded structured questionnaires to 270 customers who were selected following a purposive sampling and snowballing technique. Information collected though the questionnaires were reviewed for each respondent to ascertain quality and fit for analysis.

## Data Collection Tools

The study was conducted during 2005-07 in three seasons March-April (Spring sales), July-August (Summer sales) and November-January (Winter sales) per annum, when point of sales promotions were offered frequently by the selected retail stores as cited above. The data collection process was initiated in November 2005 and terminated in August 2007 covering 6 periods of sales during the study. A focus group session was organized with potential respondents to identify most appropriate variables for the data collection. Accordingly, 36 variables which were closely related towards influencing the shopping arousal and customer satisfaction on point of sales promotions were selected and incorporated in the questionnaires. The questionnaires were pilot tested to 32 (11.85 percent of total sample size) respondents randomly selected and finalized after refining them based on the responses during the pilot study. The variables selected for the study have been broadly classified into economic and behavioral variables as exhibited in Table 1.

A questionnaire was developed to investigate the extent to which point of sales promotions have influenced the buying behavior, derived post-buying satisfaction and augmented the volume of sales of the retail stores. The pre-test of the preliminary questionnaire on measuring the influence of point of sales promotions on stimulated buying behavior indicated that promotion offers introduced

*Table 1. Variables chosen for the study*

| **Behavioral variables** | | | **Economic variable** | |
|---|---|---|---|---|
| Product based | Application based | Arousal and Merriment | Comparative | Point of sale promotion based |
| $VS_1$ (7) | $VS_2$ (8) | $VS_3$ (8) | $VS_4$ (6) | $VS_5$ (9) |
| Appearance<br>Sensory<br>Durability<br>Newness<br>Health oriented<br>Need<br>Fun | Regular use<br>Occasional use<br>Gifts and glamour<br>Home decoration<br>Food and beverages<br>Fashion oriented<br>Recreational<br>Social status | Initial awareness<br>Product features<br>Advertising<br>Hands-on experience<br>Customer interaction<br>Self reference criterion<br>Referrals<br>Satisfaction | Value for money<br>Price sensitivity<br>Quality difference<br>Guarantee<br>Cross promotion<br>Competitiveness | Promotional attractions<br>Display<br>In-store ambience<br>Customer services<br>Availability<br>Length of promotion<br>Responsiveness<br>Value added benefits<br>Partners of promotion |

*VS=Variable Segment*

*Figures in parentheses indicate number of variables*

*Table 2. Descriptive statistics for the selected variable groups for the study*

| Variable Groups | $VS_1$ (7) | $VS_2$ (8) | $VS_3$ (8) | $VS_4$ (6) | $VS_5$ (9) |
|---|---|---|---|---|---|
| Sample Size | 234 | 234 | 234 | 234 | 234 |
| Mean | 5.309 | 7.681 | 7.443 | 6.291 | 4.836 |
| Standard Deviation | 0.875 | 0.629 | 0.643 | 0.833 | .916 |
| Standard Error | 0.082 | 0.073 | 0.051 | 0.066 | 0.068 |
| Skewness | -0.946 | -1.122 | -0.639 | -0.770 | -0.643 |
| Sample Variance | 0.655 | 0.596 | 0.482 | 0.794 | 0.804 |
| Data reliability test-Cronbach (α) scores | 0.84 | 0.76 | 0.88 | 0.82 | 0.74 |

*VS=Variable Segment*

*Figures in parentheses indicate number of variables*

by the retailers indicated strong stimuli for the regular and new shoppers. Based on responses from the pre-test, the final questionnaire necessitated no significant changes. The questionnaires were translated in Spanish. All care was taken about the terminology and language being employed in each version of the questionnaire. The variables used in the questionnaire for data collection include various perspectives of customer satisfaction and promotional practices offered by the retailers to gain competitive advantage, optimal market share and higher aggregate sales. The descriptive statistics of the data sets for the variable segments used in the analysis of the study is exhibited in Table 2.

Data was collected by means of personal interviews by undergraduate students of international commerce and marketing who hand-delivered the questionnaires to the key respondents in the self service retail stores who had agreed to be the subject of the research investigation. In most cases, the respondents completed and returned the questionnaires on the predetermined date.

## Response Trend

Questionnaires were administered to 270 respondents. However, during the process of data analysis, questionnaires of 36 respondents were omitted due to paucity of information. In all 234 respondents were covered under the study and the usable response rate was 86.66 percent. The non-response bias has been measured applying two statistical techniques. Firstly, telephonic conversations were made with 20 randomly selected non-respondents responding to some general questions about sales and services policies of the dealers (Gounaris et al, 2007). *T-tests* were used to ascertain emerging differences between respondents and non-respondents concerning the issues pertaining to market orientation and customer services strategies. No statistically significant differences in pre coded responses *(a* = 0.05) were found. A second test for non-response bias examined the differences between early and late respondents on the same set of factors (Armstrong and Overton, 1977) and this assessment also yielded no significant differences between early and late respondents.

## Construct of Measures

Effectiveness of point of sales promotion was measured with 12-variable self-appraisal perceptual scale derived originally on the basis of focus group analysis as referred in the pretext. However, motivation about this construct has been derived from an original scale developed by Narver and Slater (1990) on market orientation, who conceptualized it as a multivariate construct comprising customer orientation, competitor orientation and inter-functional coordination as principal behavioral components. This scale also comprised a dyadic decision criterion including long-term horizon and profit emphasis (*e.g.* Ruekert 1992; Hunt and Morgan 1995). Impact of post-promotional buying decision in terms of enhancing customer satisfaction and store loyalty has been measured using 11-variable 'self-appraisal perceptual scale' which included major services quality determinants-tangibility, responsiveness, trust, precision and empathy (Parasuraman et al, 1988).

In this study, a five-point Likert scale has been employed to measure the efficiency of customer services delivered by the automobile dealers in the study region. Respondents were asked, on a five-point Likert scale (anchored by strongly agree=1/strongly disagree=5), the extent to which quality management practices were implemented. The chi-square and comparative-fit index for the factor loadings have been analyzed for the model. Measures had been validated and performance construct for the point of sales promotion was developed for the scores that emerged out the data analysis. Regression analysis was performed in order to ensure that the results on these constructs become non-correlated with the mutual interaction terms (Jaccard *et.al.*, 1990).

# RESULTS AND DISCUSSIONS

Self service retail stores employ variety of point of sales promotions tools as exhibited in Table 3 to attract customers augment the store sales. Of these promotional tools, easy installment payment (EIP) and bulk purchase price (BPP) appeared to be most popular promotion tool among the customers. EIP is used by the retailers throughout the year while BPP is limited to summer sales season (July-August) and is restricted to notified products only.

The results reveal that 78.80 percent customer use EIP promotional services while 64.77 percent customers are attracted by the BPP promotions offered by the retail stores. Wal-Mart does not offer BPP promotion as it has the policy of offering every day low prices. Unlike other self service retail stores covered under this study, Wal-Mart has two major point of sales promotions which include electronic cash card (ECC) and store credit card (SCC). ECC has been introduced as gift card for use after recharging the card with cash and also the value of returned goods can be charged to this card by Wal-Mart customer services modules. ECC can be used by the customers in all the stores of Wal-Mart Group including all Wal-Mart super stores, Superama (convenience store), Bodega Aurera (super store with bulk retailing), VIPS (restaurant), and Suburbia (retail apparel stores). Hence, 78.56 percent customer use ECC within the Wal-Mart group of stores while 81.49 percent customer use SCC for continuous purchases at the store.

*Table 3. Attributes of Point of Sales Promotions Offered in Self Service Retail Stores (n=234)*

| Retail Store | Response Level | Point of Sales Promotions[b] | | | | |
|---|---|---|---|---|---|---|
| | | Electronic Cash Card (ECC) | Shopping Advantage Card[+] (SAC) | Store Credit Card (SCC) | Easy Installment Payment[#] (EIP) | Bulk Purchase Price[*] (BPP) |
| Commercial Mexicana SA de CV (**$RS_1$**) | 72 (30.77) | No | Yes (58.36) | No | Yes (83.16) | Yes (68.52) |
| Tiendas Chedraui SA de CV (**$RS_2$**) | 64 (27.35) | No | Yes (61.74) | Yes (42.93) | Yes (85.22) | Yes (52.84) |
| Gigante-Tienda Soriana** SA de CV (**$RS_3$**) | 58 (24.79) | No | No | No | Yes (60.37) | Yes (72.97) |
| Wal-Mart de Mexico (**$RS_4$**) | 40 (17.09) | Yes (78.56) | No | Yes (81.49) | Yes (86.47) | No |

[*] *Buy two get one free offer valid only in summer sales (July-August)*

[+] *Shoppers can accumulate bonus point for their purchase of the value determined by the store*

** *Soriana, the second largest self service retail store company has acquired Gigante SA de SV in January 2008*

[#] *Subject to store terms and conditions and applicable to the product (s) as determined by the retail stores administration*

[a] *Figures in parentheses are percent distribution of respondents to total sample size*

[b] *Figures in parentheses indicate percent to total sample size. These figures may not be equal to 100 as respondents might have opted for multiple responses.*

*Table 4. Regression Analysis of the Point of sales Promotional Effect and Volume of Buying*

*n*=234

| Point of Sales Promotions/ Retail Stores | $RS_1$ | $RS_2$ | $RS_3$ | $RS_4$ |
|---|---|---|---|---|
| Electronic Cash Card (ECC) | -- | -- | -- | 0.8624* (0.1992) |
| Shopping Advantage Card (SAC) | 0.6120* (0.3296) | 0.8621* (0.4725) | -- | -- |
| Store Credit Card (SCC) | -- | 0.6381** (0.1281) | -- | 0.9314* (0.1455) |
| Easy Installment Payment (EIP) | 0.9422* (0.7104) | 0.8199* (1.1409) | 0.6003** (0.7444) | 0.7518* (0.3170) |
| Bulk Purchase Price* (BPP) | 0.7631* (0.0316) | 0.8637* (0.1280) | 0.7329* (0.3904) | - |

- *p-values * >.01 and ** >.001*
- *In the above Table coefficients represent the marginal effects on the average time spread during the leisure shopping per capita*
- *Each cell represents separate regression*
- *Figures presented in parentheses indicate standard errors*

During point of sales promotion the impact of EIP promotion on volume of sales has been significant with 77.85 percent ($\bar{R}^2 = 0.7785, p > .01$) in the four retail stores while the shopping advantage card (SAC) loyalty program in two retail stores made 73.70 percent $\left(\bar{R}^2 = 0.7370, p > .001\right)$ impact on the volume of sales. The categorical analysis on point of sales promotions in the retail stores is exhibited in Table 4.

It has been observed that the longer the consumers are attracted by the point of sales promotions, product promotions, innovation and technology, and '*do it yourself*' (DIY) and *eye-track experience* (ETE), the more spendthrift they become. Many customers derived satisfaction by perceived use value and post-promotion customer relation services rendered by the retail stores. Accordingly, the results discussed in the Table 4 are consistent with the hypothesis **H1**.

Sales in response to point of sales promotions during the leisure season are stimulated also by the personal interactions with the employees of retail stores, in-store demonstrations, and hands-on experiences to customers. The post-promotion satisfaction is perceived by the customers as economic and relational advantages on products, brands and services of the retail stores. Sensitivity analysis has been performed to study which factors affect change in the buying decision of customers in reference to point of sales promotions offered by the retail stores. Variables sensitivity has been computed as a series of tests in which the different variable values were set to see how a change in the variable causes a change in the dynamic buying behavior of customers. The sensitivity coefficient $\beta$ has been computed using the following linear model:

$$MaxZ_p = Z_r + \beta\,(p_a, v_a)\Delta B_{tt} \quad (1)$$

Wherein, $Z_p$ represents maximizing promotional sales, $Z_r$ indicates regular retail sales (without promotion), $p_a$ indicates price advantage, $v_a$ shows volume advantage in buying and $\Delta B_{tt}$ represents change in the buying intensity of customers in a given time. The buying sensitivity analysis presented in Table 5 reveals that perceived advantages in reference to economic gains over price and brand have shown higher degree of response to the point of sales promotions. A small change in a variables value of price and volume of products have resulted in relatively large changes in the volume of buying, responding to the point of sales promotion, which may be said to be sensitive to variables of price and volume of products offered in the promotion.

*Table 5. Sensitivity analysis for the variables responding to point of sales promotions*
*n=234*

| Buying Sensitivity Factor | Behavioral Parameters | Sensitivity Estimation Parameters for Point of Sales Promotions | $RS_1$ | $RS_2$ | $RS_3$ | $RS_4$ | ($\chi^2$) and $\beta$ Coefficient |
|---|---|---|---|---|---|---|---|
| $BS_1$ | Compulsive Buying | Comparative advantage<br>Shopping arousal<br>Volume advantage offered<br>Perceived use value<br>Fear of not getting such bargain in near future | 0.852 | 0.721 | 0.624 | 0.939 | 79.38 (0.853*) |
| $BS_2$ | Brand value | Product attractiveness<br>Promotional product line<br>Value for money<br>Quality and uniqueness | 0.642 | 0.691 | 0.488 | 0.759 | 83.55 (0.527**) |
| $BS_3$ | Price advantage | Promotional gain on regular price<br>Affordability and repeat buying | 0.702 | 0.766 | 0.590 | 0.972 | 68.04 (0.739*) |

*p values * >.01 and ** >.001*
*Figures in parentheses indicate $\beta$ Coefficient*

The level of satisfaction derived by the customers, point of sales promotion in reference to comparative advantages, volume gains in buying, higher perceived use value and fear of not having such bargain significantly affect the buying sensitivity leading to compulsive buying [$BS_1$, ($\beta = 0.853, p > .01$)]. The buying sensitivity is also affected by the brand value of products in reference to product attractiveness, product line, value for money, quality and uniqueness of the products offered in the point of sales promotions in the retail stores [$BS_2$,($\beta = 0.527, p > .001$) ]. It may also be seen from the result exhibited in the Table that price advantage also plays significant role in stimulating the customer response on point of sales promotions [$BS_3$, ($\beta = 0.739, p > .01$)]. Accordingly, the results presented in Table 4 are consistent with hypothesis **H2 (a) and H2 (b)**.

Results of correlation metrics indicate a higher degree correlation between the interpersonal communication and in-store product experience ($V_1$, $V_2$), and variety of products and randomness, and in-store product experience ($V_4$, $V_2$). Uniqueness and perceived use value and tore brand preferences ($V_4$, $V_5$) are also highly correlated Similarly variables related to shopping arousal and impulse, store brand preference ($V_5$, $V_6$) also have shown high correlation. Comparative advantage as a variable that influenced the point of sales promotion buying decision among the customers has shown high correlation with all major variables of the study. The correlations among these variables are exhibited in Table 6.

It may be observed from the results of the Table below that the correlation coefficient has a maximum value of 0.927 which showed significant concern on multi-

*Table 6. Inter-group[a] correlation matrices (n=234)*

| Major variables influencing point of sales promotions | $V_1$ | $V_2$ | $V_3$ | $V_4$ | $V_5$ | $V_6$ | $V_7$ |
|---|---|---|---|---|---|---|---|
| Interpersonal communication ($V_1$) | **1.000** | | | | | | |
| In-store product experience ($V_2$) | 0.831* | **1.000** | | | | | |
| Uniqueness and perceived use value ($V_3$) | 0.592** | 0.621* | **1.000** | | | | |
| Variety of products and randomness ($V_4$) | 0.597** | 0.704* | 0.668* | **1.000** | | | |
| Store brand preference ($V_5$) | 0.451 | 0.574** | 0.306 | 0.682* | **1.000** | | |
| Shopping arousal and buying impulse ($V_6$) | 0.542** | 0.784* | 0.728* | 0.843* | 0.775* | **1.000** | |
| Comparative advantage ($V_7$) | 0.573** | 0.822* | 0.868* | 0.927* | 0.822* | 0.819* | **1.000** |

*p-values * >.01 and ** >.001*

[a] *Variable segments are formed from the variable groups chosen for the study as exhibited in Table 1*

colinearity between the variables- comparative advantage and variety of products and randomness in promotion ($V_7$, $V_4$). It has been observed during the study that attractive in-store ambience further escalates the shopping arousal of customer and their level of satisfaction remains high though the long term customer value is influenced by both the price and non- price factors associated with the product. However, performances of point of sales promotions in retail stores also depend on just-in-time supplies, impulsive displays, and efficient customer services. Hence, the results exhibited in Table 6 are consistent with hypothesis **H3 (a)**.

Redundancy in the results which exhibited some degree of biasness in inter-correlations among variables has been minimized using Monte Carlo (MC) method. Bias is largely affected by sample size and biasness was found to decrease by increasing the volume of data. It has been observed that inter-correlation bias tends to decrease as the inter-correlations between the two sets of variables increase. The numbers of predictors and criterion variables, as well as the size of the correlations between variables in each set, has relatively minimal effect on bias (Beth, 1982). MC method is a useful technique to compute numerical integration and sort out the redundancy in the statistical results. A procedure for averaging correlation coefficients using the Eigen value of an inter-correlation matrix was adopted in the study using Monte Carlo methods (*e.g.* Dunlap *et al*, 1987), which is known as Kaiser average. This process has substantially reduced the bias for correlations near zero and showed slightly smaller standard errors (greater efficiency) than the other averages for small correlations.

As the data has been organized following normative distribution, in many observations the biasness of inter-correlations in results was minimized. However,

*Table 7. Sales of store brands during point of sales promotions (n=234)*

| Retail Stores | Point of sales promotion led sales (in US $ per capita) | | | Percent sales of store brands against non-store brands |
|---|---|---|---|---|
| | Average sales in response to Point of sales Promotion | Distribution of volume of sales by brand categories | | |
| | | Store Brands | Non-store brands | |
| $RS_1$ | 124.63 | 80.81 | 43.82 | 64.84 |
| $RS_2$ | 129.45 | 70.38 | 59.07 | 54.37 |
| $RS_3$ | 86.92 | 43.99 | 56.25 | 46.20 |
| $RS_4$ | 95.22 | 52.29 | 42.93 | 54.91 |
| **Average** | **109.05** | **61.86** | **50.51** | **56.73** |

due to computational limitations of the data, the statistical prejudice could not be fully eliminated. The results are more likely to project a relationship from the perspectives of judgments and efficacy. The biasness of illusory correlation effect on the judgment similarity of variables relationship, or of whether the relationship of one variable induces another, has also been statistically minimized using the MC method.

It has been observed during the study that customers had experienced higher attraction towards the store brands as compared to the non-store brands due to low price and acceptable quality at par with the non-store brands. Results exhibited in Table 7 show that sale of store brands during the promotional program in a retail store is 56.73 percent on an average. This fact establishes that the customers who are loyal to particular retail store would take maximum advantage of point of sales promotional programs. The loyalty programs are largely governed through ECC, SAC and EIP promotional programs administered by the retail stores. The post-promotion satisfaction has been experienced by the customers when the promotional program benefits are combined with future events of the stores. The point of sales promotion programs in retails stores largely influence shopping arousal and contribute towards augmenting the sales of store brands among loyal customers. Hence, the results presented in the Table 7 are consistent with hypothesis **H3 (b)**.

## MANAGERIAL IMPLICATIONS

The promotional effects generated from various promotional tools may be monitored for longer periods of time and measured in reference to achieving the long-term goals of retail firms. Also, variability of promotional response in different retail markets, channels and outlets should be analyzed for making required modifications in process of delivery of promotional programs to the customers. Such management strategy would allows for better promotion planning and marketing effectiveness, with consequences that extend beyond economic benefits for the retail company itself and reverberate on relationships with suppliers and cooperative promotion decisions. Retailers must be strategic about pulling unprofitable products from the shelves and avoiding high-volume but low-profit customer segments. Retailing firms must expand aggressively into new markets and once the retailing firms saturate markets with outlets, they can sustain their earnings growth by improving the mix of products sold offering attractive sales promotions. At times, retailers also need to alter their promotion, advertising and merchandising strategies to better respond to the preferences of potential customers. Thus, sales promotion programs should be strategically conceived considering long term effects on volume of sales and building loyalty among customers.

The sales promotion programs need to be a part of the agenda of marketing managers and stretched for long period with regular intervals. Appropriate promotional strategies considering the economic and behavioral variables discussed in the study may be developed by the managers upon measuring the intensity of buying in response to sales promotions and maximizing consumer satisfaction and increase the volume of sales.

As customer satisfaction is one of the principal measures of retailing performance and buying behavior in response to sales promotions offered by the retailing firms, the focus of sales promotion need to be oriented towards augmenting the loyalty attitude and customer values. The strategy paradigm for augmenting such effect is exhibited in Figure 2. At the retail point of purchase convergence of customer loyalty, value for money and competitive product advantages drives the loyalty of retail stores. Also manager need to measure periodically the buying potential of customers and propensity of spending towards merchandise in retail store to plan the sales promotion programs effectively. Success of retail firms grow with the customer satisfaction, brand value, repeat buying behavior and increase in the sales of products. A strategic focus considering how customers and competitors will react to any promotional effort, as well as the message delivered and the stature in

*Figure 2. Point of sales promotions, consumer behavior and loyalty attitude*

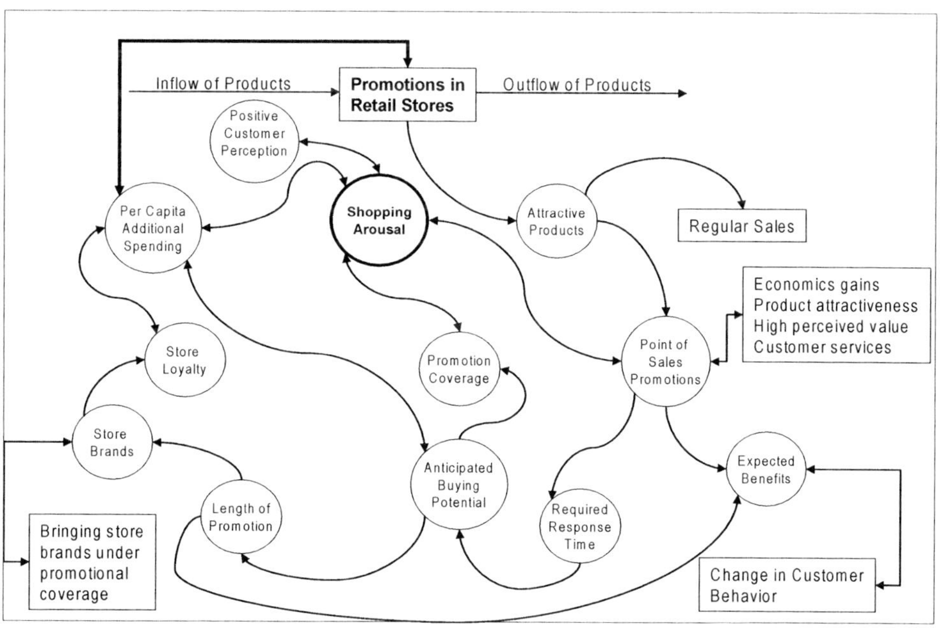

the marketplace of the brand delivering should be developed by the firms in order to strengthen and streamline the pre-purchase promotions in marketplace. Hence, managers should not only tailor promotion programs successfully to target customers, but also skillfully monitor its implementation through customer culture and competition challenges.

## CONCLUSION

Sales promotions are considered as short-term instruments usually designed to yield an immediate sales effect. Point of sales promotion programs has become the principal tool of retailers in Mexico to acquire new customers and retain the loyal customers. There is a variety of promotional strategies employed by the retailing firms during leisure seasons observed three times per annum. It is found that loyal customers are attracted to the store brands during the promotional offers while new shoppers are price sensitive and are attracted by the in-store ambience of sales promotions and volume discounts. Retail sales promotions largely are built around price or volume discount offers. Retailing firms attempt to influence buying behavior of customers by launching attractive promotional campaigns and introduce changes in their price policies, among other actions. Periodical price discounts offered by the retailers exerts greater influence on the store brand choice over the non-store brand preferences. However, type of promotion and level of retailer dominance have significant effects on volume of sales, acquiring new customers and continuing with loyalists. The discussions in study reveal that point of sales promotions significantly stimulate the buying behavior among customers towards compulsive buying driven by the factors of hidden fear of not getting such bargain in the future, product attractiveness and in-store shopping arousal. It has also been observed in the study that customers develop higher preference for store brands, enhanced use value and repeat buying behavior through hands-on experience of product.

## LIMITATIONS OF THE STUDY

Like many other empirical studies this research might also have some limitations in reference to sampling, data collection and generalization of the findings. Samples drawn for the study might have been insufficient to generalize the study results. Questionnaires were translated in Spanish for the respondents in Mexico which might have conveyed varied conceptual sense to some extent. The open ended questions were answered by the Mexican respondents in Spanish and occasionally some issues might have been overlooked during the translation of questionnaires.

The study does not indicate as how behavior control, quality differentiation, and promotion design efficiency overrule the price and volume discount stimuli among the customers. Besides, the study might also have limitation concerning some biases driving shopping arousal among the customers during the point of sales promotions such as at times virtual shopping may overweigh the price promotions. However to ensure that the data cover a wider spatial and temporal dimensions in the study region, data should be cleansed and filtered with many variability factors affecting the consumer behavior and retailer performance.

## FUTURE RESEARCH PROSPECTS

Future research could examine issues related to the customer perceptions of quality and design of sales promotion programs for sustained response. The impact of economic variables on the shopping arousal and compulsive buying behavior in response to competitive sales promotions may also be considered in reference to market orientation of a retailing firm. The role of retail competition, account retail strategy, and demographics in determining promotional response are also potential issues to be pondered over in future research. Issues related to effectiveness retail promotional programs, with the premise that level of local market dominance will impact on increasing the volume of sales and enhancing the gamut of customers may also be considered as potential for carrying further research.

## REFERENCES

Parsons, A. G., & Ballantine, P. W. (2004). Market dominance, promotions, and shopping mall group performance. *International Journal of Retail & Distribution Management, 32*(10), 458-463.

Parlar, M., Perry, D., & Stadje, W. (2007). Optimal shopping when the sales are on - A markovian full-information best-choice problem. *Stochastic Models, 23*(3), 351-371.

Rajagopal (2008). Outsourcing salespeople in building arousal towards retail buying. *Journal of Database Marketing and Customer Strategy Management, 15*(2).

Rajagopal (2007a). Influence of brand name in variety seeking behavior of consumers: An empirical study. *International Journal of Management Practice, (24)*, 306-323.

Rajagopal (2005). Buying decisions towards organic products: Analysis of customer value and brand drivers. *International Journal of Emerging Markets, 2*(3), 236-251.

Coad, T. (2006). The future for `do-it-yourself' customer service. *Journal of Database Marketing & Customer Strategy Management, 13*(4), 324-330.

MacMillan, I. C., & McGrath, R. G. (1997). Discovering new points of differentiation. *Harvard Business Review, 75*(4), 133-145.

Johnson, L. K. (2006). Successful business process outsourcing. *Sloan Management Review, 47*(2), 5-6.

Ndubisi, N. O., & Moi, C. T. (2005). Customers behavioral responses to sales promotion: the role of fear of losing face. *Asia Pacific Journal of Marketing and Logistics, 17*(1), 32-49.

Gilbert, D. C., & Jackaria, N. (2002). The efficacy of sales promotions in UK supermarkets: a consumer view. *International Journal of Retail & Distribution Management, 30*(6), 315-322.

Laroche, M., Pons, F., Zgolli, N., Cervellon, M. C., & Kim, C. (2003). A model of consumer response to two retail sales promotion techniques. *Journal of Business Research, 56*(7), 513-522.

Watkins, M., & Bond, C. (2007). Ways of experiencing leisure. *Leisure Sciences, 29*(3), 287-307.

Carpenter, J. M., Moore, M., & Fairhurst, A. E. (2005). Consumer shopping value for retail brands. *Journal of Fashion Marketing and Management, 9*(1), 45-53.

Fam, K. S. (2003). Managing an effective promotion campaign: lessons from retail advertisers in New Zealand, Portugal and Hungary. *Marketing Intelligence & Planning, 21*(5), 282-291.

Vicdan, H., Chapa, S., & de Los Santos, G. (2007). Understanding compulsive buyers' online shopping incidence: A closer look at the effects of sales promotions and bargains on Hispanic Americans. *Journal of Customer Behaviour, 6*(1), 57-74.

Kyrios, M., Frost, R. O., & Steketee, G. (2004). Cognitions in compulsive buying and acquisition. *Cognitive Therapy and Research*, 28(2), 241-258.

Dobson, J. (2007). Aesthetics as a foundation for business activity. *Journal of Business Ethics, 72*(1), 41-46.

Platz, L. A., & Temponi, C. (2007). Defining the most desirable outsourcing contract between customer and vendor. *Management Decision, 45*(10), 1656-1666.

Rajagopal (2007b). Stimulating retail sales and upholding customer value. *Journal of Retail and Leisure Property, 6*(2), 117-135.

d'Astous, A., & Jacob, I. (2002). Understanding consumer reactions to premium-based promotional offers. *European Journal of Marketing, 36*(11), 1270-1286.

Zhou, L., & Wong, A. (2004). Consumer impulse buying and in-store stimuli in Chinese supermarkets. *Journal of International Consumer Marketing, 16*(2), 37-53.

Berry, L. L. (2001). The old pillars of new retailing. *Harvard Business Review, 79*(4), 131-137.

Shoham, A., & Brencis, M. M. (2003). Compulsive buying behavior. *Journal of Consumer Marketing, 20*(2), 127-138.

Batra, R., Lehmann, D., & Singh, D. (1993). The brand personality component of brand Goodwill: Some antecedents and consequences. In Aaker & Bie (Eds.), *Brand equity and advertising : Advertising's role in building strong brands* (pp. 83-95). Hillsdale: Lawrence Erlbaum Associate Publishers.

Duncan, T., & Moriarty, S. E. (1998). A communication based marketing model for managing relationships. *Journal of Marketing, 62*, 1-13.

Saegert, J., Hoover, R. J., & Hilger, M. T. (1985). Characteristics of Mexican American consumers. *Journal of Consumer Research, 12*, 104–109.

Richins, M. L. (1994). Valuing things: The public and private meanings of possessions. *Journal of Consumer Research, 21*, 504–521.

D'Andrea, G., Schleicher, M., & Lunardini, F. (2006). The role of promotions and other factors affecting overall store price image in Latin America. *International Journal of Retail & Distribution Management, 34*(9), 688-700.

Otieno, R., Harrow, C., & Lea-Greenwood, G. (2005). The unhappy shopper, a retail experience: Exploring fashion, fit and affordability. *International Journal of Retail & Distribution Management, 33*(4), 298-309.

Liu, T. C., & Wu, L. W. (2007). Customer retention and cross-buying in the banking industry: An integration of service attributes, satisfaction and trust. *Journal of Financial Services Marketing, 12*(2), 132-145.

Anselmsson, J. (2006). Sources of customer satisfaction with shopping malls: A comprehensive study of different customer segments. *The International Review of Retail, Distribution and Consumer Research, 16*(1), 115-138.

Backstrom, K. (2006). Understanding recreational shopping, *The International Review of Retail, Distribution and Consumer Research, 16*(2), 143-158.

*Narver, J. C., & Slater, S. F. (1990). The effect of market orientation on business profitability. Journal of Marketing, 54(4), 20-35.*

Hunt, S. D., & Morgan, R. M. (1995). The comparative advantage theory of competition. *Journal of Marketing, 59*(2), 1-15.

Jaccard, J., Turrisi, R., & Wan, C. K. (1990). *International effects in multiple regression.* Thousand Oaks, CA: Sage University Press.

Parasuraman, A., Zeithaml, V., & Berry, L. (1988). SERVQUAL: A multiple-item scale for measuring consumer perceptions in services quality. *Journal of Retailing, 64*(1), 12-40.

Ruekert, R. W. (1992). Developing a market orientation: An organizational strategy perspective. *International Journal of Research in Marketing, 9*(3), 225-245.

Doron, G., Kyrios, M., & Moulding, R. (2007). Sensitive domains of self-concept in obsessive–compulsive disorder (OCD): Further evidence for a multidimensional model of OCD. *Journal of Anxiety Disorders, 21*(3), 433-444.

Otieno, R., Harrow, C., & Lea-Greenwood, G. (2005). The unhappy shopper, a retail experience: Exploring fashion, fit and affordability. *International Journal of Retail & Distribution Management, 33*(4), 298-309.

Clement, J. (2007). Visual influence on in-store buying decisions: An eye-track experiment on the visual influence of packaging design. *Journal of Marketing Management, 23*(9-10), 917-928.

Codispoti, M., & De Cesarei, A. (2007). Arousal and attention: Picture size and emotional reactions. *Psychophysiology, 44*(5), 680-686.

Wirtz, J., Mattila, A. S., & Tan, R. L. P. (2007). The role of arousal congruency in influencing consumers' satisfaction evaluations and in-store behaviors. *International Journal of Service Industry Management, 18*(1), 6-24.

Menon, S., & Kahn, B. (2002). Cross-category effects of induced arousal and pleasure on the internet shopping experience. *Journal of Retailing, 78*(1), 31-40.

Mulhern, F. J., & Williams, J. D. (1994). A comparative analysis of shopping behavior in Hispanic and non-Hispanic market areas. *Journal of Retailing, 70*, 231–251.

Deshpande, R., Hoyer, W. D., & Donthu, N. (1986). The intensity of ethnic affiliation: A study of the sociology of Hispanic consumption. *Journal of Consumer Research, 13*, 214–220.

Ganesh, J., Arnold, M. J., & Reynolds, K. E. (2000). Understanding the customer base of service providers: An examination of the difference between Switchers and Stayers. *Journal of Marketing, 64*, 65-87.

Beth, K., D-S. (1982). Correcting for BIAS in the Canonical Redundancy Statistic, *Educational and Psychological Measurement, 42*(1), 131-143.

Dunlap, W. P., Silver, C. N., & Phelps, G. R. (1987). A Monte Carlo study of using the first eigenvalue for averaging intercorrelations. *Educational and Psychological Measurement, 47*(4), 917-923.

# Chapter IX
# Internet, Reengineering and Technology Applications in Retailing

**Rajagopal**
*Monterrey Institute of Technology and Higher Education, ITESM, Mexico*

International electronic network began in 1968 by the Advanced Research Projects Agency of Department of Defense known as ARPAnet in view to connect different university networks for wider exchange of academic information world over. The ARPAnet is first step in setting up global information network through intermediate networks compatible to the personal computers. The ARPAnet, in 80's was divided into two networks called Millet and NSFnet. The former network was used for the government information purposes while the latter network was intended for information sharing in research and education. The rapid growth in computer technology and commercial needs have allowed significant changes in the information management systems. There emerged in early nineties many commercial network backbones to link with the NSFnet to provide market information to the business firms. The Internet today is a combination of NSFnet and commercially available backbone services disseminating information on the decentralized networks all over the world. It is estimated that there are over 30,000 computer networks connecting over 2 million computers with each other on the Web. In view of the increasing use of electronic information sources through the networks the Transmission Control Protocol/Internet Protocol (TCP/IP) has been designed and made essential for each user networks to abide with the protocol standards which enables the data transfer and retrieval at source. It has been estimated that about

21.92 percent of total world population is using Internet in 2008 and the usage rate has grown by 305.5 percent during 2000-2008 (Internet World Statistics, 2008). Internet usage has been extended from fixed lines to broad band, and further to mobile Internet surfing. Large number of mobile phone users have adopted mobile Internet. Interestingly, the demographics and usage patterns of consumers showed that users perceived higher importance of having mobile Internet capabilities for services marketing including retail banking (Jiang, 2008).

## THE MARKET SIZE

It is estimated that over 120 million companies and households are benefited to share information through Internet as a major communication link through interactive advertisement, bulletin boards and on-line discussions on the research and educational issues. Commercially Internet has been used by the business houses as a media for advertisements and indenting goods and services by the individuals. Internet has become the place for Direct Marketing. The net represents a market of approximately $1200 billion as estimated in 2004. The Internet serves as a catalogue shop for the business houses and it has been proved beneficial to small companies which desire to expand their market but have limited financial resources. Internet provides opportunities for inputting advertisements, contests for consumer products, marketing research results and fashion news world wide for befitting the international marketing research.

Goods sold over the Internet during 1993 were worth$100 million which tripled in 1995 endorsing the effective use of net for business to business transactions and household (Boisseau, 1995). The growth rate of users of Internet is found to be 10 percent and the projections for the year 2007 reveal that the users' number will reach 1400 million. Currently the composition of Internet users shows 75 percent business houses and 25 percent academic institutions engaged in research and development. Smaller business houses have discovered Internet cost-effective for marketing communications. Advertising on Internet is less expensive as compared to any other electronic or print media. It is projected that by the year 2000 Internet will be used by 60 percent of the large companies and 30 percent of medium and small size companies out of the total users of the business community. The increasing shares belong to business promoters who want to drive in occasionally in the international market. As regards the household users, there were 31 percent of households owning personal computers and using the Internet facilities. The communications experts have predicted that by the year 2000 about 85 percent of the household will be able to use the on-line services. Demographically Internet has attracted about 50 percent of the users of young age falling within 25 years (Paul, 1996).

## GROWTH OF SALES AND ADVERTISING

Marketing on Internet has performed $60 billion for the US business firms in 1995 through the catalogue and home shopping sales. The Home Shopping Network which has recently bought the Internet Shopping Network sells 20,000 goods and services for 1000 vendors receiving about 25 million indented per day on an average. It is expected to raise the Internet advertisement for about 10 million products by the end of 1996. The cost of advertising on Home Shopping Network ranges between $25,000 and $75,000 per annum (Computor World, 1994). The net has been used for advertising brands, retailing goods and services, political opinions, directory based sales, direct response advertisements, sales of industrial goods and services, institutional information and public interest information. Advertising on Internet is found to be less effective than on any media. The reason is that advertising on Internet is based on quality of graphics used, content of the message, sound and the overall design of the advertisement rather than time and frequency oriented unlike other media approaches. The cost of that advertisement on Internet is on an average one third of the amount spent on advertisements in any electronic or print media. The reach of the advertisement on Internet is very high and frequency is unlimited. The advertising on Internet provides global opportunities in view of its high accessibility and utility. The viewership of advertisements of goods and services are measured on hourly, monthly and yearly basis to endorse the consumer opinion. Advertisers can buy space on the Internet through the service provider-a private company. The advertising cost varies between $240 and $20,000 per annum. Internet offers the following primary shopping and advertising browsers.

- Web Shops
- Internet Malls
- Downtown Anywhere

The Web shops provide advertising and marketing opportunity to the business firms on the World Wide Web (WWW) which consists of individual home sites[1] displaying specific information of goods and services. The Web shops currently serve 400 commercial firms at a flat fee of $25,000 per annum. Virtual Shopping Centers owned like Shopping 2000, AT&T's Electronic Shop etc. also advertise text, image or audio of the site owners. These service shops are called Internet Malls and cost of advertising on these malls vary between $1200 and $25,000 per annum. The service charges include creating, maintaining and promotion of advertisements on the Internet. The Downtown Anywhere is a shopping network set up like a city on the Internet. Internet usage is frequent among urban consumers and the use of e-commerce is basically unaffected by the size of the city where the household lives. However, in some countries where terrain is difficult for supplies remote consumers are discouraged from purchasing goods on virtual shops as they cannot inspect them beforehand. Leisure activities and cultural items (i.e., books, CDs, and tickets for museums and theaters) are the only goods and services for which e-commerce is used more in isolated areas. Internet is a proactive tool for reducing shopping distances to all consumer segments (de Blasio, 2008).

The major problem which has cropped-up due to increasing number of Internet users is the security of the information disseminated on the net. In early days of exploring the net, there was little security and the business firms are risk averse of getting their products pirated, unauthorized designing, production and sales. E-commerce has witnessed extensive growth in recent years and simultaneously consumers' concerns regarding ethical issues surrounding online shopping have also grown manifold. Performance of e-ratilers is driven by the five factors co-ordination including security, privacy, non-deception, fulfillment and reliability which are strongly predictive of online consumers' satisfaction and trust (Roman, 2007). Faster penetration of new electronic applications and the inclusion of a higher number of potentially unknown users, the business processes are more vulnerable against malicious attacks than traditional systems. Economic globalization has also led to complex decentralized company structures using extensively distributed IT-systems (Herrmann and Herrmann, 2006). Security is a systematic issue which covers product design, implementation, logistic, manufacture and sales management. With the exponential growth of electronic business in the recent past, the security of e-payment which is an important part of e-supply chain management (eSCM), becomes a critical issue as a large amount of payment in transactions is made via point of sales (PoS) devices (Yang *et al*, 2007). A recent study reveals there are value-based external factors in e-trust building that consumers perceive as risks in e-commerce and value-based behavioral patterns in e-trust building. These factors help costumers to reduce perceived risks and build trust in e-commerce transactions. It is also observed that e-trust building process is different based on individuals' personal values including excitement and security (Pennanen *et al*, 2007).

## MARKETING PERFORMANCE

The innovations in the technology of production has major bearing on the quality of the product and the technology for the advertising and packaging make dent in the presentation of the goods and services of the any company in the market. The new technologies create opportunities by providing means of the new products as well as improvement in the existing products of the company. The Web marketing through Internet has added value to the advertising, distribution and retailing of the goods and services. The marketing approaches through Internet can facilitate the marketer in three ways – it provides access to the customers to the dynamically updated the technological changes in reference to the physical attributes of the goods and services, provides access to the competitor's use of advanced technology and provides a medium to understand consumer behavior and need for new technology. In the virtual market place - "Internet", the principal product is information. The role of Internet in retailing is exhibited in Figure 9.1. Most of the corporate houses across the world are now attempting to exploit the marketing opportunities of the World Wide Web (WWW) on the assumption that this network is the strongest for disseminating the data about goods and services. The digitized products and services, news, music, video clippings and general information about the company can be effectively distributed through net bypassing the traditional channels. The information on the goods and services on the net will not only provide the business to the company but also provide the source of differentiation.

Achieving an integrated e-commerce system in the industries could be accomplished by adopting a state-of-art information technology. However, it is too costly and lack of knowledge of such technology for widespread adoption by these industries. It is found that in many emerging markets e-commerce has penetrated down to the small scale industrial production section. The current usage of electronic commerce in the Hong Kong textile and clothing industries is mainly through e-mail communication (Lau *et al*, 2008). Global competitiveness places more pressure on companies to improve their delivery performance of products and services to customers. In an effort to improve the quality of delivery service, companies

*Figure 9.1 Value difference in marketing through Internet*

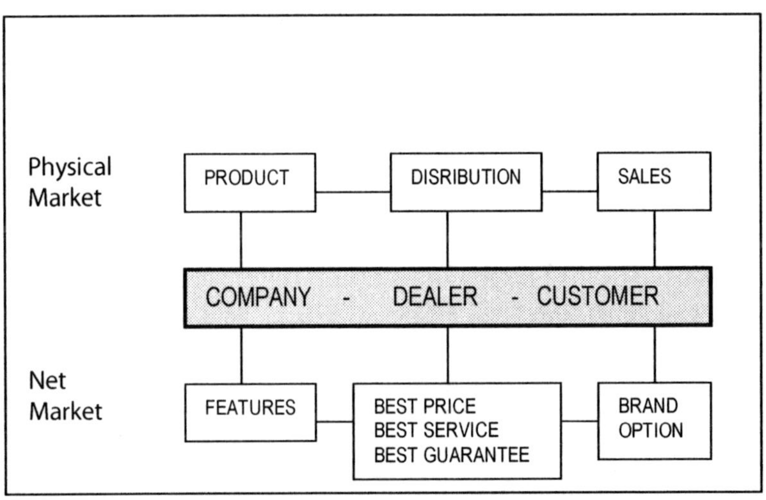

have outsourced their logistics services, including packing, inventory management and shipping of goods to customers. Communication plays an important role in integrating the activities along the logistics value chain. Information technologies such as electronic data interchange, the Internet, WWW and e-commerce have contributed greatly to improving communication with partners in the logistics chain (Gunasekaran et al, 2007). The advantage of the net market is that it provides customer the choice of the brand for the best price, service and guarantee for the product. It has been observed that the service oriented and information products are ideal to be placed on the net for marketing. The net has also enabled the dealers of small markets or niche who have significantly lower costs, to make their price competitive deals be known to the potential customers. Internet marketing also helps the customer to place his orders without incurring any costs and at the same time manufacturer can avail information. Internet is an important venue for growth and expansion among retail entrepreneurs in developing nations. Electronic markets have intensely affected competition and market structures and are capable of promoting competition in retailing and increase customized services efficiency primarily by reducing buyer and seller search costs (Li *et al*, 2006).

The Del Computers of United States which operates on the system which is linked to it's just in time manufacturing system. Only after the customer places the order the system is assembled and delivered by the Del Company. This company operates totally on the net based customer interface for promoting its sales. The net marketing helps the company also to develop strategies for product pull and push. The first generation advertising and selling initiatives of the companies involved pull strategy. The second generation strategies were more sensibly developed, but still could not match the profile of the companies, desired target audience with that of user portals, search engines or content providers. The third generation initiatives are transforming to push strategies like positioning advertising and digital store fronts on sites where there is highest probability of net visitors. The requirements of the net promotion strategy are simple - a demographic and psycho-graphic match. Marketing using Internet services have become common as virtual shopping is getting more secured in performing business transactions. Most companies have their own Websites to promote their company products and services aiming at developing their business today. Contents in customer-centered Websites are valuable asset in recognizing macro-marketing trends and real-time customers' needs. However, different semantic patterns used in various parties may have great challenges in the comprehension of the content in the Website (Li *et al*, 2007). Moreover, organizational sales transaction system such as Management Information System (MIS) can help to determine sales performance of well-known customers.

- Retail Sales
- Business to business sales
- Reducing purchasing costs
- Reducing customer support costs
- Subscription fees
- Advertising sales
- Reducing public relations, market research and recruitment costs

The marketing approaches through Internet enables the customers to browse through various options, pick new products, test the service and compare with the competing goods and services. The Internet marketing services will add value by widening the customer choice, providing flexibility, letting the customer shop as and when required without bar on the time and enabling him to look for the best deal. In this process the companies gain loyalty of the customers, offer return visits, referrals and better margins. The electronic net based marketing companies out source their operations from the customer and being paid a premium for it.

## INTERNET RETAILING

Shopping behavior of consumers has shifted with the increasing applications of Internet forcing retailers to redefine their roles to ensure their place in the Internet age. E-commerce supported with secured Internet is making an impact, providing the benefits of capturing a global audience 24 hours a day, seven days a week. Lately, the longer working day is driving customers away from queues at shopping malls and turning them to the convenience of the Internet. In travel and tourism industries, retail services stores are losing business to Internet competitors. The future losers will be the toy stores that do not have a strong online presence. The advantage of online shopping is that a shopper can check to see if the product is in stock, determine its suitability, and make a purchase, all without standing in a queue or fighting for a parking space. One characteristic of online consumer behavior is the low cost of searching for alternatives. Therefore, customer loyalty is more difficult to achieve in the online context than in the offline one (Liang *et al*, 2008). Shopping patterns are changing as customers seek added value from their shopping experience, including dramatic cost savings. Customers wishing to send a bouquet to Europe can either visit an *Interflora* accredited florist and make the purchase over the counter or visit the *Interflora* Web site. Internet retailing can be distinguished form conventional practices for the following reasons:

- Easy to place an order

- Long product-line and choices
- Competitive prices
- Faster service and delivery
- Comprehensive information about what is being offered
- No sales pressure
- Convenient payment procedures

Large manufacturers of consumer goods recognize the added benefit of the Internet, especially the one-to-one relationships that it offers. Some large manufacturers have used the Internet to introduce customized shopping options, thus becoming retailers themselves and providing yet another challenge to the traditional store owner. It is observed that shoppers can choose the hair, eye and dress color of the doll they purchase by visiting the Barbie Web site of Mattel Company where shoppers may feel different as service that the traditional stores can not offer. Customization services attract collectors or shoppers prepared to wait for their purchases to be created and delivered. Consumers through Internet shopping gradually reveal their demographics and purchasing patters, including date of birth, average spending, product preferences and hobbies. Web-based businesses largely use this information as a platform to create an interactive loyalty program and database marketing. Although consumers can research high-price items such as cars and real estate via the Internet, analyzing the information on the attributes of offerings, the deal is still more effectively done face to face as confidence of buyers is boosted in personal negotiation. A retailer provides necessary personal contact that the Internet cannot offer. However, in future a successful retail store must build upon what the Internet cannot offer and add value to its customer's shopping experience by giving them that 'something extra' to ensure continued patronage. In contrast, certain industries such as music have won a significant percentage of the market away from retail outlets. There will always be a place for retailers that serve impulse and recreational purchasers, as well as for those that sell products that don't sell well over the Internet. The conventional retail stores need to re-invent store ambience as often their online competitors compete offline and online.

## CONSUMER ACCEPTANCE OF INTERNET CHANNEL

The real breakthrough in e-commerce came with the increased commercial use of the WWW and electronic mail. The use of WWW as a new channel of distribution is still limited but continuously growing. Electronic commerce has the capabilities to function as a new type of non-store retailing, in which the Internet establishes the direct link between the consumer and the retailer or manufacturer by-passing the conventional stores. E-retailing has gained importance in recent past in order to drive consumer behaviour with innovative concepts and tools. The distinguished advantages that e-retailing offers the consumer are as below (Hoffman, 1996):

- 24 hours and 7 days a week availability of retailing
- Instant gratification because of instant information availability
- Interactivity remains with consumer which means the consumer controls the flow of information unlike the conventional retail stores

However, there exist some disadvantages in the non-store retailing in terms of perceived higher risk than the conventional retail stores and also in terms of security issues on all transactions. Large companies have announced joint efforts and task forces working on security issue and they believe that the cryptography designs in near future would help in solving the security problems to some extent (NcCarthy, 1997). There are few measures which offer distinguished risk relief to the consumers for all Web based transactions in terms of providing money-back guarantee, offering well-known brands and selling at reduced prices as compared to the on store retailing (Drik and Leuis, 1996). The retailing functions performed by the WWW may be classified into three broad groups:

- Non-store information channel,
- Non-store reservation channel with a traditional mail or courier service delivery, and
- Non-store purchasing and physical delivery channel

A growing middle class and growth in retail sales have provided high potential to cash in emerging China. Yet outside of the main cities in the vast expanse of rural China, where around 750 million people live the reliance on cash makes it difficult for consumers to spend and for retailers to sell. China has just 530 point-of-sale (POS) terminals and ATMs per million people, far below the 10,000 per million found in the United States. Accordingly, cash is used in 83 percent of all payment transactions in China, compared with just 21 percent in the United States. With most of these terminals and ATMs in China's cities, practically all rural transactions are cash based. This offeres an opportunity in China to wean rural consumers off their reliance on cash might be to add more ATMs and POS terminals. However, we estimate that such an effort would cost at least $2 billion and add just 130 terminals and ATMs per million people. Installing equipment and extending the telecommunications network in remote areas would also take a prohibitively long time. There are alternative mobile payments solutions gaining exposure around the world, but these are not well suited to the needs of rural China such as Seoul and

Tokyo have both introduced a system that allows a transaction to be completed using a mobile phone with a special built-in chip and an in-shop non-contact reader. However, the need to install the reader and to use special and expensive mobile handsets renders the solution inadequate for rural China. An SMS-based payment system, aside from its lower cost, is versatile and ubiquitous. Users simply send an SMS message specifying the mobile-phone number of the payee and the amount to transfer, along with a personal identification number. Within seconds, the payee receives both a confirmation message by SMS and the money in the designated account. The payer receives a confirmation message (Jan *et al*, 2007).

The information channel is being served currently by various powerful search engines on the Web which is largely used by the consumers and in addition to this channel the ordering/re-ordering channel is also functioning for reservation of goods and services. The Internet can not provide physical delivery for goods other than soft ware and the channels have to depend on the air or surface supply chain links. This involves bulk procedures that need to be handled like export-import duties, local laws and security of payment and delivery of goods and services. The consumer acceptance of the good and service ordered/reserved via Internet is more crucial at this juncture. The Web marketing does not help the consumers to get along with their attitude of *touch, feel and pick* the products. However, the Internet for virtual shopping is one of the preferred channels for the consumers of the same region or state or country (Rajagopal, 1999). The Web retailers should appoint the franchisee in various regions to handle the delivery of goods and establish link between the Web retailers and remote consumers. The interactive virtual retailing model is shown in Figure 9.2. Internet-based inter-organizational systems (IIOS) provide the technology infrastructure to facilitate the horizontal flow of information along strategic business partners and vertically flow of information and goods along shippers and consignees. In recent years, logistics providers are instigated to adopt their IIOS in order to cooperate and complete with their rivals. IIOS alter the rules of competition and provide opportunities that logistics providers could reduce transaction costs. However, the adoption of IIOS depends on the construction of information processing technologies to match collaborative strategies (Lai, 2008).

The Web retailers in association with the franchisees should develop interactive home system for consumers and interactive business system for the business to business transactions. However, the electronic retailing channel provides the consumers a scope for wide selection, screening of products out of long catalogue, reliability on brands presented on the net and comparison of price and product features as per the need and utility. An electronic mail survey results revealed that buying goods and services through Internet is perceived to be equivalent to the supermarkets while the mail order process is least preferred by the sample consumers

*Figure 9.2 Strategies for effective virtual shopping*

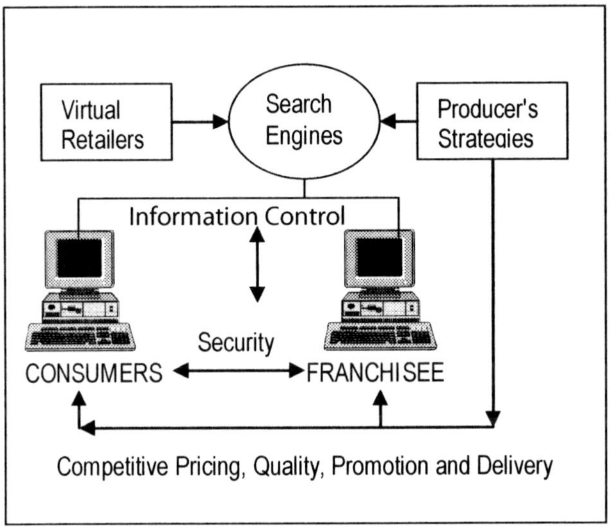


from world over ( N=200). The analysis of the data showed that the heavy Internet users, in terms of number of hours spent surfing the Web, evaluate Internet more favorably than the light users (Rajagopal, 1999). It has been observed during the study that offering money back guarantee and well-known brands are considered to be better risk relievers than simply offering the price reduction. The respondents revealed that the use of information super-highways is more acceptable media for purchasing, reservations or re-ordering with traditional courier service delivery of goods and services.

## INFORMATION SEARCH COSTS

The promise of the electronic commerce on line shopping depends to a great extent on user interfaces and how consumers interact with the computers. In particular, success depends on the understanding of marketers that consumer interaction with information technology influences subsequent consumer behavior through information search costs (Widing and Wayne, 1993). The consumer behavior is largely price sensitive to the information costs particularly in developing countries. Some information search takes longer on-line while others are shorter, depending on the design of the Web site. The consumers may become price sensitive if the on-line retailing reduces the information search costs (Alba, 1997). Internet is a convenient medium for information search or making purchases. The better-educated respondents seem to be less concerned with security issues. They also perceive that Internet shopping provides better prices and more cost savings (Hui and Wan, 2007). It has been observed that the current practices of the industry for the conventional yellow pages for placing large display advertisements is with better serial positions under their banner or selective heading for the senior clients (Abeer and Geral, 1999).

## RE-ENGINEERING BUSINESS FOR COMPETITIVE ADVANTAGE

Business performance of a company matters a lot for customer to orient himself towards its brand, product or services. A company providing aviation or health services to the customer is rated by its efficiency in delivery and recognized by the certification that the company carries to testify its quality of services. Similarly the companies manufacturing and marketing the fast moving consumer goods (FMCG) also get an advantage in gaining large customer response over their rivals on achieving the certification from an international organization for their process, quality and services. The companies operating on the competitive edge should periodically re-engineer their business strategies by adopting various measures. The companies in the developing countries which are open to global trade have started realizing the importance of re-engineering for process improvement in order to acquire competitive strength. The public sector undertakings (PSU) in India have also realized the need for process re-engineering in business while the private sector companies

*Figure 9.3a Re-engineering typology in business*

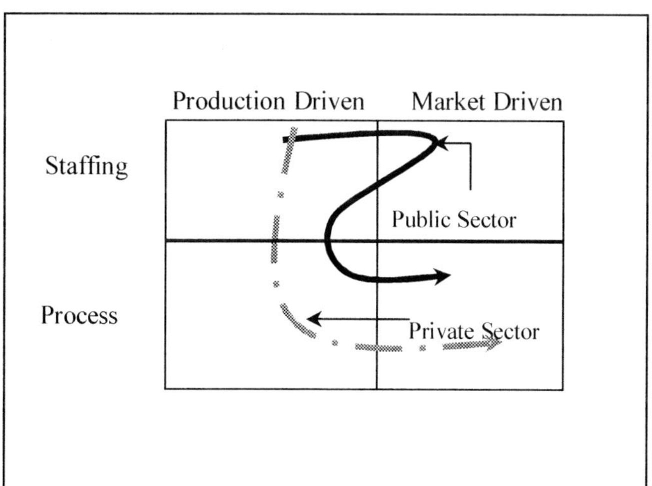

had thought of such change long back. The process orientated production has been leveraging corporate expertise in the market place for over a decade. The business re-engineering typology in Indian context may be seen as exhibited in Figure 9.3a. Initially the PSUs attempted on re-engineering by way of restructuring production and marketing functions and lately some of the PSUs like Bharat Heavy Engineering Corporation, National Thermal Power Corporation, Public Sector Banks, Power Grid, etc. are thriving on process oriented re-engineering to make their stand more competitive in the market. The private sector has re-engineered its business process since long on the line of process change for implementing better product and market driven strategies. The process driven dynamics has been proved to be effective to build the competitive strategies and sustain amidst market competition.

Wireless identification and tracking with radio frequency identification (RFID) technology represents a new way to conduct operations, which creates new benefits and challenges. This technology operates with a reader that identifies the product tag in the warehouse and sends the signal about its movement through a computer based tracking tool as exhibited in Table 9.1. The identification is accomplished by an interrogator, also called a reader or "master," and a tag, also called a transponder or "slave" that has a unique identification code. Data is exchanged between tags and readers using radio waves between the tag and interrogator, and no direct line of sight is required for the transaction. The interrogator asks the tag for the code, or processes the signal being broadcast by the tag, decodes the transmission and transfers the data to a computer. The computer, in turn, may simply record the reading, or look up the tag identification in a database to direct further action, and may also direct the interrogator to write additional information to the tag. The latest generation of RFID allows the dozens of individual objects within a group to be uniquely identified at the same time. This is in contrast to bar codes, which must be read one by one, and can be very advantageous in high-speed reading, sorting and material handling applications.

*Table 9.1 Re-engineering customer value*

| Quality | Service | Cost | Cycle Time |
|---|---|---|---|
| • Customer relationship | • Customer support | • Innovation | • Market preparation |
| • Useful applications | • Flexibility in meeting | • Quality assurance | • Lead time |
| • Minimum variance | customer demands | • Logistics | • Ordering and delivery |
| • Process integrity | • Delivery and service | • Staffing | • Response analysis |
| • Minimizing waste | • Information flow | • Materials management | |
| • Regular improvement | • Value assessment | | |

The low-cost tags generally are have limited data storage capacity, typically 32 to 128 bits, which are read-only (not rewriteable) like bar codes, and have limited read range. On the contrary, high-cost tags are available for many more complicated longer read applications. They often have their own power source for managing large storage databases. RFID systems are available in a wide range of frequencies to suit various performance needs. Frequency is an important factor in transmission range and speed. This is an important consideration when planning logistics and supply chain applications. Most RFID technology used in warehousing and distribution operates at 13.56 MHz (high frequency), 860-930MHz (ultrahigh frequency, or UHF) or the 2.45GHz (microwave) band. Wal-Mart has already begun its RFID pilot with selected distributors in 2006 while other eight suppliers that started shipping a handful of RFID-enabled pallets were Gillette, Hewlett-Packard, Johnson & Johnson, Kimberly-Clark, Kraft Foods, Nestle Purina PetCare, and Procter & Gamble.

## CUSTOMER VALUE AND REENGINEERING PROCESS

In the era of global competition, regardless of whether the company operates in FMCG, industrial goods or services, leading organizations around the world are being driven to rethink their business strategies and reorient them towards process change for reaching higher efficiency levels. In order to engineer their process change it is essential to consider the customer value criteria based on the attributes of four major business determinants - quality, service, cost and time . The customer value metrics is detailed in Table 1.4 among various attributes of quality the companies must look for continuous improvement in the products deliverables and minimize the variances. The customer support in terms of product and price should be prioritized for achieving competitive excellence. The cost factors may need very important consideration in the processes re-engineering as the quality improvement efforts would lead to price rise due to design improvement, quality assurance, restructuring the distribution and logistics strategies, inventory and staffing. The customer value largely depends on the cost of time involved in the change process. Doing re-engineering forces the companies to quantify the business efforts by way of quality, service and cycle time reducing the cost to the customer at the same time increasing the speed of innovation and new-product development. The time required for market preparation includes the concept selling, pre-positioning advertising and information for market initialization. The lead time is the time taken for stabilizing the sales and customer response to the changes engineered in order to outwit, out maneuver and out perform the competitors in the market. In the process of re-engineering the business strategies it is essential for the companies to analyze the customer response to the innovation and modify the entire the process accordingly before finally setting the changes in the market. In all, reengineering the customer value may be expressed in the simple notation as:

$$CV = \frac{Q(S)}{C(T)}$$

Wherein, CV represents customer value. Q and S denote quality of goods and services, and customer services efficiency respectively. Also, in the above equation, cost of goods and services is represented by C in a give time T. The process reengineering concept broadly include the philosophies of *just-in-time* (JIT), *total quality management* (TQM), *break even point analysis* and most recently introduced application of *enterprise resource planning* (ERP). These applications and strategies generate pull and push effects in the market releasing signals to the competitors.

## CORPORATE CONCEPTS OF REENGINEERING BUSINESS

Reengineering business strategies for competitive advantage necessarily makes a company redefine its corporate objectives and bring some differentiation in terms of quality of the products, services offered and the customer governance in the process. A company has to define the following corporate objectives while doing the process of production and marketing reengineered:

- Customer satisfaction and service
- Business safety from the new entrants and existing competitors
- Production efficiency, quality assurance and innovation
- Financial performance and growth
- Customer relationship management and grievances solving
- Creativity in marketing
- Organizational development and human resources

It is possible for a company to take advantage of implementing the process improvements either to enhance its lead in the existing market or to enter new markets, once the company successfully implements the reengineered process along with the value chain elements. The enablers in the process change in a company are people, management, leadership skills, organizational culture, expertise, market place stimuli and the performance measurements. The companies getting prepared to reengineer the business process and sustain in the competition have to give away the bureaucratic way of thinking and must put efforts to shift to the new market

*Figure 9.3b Engineering market interplay*

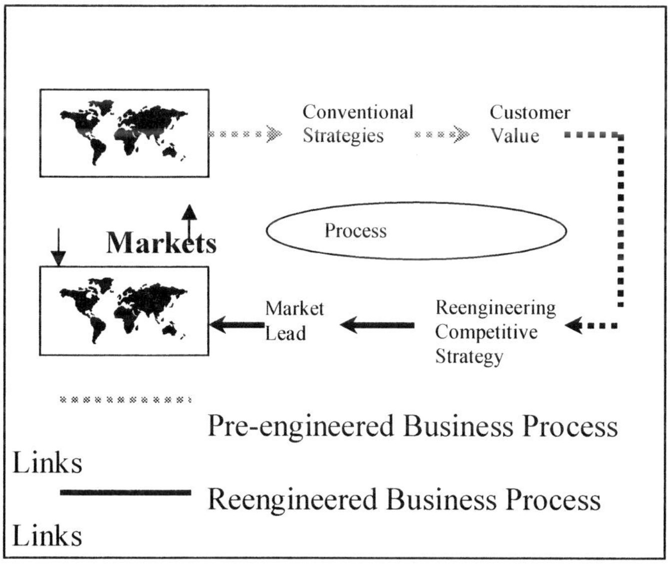


driven paradigms. The Figure 9.3b exhibits the market interplay engineering path for the companies looking to adopt process change strategy for regaining the competitive strength. In this process it is necessary for a company to reorient its team leaders with new paradigm elements and process oriented operations to stand ahead in the competition and outperform the business rivals. Such reorientation must be towards creating vision, articulating and sharing values, transparency in the team work, and relationship management at all levels - customers and channel managers. The company has to develop corporate core team for building functional expertise among the managers implementing the competitive strategies. The company has to establish direct contacts between the market place and customers to have direct control over the flow of goods and services and customer reactions.

The companies open to global trading must accept the challenge of competition. The competitive pressures drive the companies to look at their process and determine that they can become competitive or even leapfrog the competition by focusing on the process, lead attribute and quality. For example, the *Baskin Robbins* Ice Cream Company in its logo writes *31*, the number indicates their distinguished 31 flavors (one flavor a day) which adds to its performance and lead in the market. The Hewlett Packard computers in the early 90's thoroughly redesigned its printers and reengineered by simplifying the process and are now leading in Indian markets. In many instances, competition goes hand in hand with the customer service as the competition is also related to the customer needs. Hence the companies need to redefine their process to connect to the customers and subsequently reengineer them.

Reengineering business process for a company is a systematic approach for gaining strength in three basic areas comprising optimization of cost, handling renewed competitiveness and building competitive dominance in the market. Of many competitive dimensions the product performance, market reach, rate of new product development and innovation, resource leverage and customer loyalty are major ones which need to be emphasized by the company for achieving competitive advantage. The reengineering strategy gives an opportunity to the company to reduce their cost to the optimal level by process improvement and provided competitive focus in achieving best in the market or to be a class brand. The process improvement is fundamentally an approach to clean-up the redundant activities in the business and set up swift process to reach the market. The supply chain management as a function of re-engineering process has been exhibited in Figure 9.4.

## COMPETITIVE FOCUS

The company planning to take lead in the market should develop a strategic vision for dominance in the market place. It should also plan to achieve the output by implementing the strategy successfully. This phase may be viewed as ***discovering*** the competitive strength of the company. Later on the basis of results of discovery the business process need to be ***reengineered*** and ***executed***. These are the three important phases in the reengineering the business function with competitive focus, a company has to be prepared for planning to outwit, outmaneuver and outperform

*Figure 9.4 Reengineering Supply Chain Management Function*

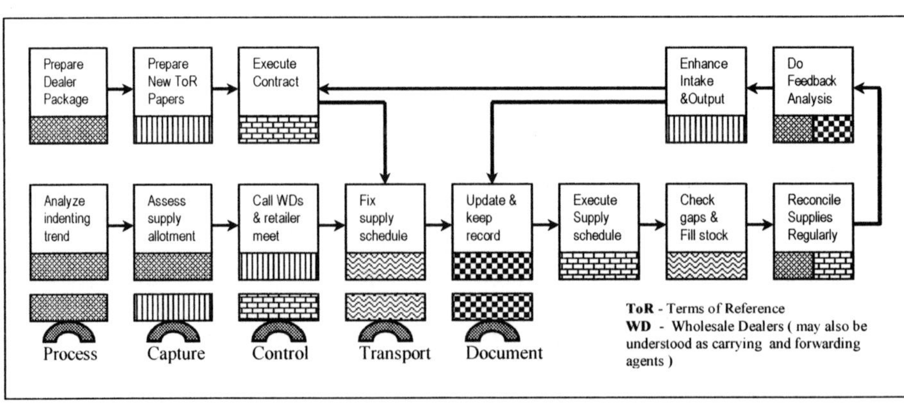

the competitor. There are various factors associated with these phases of change in business strategy for a company to be one of the best companies surviving in the market. The Table 9.2 exhibits the factors associated with the business reengineering phases of dominance redesign and realize.

A company making efforts to become the market leader has to put substantial energy and resources in learning the competitor's move and later unlearn the same among the core team responsible for building strategies. In this process it is necessary to generate new ideas and assess their suitability to administer in the market and adaptability in the work environment of the company. Once the appropriate strategy is selected the core team has to take all steps to apply the same against the move of the competitors. These steps will help the company to play its dominance in the market against the competing forces. The dominance will also help the company to redefine the engineered strategy to its suitability in the market and commitment to apply the same against the competitors. The time taken for realizing the reengineered strategy results against competitors vary according to the intensity of business penetration and customer relationship. However, to get a quick realization to the reengineered business efforts a company has to build teams, plan execution of strategy in detail, confirm investment (if any), assess and recognize the impact. The company, during such market intervention operations has to handle the communications very carefully among the staff members and channel managers to avert any fowl interpretations and actions thereby. Communications to the staff members and channels should be comprehensive in the context of strategy reengineering, the vision of work has to be made known to the concerned, explain rationale and assess the impact. The core team has to be trained to execute the task, control strategic points of the plan and to provide continuous inflow of the impact information to the top management of the company. Any business strategy implemented in the market should have strict measures against the task, time and target. Nevertheless, the cost-benefit assessment is important to evaluate the success of the interventions moved against competitors and redefine the next moves. The ongoing management reviews and key indicators analysis are essential for a company

*Table 9.2. Framework of Reengineering Business Process*

| Dominance | Redesign | Realize |
|---|---|---|
| • Learn and unlearn new ideas<br>• Assess suitability<br>• Make appropriate selection<br>• Apply against competitors | • Learn and unlearn new ideas<br>• Analyze suitability<br>• Redefine and engineer strategy<br>• Commit | • Mobilize people/ staff<br>• Communicate and PR<br>• Execute redesigned packages<br>• Measure performance<br>• Sustain |

to count its sustainability amidst competition in the market. The company must prepare a checklist of strength, weakness, opportunities and threats of in reference to the moves of the competitor. Some of the variable of the SWOT is illustrated in Table 9.3. The company has to prepare for the opportunities and build strategies to overcome the threats from the competitors. There are some factors like advertising and communication where equal opportunities exist for both the potential and rival business companies. This is an innovative sector where higher the creativity and reach larger is the impact on market.

*Table 9.3. Competitor learning: SWOT analysis*

| Indicators | Strong | Weak | Opportunity | Posing Threat |
|---|---|---|---|---|
| Process Technology | | A | B | |
| Quality | | A | B | |
| Cost | A | | | |
| Lead time | B | A | | |
| Delivery time | B | | | A |
| Delivery system | B | A | | |
| Information management | A | | | B |
| Work Team | A | | | B |
| Product support/services | B | A | | |
| Merchandising | A | | | B |
| Marketing and sales | A | | | B |
| R&D | | | B | A |
| Customer price | A | | B | |
| Advertising | | | A B | |
| Robustness | | A | B | |
| Flexibility | A | | B | |
| Differentiation Policy | | A | B | |
| Customer response | B | | | A |
| Customer relationship | A | | | B |
| Correctness to customers | | A | B | |
| Channel management | B | | A | |
| Profit and performance | | A | B | |
| A - Competitor Firm | | B - Your Company | | |

## TECHNOLOGY APPLICATIONS IN RETAILER SERVICES: A CASE STUDY[2]

In general terms, increasing convenience is a way of raising consumers' surplus provided new technology is adopted by the banks in order to offer convenience to the customers may be through an electronic transaction as a substitute for a trip to the branch. The technology based services imply different combinations of accessibility attributes (time, distance, and search costs), ease of use and price. Another factor in determining the magnitude of the surplus that the bank can seize is the relative importance of cross-selling. The bundle of services provided electronically is usually not the same as the one available at a branch. For this reason new technology based banking services with high customer value may offer better service conditions to harmonize the flow of information and services across the spatial and temporal dimensions.

The main financial goals of ING Insurance Americas for 2004 in Mexico were to improve sustainable and profitable growth and value creation in its core business lines and objectives were achieved. Operating expenses rose 4.1% on a comparable basis, due to higher sales costs. In Latin America, premium income declined 10.3% and operating profit before tax fell 23.5% to €231 million, also due to currency effects. In Mexico, the largest contributor to premium income and profits in Latin America, operating profit before tax declined 39.3%. Apart from currency effects, the result was influenced by the profitable sale of the *Seguros Bital* joint venture in 2003, reserve strengthening, higher acquisition costs, and higher claims, particularly in health insurance. Operating profit before tax from Chile, Brazil, Peru and Argentina increased 40.0%. ING Mexico and ING Global Pensions explored a business case to broaden the distribution of life insurance via tied agents. In Brazil, ING and its joint-venture partner, Sul America, began to offer pensions and life insurance in the wake of the reform of the pension system. The first-time value of new business and embedded value for Mexico, Peru and Chile showed healthy pension activities in these countries. In 2004, total fund inflows into the pension funds in Chile, Mexico and Peru increased 33.5% to € 1,542 million (Rajagopal, 2005).

*ING Comercial America* is a Mexican company and a, leader in the insurance, pension benefits and guaranties industry, providing financial services to people who are engaged in developing new projects in Mexico. Recently ING has consolidated its database, providing its employees with real-time availability and easy access to the credit history of its customers. The businesses of the company in Mexico reported very strong performance, with results of US $192.6 million before tax in 2002 due to sustained, favorable underwriting results and expense reductions resulting from operating centralization initiatives. The results of before tax performance shows US $59.9 million for the same period in 2001 reflected in the company's then 49 percent minority ownership in Seguros Comercial America. In June 2001, ING increased its shareholding of Seguros Comercial America and currently wholly owns this business which has been re-branded as ING Comercial America. The company has shown high performance underwriting in Canada and Mexico in reference to property/casualty businesses including successful integration of new acquisitions in markets of both countries. The company has catered to 70 percent of corporate clients and remaining individual customers during 2002. The product-mix of the company included properties/causalities (30 percent), life/health (41 percent) and automobile insurance (29 percent).

## MANAGING AGENTS IN INSURANCE MARKET

In view of increasing competition in insurance companies, it may be argued that different insurance marketing organizations emerge as a means to minimize the costs of correctly matching policyholder risks with insurance coverage. A company may prefer corporate dealing with the prospects and large accounts when the role of agents and promoters is unclear and look for setting-up independent agencies for information dissemination and wider prospecting of new customers. Exclusive dealers are found to be prevalent in relatively standardized, homogeneous product lines and markets, and their agents receive less profit-based compensation than those of independent agency insurers (Laureen and Sharon, 1996). Any company that relies on agents or brokers to bring in business knows how important it is to keep them happy. This goal is critical in the insurance industry, where carriers depend on networks of agents to sell policies and deliver customers. The $600 billion North American property and casualty market is mature, fiercely competitive, and highly fragmented. Given that policies, pricing, and agent compensation within the industry are fairly standardized, why would an agent choose one carrier over another? An answer may lie in the policy of flexibility in business and personalized service. The challenge for insurers is to offer both while increasing the efficiency and cost effectiveness of their operations.

Since agents control the customer relationships and the placement of premium dollars, they wield a growing amount of power. Moreover, as agencies grow in size and bargaining clout, their needs become more sophisticated and they seek carriers that are responsive and flexible, minimize paperwork, make fewer errors, and offer online processing and support. While policy pricing is also important, it is becoming less differentiated and more transparent, thus making agent capabilities and customer service more important. Automated decision making—the norm in personal insurance and currently being adopted by the more complex small commercial lines—can also speed up the application process. Emerging business-rule-engine technologies allow carriers to translate the expert judgment of underwriters into algorithms that can be modified without rewriting core systems (Andre et al, 2005). Leading personal-insurance carriers such as Allstate and Progressive use automated decision making to process up to 95 percent of their applications. The *Consult-Ing* program is one of the automation support provided to the agents of the ING for offering vale added and quick services to the prospects. The automation support to the agents of ING helps the agents to drive the prospects to their quick and sustainable decision on buying the services of the company. Every company knows that it costs far less to hold on to a customer than to acquire a new one and this notion is gradually getting implanted in the services industries. Yet defector customers are far less of a problem than customers who change their buying patterns and incline towards switching. The *Conslut-Ing* of the company is implemented as a tool used to retain the customers and fence the switching options with the customers.

## *Consult-Ing* PROJECT

This is wide area network (WAN) based software for use thorough the computers and PDAs by the sale force which has been introduced by the company in Mexico in order to support the prospecting skills of the sales force of ING. This innovative IT sales force automation has been offered to the sales force of the company for improving the retail business. This project has been launched for 2100 agents and promoter in 2003 which enhanced its outreach to 6464 users in the sales force by the end of 2004 representing 66 percent of the total sales force of the company.

## On-line Solutions

In *Consult-Ing* Web site, agents and promoters carry diverse activities from prospecting to closing the deal and servicing the existing policies by offering on-line solutions to the clients. The sale personnel look for the necessary information on-line to perform their sales daily operations. The on-line solutions to the agents and promoters also include the customization and printing of insurance policies for quick document delivery to the customer after closing the deal. The benefits associated with the use of this software loaded Website has been described in Appendix-A. This Web site has a featured link as "My Production" to view the sales growth and customer reactions on negotiations. This section of the site has been updated every morning at 0800 hr. since December 2003. The number of users for this Web site increased by 62 percent during July 2002 to December 2004 and also marked a 32 percent increase towards the visit to "My Production" link. This link allows the agents and promoters to review accounts and the status of paid and due premiums. The incentives and commissions as per the policy of the company also may be viewed through the link on "My Production". As a sales support Internet tool of ING, *Consult-Ing* provides different services to the agents and promoters which include:

- Surfing on-line information about all insurance products, service branches and about their own performance, and
- To quote and write policies instantly for automobiles and home insurance and make electronic requests for universal variable life (VUV-ING) insurance products.

In October 2003 the company has enhanced the band width of the WAN servers to speed-up the response time of *Consult-Ing* Web site. ING has developed a customized helpdesk for the sales force to provide on-line solution on business issues while prospecting or serving a customer. The link-wise usage of the *Consult-Ing* has been exhibited in the Appendix-B. The software has also featured with useful downloads on financial resources available as "Assesor@" link. This information may also be installed through a CD externally. The package Assesor @ allows initial compilation of the information of prospects as well as knowing the client profile and his product needs to customize the most appropriate solution. The "Portfolio Life Consult" link may be used by the agents and promoters on-line while using the Web-site to know their status on collected premiums, additional benefits, validity of policies, funds market value and insured clients. The *Consult-Ing* software provides mailing facility for fast-tracking the customer inquiries and suggestions. The Web site has been designed also to perform the on-line tasks related to training, options exercise on product preferences, utilities, printing, quoting premiums to the prospects, writing desk to support the task scheduling, calculations, directory listings and dictionary to help conversing with the customer without language barriers to build more profitable orders and improve customer experience in the following ways:

- Enable sales and service professionals to cross-sell and up-sell more effectively
- Improve accuracy and speed during quote and order capture
- Simplify product catalog management and product configuration
- Improve productivity with improved pricing management

The *Consult-Ing* software based Web site also provides scope for developing the large accounts to serve on the business-to-business platform. A multi-level selling program can also be developed by the agents and promoters of the company scheduling the conference involving hierarchical negotiations among the executives of the company and the client organization. Developing accounts is inherently more important than customer acquisition. That means a customer-focused B-to-B site will need a sales force that is differently trained, structured, and compensated. The sales force must orient itself around the goal of finding products for its customers by using efficiently the *Consult-Ing* Web site. The sales force of the company may look into the possibilities of concentrating first on relationships with a few, very-high-value clients.

## REFERENCES

Abeer, Y. H., & Lohse, G. L. (1999). Information cost search perspective for designing interface for electronic commerce. *Journal of Marketing Research, 36*, 387-394.

Alba, J. (1997). Interactive home shopping: Consumer, retailer and manufacturer incentives to participate in electronic market places. *Journal of Marketing, 61*, 38-53.

Andre, A., Bradford, B.,, Choolszian, J., & Davine, T. Y. (2005). An operating edge for insurers. *The McKinsey Quarterly.*

Boisseau, C. (1995). Internet rife with cyberspace. *The Dallas Morning News.*

Computer World (1994). Business on the Internet. *Computer World* (pp. 78-80).

de Blasio, G. (2008). Urban-rural differences in Internet usage, e-commerce, and e-banking: Evidence from Italy. *Growth and Change, 39*(2), 341-367.

Gunasekaran, A., Ngai, E. W. T., & Cheng, T. C. E. (2007). Developing an e-logistics system: A case study. *International Journal of Logistics, 10*(4), 333-349.

Herrmann, P., & Herrmann, G. (2006). Security requirement analysis of business processes. *Electronic Commerce Research, 6*(3-4), 305-335.

Hoffman, D. L., & Novak, T. P. (1996). Marketing in hypermedia computers. *Journal of Marketing, 60*, 50-68.

Hui, T-K., & Wan, D. (1997). Factors affecting Internet shopping behaviour in Singapore: Gender and educational issues. *International Journal of Consumer Studies, 31*(3), 310-316.

Internet World Statistics (2008). *Internet world statistics.* Miniwatts Marketing Group. http://www.Internetworldstats.com/stats.htm.

Bellens, J., Ip, C., & Yip, A. (2007). Developing new rural payment system in China. *South China Morning Post.*

Jiang, P. (2008). Adopting mobile Internet: A demographic and usage perspective. *International Journal of Electronic Business, 6*(3), 232-260.

Lai, I. K. W. (2008). The information processing infrastructure for Internet based collaboration. *International Journal of Logistics Systems and Management, 4*(6), 634-649.

Lau, T. W., Hui, C. L., Ng, S. F., Moon, K. L., & Taylor, G. (2008). An implication of e-commerce in textile and clothing industries: A relational online analytical processing (OLAP) approach. *International Journal of Information Technology and Management, 7*(20), 231-243.

Liang, C-J., Chen, H-J., & Wang, W-H. (2008). Does online relationship marketing enhance customer retention and cross-buying? *The Service Industries Journal, 28*(6), 769-787.

Li, F. L., Cheung, C. F., Lee, W. B., & Kwok, S. K. (2007). Business intelligence for new market development: A Web Semantic network analysis approach. *International Journal of Enterprise Network Management, 1*(3), 261-282.

Li, X., Gupta, J., & Koch, J. (2006). Effect of technological breakthroughs on electronic markets. *Electronic Commerce Research, 6*(3-4), 389-404.

McCarthy, V. (1997, January). Web security: How much is enough? *Datamation, 43*, 112-117.

Pallab, P. (1996). Marketing on Internet. *Journal of Consumer Marketing, 13*(4), 27-39.

Pennanen, K., Tiainen, T., & Luomala, H. T. (2007). A qualitative exploration of a consumer's value-based e-trust building process: A framework development. *Qualitative Market Research: An International Journal, 10*(1), 28-47.

Rajagopal (1999). *Virtual shopping: Strengths and weaknesses.* Working Paper, Administrative Staff College of India, (pp. 5-18).

Rajagopal (2005). *Virtual sales offices for insurance services in Mexico: A case of ING Commercial America.* ITESM, Marketing Case Studies Series, (pp. 1-21).

Regan, L., & Tennyson, S. (1996). Agent discretion and the choice of insurance marketing system. *Journal of Law and Economics, 39*(2), 673-666.

Roman, Sergio (2007). The ethics of online retailing: A scale development and validation from the consumers' perspective. *Journal of Business Ethics, 72*(2), 131-148.

Van den Poel, D., & Leuis, J. (1996). Mail order verses retail store buying- The role of perceived risk and risk reduction strategies. *International Review of Retail, Distribution and Consumer Research, 4*, 351-371.

Widing, R. E., & Wayne, W. T. (1993). Electronic information system for consumers- An evaluation of computer assisted formats in multiple eecision environments. *Journal of Marketing Research, 30*, 125–141.

Yang, C., Tian, G., & Ward, S. (2007). Security systems of point-of-sales devices. *The International Journal of Advanced Manufacturing Technology, 34*(7-8), 799-815.

## ENDNOTES

1 Any firm or individual can by home site on the Internet and use it for disseminating and receiving information. The information of the site owners is displayed on *Internet pages.*

2 This case has been written as the basis for class discussion rather than to illustrate either effective or ineffective handling of an administrative situation of the company.

# Chapter X
# Performance Enhancement of Team Retailing Through Six Sigma Applications

**Amritanshu Rajagopal**
*Dentalia, Mexico*

'Team' conceptualizes group of people engaged in delivering a common task. In ideal situations the individual and group behavior in a team is integrated towards common objectives and the task delivery process is shared which leads to set the group dynamics. The basic attributes of a good team include clear identification of goals, clarity of roles, common feeling, motivation, commitment and collaborative attitude (Rajagopal and Rajagopal, 2006[a]). The team selling approach is followed by many multinational companies for various products and services, which the customer faces as a first-time buy and salespeople need to support such negotiations with comprehensive information needs. Team selling would also be advantageous when an account requires special treatment or a large number of people are involved in the process of buying decision. In addition, team selling is more likely to be employed when the potential sale is large for the representative firm and when the product is new to the product line of salespeople (Rajagopal, 2007). In a sales team each member of the group shows interest in the achievement and follows a systems approach which provides the framework or organizational principal for evaluating task in parts (Cummings, 1980). The members develop confidence, trust, and commitment to work in a team and rely on group communication on the given tasks and schedule.

Team may not function effectively if any of the above factors or associated variables are incoherent. The reward and punishment issues in a team emerge as a post-process synergy of all associated variables and are largely governed by the factors such as common feeling, motivation, commitment and collaborative attitude (Rajagopal, 2006[b]). Hence teams are collections of people who must rely upon group collaboration, if each member is to experience the optimum success and goal achievement. Changing technology and markets have stimulated the team approach in multinational companies for performing the organizational tasks. Moreover, complexity of the society and human needs has prompted team work as a significant tool in managing the corporate tasks (Dyer, 1987). Team management is employed largely in the organizations where activities are less repetitive and predictable. Such an approach demands effective liaison, appropriate delegation of powers, judicious allocations of roles of team members, sharing of information and accuracy in evaluation of team performance (Harris and Moran, 1999).

Team control has emerged as a behavioral control mechanism. The sales engineers become a part of a quasi-firm arrangement, along with the client's engineers and managers, who supervise their work. Management efforts to ensure detailed documentation emerge as a second control mechanism (Darr, 2003). Industrial organizations largely implement direct management control and influence the activities of employees leading towards improving their efficiency (Anderson and Oliver, 1987; Eisenhardt, 1985; Ouchi, 1979). The extent monitoring of sales managers, and directing, evaluating, and rewarding activities in an organization intend to guide sales team behavior through team control processes to achieve favorable results to the organization and the employees (Anderson and Oliver, 1987). Team control in a sales organization, is thus recognized as an important performance indicator of the task performed by the salespeople (Cravens *et al.,* 1993; Oliver and Anderson, 1994).

Result oriented control and market volatility are positively related to new product selling performance. The effect of sales team adoption on selling performance is stronger where outcome based control is used and where the firm provides information on the background of the new product to salespeople through internal marketing (Hultink and Atuhene, 2000). It has been observed that salespeople, who simultaneously exhibit commitment and effort, achieve higher performance in sales activity. Measuring sales performance has been emerged as significance managerial control to sustain competitive advantage (Magrath, 1997).

High technology sales organizations evolve in a highly turbulent environment, hence external conditions can be expected to modify the relationships between the antecedents and the control system in these industries. The uncertainty of environment and technological turbulence modify the relationships between most of the antecedents and the control system (Lapierre and Skelling, 2005). A study of sales team working in the pharmaceutical companies in UK and Ireland explores how changes in the nature of the customer and the competitive environment are impacting on the way managements are structuring the work process and the nature of skills required (Lloyd and Newell, 2001). The SMART variables may be considered to administer sales teams which include-strategy orientation, measurability, approach, reality and time frame. The strategy orientation would drive the brainstorming discussion to result orientation and the measurability would count on the success of the deliberations (Rajagopal, 2006[a]). Teams which need to work within an organization and across functional activities such as sales, marketing, purchasing, personnel and finance find that team working fosters as collaborative tool rather than a competitive approach. It is important that terms of reference of teams must be capable of doing the job for which they have been selected and this clearly implies that the membership should include people that are able to contribute towards the completion of task (McGreevy, 2006).

## DMAIC ANALYSIS

DMAIC is an analytical, data driven approach to eliminate weaknesses in active processes, products and services. This methodology is an acronym for the following five interconnected phases:

- Define the process improvement goals that are consistent with customer demands and enterprise strategy.
- Measure the current process and collect relevant data for future comparison.
- Analyze to verify relationship and causality of factors. Determine what the relationship is, and attempt to ensure that all factors have been considered.
- Improve or optimize the process based upon the analysis using techniques like Design of Experiments.
- Control to ensure that any variances are corrected before they result in defects. Set up pilot runs to establish process capability and thereafter continuously measure the process and institute control mechanisms.

The purpose of the Control phase is to maintain the changes that the team made in the X's in the transfer function equation in order to sustain the improvements in the Y's. The team must document and monitor the process using the metrics defined earlier in DMAIC, evaluate the solution, assess the capability of the process over time, establish control systems to ensure that the solution works for the long term, standardize procedures, hand over the process to the process owners, and then calculate and document the gains. The objective of the Control phase is to establish the required action plan that reflects the finding from the Improve phase and to drive controls to sustain the improved performance. The team must ensure that the new process conditions are documented and then monitored via statistical process control methods. After a "settling in" period, the process capability should be reassessed. Depending upon the outcomes of such a follow-on analysis, it might be necessary to revisit one or more of the preceding phases.

## STAGES OF CONTROL PHASE

The team assesses the results of the implementation according to the implementation plan developed in the Improve phase. The most important thing is to ensure that the improvements enabled the process to achieve the business goals of the project. At this point, the team might find it necessary or wise to make minor adjustments, to tweak the process a little. The process team should ensure the stability of the process. If the team verifies that the process is stable, it then can determine process capability/process sigma. In the Control phase, the process of evaluating capability is repeated to ensure that improvement occurred. Calculate and document improved process capability:

- Capability analysis (Cpk) study
- Confidence intervals (review)

Monitor the process for sustainability to sustain the gains. Maintain the quality levels, and prevent the recurrence of problems. Validate the measuring system: In the Control phase, the process of validating the measurement system is repeated to ensure that improvement occurred.

## CONTROL PLAN

The *control plan* is one of the marquee tools of the DMAIC process. It is of the important elements that differentiate Six Sigma projects from traditional projects. The control plan should extend well beyond control charts. It should, include procedures for process setup, monitoring, control, and troubleshooting. The plans need to be complete enough to ensure that the process owners and operators can maintain over time the gains achieved by the Six Sigma team. The control plan is a management tool to ensure that the process changes are maintained. Control plans provide a written description of the actions that are required at each phase of the process to ensure that all process, inputs and outputs will be in a state of control. Control plans are living documents maintained and updated throughout the life cycle of a process. Updates are made as measurement and processing systems are improved. Control plans ensure that improvements are sustained over time and that plans are in place that will continue to identify opportunities within the process.

These are the five elements of a complete control plan:

- Training plan
- Documentation plan
- Monitoring plan
- Response plan
- Institutionalization plan, to align systems and structures

The team working on the project is responsible for creating the plan. Anyone who has a role in defining, executing, or changing the process could be involved. The team develops the control plan using all available information from the results of the measure, lessons learned from similar products and processes, team's knowledge of the process, and design reviews.

## STATISTICAL PROCESS CONTROL (SPC)

Statistical process control was developed by Walter Shewhart in 1924. SPC is very similar to hypothesis testing. It's a statistically based graphing technique that compares current process data with a set of stable control limits established from normal process variation. Those control limits are statistically based limits to detect a shift in the process in terms of the critical statistic of interest (e.g., mean, variance, etc). The state of statistical control is considered the null hypothesis and an, out-of-control situation is the alternate hypothesis. Type I and type II errors exist in control charts. (A type I or alpha error occurs when a point fall, outside the control limits even though no special cause is operating. A type II or beta error occurs a special cause is missed because the chart isn't sensitive enough to detect it.)

Control performance is measured by average run length statistics, which are the average number of samples taken until the average number of sample taken before detecting a one-sigma shift. A process is in *statistical control,* there is no uncontrolled or special cause variation present. Attentive use control charts can identify assignable causes. Control charts only deter processes that are out of control; they don't show why. Control charts to track process statistics over time and to detect the presence of special causes. A control chart plots a process statistic, such, a subgroup mean, individual observation, weighted statistic, or number of defects, versus sample number or time.

- Center line at the average of the statistic by default
- Upper control limit, 3s above the center line by default
- Lower control limit, 3s below the center line by default

*Controlled* or *common cause variation* occurs naturally and is inherent and expected in a stable process. This type of variation can be attributed to "chance" or random causes. *Uncontrolled* or *special cause variation* occurs when an abnormal action enters a process and produces unexpected and unpredictable results.

## CONTROL CHARTS

SPC refers to a group of graphical tools called control charts, which display process input or output continuous characteristics over time with points plotted to represent statistical values of subgroup measurements *(X, X-bar, R, S,* etc.) through time. The charts can serve three different purposes. They are used to control the CTP (critical-to-process) characteristic; in that case, we call this *statistical process control.* They can also be used to monitor CTQ, CTC (critical-to-cost), or CTD (critical-to-delivery) characteristics; then we call it *statistical process monitoring (SPM).* Finally, they are also used as diagnostic tools for any CT characteristics.

Control charts form data into patterns that can be statistically tested and, as a result, lead to information about the behavior of product and/or process characteristics. In order to evaluate this behavior, *we* use historical statistics of the process such as the mean, the standard deviation, statistical control limits, and different tests of out-of-control situations. Control charts enable the project team to detect assignable causes that affect the central tendency and/or the variability of the cause system and identify when action is needed on the process. To sustain the use of SPC, the charts have to be reviewed, changes must be made as indicated (such as adjusting the sampling interval, combining charts, and eliminating charts found unnecessary), and the team or the process owners must act on the information provided by the charts.

### Variables Charts

- **Xi–MR chart (individuals and moving-range chart).** Can be used for tracking both X and Y The method incorporates two separate charts: The individuals chart tracks individual measurements and the moving-range chart tracks the moving range between individual measurements.
- **X-bar–R chart (average and range chart).** Used for tracking *X* and/or Y. The method incorporates two separate charts: The average chart tracks the subgroup average, and the range chart tracks the range within each subgroup.

- **Precontrol chart.** Used mainly during setup to make run or no-run decisions on the production line. The output Y is the variable of interest.
- **EWMA chart (exponentially weighted moving average).** Can be used to monitor both *X* and Y .Used to detect small shifts and drifts in the process: WWMA is a statistic that averages data in a way that gives progressively less weight to data as they become further removed in time.

### Using Control Charts

Here are the basic steps for using control charts:

1. Select the appropriate variable to chart. Ideally, this should be a critical X
2. Select the type of control chart to use.
3. Determine rational subgroup size and sampling interval/frequency.
4. Determine measurement method and criteria.
5. Do a gage capability study if necessary.
6. Calculate the parameters of the control chart.
7. Gather the data.
8. Calculate the control limits.
9. Train the necessary people.

## MISTAKE PROOFING

Mistake proofing (or *poka-yoke* as it is known in Japan) is one of several control concepts where the solution is not dynamic, as is the case with a closed loop feedback control system. It should be noted that *poka-yoke is* very consistent with the fundamental aims and philosophy of Six Sigma and widely applied in manufacturing, engineering, and transactional processes. It involves actions designed to eliminate errors, mistakes, or defects in activities and processes. Mistake proofing is the use of experience, wisdom, and ingenuity to remove opportunities for errors. The methodology involves complete understanding of the cause-and-effect relationship and identification of the simplest remedy that can be applied to eliminate that particular error in the future. Sometimes this involves adding a simple feature, changing the sequence of an operation, programming a software message that reminds the operator anything to help to totally eliminate or substantially reduce mistakes. The traditional application of mistake proofing is in a production environment. Here are some examples:

- A stop is added to a drill press.

- A hydraulic ram is added to align a component during assembly.
- A lever is designed into an assembly fixture to index the part.
- A pin is added so the part cannot be installed backwards.

Control phase is to establish the required action plan that reflects the finding from the Improve phase and to drive controls to sustain the improved performance. The team must ensure that the new process conditions are documented and then monitored via statistical process control methods. After a "settling in" period, the process capability should be reassessed. Depending upon the outcomes of such a follow-on analysis, it might be necessary to revisit one or more of the preceding phases. The major Control phase tools are:

- Statistical process control (SPC)
- Mistake proofing
- Control plans

The purpose of the Control phase is to maintain the changes that the team made in the X's in the transfer function equation in order to sustain the improvements in the Y's. The team must document and monitor the process using the metrics defined earlier in DMAIC, evaluate the solution, assess the capability of the process over time, establish control systems to ensure that the solution works for the long term, standardize procedures, hand over the process to the process owners, and then calculate and document the gains. DMAIC is an analytical, data driven approach to eliminate weaknesses in active processes, products and services. *Control* is done to ensure that any variances are corrected before they result in defects. Set up pilot runs to establish process capability and thereafter continuously measure the process and institute control mechanisms.

## ORGANIZATIONAL PERFORMANCE

Organizational commitment and sales territory design are significantly related to sales team performance and the study highlights the growing emphasis on building long-term, collaborative buyer-seller relationships that favor the use of behavior-based control systems in many sales management situations, and suggests a new agenda for management attention in improving sales team effectiveness. The importance of designing effective sales territory is widely supported in the process of organizational restructuring (Bailey, 1989). Despite this importance, the impact of sales territory designs on salesperson and organizational consequences has not gained significant research attention. There is a significant relationship between the different behavioral attributes of work-related activity in team-work and team performance (Ntayi, 2005). However, the role of designing effective sales territories in the multinational sales organization is growing substantially which includes the challenges towards integrating the local market differences in sales infrastructure and other competitive market attributes

Sales performance in an organization is largely associated with the derived customer value, delivery of goods and services, and customer relations. Market dynamics and growing competition have led to the evolution of a new sales operation which manages a complex strategic customer portfolio and works across functions to deliver value to customers. Evidence suggests that many important decisions and responsibilities associated with marketing strategy are now located in the sales organization (Piercy, 2006). As the multinational companies are getting closer to the customer oriented selling strategies, the sales teams have increasing responsibility on building customer value and customer retention. The outcome performance of the salespeople is thus reflected through the customer value generated either in business to consumers or business to business sales operations.

Value measurements have been used as one of the principal tools to assess the trend of consumer behavior for the non-conventional products. Value syndrome influences the individual and group decisions in retail and bulk deals, and conditionalizes the decision process of consumers. Conditional consumption behavior suggests that consumption depends heavily on the utility function and on the source of uncertainty (Carroll and Kimball, 1996 and Deaton 1992). The dynamics of retail consumption behavior may be expressed as:

$$c_t = \alpha_0 + \alpha_1 y_t + \alpha_2 w_t + u_t \qquad \text{(i)}$$

Where $c_t$ is a log of real per capita total consumption, $y_t$ is the log of real per capita disposal income, $w_t$ is the per capita expenditure on buying and $u$ denotes the random error term. Under this assumption $c_t$, $y_t$, and $w_t$ are co-integrated, $u_t$ is $\leq 0$ in the process of measuring the consumer behavior in reference to preference variables leading to price and non-price determinants, the dependent factor is the rate of change in the consumption ($\Delta_{ct}$). In view of the above discussion the dynamic consumption function that reflects the retail consumer behavior for particular products may be estimated as [deriving from equation (i)]:

$$\Delta_{ct} = \beta_0 + \beta_1(L)u_{t-1} + \beta_2(L)\Delta_{yt} + \beta_3(L)\Delta_{wt} + \beta_4(L)\Delta_{rt} + \varepsilon_t \qquad \text{(ii)}$$

Where $\Delta$ is the change factor, r is the concentration ratio of retail stores in a given location and $\varepsilon_t$ is a random error term. Test of this model requires time series data to be analyzed for trend values, taking (L) as polynomial log operator (Rajagopal,

2007 b). It has been observed in previous studies that value to expenditure ratios increase consumer sensitivity in volume of buying and driving repeat buying decisions for the regular and high-tech products (Carroll and Dunn 1997). Belessiotis (1996) had explained in one of his studies that consumer confidence index derived of value factors, forecasts more than changing expectations. Consumer decision making with respect to 'which store to buy from' and 'how much to buy from that store' is assumed to depend only on the distance between the consumer's ideal store practices and the actual practices of stores. The Euclidean distance which takes the form $\sqrt{\sum_{k=1}^{N}(z_k - w_k)^2}$ for a consumer of type $\underline{w} \equiv (w_1,...,w_N)$ and a store with practices $\underline{z} \equiv (z_1,....,z_N)$ has been used to measure the impact of retail store practices on variety seeking and repeat buying behavior of consumers (Rajagopal, 2005). A consumer ranks stores according to this metric. Furthermore, it is assumed that the number of units demanded by a consumer equals $\left[A - \sqrt{\sum_{k=1}^{N}(z_k - w_k)^2}\right]^{\sigma}$ and such decisions are largely governed by the convenience factor associated with buying the products and services; where $\sigma > 1$ and $A \geq \sqrt{N(R-1)^2} + 1$ so that $\left[A - \sqrt{\sum_{k=1}^{N}(z_k - w_k)^2}\right] > 1$ for all $(\underline{w}, \underline{z})$.

A retail firms learns, intentionally or unintentionally, from the process the multinational firms build new capabilities to adapt to changing environments through the technology applications as a core of strategic business management. However, contemporary research has addressed this question only recently. Many multinational firms develop a capability to create and develop retail ventures through investment in technology, alliances, and customer acquisitions have been addressed in an integrated model (Rajagopal, 2006). The model is based on two longitudinal case studies of large corporations operating in the information and communication technology sector in Europe. The model envisages learning processes, which enable the firm to build up an external corporate venturing capability, by utilizing learning strategies both within and outside venturing relationships. Retail venture firms often rely heavily on their ability to develop firms around "winning" ideas and too little on how they can promote the development of a continuous flow of high quality ideas. Contemporary trends in the organization of multinational retail enterprises (MNREs), developments in regional economic integration, and evidence pertaining to the globalization of innovative activities are suggestive of the need to revisit the question of the contribution of overseas MNRE affiliates to the technological capacity of developing countries.

## DOMINO'S PIZZA RETAILING EFFICIENCY: CASE STUDY[1]

The cause and effect diagram is used to explore all the potential or real causes (or inputs) that result in a single effect (or output). Causes are arranged according to their level of importance or detail, resulting in a depiction of relationships and hierarchy of events. The fishbone diagram identifies many possible causes for an effect or problem. It can be used to structure a brainstorming session. It immediately sorts ideas into useful categories.

The main causes for delays presented in the Domino's Pizza belong to all the 6M's which include materials, methods, machines, measurement, mother nature and manpower of the fishbone diagram. It is observed that the main causes for the problem are due to the factors concerning the manpower and methods applied by them for preparation of the order. Poor attitude, inadequate training and personnel distraction contribute in major part to this problem on behalf of manpower whereas inappropriate materials handling, wrong work sequence and poor organization of the chef to handle the orders received pertain to factor of methods. Apart from the causes mentioned above, incorrect measurement of raw materials required, poor quality materials and untimely supply of those along with malfunctioning of order generation systems such as printer and computer also contribute in a huge manner, to the delay in delivery of Domino's Pizzas. Occurrence of disaster in the area creating power failures and system shut downs along with delays in the delivery of raw materials from the supplier are one of the major concerns in the business these days and these issues are to be addressed as soon as possible by generating backup plans to avoid loss of reputation in front of the customers

SIPOC (supplier, inputs, process, output and consumers) tool helps a lot to understand the whole process along with some added details such as suppliers and customers and a flow chart. This tool is an excellent aid to visualize the whole scenario and proceed with fish bone diagram to completely understand the situation we are dealing with. In case of the Fishbone diagram, as mentioned above, the factors that contribute to delays in the delivery time of pizzas are a lot and have to be addressed on time in order to comply with the promise made to the customer about timely delivery of their order. Some of the issues can be solved in the near future and are relatively easy to implement. For example, offering adequate training to cashier, cook and all other personnel could be a good start followed by implementing timely recess system for the employees in order to avoid fatigue and create a

*Figure 10.1 Fish bone diagram of process reengineering*

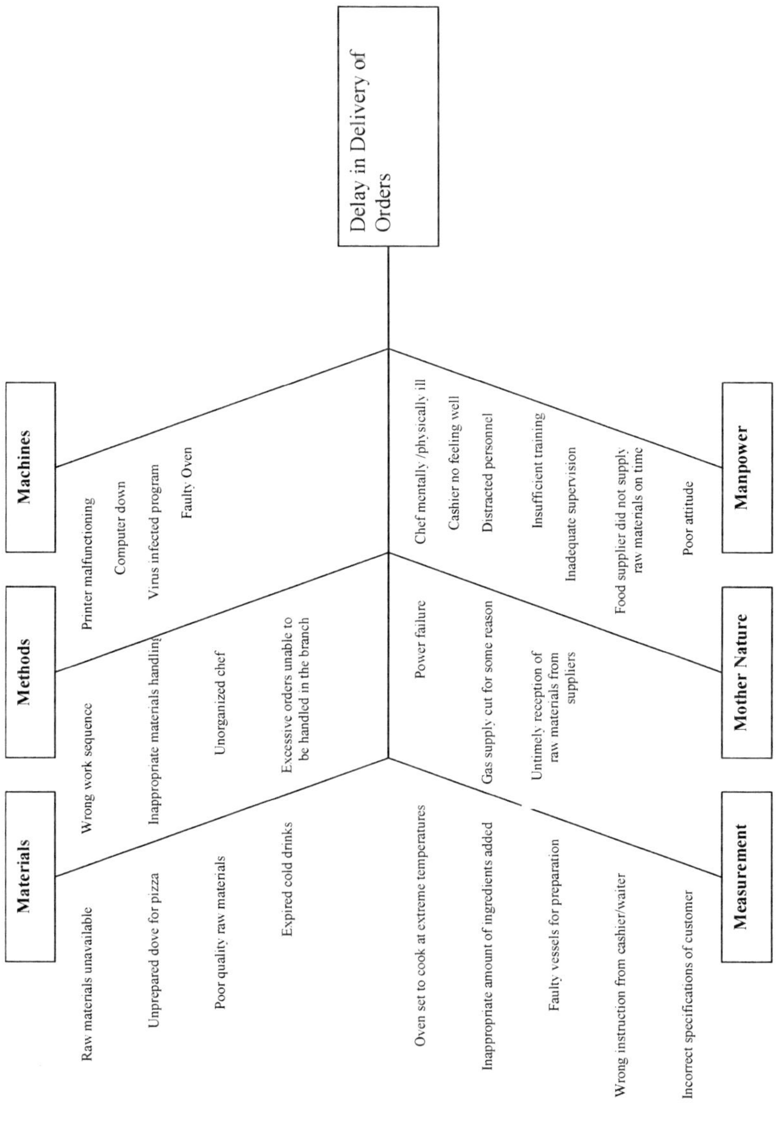


friendlier environment at the work place. Agreement with the suppliers for timely delivery of raw materials and of good quality is essential to avoid getting surprised at the last hour, while committed with a customer to hand in the order on time to increase the retailing efficiency.

## REFERENCES

Anderson, R. E. (1996). Personal selling and sales management in the new millennium. *Journal of Personal Selling and Sales Management, 16*(4), 17-32.

Anderson, E., & Oliver, R. L. (1987). Perspectives on behavior-based versus outcome-based sales team control systems. *Journal of Marketing, 51*, 76-88.

Bailey, E. L. (1989). Getting closer to the customer. *Research Bulletin, 229*. New York: The Conference Board, Inc.

Churchill, G. A., Ford, N. M., Walker, O. C., Johnston, M. W., & Tanner, J. E. (2000). *Sales team management* (6th ed.), Chicago: Irwin.

Crow, K. (2002). *Failure mode and effects analysis.* DRM Associates http://www.npd-solutions.com/fmea.html

Cummings, T. (1980). *Systems theory for organizational development.* Chi Chester, UK: Wiley, (pp. 19-25).

Darr, A. (2003). Control and autonomy among knowledge workers in sales: An employee perspective. *Employee Relations, 25*(1), 31-41.

Cravens, D. W., Ingram, T. N., LaForge, R. W., & Young, C. E. (1993, October). Behavior-based and outcome-based salesteam control systems. *Journal of Marketing, 57*, 47-59.

Dyer, W. (1987). *Team building,* (pp. 20-23). Reading, MA: Addison-Wesley.

Eisenhardt, K. M. (1985, February). Control: Organizational and economic approaches. *Management Science, 31*, 134-149

Harris, P. R., & Moran, R. T. (1999). *Managing cultural difference- Leadership strategies for a new world of business,* (pp. 106-273). Houston, TX: Gulf Publishing Company.

Hultink, E. J., & Atuahene-Gima, K. (2000, November). The effect of sales team adoption on new product selling performance. *Journal of Product Innovation Management, 17*(6), 435-450.

Magrath, A. J. (1997). From the practitioner's desk: A comment on personal selling and sales management in the new millennium. *Journal of Personal Selling and Sales Management, 17*(1), 45-47.

Lapierre, J., & Skelling, J. (2005, June). Sales team control system in high-tech contexts: Do environment and industry matter? *Journal of Business and Industrial Marketing, 20*(6), 297-306.

Lloyd, C., & Newell, H. (2001). Capture and transfer: Improving the performance of the pharmaceutical sales representatives. *International Journal of Human Resource Management, 12*(3), 464-483.

McGreevy, M. (2006). Team working: How are teams chosen and developed? *Industrial and Commercial Training, 38*(7), 365-370.

Ntayi, J. M. (2005). Work ethic, locus of control and sales team task performance. *Journal of African Business, 6*(1-2), 155-176.

Ouchi, W. Z. (1979, September). A conceptual framework for the design of organizational control mechanisms. *Management Science, 25*, 833-847.

Piercy, N. F. (2006). The strategic sales organization. *The Marketing Review, 6*(1), 3-28.

Rajagopal & Rajagopal, A. (2006a). *Trust and cross-cultural dissimilarities in corporate environment. Team Performance Management-An International Journal, 12(7-8),* 237-252.

Rajagopal (2006b). Innovation and business growth through corporate venturing in Latin America: Analysis of strategic fit. *Management Decision, 44*(5), 703-718.

Rajagopal (2006c). Leisure shopping behavior and recreational retailing: A symbiotic analysis of marketplace strategy and consumer response. *Journal of Hospitality and Leisure Marketing, 15(2), 5-31.*

Rajagopal (2007). Sales management in developing countries: A comparison of managerial control perspectives. *Journal of Asia Pacific Business, 8(3), 37-61.*

Six Sigma Quality Resources for Achieving Six Sigma Results. *Fishbone diagram.* http://www.isixsigma.com/tt/cause_and_effect/

## ENDNOTE

1 This case has been written as the basis for class discussion rather than to illustrate either effective or ineffective handling of an administrative situation of the company.

# Chapter XI
# Consumer Response to High Technology Mobile Phones in Emerging Markets

**Ernesto Fierros**
*Monterrey Institute of Technology and Higher Education, ITESM, Mexico*

**Rajagopal**
*Monterrey Institute of Technology and Higher Education, ITESM, Mexico*

## INTRODUCTION

Information and communications technologies (ICT) are concerned with the use of technology to gather and process information, they help people all around the world to communicate with others, keep a fresh look of what is happening out there. The new information technology is becoming an important factor in the future development of financial **services** industry, and especially **banking** industry. The developments on information and communication technology have significantly contributed to the exponential growth and profits of the financial institutions worldwide. This evolution had transformed the way banks deliver their services, using technologies such as automated teller machines, phones, the Internet, credit cards, and electronic cash. However, banks face a number of important questions on strategies for deriving full advantage of new technology opportunities and tracking electronic development changes affecting interactions with the customers (Rajagopal, 2007).

Growth of the ICT sector means that new products will appear for the users of communications products, in other words more IC technologies means more products and a change on the consumer's behavior, as well as on the market. As all new products, they can have a positive or a negative impact on the consumer, not only this impact can affect the companies, there is also a financial risk; with all the users having access to all the information for all the products combined with the fact that most users are looking for the newest products allowing that the consumers adopt the new products (Hirunyawipada and Paswan, 2006). The principal objective of the study is to identify the primary variables that can make an impact on the buying decision for a mobile phone. The focus of this study is to suggest developing a high performing customer-centric marketing plan to guide the mobile telecommunication companies to gain competitive advantage in the market.

## REVIEW OF LITERATURE

### Growth of Information Technologies

Currently, the world is a place where information and communication technology (ICT) is being diffused into all human activities at an unprecedented rate. Along with this development, there is also an intense debate on the contribution of ICT towards productivity and growth in both developed and developing countries (Joseph, 2002). Given the rapid growth of technology markets, the ICT industry is growing. The importance of the information is critical, everybody needs information, about the work, school or personal issues, and there is a need for information. The access to information can give a company a strategic advantage over the others, so investments on ICT have been increasing over the years (Rao *et. al.*, 2004). It is important that developing countries, as Mexico invest on ICT since it has a critical role to play in development efforts around the world. Developing countries that use ICT grow faster, invest more and are more productive than those that do not (World Bank, 2006). In recent years, developing countries and the international development community have started taking concrete actions to incorporate ICT into their economic policies and development agendas. Many countries are preparing and implementing national e-strategies that emphasize the ubiquity of connectivity as well as new applications in areas like e-business. ICT has become the key driver for socioeconomic development in recent years (Kuppusamy and Santhapparaj, 2005). The benefits of ICT can be for economic growth and development. The rapid diffusion of the Internet, of mobile telephony and of broadband networks all demonstrates how pervasive this technology has become (OECD, 2003). All countries are investing on ICT in order to increment the Gross Domestic Product

(GDP), Mexico has done ICT investment over the years, to provide an infrastructure to support the growth of mobile users.

The impact of the ICT capital can be shown on real output growth; the benefits gained from the ICT-based investment made by the countries over the years. The growth on ICT has made a positive impact on the economic growth of the countries that made the investments (O'Mahoney and Vecchi, 2005). Another key factor for ICT growth, besides economic factors, is the growth on the service industries; this growth is responsible for the acceleration in ICT capital, and as a consequence the economic growth. The ICT can also boost the labor productivity when used (Inklaar *et. al*., 2005). The contribution of ICT on productivity growth has increased in production and investment, not only ICT contributes to increment the production but also the investment received by the countries thanks for the new ICT adoption (Viljselaar and Albers, 2004). In order to achieve high performance, while implementing ICT there should be considerations associated with the adoption and use of this ICT, and not only the direct effect on problems associated with information flow, distribution and management; in other words, the ICT by themselves cannot achieve any goal, the people who use them achieve them, and in order to do this, they need to know what does the new ICT can provide them (Cordella, 2006). Over the last few years there has been a growth of ICT investment, mainly due the fact that ICT can help a country on his economics and productivity. ICT can make people lives easier allowing them to do more functions and tasks therefore ICT has been incorporated as a part of ordinary life.

## Customer Value and Technology

The role of consumer value can be used by the companies as an instrument to stimulate the market and improve their profit the companies need to ascertain a continuous organizational learning process with respect to the value creation and measure performance of new products introduced in the market (Rajagopal, 2005). Value is a subjective perception of the trade off between multiple benefits and sacrifices, relative to competition (Ulaga, 2003). The customer value can be related to a single purchase of a good or service, or to the relationship between customer and a supplier. The customer values are created towards the new products through individual perceptions, and organizational and relational competence. Technological development and especially the fast development of IT is one of the forces changing the value creation in the services. Innovations in information technology continue to open up areas for new kinds of professional services (Komulainen *et. al.,* 2004).

Convergence represents an important trend in information technology. In service convergence various services are incorporated into one converged service. There is also a device convergence, where many kinds of extant devices and terminals used for various devices are incorporated into a new, converged device that enables consumers to use the converged services and connect to the converged network (video, audio and data). The new technologic device allows multiple applications with just one device, making it easier for the user adding customer value to them (Yeonabe *et. al.*, 2005). The mobile communication providers need to give more applications to the users, some new features, as paying by mobile phones; new products and services will be designed to tap into the convenience of "non-contact" payment technologies, particularly those that leverage the growing array of cell phones and other mobile data devices. In a near future, consumers will be able to pay for a variety of Internet, mobile and physical goods with a single contact-less device, allowing them to do more with their mobile phones, adding costumer value (CRM Today, 2003).

The investments in information technology (IT) create consumer value; the magnitude of the benefits that have been passed on the consumers. There are only two ways to obtain value: value can be created, and value can be redistributed from others. While the processes of value creation and value redistribution are often linked, they can also be considered separately (Hitt and Brynjolfsson, 1995). Consumer value will be a critical factor for the mobile operators in the future, since all service providers are having almost the same services, as the technology advances. An example of adding consumer value is the adoption of new payment methods; these can add tangible value over existing consumer payment habits, adding more value with just a little investment on technology infrastructure (Tower Group, 2003).

Innovation makes companies achieve future performance; if they achieve this the company creates value and can satisfy customers better than before (Sahut and Lantz, 2003). Innovate on the ICT can add value to a customer, by making easier the processes, devices easier to use, and so. Examining the customer perceived value elements in the emerging mobile advertising business is an important topic. Mobile devices can help to transmit customer value, thanks to mobile advertising (Durlacher Research, 2000). This kind of advertising can give the users the information needed or wanted. The technology can be used not only to create new services it can also be used to improve the actual ones. If the service gets improved, the perception from the customer side will be that the service is better, adding value to him (Parasuraman and Grewal, 2000). Technologic innovations can help the companies to add value to their customers, creating loyalty. Technology is close related to customer value since technology can give more applications, make process easier, allow customers to do more things, in other words technology can add value to the customer.

## Technology Services and Consumer Behavior

The Mexican mobile providers offer the Short Message System (SMS) service which allows users to send a text message to another user. Text messaging is an enormously popular service. Sending and receiving text messages requires users to look at the display; the text message needs to be written using a numeric keypad (the one from the mobile phone) and the user has to tap the keys in order to write a message (Mc Connell, 2005). The Mexican SMS market has been growing since 2004, when the operators in Mexico decided to focus on domestic SMS interoperability (Chavez, 2006). According to Telcel, SMS traffic grew ten times in three years, from 3.3 million messages daily in 2002 to 33 million messages every day in 2005.

Multimedia Message System (MMS) is the evolution of SMS. With MMS the mobile device can send not only pure text messages, but can send and receive multimedia messages such as graphics, video, audio and so on (Le Bodic, 2005). Mobile subscribers are beginning to embrace MMS and are becoming aware of its potential as a platform for delivering much more rich content and services, like ringtones, background images and even applications, directly to the handset. Most mobile operators have limits on the overall size of an MMS message; these limitations are increasing, allowing for a significant variety of content to be delivered to the hand set (Dudley, 2005). General Packet Radio Service (GPRS) is a service available for GSM mobile phones and is a mobile data service, is a GSM packet-based data transmission technique that offers continuous connection to the Internet for mobile phone and computer uses. It uses the existing GSM network to transmit and receive TCP/IP based to and from GPRS mobile devices (Comtech, 2006).

WAP (Wireless Application Protocol) is an open international standard for applications that use wireless communication, its principal application is to enable access to the Internet from a mobile phone (Romo, 2004). WAP is the protocol used for the majority of the world's mobile internet sites, known as WAP sites. The trend is that every site creates his WML (Wireless Markup Language) versions in order to be viewed with WAP (Van Der Henst, 2004). A WAP service allows mobile phones to browse over Internet. PTT (Push to Talk): PTT is a two-way communication service that works like a "walkie talkie". Is a method based on half-duplex (communication can travel in only one direction at a given moment) using a momentary button to switch from voice reception mode to transmit mode (press the button for talking and release it for receive); in other words PTT is a one way communication service, while one person talks the other listens (NOKIA, 2005). Operators use VoIP technologies to provide the service over high-speed data networks. Enhanced Data for GSM Evolution (EDGE) is a digital mobile phone technology that allows increased data transmission rate and improved data transmission reliability. EDGE provides up to three times the data capability of GPRS and offers data transmissions speeds up to four times faster than GSM (GSM World, 2006).

High capacity mobile voice/data services (1xRTT) is short for Single Carrier (1x) Radio Transmission Technology (RTT), 1xRTT has the capability of providing greater speeds, up to 144kbps. 1xRTT qualifies as a 3G technology, although sometimes it is considered as a 2.5 – 2.75G (TECH-FAQ, 2004). Broadband wireless data service (1xEV-DO): 1xEV-DO is short for Single Carrier Evolution Data Optimized, is an evolution of 1xRTT with High Data Rate (HDR) capability added and where the forward link is time-division multiplexed. It's a 3G technology. The data transmission speeds can be up to 2.4Mbps (download) and 155kbps (upload) and has compatibility with the 1xRTT standard (Telefonica Móviles, 2005). Because of his higher data transmission rates, it is used to transmit television signals on mobile phones over the 1xEV-DO networks. Location-Based Services (LBS) are the path to send some information to cell-phone subscribers pertaining to billing options, tracking people, etc in reference to their current location. The provider gets the location form a GPS chip on the phone or using radiolocation, based on the signal-strength of the closest cell-phone towers (Steiniger *et. al.*, 2005). Those are the services that Mexican mobile providers are offering to their customers at this moment. Although some of those services are only offered by mobile providers under contract, some of them don't need any contract, just a phone that supports the service. Table 1 shows the growth of mobile subscribers in prepaid and postpaid services.

There are various factors for the mobile success in Mexico: the Mexican economic recovery, increased competition that lead to reduced services prices (prepaid

*Table 1. Profile of mobile phone subscribers*

| Year | Prepaid Subscribers ('000) | Change per Annum (in percent) | Post-paid Subscribers ('000) | Change per Annum (in percent) |
|---|---|---|---|---|
| 1997 | 1000 | - | 741 | - |
| 1998 | 2315 | 132 | 1035 | 40 |
| 1999 | 6370 | 175 | 1362 | 32 |
| 2000 | 12450 | 95 | 1628 | 20 |
| 2001 | 19974 | 60 | 1784 | 10 |
| 2002 | 23992 | 20 | 2006 | 12 |
| 2003 | 28069 | 17 | 2029 | 1 |
| 2004 | 35943 | 28 | 2508 | 24 |
| 2004 | 43873 | 22 | 3268 | 30 |

*Source: Adapted from Dirección de Información Estadística de Mercados, COFETEL, 2005*

and post paid), the introduction of SMS and the migration to GSM technology. The prepaid method contributed to the growth of the mobile market in Mexico. Mexico has one of the largest prepaid bases in Latin America, it was the first Latin American country to introduce this service, and the Mexican operators have been really effective in developing successful prepaid programs (Budde, 2006). Prepaid card have made mobile phones accessible to those segments that have limited budgets, or make few outgoing calls and that don't want to make a contract with one of the mobile providers. In September of 2005 prepaid subscribers made up 93 percent of the country's total subscriber base (COFETEL). Prepaid method became so popular that operators have been unable to migrate subscribers from prepaid to contract plans.

It has been observed that consumer's behavior is heading more towards the prepaid option and it has been impossible for the mobile providers to shift the users from prepaid to a postpaid (contract plan). Prepaid has some advantage for the operators, as lower acquisition costs, the elimination of bad debt problems since subscribers pay up-front for airtime and wider distribution as operators can sell their prepaid packages. The disadvantage of prepaid for operators is the lower ARPU, short for Average Revenue per User (Infoamericas, 2002).

## MOBILE PHONES TECHNOLOGIES AND MARKET BEHAVIOR IN MEXICO

In Mexico there are four mobile phone technologies as state below are under operations with the service providers.

- Analogue
- Advanced Mobile Phone Service (AMPS)
- Digital:
- Time Division Multiple Access (TDMA)
- Code Division Multiple Access (CDMA)
- Global System for Mobile Communications (GSM)

The mobile phone operators in Mexico include Telcel (America Movil Group), Telefónica Movistar, Iusacell and Unefon. Telcel and Telefónica Movistar adopted GSM technologies, while Iusacell and Unefon choose CDMA. Besides GSM Telcel also uses TDMA, while Movistar also uses CDMA; however both of them are trying to encourage their users to GSM. It is found that in Mexico among four major mobile communication operators Telcel is leading the market with highest market share ranging form 81 to 79 percent during 2001-2006 (declining trend) while the bottom line market share is held by Unefon ranging between 4 to 3 (declining trend) percent during the above reference period (Budde, 2006).

GSM is the fastest growing mobile technology in Mexico. During 2004, it grew by 221 percent and continued growing at a 40 percent rate in 2005. CDMA fell by 5 percent in 2004 and continued falling by a 4 percent rate in 2005. TDMA fell by 8 percent in 2004 and continued by about 9 percent in 2005, mainly due to migration from TDMA to GSM system. AMPS is on his way out of the Mexican mobile market, falling 55 percent in 2004 and 160 percent in 2005, currently has less than 1 percent of the total subscriber base (Frost and Sullivan, 2006). Those were the called 2G technologies; however some mobile operators are using 2.5G and 3G technologies as well. In July of 2004 Movistar was the first operator in Mexico to launch EDGE technology, providing high-speed mobile Internet access on its GSM network (Yankee Group, 2005) but by 2006 all the operators had 3G technologies. Mobile communications operate within a competitive environment in Mexico, although the market is clearly dominated by Telcel, with movistar in second place. GSM covers 50 percent of the market, and the goal is to make the entire market GSM, except for Iusacell, which has incorporated 3G technology under CDMA (Chavez, 2006).

The mobile market in Mexico is growing; according to COFETEL in 2006 there was an increment of 3 percent on the number of mobile phones users, leading to 48,600,000 users. The projections of the users for the year 2007 is an increment

*Figure 1. "Growth of Mobile Phone Users in Mexico"*

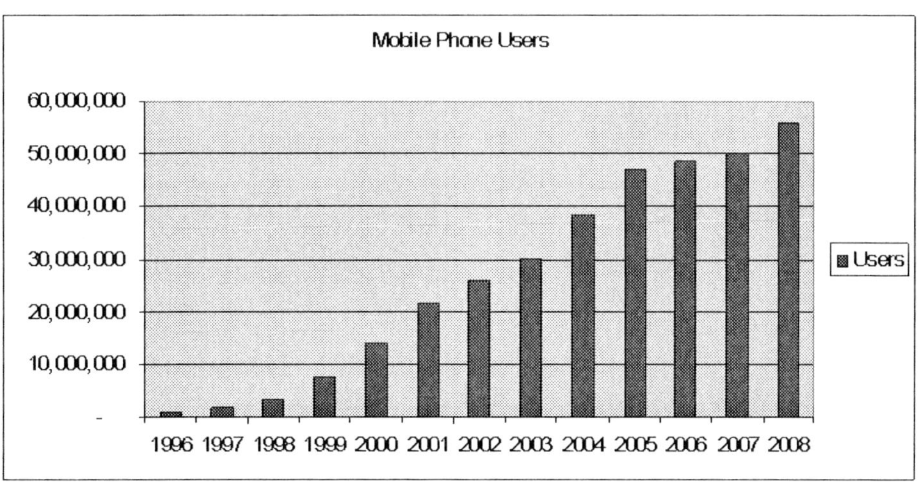


*Source: Table based on COFETEL data, 2007*

of another 3 percent on the total number of mobile phones users and for the year 2008 is of 15 percent, resulting on 56,000,000 users for 2008 (Select, 2002). Figure 1 shows the increment of the mobile phone users over the years; this figure shows that the mobile market is growing every year.

Currently, Mexico is the number two mobile market in Latin America behind Brazil. Mobile subscribers in Mexico overtook fixed-line phones in mid-2000 (Pyramid Research, 2003). Driven by a booming GSM market, the Latin America mobile industry is growing at a rate of around 22 percent annually, with a mobile penetration rate of around 43 percent in February 2006 (Ramirez, 2006). The growth of the Mexican mobile market is fragmented because of the youth is taking advantage of lower cost of ownership of a mobile phone, contributing to a 50 percent increment in subscribers and an $850 million increase in data revenues by 2007 (Wireless World Forum, 2006). Another factor was the introduction of CCP (Calling Party Pays) implemented by all mobile operators, this caused a massive buying trend of mobile phones (Comisión Federal de Telecomunicaciones, 2000). The growth after the CCP was introduced by Mexican mobile providers, according to COFETEL (2006). On the figure it can be seen that after CCP was introduced the mobile subscribers growth. According to the World Fact Book, Mexico was until recently the world leader in wireless growth. Between 1998 to the end of 2003, the number of handsets increased 1178 percent from 2.2 million to a little more than 28 million. Despite these stunning growth figures, only about a third of Mexico's nearly 105 million inhabitants have a mobile subscription. And almost 90 percent of these are prepaid, which is largely responsible for the rapid initial growth (ERICSSON, 2005). The Mexican telecom industry is developing rapidly and has enormous growth potential, making it one of the most interesting telecom markets in the world (Bharat Book Bureau, 2006). With the improvement of technology and the steady growth of subscribers, Mexico has a lucrative mobile market. The youth and corporate markets are the segments where operators will likely concentrate and so developers can also expect to find business opportunities there.

## HYPOTHESES

Since most of the people have limits on what they'll spend, cost plays a big role in most of the people buying decisions, it can be said that the price it's a key buying factor. From a consumer's perspective the price of a product is one of the key buying factors (Fetscherin and Vlietstra, 2004). The companies work on competitive marketing strategies (product positioning, product improvements, new product development, value pricing, branding, marketing communications, to name a few) and they use the techniques and tools to execute their strategies to outperform competitors (Gale, 1994). Price can be an indicator of product quality, if a price is high, then the product has high-quality, if it is low, then it has low-quality; and status, higher price usually means premium products (Nagale and Holden, 2002). Therefore, the price that a buyer is willing to pay for a product also depends on what customer wants; different economic profiles will have different needs. The hypothesis can be stated as:

**H1:** *The people of certain economic profile choose the products to buy for price.*

Service providers are working with mobile phones manufacturers in order to create mobile phones compatible with their networks and the services they offer (PC World LA, 2005). Some extra functions that mobile phones can do are email and Internet access. But in order to have these services the service provider must support them. Another service that needs to be compatible with mobile phones and service providers are the Multimedia Message Service (MMS) or picture messaging (images, video, audio and text), some mobile phones support this service, but if the service provider don't support them, the mobile phones capabilities are useless. Users of mobile phones are looking for more and new services, so they are looking for phones that have the services and a service provider that can support the service. Therefore, a hypothesis can be stated as follows:

**H2:** *Demands of the mobile phones depend on the service offered by the service providers.*

Consumer needs and preferences change with age and life style. The preferences when a person is young are different that the preference of the same person when he is older. People have different wants and needs at different ages. Just like preferences changes with the age, also change with the gender. Men and women tend to have different attitudinal and behavioral orientations. The preferences of men are not the same as the preferences of women (Kotler and Keller, 2006). The product with certain characteristics should be attractive for certain ages and certain gender. Hence the hypothesis can be stated as:

**H3:** *Product attractiveness is closely related to the consumer preferences.*

Advertising can be used to build up an image for a product and to trigger quick sales. There are many forms and uses of advertising (massive channels like TV, radio, and others) and just the presence of advertising might have an effect on sales. The objective of advertise something is to communicate the values offered by the product to the possible consumers. Hence a hypothesis can be stated as:

**H4:** *Consumer decision of buying mobile phones is a fact of communication by the brands (advisement).*

## STUDY DESIGN

This study will be a descriptive study, since this kind of studies pretend to specify the important properties, characteristics and profile of the people, groups, communities or any other thing that it is analyzed (Hernández *et. al.*, 2002). On this type of studies a series of questions are selected and measured or data collected about all of these questions. A non-experimental study is the one were the research is made without intentional manipulation of the variables; in other words is a study where the independent variables don't change, at least not willingly. A cross-sectional study is a descriptive study were data is collected for a certain moment in time only once in a time. Its purpose is to describe variables and analyze their incidence and interrelation on a certain moment; they are often related with a "snapshot" for a certain period of time, giving the frequency and characteristics of a variable in a population at a particular point in time. The data obtained on this study can be used to assess the prevalence of chronic condition in a population. The Table 2 shows the variables groups and the variable on each group that will be used on this work; these variables are the most significant variables that are closed related to buy a mobile phone.

*Table 2. "Variable Groups"*

| IT Variables | Economic Variables | Relational Variables |
|---|---|---|
| Technology | Price | Social Status |
| Physical Attributes | Durability | Communication |
| Size | Social Status | Promotion |
| Weight | Ownership | Style |
| Accessories | Appearance | Brand loyalty |
| Compatibility | Guarantee | Age |
| Use Application | Availability | Gender |
| Upgrading | Payment Method | Color |
| Security | Occupation | Product Attractiveness |
| Self-Service Technologies | | Service Efficiency |
| Innovation | | |

These 30 variables were chosen because of the effect they have on the mind of the consumer on their buying decision. All the data collected on this study will have something to do with these variables. On this study the data has been collected through questionnaires; this means that the data will be collected directly from the users or potential users of mobile phones. The number of questionnaires that will be applied will be explained on the sampling section. The secondary data has been obtained through INEGI, COFETEL, and some data provided by the national mobile service providers. This study is confined to the population of Mexico City that uses mobile phones (people from economic classes from A to D). According to the INEGI the number of people (total, sum of all the classes) on Mexico City that of those characteristics is 7,661,807 (INEGI). This number will help us to get the total population used on the formula showed above. Since this study is largely based on the primary data it is necessary to define the sample size to administer the questionnaires. This sample has been calculated through the following formula (Weiers, 1996):

$$n = \frac{P*(1-P)}{\frac{E^2}{Z^2} + \frac{P*(1-P)}{N}}$$

Where:
n = sample size
Z = Standard deviation
E = Error
P = Population proportion trying to estimate.
N = Total population

On this case for a 95 percent of credibility, and for México City citizen's economic classes, the formula can be with the following data:

Z = 1.96
E = .07
P = 0.5
N will be calculated here:
Economic Class population:

A = 2,842,874 B = 2,421,537 C = 1,976,059 D = 421,337

$$N = \frac{4A + 3B + 2C + D}{10} = 2,300,956.2 \approx 2,300,956$$

Therefore;

N = 2,300,956

$$n = \frac{0.5 * (1 - 0.5)}{\frac{(.07)^2}{(1.96)^2} + \frac{0.5 * (1 - 0.5)}{2300956}} = 195.98 \approx 196$$

Therefore the sample size is confined 196. The questionnaires will be applied to 200 people from different delegations of Mexico City. To analyze the data collected from the questionnaires (primary data) the data has been gathered on spreadsheet software; this will facilitate the data analysis. Each question of the questionnaire is related to one or more of the variables of the study, also the variables are related to the hypothesis therefore it will be possible to find a trend of the data. The secondary data has been collected to quantify the market share of the companies, the market trends, and some other useful information that will support the primary data while supporting the hypothesis.

## FINDINGS AND DISCUSSION

This is an empirical study based on the primary investigation around the selected respondents in Mexico City. The study area has been divided into four regions considering demographic and economic profile of the respondents on one have and the geographic distribution of sales outlets on the other. In all the information of 200 respondents have been analyzed and qualitative dimensions of sales outlets of mobile phones have been discussed in the following text.

### Attributes of Respondents

Data of respondents has analyzed in reference to anthropometric and economic variables in the study regions. Income has close relationship with the acquisition and type of mobile phone owned by the respondents. It has been observed during this study that the people with higher income spent more on their mobile phones than those with lower income, as stated on hypothesis 1 (H1). In this study the income of respondents constituted for 9001-11000 (30.5 percent), more than 11001 (23.5 percent), and between 100-3000 and 3001-9000 (23 percent each) as exhibited in Table 3.

The most important results from this part of the study are the following: from the 200 respondents 64.5 percent were males and 35.5 percent females, the majority

*Table 3. "Distribution of Respondents by Income in the Study Area" n=200*

| Region | INCOME | | | |
|---|---|---|---|---|
| | 100-3000 | 3001-9000 | 9001-11000 | 11001+ |
| West | 8 (4) | 8 (4) | 14 (7) | 20 (10) |
| North | 14 (7) | 19 (9.5) | 9 (4.5) | 8 (4) |
| East | 7 (3.5) | 12 (6) | 18 (9) | 13 (6.5) |
| South | 17 (8.5) | 7 (3.5) | 20 (10) | 6 (3) |
| | | | | |
| *TOTAL* | 46 (23) | 46 (23) | 61 (30.5) | 47 (23.5) |

*The number in the parentheses indicates the percentage of the respondents in terms of n*

from the respondents had between 18 and 30 years old. The principal occupations on the area of the study were field executive and students, which can be understood due the age of the respondents. The majority of the respondents claimed that their income was from $9001 to $11000; however the other amounts were almost the same percentage as this one. With this data we can have an idea of the kind of people were the respondents, this will be useful later in order to identify the factors that contribute the users to buy new mobile phones.

## Consumer Preferences Towards Product and Services

The features that a user of the mobile phone depends on certain factors, such as main use and age of the users therefore the features on a mobile phone will depend on the respondents. For the respondents that thought that the physical attributes are a key factor while buying a new mobile phone, the first choice for the respondents of the physical attributes where like this: 57.8 percent of the respondents choose brand, 53.7 percent thought that accessories were the most important attribute, 48.3 percent appearance, 27.9 percent style of the mobile phone, 21.1 percent size, 17.7 percent color and 8.2 percent weight as shown on Table 4. It can be observed that the physical attributes changes mainly because users were different in ages, gender and so, therefore the Hypothesis 3 (H3) was fulfilled.

Respondents of this question could choose more than one option of the physical attributes, so there will be more tables of the same variable. Since only 147 cared about the physical attributes, as a key factor, the percentage shown were calculated as if 147 were the only responses, but since some user choose more than 1 option, the number will be higher than 147. Table 5 exhibits the importance of the service

*Table 4. "Important Physical Attributes for Respondents" n=147*

| Region | PHYSICAL ATTRIBUTES | | | | | | |
|---|---|---|---|---|---|---|---|
| | Appearance | Brand | Style | Size | Color | Weight | Accessories |
| West | 18 (12.3) | 19 (12.9) | 13 (8.8) | 8 (5.4) | 6 (4.1) | 5 (3.4) | 15 (10.2) |
| North | 21 (14.3) | 17 (11.6) | 15 (10.2) | 4 (2.7) | 10 (6.8) | 4 (2.7) | 19 (12.9) |
| East | 12 (8.2) | 22 (15) | 6 (4.1) | 5 (3.4) | 3 (2) | 1 (0.7) | 21 (14.3) |
| South | 20 (13.6) | 27 (18.4) | 7 (4.8) | 14 (9.5) | 7 (4.8) | 2 (1.4) | 23 (15.6) |
| | | | | | | | |
| *TOTAL* | 71 (48.3) | 85 (57.8) | 41 (27.9) | 31 (21.1) | 26 (17.7) | 12 (8.2) | 79 (53.7) |

*The number in the parentheses indicates the percentage of the respondents in terms of n.*

*Table 5. "Service Provider as Key Factor for Respondents" (n=200)*

| Region | SERVICE PROVIDER AS KEY FACTOR | |
|---|---|---|
| | Yes | No |
| West | 37 (18.5) | 13 (6.5) |
| North | 38 (19) | 12 (6) |
| East | 42 (21) | 8 (4) |
| South | 43 (21.5) | 7 (3.5) |
| *TOTAL* | 160 (80) | 40 (20) |

*The number in the parentheses indicates the percentage of the respondents in terms of n.*

provider of the mobile phone for the respondents. As shown on the table, 80 percent of the respondents think that the service provider is a key factor when buying new mobile phones while 20 percent don't think as that. As stated on Hypothesis 2 (H2), most of the users think that the service provider is a key factor while making a decision to buy a new mobile phone.

For the respondents that thought that the service provider is a key factor while buying a new mobile phone has several factors, the respondents answered like this: 52.5 percent of the respondents said that promotional packages is the most important factor while choosing a new mobile phone while 51.9 percent of the respondents thought that the service efficiency was a key factor, 35 percent advertising from the service providers, 33.2 percent payment facilities, 26.9 percent for the availability of certain equipments and 20 percent because of the guarantee that the service provider gives. With this group of factors we can identify some of the consumer preferences in terms of products and services; these factors can show what is what the buyers are looking in their products and services in order to understand the needs of the buyers.

## Economic Issues Guiding Buying Behavior

Price is one of the key factors for most of the respondents while making a decision to buy a new mobile phone, 66 percent of the respondents in this study stated that the price was a key factor while 34 percent said that the price wasn't a key factor as exhibited on Table 6. This table can also help to explain the fulfillment of Hypothesis 2 (H2).

Perceived value for money from the respondents is exhibited in Figure 2, it is interesting see that getting a good price is value for the users, meaning that if they think that they had a great deal or promotional package then they are getting more value almost the same number of respondents thought that getting a better service added value to their purchase. Respondents get information about the new mobile phones from different sources; this is an important thing for the companies, in order to place the right information on the right source. This study shows that: 38.5 percent of the respondents get the information on TV ads, 20.5 percent from service providers, 13.5 percent from personal references, 11.5 percent from brochures on sales points, 10.5 percent from Internet and 5.5 percent from magazines as exhibited on Table 7.

Sources of acquiring the information about the new mobile phones on the market as adapted by the customers are exhibited in Figure 3. It may be observed that the majority of mobile phone users get the information of mobile phones from television, but also from the service provider were they can ask the personnel there about specific doubts from the model or technology. One important thing shown here is that a big number of users (13.5 percent) ask their relatives or friends about new

*Table 6. "Price as Key Factor for Respondents"*
*n=200*

| Region | PRICE AS KEY FACTOR | |
|---|---|---|
| | Yes | No |
| West | 27 (13.5) | 23 (11.5) |
| North | 38 (19) | 12 (6) |
| East | 34 (17) | 16 (8) |
| South | 33 (16.5) | 17 (8.5) |
| | | |
| *TOTAL* | 132 (66) | 68 (34) |

*The number in the parentheses indicates the percentage of the respondents in terms of n.*

*Figure 2. Value for money*

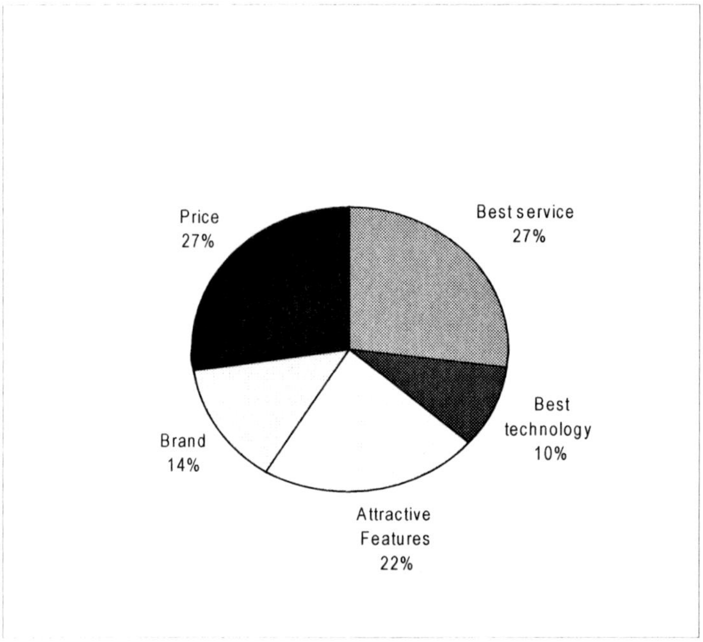


*Table 7 "Information Acquisition"*
*n=200*

| Region | INFORMATION | | | | | |
|---|---|---|---|---|---|---|
| | Service provider | TV | Brochures | Magazines | Personal references | Internet |
| West | 9 (4.5) | 18 (9) | 3 (1.5) | 5 (2.5) | 12 (6) | 3 (1.5) |
| North | 13 (6.5) | 21 (10.5) | 6 (3) | 2 (1) | 6 (3) | 2 (1) |
| East | 11 (5.5) | 24 (12) | 9 (4.5) | 1 (0.5) | 3 (1.5) | 2 (1) |
| South | 8 (4) | 14 (7) | 5 (2.5) | 3 (1.5) | 6 (3) | 14 (7) |
| | | | | | | |
| *TOTAL* | 41 (20.5) | 77 (38.5) | 23 (11.5) | 11 (5.5) | 27 (13.5) | 21 (10.5) |

*The number in the parentheses indicates the percentage of the respondents in terms of n.*

*Figure 3. Information acquisition*

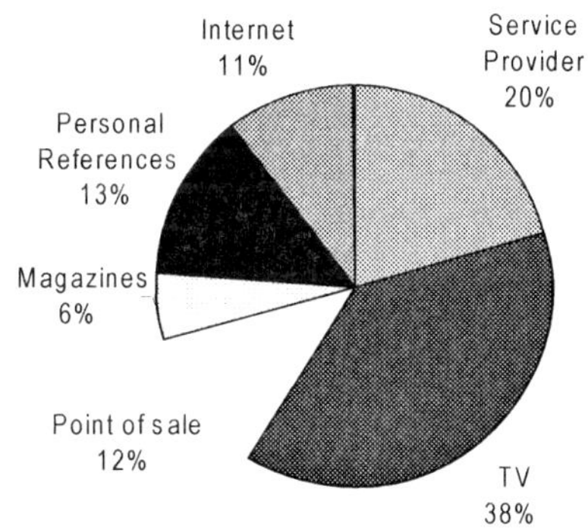


mobile phones and they consider this as a source of information. The last group of factors shows the importance of the technology as a factor for buying new mobile phones. The group shows what technological factors are important for the mobile phone users as well as what they consider a great deal in terms of "value for money" for the respondents of the questionnaire. On this group also it's shown where the users get the information in order to acquire a new mobile phone.

## Variable Correlations

It has been observed during the study that some economic and relational variables play major role in determining the buying decision on mobile phones. These key variables include: occupation, income, buyer's compliance to price, price factor, buying frequency, service factor, technology factor and manufacturer support and service provider factors. The correlation indicates the degree of relationship between two variables which shows the strength of association among variables. Table 8 shows the correlation matrix between the key variables described above.

The above results shows that the highest correlation of the variables is the one regarding with service and technology, meaning that users of mobile phones think that service providers gives them the best technology and this makes them a key factor for some users while buying mobile phones. The Table also shows that the

*Table 8. "Correlation between Key Variables"*

| Variables | Occupation | Income | Buyers compliance to price | Price factor | Buying frequency | Service factor | Technology factor | Manufacturer Support |
|---|---|---|---|---|---|---|---|---|
| Occupation | 1 | | | | | | | |
| Income | 0.7576292 | 1 | | | | | | |
| Buyers compliance to price | 0.80962082 | 0.97468394 | 1 | | | | | |
| Price factor | 0.88166375 | 0.98551969 | 0.98397548 | 1 | | | | |
| Buying frequency | 0.75738095 | 0.91369535 | 0.96502478 | 0.91894508 | 1 | | | |
| Service factor | 0.60928893 | 0.97562869 | 0.93207778 | 0.90737128 | 0.87039756 | 1 | | |
| Technology factor | 0.61481314 | 0.97815322 | 0.94618041 | 0.90801832 | 0.8765335 | 0.99923501 | 1 | |
| Manufacturer Support | 0.99842968 | 0.72142217 | 0.77551523 | 0.85478081 | 0.72190785 | 0.56241172* | 0.57168733* | 1 |

**Significant at 5 percent level and rest of the results are significant at 1 percent level.*

variables less correlated are Service and Manufacturer Support this means that users don't think that the service provider is related with the service that manufacturers give to their mobile phone users. The variable "service factor" is the importance that service provider attention towards the users has while new users are trying to buy a new mobile phone, while manufacturer support refers to the attention given by the manufacturer and service providers, like help to solve problems, manuals, guarantee, etc. Variables which are highly correlated are associated with occupation, manufacturer support, income and price factor. Occupation is highly correlated with Manufacturers support so for certain persons (with different occupations) the manufacturer support is needed; Income is highly correlated with the price of the mobile phone as a key factor, for certain income levels the price is a key factor while buying a new mobile phone and another interesting finding from this table is that Price is highly correlated with buying frequency.

## Retailers Perspectives in Selling Mobile Phones

Besides the 200 respondents for this study, an additional questionnaire (see appendix A.3) was given to mobile phone sellers from the service providers Telcel and Movistar; five questions were asked in order to get more info about the customers.

According to the service providers the customers preferences for a specific mobile phone change as they are different kind of people; if the customer is young the mobile phone selected will be different than if the customer is old, in other words, the selection for buying a new mobile phone depends on the characteristics of the users, such as age, gender, economic profile, etc; this can also be observed on this study, since the respondents were different, some were males other females, different ages, occupations, etc, and they all choose different mobile phones. Another interesting thing stated by the service providers was that according to them, the service provider makes a huge difference as a factor when buying a new mobile phone; most of the users take the service offered by the service providers as a key factor, as well as the attention given by them, according to this study 80 percent of the respondents thing that the service provider is a key factor.

Advertising from part of either service providers or mobile phones brands make a huge impact on the potential buyers; according to the service providers, when a new advertising campaign is out, an increase on sales can be observed on the specific mobile phone shown on the add. Another important thing said by the service providers is that whenever a promotional package (free time, free DVD, free accessories, etc) is out, sales on that equipment goes up, this can show us that for most of the users, if they get something for free then they get more value for their money. Although users didn't state this on the questionnaires applied, the people from the service providers claimed that advertising campaigns do make an impact and can affect a decision of buying a new mobile phone from the users, fulfilling the Hypothesis 4 (H4).

## MANAGERIAL IMPLICATIONS

Services are dynamic by nature, so to maximize overall service employment companies must be free to start up, grow, and create more jobs or if they can't compete, they must be free to shrink, lay off workers and eventually to close. Service industries are mostly composed of small companies, which are particularly likely to operate informally, ignoring tax requirements, employee benefits, and other regulations. Informality is a much larger barrier to growth than most policy makers in Latin America acknowledge. Steps to make informality less common will be rewarded with significant gains in productivity, growth and employment. Less informality will also make companies to give better services to their clients, improving loyalty and creating stronger brands which will help them to make the companies different from their competitors. Therefore the biggest challenge for Latin America is to help services become the engine of growth in high value added jobs, something that most of Latin America's countries need.

The trend of the Mexican mobile phone market is quite simple; stay communicated during all time in all places and available all the time. Manufacturers know this so there has been an increment on the number of competitors, as well as the number of mobile phone numbers. Service providers in Mexico are creating new ways to improve the services offered by them, and they are creating more support centers, points of sales, etc.

Mobile phones are creating new ways for doing business and new ways to communicate with others. In order to achieve these new ways prepared personnel is required, as well as investment in certain areas, like technology in order to create new features which can make a difference to the users and with this retain and obtain new users.

An augmented and sustainable customer value builds the loyalty towards the product and brand implying that bank managers should develop customer driven strategies so that relationship augmentations can be achieved. This is not simply a matter of segmenting customers, but also signals the need to manage the reciprocities of relationship. It has been argued that relationships are constituted by value creating transformations in which the customer may contribute in different ways. Relationship development is to improve these processes by capitalizing on an increasing customer involvement in adoption of new technology used in the telecommunication services. However, acquiring new customers is the easiest way to develop enhanced customer-technology relations favoring the growth of the

*Figure 4. Marketing operations and strategy*

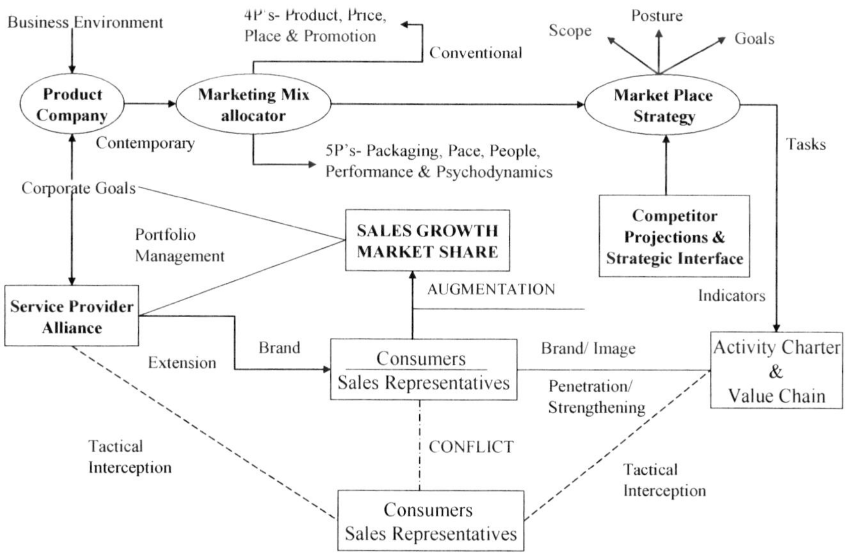


telecommunication services industry (Rajagopal, 2005b). Marketing operations and strategy implementation process in gaining competitive advantage to acquire new customers, retain existing users and enhance the customer value is exhibited in Figure 4.

Systematically explored concepts in the field of customer value, and market driven approach towards new products would be beneficial for a company to derive long-term profit optimization strategy over the period. Hence, a comprehensive framework for estimating both the value of a **customer** and profit optimization need to be developed. On a tactical level, managers need to consider the optimum spread of customers on a matrix of product attractiveness and market coverage. This needs careful attention and the application of managerial judgment and experience to measure the value driven performance of the product of the firm. It is necessary for the managers to understand that customer value is context dependent and there exists a whole value network to measure, not just a value chain. This value network will contain important entities far beyond the ones commonly taken into consideration in financial projections and business analyses (Rajagopal, 2006).

## SUGGESTED MARKETING PLAN

The marketing plan process begins with a *situation analysis* of a specific product or market. Whereas the strategies plans look ahead three to five years, the situation analysis requires that you look back three to five years to obtain a historical perspective of business. The situation analysis is divided into three parts: marketing mix analysis, market background, and competitor analysis. *Marketing mix analysis* may be done *objectively* in reference to pricing, promotion and distribution strategies. *Market background* deals with the nature of audience, human factor, the image you convey, what customers think of product, and the frequency of its use. The examination of the background permits the firm to think extensively about marketplace and customers. The third part comprises *analyze competitors* in detail. The main sections of a marketing plan and the process to follow in developing a plan has been exhibited in Figure 6.1. A marketing plan should include product name, activity schedule and time allocation for performing tasks.

Figure 5 shows the basic sections (components) of a marketing flowchart. Each one of the sections of the flowchart has been described below.

Information inputs: The quality of the marketing plan will be determined by the quality of the market research and the information that goes into it through the following stages:

- **Origin and objectives of the project:** It describes the marketing plan and its reason of being. The objectives, guidelines or constraints imposed by management should be identified here.

*Figure 5. Strategic Marketing Planning*

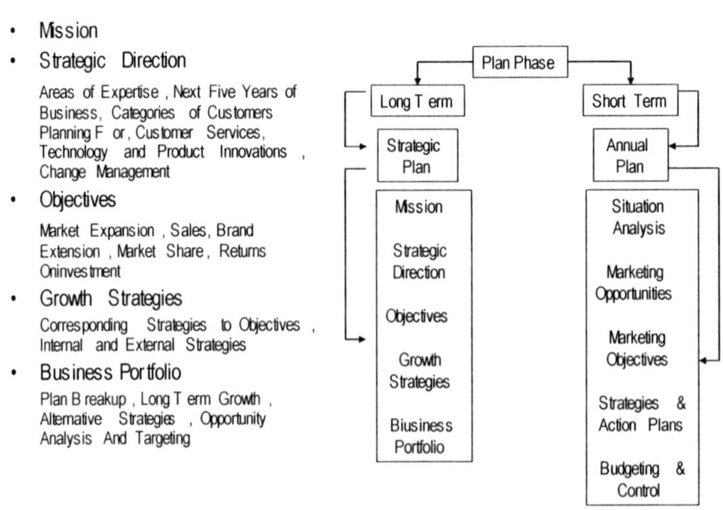

- **Market size:** If it's an existing market it should be expressed size in terms of money, showing historical sales. Type(s) of product(s).
- **Analysis of the market environment:** Demographic trends, economic trends, social and cultural trends, political and legal forces, competitors and technology.
- **Consumer:** Understanding the consumer is vital in order to create a good marketing plan (understanding of this needs, attitudes, perceptions, purchase/usage behavior, satisfaction, what he likes, dislikes, etc.). Usually to get this information a market research is needed.
- **Company analysis:** SWOT analysis.
- **Assumptions:** Critical assumptions made while developing a marketing plan.

Customer motivation and market segmentation: The motivation describe the consumer's buying motive, the fulfillment of a need or want, the solution to a problem, etc; The segment describe the group of people who are seeking a solution for a need. The segmentation can be done in terms of lifestyle, activities, interests, attitudes, opinions, demographic characteristics, value, etc. It also includes the size of the market (number of people in the segment). Financial, marketing and customer objectives: these objectives must be consistent with the corporative objectives. The financial objectives may include money sales, gross profit, net profit, return on investment, etc; The marketing objectives may include unit sales, share of market, rate of repeat purchases, awareness, levels of satisfaction, etc; The customer objectives may include acquisition of new customers, retention of existing customers, stimulation of existing customers or re-activation of lapsed customers. Marketing strategy need to be considered in reference to the following functions:

- **Overall marketing strategy:** Competing mainly on service, product differentiation, innovation, price, etc.
- **Definition of competition:** Identify those products which are your main competitors.
- **Market demand:** Achievement of sales target mainly by expanding the total market (primary) or by gaining a share of the existing market (secondary).
- **Competitive positioning:** How to position the product relative to competitive products.
- **Promotional strategy:** Use a pull strategy (heavy advertising and promotion to the end consumer), a push strategy (offer of special incentives to middlemen) or a combination of those two.
- **Communication theme:** State the theme or message to communicate to the consumer via your advertising, packaging, promotion, point-of-sale material, public relations, direct mail, etc.

- **Elements of the marketing mix** including the core and extended operations elements as following (4 traditional elements plus an additional 7 more):
  - *Product:* The main features of the product cost per unit. The brand name, packaging, etc.
  - *Place:* Distribution, where the product will be bought, middlemen's, points of sale, etc.
  - *Price:* Retail price, the price that the consumer is willing to pay.
  - *Promotion:* Costumer advertising, media that will be used on the campaigns, media cost per period. The promotion for each type of costumer, public relationships, etc.
  - *Packaging:* How the product is presented to the consumers.
  - *Pace (competitive dynamics):* Series of competitive actions and responses among firms in the same industry.
  - *People (sales force performance):* The training of the sales force, the quality of the attention, the number of sales made, preparation of the sales force personnel.
  - *Performance:* Market share of related brands of the company.
  - *Psychodynamics:* Consumer to consumer dynamics, the word of mouth, comments of certain products based on personal experience, etc.
  - *Posture:* The image of the company/service providers to the eyes of the consumers.
  - *Poliferation:* expansion of marketing area.

Marketing plan need to consider also the factors associated with dynamics of the market. The dynamics of a market includes Costumer to Costumer (C2C), Business to Costumer (B2C), Business to Business (B2B) and Costumer to Business (C2B). When a customer makes a buying decision, he moves through a process. Usually such decision can take place instantly or it could take a long period of time, nonetheless it's a process not a single event. The buying decision process begins when buyer recognizes the need Once the need is identified a search is made in order to find possible products for meeting that need. The information can be gathered from several sources (Word of mouth from other users, personal experience, expert referrals or expert users, etc.). Customers' match the products offered by the companies with the identified need, cost-benefit ratio, competitive gains, etc. which determines the decision to purchase and narrow the choice to a few "best" alternatives. The customer will choose then the best alternative and make a purchase. The final step in this process involves a re-evaluation of the decision and its results, which may lead to decision on repeat buying.

Figure 6 represents the process described above. It consists on 3 blocks (C [Customer Environment], M [Manufacturer] and S [Service Provider/Retailer En-

*Figure 6. Buying decision process*

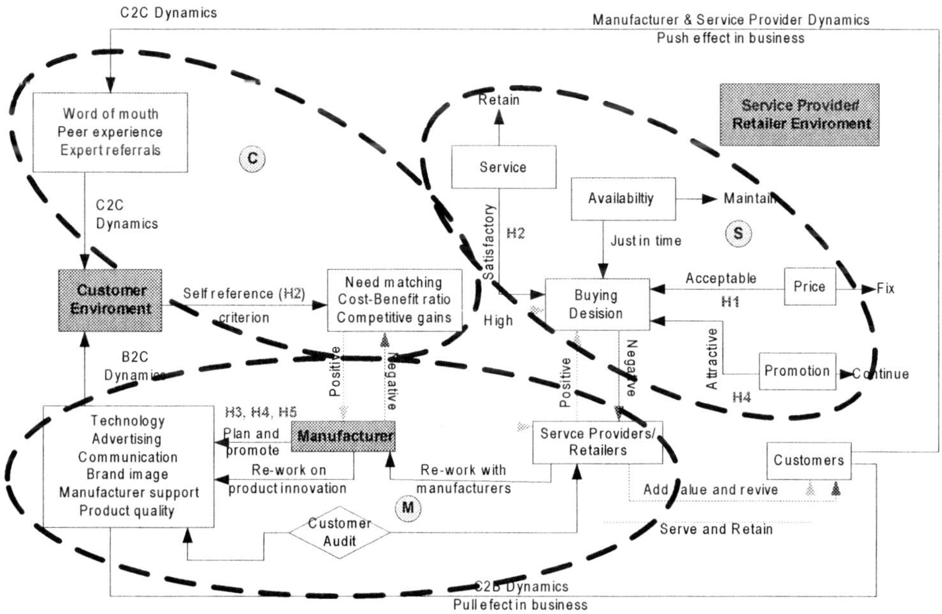


*Adapted conceptually from Rajagopal (2008), Point of Sales Promotions and Buying Stimulation in Retail Stores, Working paper, ITESM, July, Available at http://ssrn.com/abstract=1261570 with permission from the author who holds the copyright*

vironment]). Each block has the different dynamics on the retailing business (C2C dynamics, B2C dynamics and C2B dynamics), as well as the process involving the buying decision and the retention and acquisition of customers. For the service provider and manufacturers the process is little bit different. Once they have identified the consumer needs they need to make their clients aware of them (improving quality, differentiation [technology, brand image, service, price, promotional packages], add value, and so. It must be important to remind that although every consumer is different (in terms of their needs) they can be grouped into different segments; these segments will help to direct the advertising campaigns (once identified the needs of each segments, the advertising campaigns can be focused on features, brand, colors, size, technology, prize, etc.).

## ACKNOWLEDGMENT

Ernest Fierros thanks Dr. Rajagopal, Professor of Graduate School of Administration and Management (EGADE), Monterrey Institute of Technology and Higher

Education (ITESM), Mexico City Campus for supervising this research work and offering his valuable suggestions in further improvement.

## REFERENCES

Anderssen, H. (2006). ICT and Australia's productivity growth: Understanding the relationship. *Prometheus,* 24(2), 189-212.

Bharat Book Bureau (2006). Latin America telecoms. *Mobile and broadband in Mexico and the Caribbean 2006.*

Blaine, T. W., Lichtkoppler, F. R., & Stanbro, R. (2003). An assessment of residents' willingness to pay for green space and farmland preservation conservation easements using the Contingent Valuation Method (CVM). *Journal of Extension, 41*(4).

Budde, P. (2006). Mexico mobile market, overview and statistics. *Communications Pty Ltd.*

Campos, R. (2004). Niveles Socioeconómicos por Entidad Federativa. *Consulta Mitofsky.*

Capon, N., & Glazer, R. (1987). *Marketing and technology: A strategic coalignment.*

Chavez, A. (2006). Country focus: Mexico. *Mobile 365 Viewpoint, 2*(4), Fourth quarter.

Cordella, A. (2006). Transaction costs and information systems: does IT add up? *Journal of Information Technology, 21*(3), 195-202.

Comisión Federal de Telecomunicaciones (2000). La calidad en el servicio celular.

Comtech (2006). *GPRS TUTORIAL.*

Cooper, R. G. (1990). New products: What distinguish the winners? *Research Technology Management.*

CRM Today (2003). Consumer value – Not underlying technology – Will be top driver for new consumer payment tools.

Dewenter, R., Haucup, J., Luther, R., & Rötzel, P. (2004). *Hedonic prices in the German market for mobile phones.*

Duddley, W. (2006). *Market trend: The MMS gold rush.*

Durkin, M., & O'donnell, A. (2005). Towards a model of adoption in internet banking: Strategic communication challenges. *The Service Industries Journal, 25*(7), 861-878.

Durlacher Research (2002). UMTS report an investment perspective.

ERICSSON (2005). Market update: Mexico.

Farrel, D., & Remes, J. (2007). Tapping Latin America's potential in services. *The McKinsey Quarterly.*

Fetscherin, M., & Vliestra, C. (2004). *DRM and music: How do rights affect the download price?*

Frost and Sullivan (2006). Communications & IT markets - Latin America.

Frost and Sullivan (2004). Mexico telecommunications services market.

Gale, B. T. (1994). Managing customer value: Creating quality and service that customers can see. *Simon & Schuster.*

GSM World (2006). *EDGE Platform.*

Haucap, J. (2003). *The economics of mobile telephone regulation.*

Hernández, S. R., Fernández, C. C., & Baptista, L. P. (2001). *Manual para elaborar un plan de mercadotecnia: un enfoque latinoamericano.* Ecafsa Thomson Learning.

Hirunyawipada, T., & Paswan, A. K. (2006). Consumer innovativeness and perceived risk: implications for high technology product adoption. *Journal of Consumer Marketing, 23*(4), 182-198(17).

Hitt, L., & Brynjolfsson, E. (1995). *Productivity, profit and customer welfare: Three different measures of information technology's value.*

Horváth, C., Leeflang, P. S. H., & Wittink, D. R. (2004). *Dynamic analysis of a competitive marketing system.*

Hunt, C. E. (1992). *Defining and costing pots: A common carrier approach using the Joint Products Method.*

Infoamericas (2002).The prepaid mobile revenue problem: the answer may be in the cards. *Infoamericas tendencias, 33.*

Inklaar, R., O'Mahony, M., & Timmer, M. (2005). ICT and Europe's productivity performance: Industry-level growth account comparisons with the United States. *The Review of Income and Wealth,* 51(4), 505-536(32).

Joseph, K. J. (2002). *Growth of ICT and ICT for development.*

Kim, Y., & Lee, J-D. (2005). Effects of consumer preferences on the convergence of mobile telecommunications devices. *Applied Economics, 37*, 817–826.

Komulainen, H., Mainela, T., Tähtinen, J., & Ulkuniemi, P. (2004). *Exploring customer perceived value in a technology intensive service innovation.*

Kotler, P., & Keller, K. L. (2006). *Marketing management 12e.* Pearson Prentice Hall.

Kuppusamy, M., & Santhapparaj, A. S. (2005). Investment in information and communication technologies (ICT) and its payoff in Malaysia. *Perspectives on Global Development and Technology,* 4(2), 147-168(22).

Le Bodic, G. (2005). *MMS Resources.*

Lee, B-Y., & Lee, S-J. (2004). *Samsung mobile phone business.*

Lin, W., Somwaru, A., & Tuan, F. (2006). Consumers' willingness to pay for biotech foods in China: A contingent valuation approach. *Journal of Agrobiotechnology Management & Economics,* 9(3), 4.

Lohmann, C. C., & Arbache, S. J. (2006). *Are fixed and cell phones substitutes or complements? The case of Brazil.*

Macalister Hall Malcolm (2001). Selling by stealth. *Business Life*, (pp. 51-55).

Mc Connell Brian (2005). *Back to the future: Morse code and cellular phones.*

Mort, G. S., & Drennan, J. (2005). Marketing m-services: Establishing a usage benefit typology related to mobile user characteristics. *The Journal of Database Marketing & Customer Strategy Management, 12*(4), 327-341(15).

Nagle, T. T., & Holden, R. K. (2002). *The strategy and tactics of pricing: A guide to making profitable decisions.* 3rd Edition, Prentice Hall.

NOKIA (2005).*Push to talk over cellular: Stay connected.*

O'Mahony, M., & Vecchi, M. (2005). Quantifying the impact of ICT capital on output growth: A heterogeneous dynamic panel approach. *Economica,* 72(288), 615-633(19).

OECD (2006). *ICT industry growth set to increase by 6 percent in 2006.*

OECD (2003). The Economic impact of ICT measurement, evidence and implications: ICT investment in OECD countries and its economic impacts. *General Economics & Future Studies.* The Economic Impact of ICT : Measurement, Evidence and Implications (ISBN 9264021035), pp. 129-361(233).

Otero, J. F. (2004). The Latin American prepaid mobile services market. *Infoamerica.*

Parasuraman, A., & Grewal, D. (2000). *The impact of technology on the quality-value-loyalty chain.*

PC World LA (2005). *Conectados, una necesidad de la vida moderna.*

Price, J. (2001). The Mexican cellular market challenging times ahead. *Infoamerica Poder Magazine.*

Pyramid Research (2003). *Communications markets in Mexico.*

Rajagopal (2006). Measuring customer value and market dynamics for new products of a firm: An analytical construct for gaining competitive advantage. *Global Business and Economics Review, 8(3-4), 187-205.*

Rajagopal (2005). *Measuring customer value gaps: An empirical study in Mexican retail market.*

Rajagopal (2005b). Measuring variability factors in consumer values for profit optimization in a firm: A framework for analysis. *Journal of Economics and Management, 1(1), 85-103.*

Rajagopal & Sanchez, R. (2004). Conceptual analysis of brand architecture and relations within product categories. *The Journal of Brand Management, 11*(3), 233-247.

Ramirez, M. (2006). Regional perspective: Latin America. *Mobile 365 Viewpoint, 2*(4), Fourth quarter.

Rao, V. V., & Galvin, P. (2004). The changing technological profile of the leading ICT firms: Evidence from US patent data, 1981-2000. *Industry and Innovation, 11*(4), 353-372(20).

Research and consultancy outsourcing services (2006). *World Mobile Market.*

Romo, F.(2004). *WAP la unión de Internet y el celular.*

Sahut, J-M., & Lantz, J-S. (2003).Value Creation in High-Tech: The Case of the Telecommunication Sector. *International Journal of Business.*

Sangwan, S., & Pau, L-F. (2005). Diffusion of Mobile Phones in China. *Erim report series research in management.*

Savvides, S. C. (1990).*Marketing analysis in Project Evaluation.*

Select (2002). *Modelo de la Oferta de Servicios de Telecomunicaciones.*

Sigala, M. (2006). Mass customization implementation models and customer value in mobile phones services: Preliminary findings from Greece. *Managing Service Quality, 16*(4), 395-420(26).

Steiniger, S., Neun, M., & Edwardes, A. (2005). *Foundations of location based services.*

Talukdar, D. S., & Ainslie, A. (2002).. Investigating new product diffusion across products and countries. *Forthcoming, 21*(1), (Winter).

TECH-FAQ (2004). *What is CDMA-2000 1Xrtt?*

Telefonica, M. (2005). *1xEV-DO.*

Tower Group (2003). *Lessons from current consumer payments market for financial institutions, mobile operators.*

Ulaga, W. (2003). *Capturing value creation in business relationships: A customer perspective.*

Van Der Henst, C. (2004). *WAP, el protocolo para aplicaciones inalambricas.*

Vijselaar, F., & Albers, R. (2004). New technologies and productivity growth in the euro area. *Empirical Economics*, 29(3), 621-646(26).

Wagner, J. (1990). *New products are not the only way to grow.*

Wang, Y-S., Lin, H-H., & Luran, P. (2006). Predicting consumer intention to use mobile service. *Information Systems Journal, 16*(2), 157-179(23).

Wang, Z. (2005). *Technology innovation and market turbulence: A dot com example.* Federal Reserve Bank of Kansas City, Payments System Research Working Paper # PSR-WP-05-02, 1-49.

Weiers, R. M. (1996). *Investigación de mercados.* Prentice-Hall

Wireless World Forum (2006). *Mexico mobile market statistics.*

World Bank (2006). *Information and communications for development 2006: Global trends and policies.*

Yankee Group (2005). *Telefonica Moviles is first in South America and second in Latin America.*

# Chapter XII
# Building Shopping Arousal Through Direct Marketing in Retail Environment

**Rajagopal**
*Monterrey Institute of Technology and Higher Education, ITESM, Mexico*

## INTRODUCTION

Customer centered companies are increasingly engaged in direct marketing activities by outsourcing sales people to enhance the market coverage and augment volume of sales in the competitive business environment. By outsourcing sales people commonly known as promoters to perform certain activities targeted toward customers, firms are engaging in service networks. Outsourced sales people are engaged in disseminating brand image of the company and bringing more customers in the business fold by delivering satisfaction and caring their buying intentions. They are deployed by the companies and distributors at strategic locations such as in front of malls, large self-service stores, departmental stores and traffic islands in the city. Services provided by the sales promoters directly to the customer are likely to play an important role in building a firm's brand image and equity (Morgan *et al*, 2007).

Many firms have discovered that outsourcing sales promotion activities can also backfire loudly and put reputations at risk if promoters mismanage the process. Yet despite the apparent risks, managers in a widening range of industries are exploring the scope of sales outsourcing. This strategy of promoting sales has helped many companies to slash costs on advertising and publicity, and sharpen their focus on core competencies (Johnson, 2006). Personal shopping motives, values and perceived shopping alternatives are often considered independent inputs into a choice model, it is argued that shopping motives influence the perception of retail store attributes as well as the attitude towards retail stores (Morschett *et.al*, 2005). In the process of making buying decisions in the leisure shopping, the purchase acceleration and product trial are found to be the two most influential variables.

Firms and their distributors outsource salespeople intending to influence customer behavior and buying decision process in such a way that higher sales targets are achieved. Sales systems can be classified as behavior-based sales system (BBSS) and outcome-based control system (OBSS) which explain the selling process in a market (Anderson and Oliver, 1987). A BBSS aims at the selling process inducing buyers at the pre-purchase stage, and helps retailers to sell higher volume in view of the customer pull effect generated by salespeople. On the contrary, OBCS evaluates the sales force in light of end results, and compensation is usually incentive-based. However, in view of the growing competition among firms, the OBCS is widely used together with the BBCS in a continuum between the two sales systems (Krafft, 1999). Growing use of the BBCS is driven by such economic principles as Agency Theory. The Agency theory envisages the sales manager with predetermined guidelines for outsourced sales people to act on his behalf and accordingly the firm's objectives are affected by the outsourced salespeople or sales promoters (Wright et al., 2001).

This study attempts to analyze behavioral drivers which influence consumers' leisure shopping behavior and measure customers' value through empirical investigation in Mexico. The role of outsourced salespeople who act as sales promoters in stimulating arousal and satisfaction as behavioral drivers, which influence buying behavior of consumers and measures the extent of satisfaction, has been analyzed. Also, customer prospecting as direct marketing strategy through outsourced salespeople in swaying the leisure shopping and driving brand loyalty is discussed in the study.

## PREVIOUS CONTRIBUTIONS

### Defining Leisure Shopping

Leisure shopping is observed in a variety of circumstances in reference to buyer characteristics, shopping motivations, the social setting of shopping practices (*e.g.* shopping with family and friends) and the nature of the shopping destinations such as self-service super retails stores, departmental stores or shopping malls (Howard, 2007). Leisure shopping is a major source of relaxation as well as a household chore and is different from regular or planned shopping. In the process of leisure shopping customers intend to learn and respond to the new product and associated technologies (Dholakia, 1999). Leisure time is influenced by many variables viz. hours of work, public holidays, paid leave entitlements and retirement arrangements. These factors vary widely in reference to consumer segments and markets attractiveness. Leisure is judged by the satisfaction in spending and perceiving pleasure of buying occasionally exercising choice and passing time in knowing new products, services, technologies and understanding fellow customers (Watkins and Bond, 2007).

Leisure shopping is a recent development which attracts customized experience and merriment from shopping. It is argued that leisure shopping has emerged as a multifaceted activity that may be performed in various ways and embody different types of consumer meanings. Marketing communication has dynamic relationship with leisure shopping as customers experience interface with products, services and salespeople in a relaxed manner. Such process helps in prospecting and acquiring customers by attracting leisure activities like sports, amusement and *DIY* promotions. The recreational facilities to attract leisure shopping may play a pivotal role to deliver a divulging impact of consumer behavior on building brand loyalty (Rajagopal, 2007a). Retailers using a "store as the brand" strategy invest in creating a specific, unique shopping experience for their target customer and encourage leisure and group buying behavior where delivery of customer satisfaction seems to be an effective source of differentiation (Carpenter *et al*, 2005).

## Developing Buying Arousal

Arousal in shopping makes consumers stay longer in the stores, derive product and make buying decisions. Perceptions of shopping duration, emotional levels, and merchandise evaluations are derived from the level of arousal experienced by the consumers while interacting with the sales promoters (Rajagopal, 2007). Five essential qualities of aesthetic judgment, which include *interest, subjectivity, exclusivity, thoughtfulness, and internality,* need to be nurtured among consumers to develop conviction in buying. The quality of aesthetic judgment driven by in-store aura and arousal on new products, exercised by the customers in association with the sales promoters, determines the extent to which new products and brands promoted enhances quality of life (Dobson, 2007). The three distinct dimensions of emotions, which include pleasantness, arousal and dominance, have been identified as major drivers for making buying decisions among consumers. Convergence of sales promotion, customer's perceptions, value for money and product features drive arousal among customers (Rajagopal, 2007).

There are some common strategies adopted by retailers to overcome the problems of fickle consumers, price-slashing competitors, and mood swings in the economy.

Such wishful thinking holds that sales promoters can thrive only if they communicate better with consumers during pre-purchase situations and assist in product demonstrations involving consumers to help their purchase decisions (Berry, 2001). The negotiations with sales promoters whether pleasant or unpleasant, moderate the arousal effect on satisfaction and buying behavior of customers.

## Role of Outsourced Salespeople

Relationship advancement through sales promoters in the firm has a positive significant impact on the growth of sales and developing customer value. Outsourced salespeople identify appropriate customer from different markets, facilitate the dialogue with the firm and bring customers together with the firm to process the sales. Sales promoters support interactive learning processes and bridge the gap between the customers and firm (Walter and Gemnden, 2000). The bargaining power of firms increases with outsourced salespeople who stimulate demand for products and contribute to the enhanced sales at retail outlets. It has been observed that pull effect for the brands supported by sales promoters increases at the retail stores as customers gather the pre-buying information form sales promoters (Gomez *et al*, 2007). Sales promoters offer samples and giveaways of many consumer products during leisure shopping to catalyze consumer buying behavior towards these products. Many types of promotions were measured in a study within seven food categories including sweet biscuits, snack foods, confectionery, chips/savory snacks, cereals, dairy snacks and ice cream. Foods that utilized promotional tactics were categorized as either healthy or unhealthy, according to set criteria. Giveaways accounted for 13 percent of all promotions and were commonly used in conjunction with another promotional method by the sales promoters outsourced by the manufacturing firm (Chapman *et al*, 2006).

Firms that introduce new products frequently or emerge as less familiar brands in the marketplace, engage in pushing sales by working with customers, and outsourced salespeople. A broad set of process standards makes it easy to determine the selling strategies for the outsourced teams in a given market. Such standards help firms evaluate the costs vs. the benefits of outsourcing. Eventually these costs and benefits will be visible to buyers in terms of satisfaction and develop demand pull effects (Davenport, 2005). Firms must consider and alter four factors over time: the differing roles that internal salespeople and external selling partners should play, the size of the sales force, its degree of specialization, and the way salespeople apportion their efforts among different customers, products, and activities. These variables are critical because they determine how quickly sales forces respond to market opportunities, influence salespersons' performance, and affect companies' revenues, costs, and profitability (Zoltners *et al*, 2006).

A new strategy has emerged among the multinational companies engaged in competition of identical products like carbonated drinks and purified bottled water, which can be explained by two-dimensional framework in reference to distributors' capability levels (low, medium, and high) and outsourcing sales force to enhance market coverage. A match between distributor capability levels and outsourcing sales force needs is considered to be the key to a sustainable relationship between suppliers and their customers (Kim *et al*, 2007). However, some researchers have found that relationship of customers with the outsourced salespeople may not be sustainable in the long run. There is a common set of key contractual elements in most of the outsourcing contracts. The nature of customer-promoter relationship functions as the key in the selling process for new products. In this process the perceptional problems with customers can greatly devalue the customer-promoter relationship and brand as a whole (Platz and Temponi, 2007).

## Driving Prospecting Buyers

Driving consumer arousal and merriment as a major influencing factor in making buying decision is a recent strategy of retailers and an innovative concern as these factors reveal personalized enjoyment during shopping. Arousal during shopping may be seeded through multifaceted activity that may be performed in various ways and embody different consumer feelings. It is also argued that outsourced salespeople need to focus more on the consumers engaged in leisure shopping (Backstrom, 2006). It has been observed in some studies that consumers who intend to do shopping in short notice, generally lean towards impulsive or compulsive buying behavior driven by arousal effect in the retail stores. Gender, age, leaning towards unplanned purchases, and tendency to buy products not on shopping lists, serve to predict compulsive tendencies (Shoham and Brencic, 2003). However, sales promoters at times fail to recognize that what influences buyers' satisfaction is not the same as what engenders store loyalty, and consequently do not effectively develop the cognitive drive to stimulate buying decisions. Hence, they need to vigilantly manage the quality of arousal by developing adequate customer involvement in the buying process (Miranda *et al*, 2005).

Customer values towards new products are created through individual perceptions, and organizational and relational competence (Johanson *et.al.*, 2001). Firms need to ascertain a continuous organizational learning process with respect to the value creation chain and measure performance of the new products introduced in the market. In the growing competitive markets the large and reputed firms are developing strategies to move into the provision of innovative combinations of products and services as 'high-value integrated solutions' tailored to each customer's needs than simply 'moving downstream' into services (Davies, 2004). The product attractiveness may include product features like improved attributes, use of advance technology, innovativeness, extended product applications, brand augmentation, perceived use value, competitive advantages, corporate image, product advertisements, and sales and services policies associated therewith which contribute in building sustainable customer values towards making buying decisions on the new products (Lafferty and Goldsmith, 2004). Attractiveness of new products is one of the key factors affecting the decision making of customers and in turn is related to market growth and sales. The higher the positive reactions of the customers towards the new products in view of their attractiveness, the higher the growth in sales.

It has been observed in some studies that consumers intend to do shopping in short notice generally lean towards impulsive or compulsive buying behavior. Consumer's compulsive buying is an important area of inquiry in consumer behavior research. The importance of studying compulsive buying stems, in part, from its nature as a negative aspect of consumer behavior (Backstrom, 2006). Practically consumers react favorably to leisure sales campaigns of goods and services. However, customer value plays a decisive role in the shopping process. It may be argued that individual consumer behavior to a buying option is a function of preference for the option, whether it is a considered option or any choice constraint is personally directed. Consumer response is also affected by search associated with making a decision on leisure shopping in reference to the innovative products and campaign through the sales promoters creating the shopping arousal (Rajagopal, 2006).

The importance of building behavioral thrust among the potential buyers through effective communication and sales induction at customers' convenience is increasing. This process is largely managed by the outsourced sales people with focus on eight underlying factors of varying character important to customer satisfaction. These are awareness, selection, persuasion, convenience, trial, attention, location, promotional activities and merchandising policy (Anselmsson, 2006). Sales promoters instill emotions among customers in terms of merchandise choice, visual merchandising, store environment, sales personnel attitude, pricing policies and promotional activities during the pre-purchase stage. These factors are the very foundations of consumer satisfaction and decision drivers towards buying products (Otieno *et al*, 2005).

## CONCEPTUAL MOTIVATION

Direct marketing strategy towards prospecting new customers and generating shopping arousal through outsourced salespeople involves an interacting selling process. The effects of location convenience, one-stop shopping convenience, firm reputation, in-store ambience, and direct mailings generate shopping arousal

*Figure 1. Direct marketing interactions in customer prospecting and creating shopping arousal*

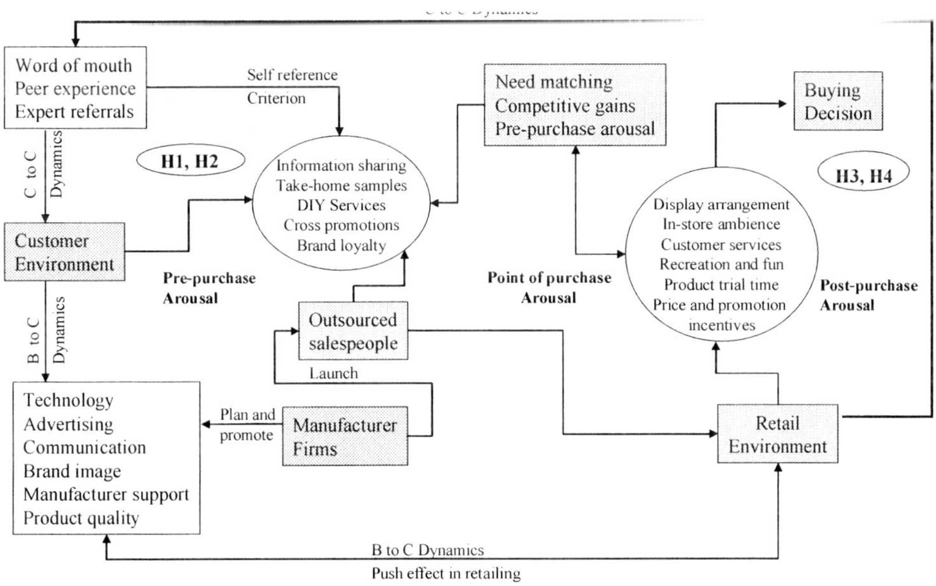


among the leisure shoppers. Satisfaction and trust developed by the outsourced salespeople during pre-purchase phase of buying help persuading brand orientation among customers (Liu and Wu, 2007). Consumers react encouragingly to leisure sales campaigns run by the outsourced salespeople, however, in-store arousal and perceived values play a decisive role in the leisure shopping process (Rajagopal, 2006; Anselmsson, 2006). Arousal during shopping begins through multifaceted activities that stimulate consumer feelings. It is observed that outsourced salespeople largely target leisure shoppers who are bent towards experimenting new products (Backstrom, 2006). The role of outsourced salespeople in building pre- and post-purchase shopping arousal, derived from the previous research studies reviewed in the pretext is exhibited in Figure 1.

The above figure illustrates that the pre-purchase shopping arousal is created by the manufacturing firms through direct marketing approaches engaging outsourced salespeople. Such interactions drive business-to-consumer (B-to-C) marketing approaches. Retailing firms develop the point of purchase satisfaction and pos-purchase arousal which prompts consumer-to-consumer (C-to-C) interactions and help in building brand loyalty. The hypotheses H1 and H2 have been framed considering pre-purchase arousal and the construct of hypotheses H3 and H4 is based on the post-purchase arousal process as an impact of direct marketing.

# STUDY DESIGN

## Framework of Hypothesis

Consumption among consumers has often been dichotomized in terms of its arousal-hedonic nature and has been closely associated with the level of satisfaction leading to determine the customer value (Wakefield and Inman, 2003). As new and exciting products are introduced, firms prospect the consumers through inter-personal negotiations managed by the sales promoters and inculcate high arousal among customers towards buying these products. The *Do-it-yourself* (DIY) and computer aided simulations act as stimuli to consumers who intend to elicit a positive response. Further, it is predicted that the magnitude of such positive response will be proportional to the value of an option to make buying decision at the available price (Rajagopal, 2006). Accordingly, hypothesis may be framed as:

**H1:** *Consumers are influenced in making buying decisions by the product attractiveness and pre-purchase arousal generated by the sales promoters during leisure shopping.*

Visual effects associated with products often stimulate the buying decisions among young consumers. Point of sales brochures, catalogues and posters build assumption on perceived use value and motivational relevance of buying decisions of product. Emotional visuals exhibited on contextual factors such as proximity or stimulus size, drive perception and subjective reactions on utility and expected satisfaction of the products (Codispoti and De Cesarei, 2007). A pleasant negotiation ambience with sales promoters where music, hands-on experience facilities and recreation are integrated helps in maximizing the consumer arousal towards buying. It has been observed that consumers perceive positive effect during interaction with sales promoters if arousal is high (Wirtz *et al*, 2007). Hence, it may be hypothesized as:

**H2:** *Consumers also develop higher brand loyalty during pre-purchase interaction with the sales promotes which boosts up higher arousal and conformity towards buying decision.*

The impact of initial interaction of customers with the sales promoters can be measured in reference to degree of stimulation and pleasure gained by customers. Interactive tools on product learning provided by the sales promoters significantly affect the level of arousal and pleasure which contribute towards experience, and thereby influence the buying behavior. As higher stimulation or interactive learning provided by the sales promoters focuses on gaining initial experience on the product use, consumers tend to engage in higher arousing activities by acquiring the product (Menon and Kahn, 2002). In view of such consumer arousal led behavior in retail buying, the hypothesis may be delineated as:

**H3:** *Product information and experience offered to the customers during leisure increase randomness of variety-seeking behavior.*

However, difficulty in buying decisions increases during leisure shopping overruling the brand loyalty, which may pose a threat on consumer satisfaction in the long run. Sometimes a negative response to the leisure time sale is expected, independent of any short-run price advantages at the retail outlets (Shugan, 1980). Hence, the hypothesis may be derived as:

**H4:** *Consumers are attracted by innovative sales techniques and gain higher in-store arousal but they sometimes feel lower satisfaction during post-purchase usage.*

The magnitude of consumer response to clearance sales is weighed in two ways-evaluative and behavioral. Firstly, consumer satisfaction with the decision process leading to the expected level of *satisfaction* is measured, which may be expressed as one of a number of cognitive and affective responses. Satisfaction is the customer's perception of the value received in a transaction or relationship and it helps in making re-patronage decisions on the basis of their predictions concerning the value of a future product. Hence, many retailers develop innovative approaches to prospect new customers for new products by strengthening customer relationship and value management strategies (Ganesh, *et al*, 2000).

## Sample Size

In order to measure the effectiveness of the outsourced salespeople in stimulating buying decisions of customers during shopping, a preliminary investigation has been conducted in 11 retail self-service stores in the Mexico City including 4 departmental stores and 2 self-service stores on construction material spread over 3 retail locations. The September – December period has been identified as leisure period when companies and distributors engage maximum outsourced salespeople in Mexico, which contribute to 18-22 percent of regular salespeople of the firm. The data has been collected on 31 variables closely related towards influencing the customer values. These variables include various perspectives of customer satisfaction and sales strategies for the new products in order to increase retail sales. The data sets have been categorized in reference to pre-purchase and point of purchase variables for the study as illustrated in Table 1

Data has been collected from 210 outsourced sales people engaged in selling products of various companies. The products handled by the outsourced salespeople have been categorized into processed food products, toiletries and personal hygiene. The respondents belonged to the Kraft (Cheese), DANONE (Frozen milk food), Cadbury's (Chocolates), Nestlé (Ice cream), Kellogg (Energy bar), and Unilever (Knorr processed food) companies among the processed food products category, salespeople from S C Johnson (Cleaning liquids), Colgate Palmolive (Toilet soaps) and Proctor and Gamble (Detergent) were engaged in promoting toiletries while respondents were covered promoting personal hygiene products of Kimberly Clark (Kotex sanitary towels), Proctor and Gamble (Skin Care) and BDF (Nivea Face wash). Accordingly, questionnaires were administered to 70 respondents in each category of industry. Filled-in responses were carefully examined and 22 responses of 28 samples were eliminated from the study due to inconsistency and paucity of information. Hence, information of 182 respondents was considered for data processing and analyzing the results. It has been found that the overall response rate in the survey was 86.66 percent. The descriptive statistics of the data sets for the variable segments used in the analysis of the study is exhibited in Table 2.

*Table 1. Variables chosen for the study*

| **Pre-purchase Variables** | | | **Point of Purchase Variables** | |
|---|---|---|---|---|
| Product based | Innovation related | Arousal and Merriment | Comparative | Retailer based |
| $VS_1$ (7) | $VS_2$ (4) | $VS_3$ (8) | $VS_4$ (7) | $VS_5$ (5) |
| Appearance<br>Sensory<br>Durability<br>Newness<br>Health oriented<br>Need<br>Fun | Organic<br>New ingredients<br>Process technology<br>Value based | Initial awareness<br>Product features<br>Advertising<br>Hands-on experience<br>Take-home trials<br>Social status<br>Referrals<br>Satisfaction | Value for money<br>Price sensitivity<br>Buying cost<br>Guarantee<br>Cross promotion<br>Value additions<br>Competitiveness | Display<br>Retailer support<br>Availability<br>In-store promotion<br>Responsiveness |

*VS=Variable Segment*
*Figures in parentheses indicate number of variables*

*Table 2. Descriptive statistics for the Selected Variable Groups for the Study*

| Variable Groups | $VS_1$ (7) | $VS_2$ (4) | $VS_3$ (8) | $VS_4$ (7) | $VS_5$ (5) |
|---|---|---|---|---|---|
| Sample Size | 182 | 182 | 182 | 182 | 182 |
| Mean | 6.720 | 4.288 | 5.761 | 4.503 | 6.065 |
| Standard Deviation | 1.030 | 0.735 | 0.810 | 0.879 | 1.226 |
| Standard Error | 0.054 | 0.038 | 0.042 | 0.046 | 0.064 |
| Skewness | -0.906 | -1.085 | -1.050 | -0.610 | -0.463 |
| Sample Variance | 1.061 | 0.540 | 0.656 | 0.773 | 1.504 |
| Data reliability test- Cronbach (α) scores | 0.849 | 0.781 | 0.866 | 0.824 | 0.762 |

*VS=Variable Segment*

*Figures in parentheses indicate number of variables*

Initially focus group discussion of a representative sample from selected companies was carried out to understand their role in prospecting customers. Based on the pre-purchase promotion activities carried out by outsourced salespeople, major variable segments were identified keeping in view the objectives of the study. Accordingly pre-coded questionnaires were developed for the study and administered to the respondents. Besides questions with pre-coded options, some open ended questions were also administered separately for qualitative assessment of the responses. Content analysis was done to summarize the open ended questions using software QSR NVivo2. This software has powerful tools for combining subtle coding with qualitative linking, shaping and modeling qualitative information. The analysis of qualitative responses has largely benefited in deriving appropriate managerial implications of the study.

The questionnaires were initially drafted in English and later translated in Spanish for use in Mexico. The questionnaires have been translated from English to Spanish using the literal translation and transposition techniques. In translating some questions the technique of equivalence or reformulation has been used to give a correct sense to the sentence. While translating the questions, bilingual advisors help from an agency providing multi-lingual translation services was taken to ensure correctness of the meanings of complex words and accuracy in the transcription of qualitative data. Later the responses collected on the structured question were coded for analysis purpose.The data collected from respondents were tested for its reliability applying the Cronbach Alfa test. Variables derived from test instruments are declared to be reliable only when they provide stable and reliable responses over a repeated administration of the test. The test results showed high reliability

$(\alpha = 0.816)$ on an average for all observations included for analysis in reference to all variables pooled under different segments.

## RESULTS AND DISCUSSIONS

During pre-purchase period arousal tends to increase about 3.27 percent retail sales on the processed food products, toiletries and personal hygiene products per person upon interacting with sales promoters. Sales promoters operate in strategic locations such as in front of malls, large self-service stores, departmental stores and traffic islands. The implied difference between the pre-purchase arousal-led shopping and regular shopping is 16.24 percent additional spending over regular spending on an average. It has been observed that the longer the consumers are attracted by the sales promoters, product promotions, innovation and technology, and '*do it yourself*' (DIY) experience, the more spendthrift they become. The categorical expenditure on shopping influenced by the in-store arousal in the referred period as observed during the study is exhibited in Table 3.

*Table 3. Regression Analysis of the Arousal Effect and Time Spread in Buying Products*

*n=182*

| Arousal Indicators/ Product Category | Processed Food | Toiletries | Personal Hygiene |
|---|---|---|---|
| Interaction with Sales Promoters | 0.5296 (0.8881) | 0.6419** (1.1620) | 0.7204 * (0.9294) |
| Pre-purchase Stimulus | 0.6120 (0.3296) | 0.8621* (0.4725) | 0.7329** (0.3904) |
| Product Promotion | 0.7738* (0.0324) | 0.6381** (0.1281) | 0.5579** (0.1082) |
| DIY Experience | 0.3774* (0.3321) | 0.8199* (1.1409) | 0.6003** (0.7444) |
| Take Home Trial | 0.9411** (1.2104) | 0.8637* (0.1280) | 0.7146 (1.3621) |
| Referral Influence | 0.5238 (1.3170) | 0.9314* (0.1455) | 0.8624* (0.1992) |
| Post-purchase recreation by sales promoters | 0.3228 (0.7460) | 0.5986 (0.8781) | 0.5311 (0.4981) |

– *p-values * >.01 and ** >.001*
– *In the above Table coefficients represent the marginal effects on the average time spread during the leisure shopping per capita*
– *Each cell represents separate regression*
– *Figures presented in parentheses indicate standard errors*

It may be seen from the Table 3 that buying decisions influenced by pre-purchase stimulus influences 86.21 customers towards buying toiletries suggested by the sales promoters while take home trials offered by the sales promoters induce 94.11 percent customers towards buying the processed food. However, many customers derive satisfaction by post-purchase recreation or fun provided by the sales promoters and customers perceive value addition to their decision on buying the products suggested by the sales promoters. Results exhibited in the above Table show that 59. 86 percent of customers derive satisfaction during the post-purchase recreations and fun activities associated with the buying of toiletries prospected by the sales promoters. However, customer derived lower level of satisfaction from the post-purchase activities conducted by the sales promoters of processed food and personal hygiene products. In addition, the results reveal that per capita sales tend to increase in all product categories, though marginal in case of personal hygiene products as compared to other products, during the leisure shopping season. Sales during the leisure season are stimulated by the sales promoters through personal interactions, take-home trials, hands-on experiences to customers and post-purchase recreations which are perceived by the customers as economic and relational advantages on products, brands and services of the companies. Accordingly, the results discussed in the Table 3 are consistent with the hypothesis **H1**.

It may be observed from the Table 4 that significant values of the change factor representing the perceived advantages in reference to appropriate product position-

*Table 4. Sensitivity Analysis for the Variables affecting Pre-purchase Decisions n=182*

| Change Factor | Perceptional Change Parameters | Value Estimation Parameters for Sales Promoters | Location-1 (3 Retail stores) | Location-2 (4 Retail stores) | Location-3 (4 Retail stores) | *p* | Chi-Square |
|---|---|---|---|---|---|---|---|
| $C_1$ | Product knowledge | Customer interactivity, information dissemination, referrals | 0.836 | 0.821 | 0.921 | 0.598* | 84.22 |
| $C_2$ | Brand value | Trial response, product line of company, value for money, quality and uniqueness | 0.913 | 0.869 | 0.626 | 0.491* | 87.26 |
| $C_3$ | Price sensitivity | Competitive advantage, affordability, repeat buying | 0.942 | 0.824 | 0.511 | 0.366** | 64.02 |

*p values * <.05 and ** <.01*

ing strategies associated with the quality, pricing and communication would help driving positive customer influence during pre-purchase stage. Effective interactions with the sales promoters, strong product differentiation revealing uniqueness, value for money and stimulating product trial response help in building brand value among customer during the pre-purchase decision process.

The level of satisfaction derived by the customers during pre-purchase stage through interactions with the sales promoters at retails stores may be seen as a significant change factor ($C_2$), which largely keeps the brand value of products high at the retail stores location 1 and 2 as compared to retailers in location 3. It may also be seen from the result exhibited in the Table through the change factor ($C_1$) that interpersonal communication, information spread and referrals influence significantly pre-purchase decisions of customers in all the retail store locations except in location 3. This may be due to the lower level of involvement of the customers with the sales promoters in these retail stores. However, the results presented in Table 4 are consistent with hypothesis **H2**.

Results of the correlation matrices indicate a higher degree correlation between the variety of products and perceived brand difference ($V_{1,}$ $V_2$), innovativeness in the products and perceived brand difference ($V_{3,}$ $V_2$), and product varieties and perceived use values ($V_{1,}$ $V_3$). Similarly variables pertaining to take-home trial experiences and perceptions on repeat buying ($V_4$, $V_6$), recreational value and influence of referrals ($V_5$, $V_7$) are also observed to have correlation of higher degree. The correlations among these variables are exhibited in Table 5.

*Table 5. Inter-group[a] correlation matrices (n=182)*

| Variable Segments | $V_1$ | $V_2$ | $V_3$ | $V_4$ | $V_5$ | $V_6$ | $V_7$ |
|---|---|---|---|---|---|---|---|
| Variety products with value additions ($V_1$) | **1.000** | | | | | | |
| Perceived brand difference ($V_2$) | 0.829* | **1.000** | | | | | |
| Innovativeness and perceived use value ($V_3$) | 0.671 | 0.694* | **1.000** | | | | |
| Customer satisfaction on take-home trials ($V_4$) | 0.827* | 0.510 | 0.735* | **1.000** | | | |
| Recreational value during post purchase ($V_5$) | 0.251 | 0.294 | 0.306 | 0.682* | **1.000** | | |
| Brand value and repeat buying ($V_6$) | 0.542** | 0.791* | 0.728* | 0.843* | 0.475 | **1.000** | |
| Influence of referrals ($V_7$) | 0.573** | 0.451 | 0.915* | 0.868* | 0.822* | 0.819* | **1.000** |

*p-values * >.01 and ** >.001*

[a] *Variable segments are formed from the variable groups chosen for the study as exhibited in Table 1*

It may be observed from the above matrix that the coefficient has a maximum value of 0.915 which showed significant concern on multi-colinearity between the variables- innovativeness in the product offered by the sales promoters and influence of referrals ($V_3$, V7). It has been observed during the study that initial consumption of the innovative products introduced by the sales promoters at strategic shopping locations enhances shopping arousal of the customers. Attractive in-store ambience further escalates the shopping arousal of customer and their level of satisfaction remains high. However, the long term customer value is influenced by both the price and non- price factors associated with the product. However, performances of the company in retailing management of the product in terms of just-in-time supplies, display, point of sales approaches and customer services also help in building the customer values for the product in a given market. Therefore, the results exhibited in Table 4 are consistent with hypothesis **H3**.

It has been observed during the study that consumers had experienced shopping arousal at two different stages of buying process. The pre-purchase arousal was felt by the consumers through product advertisements, inter-personal communications and product simulations provided by the sales promoters. The post purchase arousal has been experienced by the consumers as an extended benefit associated with purchase of the product. Table 6 exhibits the results of shopping arousal experienced by the consumers in a phased manner during exploring their leisure.

The $\beta$ coefficients, derived through linear regression model in the above Table show that pre-purchase arousal (0.745) significantly influences the buying decision of toiletries while the post-purchase arousal (0.732) induces the decision making of

*Table 6. Measure of Shopping Arousal and Buying Intensity among Young Consumers (n=182)*

| Product Categories | $\beta$Coefficients | | | | Arousal led sales⁺ (in US $) | | | $\Delta$% in Leisure as compare to Non-leisure sales |
|---|---|---|---|---|---|---|---|---|
| | Pre-purchase arousal | Post-purchase arousal | Point of sales arousal | In-store ambience led arousal | Average Arousal led sales | Regular sales | Arousal led Excess | |
| Processed Food | 0.537 | 0.472 | 0.498 | 0.536** | 43.28 | 37.60 | 5.68 | 15.10 |
| Toiletries | 0.745* | 0.345 | 0.872* | 0.781* | 85.10 | 68.46 | 16.64 | 24.30 |
| Personal Hygiene | 0.685** | 0.732* | 0.893* | 0.921* | 80.94 | 62.60 | 18.34 | 29.41 |

*p-values * >.01 and ** >.001*

hygiene products. The point of sales stimulation (0.893) and in-store ambience (0.921) also influence significantly the decision of consumers towards buying innovative personal hygiene products. However, the post-purchase stimuli have been found lower for the toiletries (0.345) and processed food products (0.472), as consumers did not find any amusements or challenging activities organized by the sales promoters. Still all factors influencing shopping arousal contribute towards augmenting the sales of products during leisure shopping. Hence, the results presented in the Table 6 are consistent with hypothesis **H4**.

## MANAGERIAL IMPLICATIONS

Systematically explored concepts in the field of customer value and market driven approach towards new products would be beneficial for a company to derive long term profit optimization strategy over the period. On a tactical level, managers need to consider the optimum spread of customers on a matrix of product attractiveness and market coverage. A Company may also need to consider emphasizing an integrated promotion strategy for new brands in reference to attributes, awareness, trial, availability and repeat (AATAR) principle. One of the challenges for the manager of a retail store is to enhance the in-store ambience to influence the consumers for prolonged stay in the store for shopping and explore the zone of experience of new products. An augmented and sustainable customer value builds loyalty towards the product and the brand. Systematically explored customer preferences and arousal driven retailing approach towards new products would be beneficial for a company to derive long term profit optimization strategy over the period. This needs careful attention and application of managerial judgment and experience to generate consumer arousal and develop appropriate point of sales strategies for stimulating the buying decision.

Appropriate promotional strategies considering the economic and relational variables discussed in the study may be developed by the managers upon measuring the intensity of leisure shopping and the scope of expanding the tenure of leisure shopping in view of maximizing consumer satisfaction and increase the volume of sales. As customer satisfaction has become one of the principal measures of retailing performance and leisure shopping behavior towards buying innovative and fashion products, the retail promotion need to be oriented towards augmenting the customer values and in view of the various factors affecting shopping arousal of customers, a strategy paradigm for augmenting such effect is exhibited in Figure 2.

At the retail point of purchase convergence of customer loyalty, value for money and competitive product advantages drives the loyalty of retail stores. Success of retail firms grow with the customer satisfaction, brand value, repeat buying

*Figure 2. Sales promotions and buying decision process*

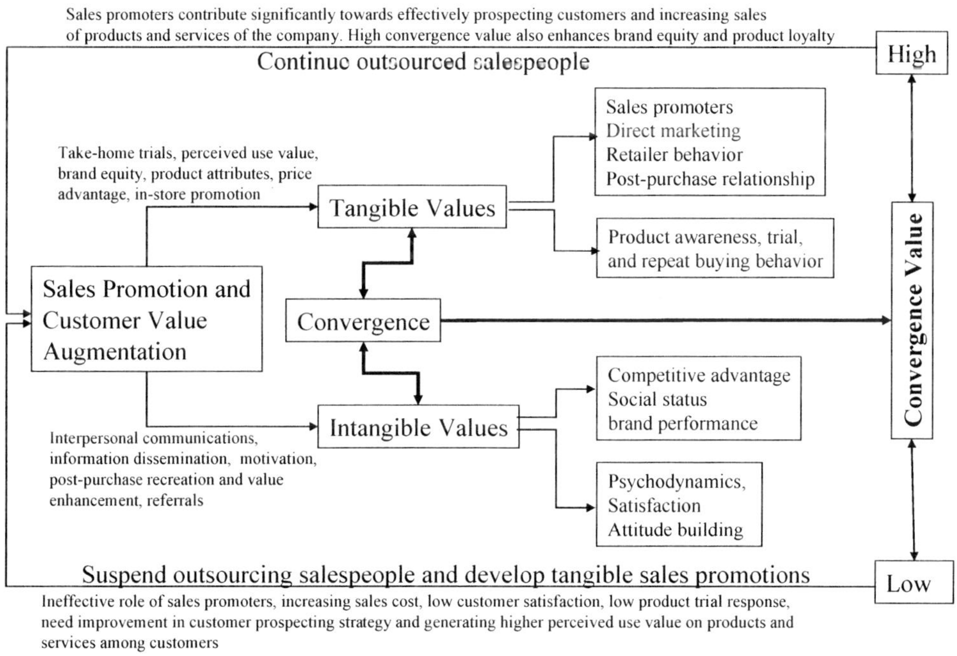


behavior and increase in the sales of products. By making effective pre-purchase interaction with the customers, planning appropriate sales promotions, user friendly packaging, generating adequate shopping arousal, and focusing in-store ambience, marketers can effectively serve various interests of the manufacturer, the retailer, and the customers. A strategic focus considering how customers and competitors will react to any promotional effort, as well as the message delivered and the stature in the marketplace of the brand delivering should be developed by the firms in order to strengthen and streamline the pre-purchase promotions in marketplace. Hence, managers should not only tailor promotion programs successfully to target customers, but also skillfully monitor its implementation through customer culture and competition challenges.

## CONCLUSION

Outsourcing salespeople as sales promoters is commonly practiced by the multinational companies to conduct direct sales promotion activities with target customers to develop pre-purchase shopping arousal. The sales promoters are deployed by the companies and distributors at strategic locations such as in front of malls, large self-service stores, departmental stores and traffic islands in the city. The paper discusses major factors affecting shopping decisions of customers in reference to interactive sales promotion approaches, shopping behavior, brand value, perceived values and price. The discussion in study reveals that sales promoters significantly stimulate interest among customers towards buying products and trigger shopping arousal. Consumers are influenced in making buying decisions by the product attractiveness and pre-purchase arousal generated by the sales promoters during leisure shopping. Sales promoters disseminate product information through inter-personal communications, brochures, referral videos and virtual resources to potential customers to develop conviction towards buying. It has been observed in the study that customers develop brand value and repeat buying behavior through hands-on experience of product, innovative sales techniques and gaining higher in-store arousal during shopping. The framework for measuring the customer values discussed in this paper provides analytical dimensions for establishing the customer relationship by the firm and to optimize its profit levels by gaining the competitive advantage in the short run.

## LIMITATIONS OF THE STUDY

Like many other empirical studies this research might also have some limitations in reference to sampling, data collection and generalization of the findings. Samples drawn for the study might have been insufficient to generalize the study results. Questionnaires were translated in Spanish for the respondents in Mexico which might have conveyed varied conceptual sense to some extent. The open ended questions were answered by the Mexican respondents in Spanish and sometimes transcription of the audio might have overlooked some issues. The study does not indicate as how behavior control, price differentiation, and promotion design efficiency cause changes in the consequences leading to leisure shopping behavior among the customers. Besides, the study might also have limitation concerning some biases driving buying stimuli among the customers during the direct marketing process such as at times take home trials may overweigh the price promotions. However to ensure that the data cover a wider spatial and temporal dimensions in the study region, data should be cleansed and filtered with many variability factors affecting the consumer behavior and retailer performance.

## REFERENCES

Anderson, E., & Oliver, R. L. (1987). Perspective on behavior-based versus outcome-based sales force control system. *Journal of Marketing, 51*(4), 76-88.

Anselmsson, J. (2006). Sources of customer satisfaction with shopping malls: A comprehensive study of different customer segments. *The International Review of Retail, Distribution and Consumer Research, 16*(1), 115-138.

Backstrom, K. (2006). Understanding recreational shopping. *The International Review of Retail, Distribution and Consumer Research, 16*(2), 143-158.

Berry, L. L. (2001). The old pillars of new retailing. *Harvard Business Review, 79*(4), 131-137.

Carpenter, J. M., Moore, M., & Fairhurst, A. E. (2005). Consumer Shopping Value for Retail Brands. *Journal of Fashion Marketing and Management, 9*(1), 45-53.

Chapman, K., Nicholas, P., Banovic, D., & Subramaniam, R. (2006). The extent and nature of food promotion directed to children in Australian supermarkets. *Health Promotion International, 21*(4), 331-339.

Codispoti, M., & De Cesarei, A. (2007). Arousal and attention: Picture size and emotional reactions. *Psychophysiology, 44*(5), 680-686.

Davenport, T. H. (2005. The coming commoditization of processes. *Harvard Business Review, 83*(6), 100-108.

Davies, A. (2004). Moving base into high-value integrated solutions: A value stream approach. *Industrial and Corporate Change, 13*(5), October, 727-756.

Dholakia, R. R. (1999). Going shopping: Key determinants of shopping behaviors and motivations. *International Journal of Retail & Distribution Management, 27*(4), 154-165.

Dobson, J. (2007). Aesthetics as a foundation for business activity. *Journal of Business Ethics, 72*(1), 41-46.

Ganesh, J., Arnold, M. J., & Reynolds, K. E. (2000). Understanding the customer base of service providers: An examination of the difference between switchers and stayers. *Journal of Marketing, 64*, 65-87.

Gómez, M. I., Maratou, L. M., & Just, D. R. (2007). Factors affecting the allocation of trade promotions in the U.S. food distribution system. *Review of Agricultural Economics, 29*(1), 119-140.

Howard, E. (2007). New shopping centres: Is leisure the answer? *International Journal of Retail & Distribution Management, 35*(8), 661-672.

Johnson, L. K. (2006). Successful business process outsourcing. *Sloan Management Review, 47*(2), 5-6.

Johnson, U., Martensson, M., & Skoog, M. (2001, September). Measuring to understand intangible performance drivers. *European Accounting Review, 10*(3), 407-437.

Kim, K. I., Syamil, A., & Bhatt, B. J. (2007). A resource-based theory of supplier strategy. *International Journal of Logistics Systems and Management, 3*(1), 20-33.

Krafft, M. (1999). An empirical investigation of the antecedents of sales force control system. *Journal of Marketing, 63*(3), 120-134.

Lafferty, B. A., & Goldsmith, R. E. (2004). How influential are corporate credibility and endorser attractiveness when innovators react to advertisement for a new high technology product? *Corporate Reputation Review, 7*(1), spring, 24-26.

Liu, T. C., & Wu, L. W. (2007). Customer retention and cross-buying in the banking industry: An integration of service attributes, satisfaction and trust. *Journal of Financial Services Marketing, 12*(2), 132-145.

Menon, S., & Kahn, B. (2002). Cross-category effects of induced arousal and pleasure on the internet shopping experience. *Journal of Retailing, 78*(1), 31-40.

Miranda, M., Konya, L., & Havira, I. (2005). Shopper's satisfaction levels are not only the key to store loyalty. *Marketing Intelligence and Planning, 23*(2), 220-232.

Morgan, F., Deeter-Schmelz, D., & Moberg, C. R. (2007). Branding implications of partner firm-focal firm relationships in business-to-business service networks. *Journal of Business and Industrial Marketing, 22*(6), 372-382.

Morschett, D., Swoboda, B., & Foscht, T. (2005). Perception of store attributes and overall attitude towards grocery retailers: The role of shopping motives. *The International Review of Retail, Distribution and Consumer Research, 15*(4), 423-447.

Otieno, R., Harrow, C., & Lea-Greenwood, G. (2005). The unhappy shopper, a retail experience: Exploring fashion, fit and affordability. *International Journal of Retail & Distribution Management, 33*(4), 298-309.

Platz, L. A., & Temponi, C. (2007). Defining the most desirable outsourcing contract between customer and vendor. *Management Decision, 45*(10), 1656-1666.

Rajagopal (2006). Leisure shopping behavior and recreational retailing: a symbiotic analysis of marketplace strategy and consumer response. *Journal of Hospitality and Leisure Marketing, 15*(2), 5-31.

Rajagopal (2007). Stimulating Retail Sales and Upholding Customer Value. *Journal of Retail and Leisure Property, 6*(2), 117-135.

Shoham, A., & Brencis, M. M. (2003). Compulsive buying behavior. *Journal of Consumer Marketing, 20*(2), 127-138.

Shugan, S. M. (1980). The cost of thinking. *Journal of Consumer Research, 7*(2), 99-111.

Wakefield, K. L., & Inman, J. J. (2003). Situational price sensitivity: The role of consumption occasion, social context and income. *Journal of Retailing, 79*(4), 199-212.

Walter, A., & Gemnden, H. G. (2000). Bridging the gap between suppliers and customers through relationship promoters: theoretical considerations and empirical results. *Journal of Business and Industrial Marketing, 15*(2), 86-105.

Watkins, M., & Bond, C. (2007). Ways of experiencing leisure. *Leisure Sciences, 29*(3), 287-307.

Wirtz, J., Mattila, A. S., & Tan, R. L. P. (2007). The role of arousal congruency in influencing consumers' satisfaction evaluations and in-store behaviors. *International Journal of Service Industry Management, 18*(1), 6-24.

Wright, P., Mukherji, A., & Kroll, M. J. (2001). A re-examination of agency theory assumptions: extensions and explorations. *Journal of Socio-Economics, 30*(5), 413-429.

Zoltners, A. A., Sinha, P., & Lorimer, S. E. (2006). Match your sales force structure to your business life cycle. *Harvard Business Review, 84*(7-8), 80-89.

# Chapter XIII
# Marketing Strategy, Technology and Modes of Entry in Global Retailing

**Rajagopal**
*Monterrey Institute of Technology and Higher Education, ITESM, Mexico*

A firm, which would like to involve itself in the international business, may look for its entry into international marketing in many possible ways including exporting, licensing, franchising, or as a production firm with multi-national plant locations. However, at any level of market entry the managerial trade-off lies between extent of risk and operational control. The low intensity modes of entry minimize risk *e.g.* contracting with a local distributor requires no investment in the destination country market as the local distributors may own offices, distribution facilities, sales personnel, or marketing campaigns. Under the normal arrangement, whereby the distributor takes title to the goods or purchases them as they leave the production facility of the international company, there is not even a credit risk, assuming that the distributor has offered a letter of credit from his bank. At the same time such arrangement to enter a destination country may minimize control along with the risk factor. In many cases, low-intensity modes of market participation cut off the international firm with information network while operational controls can only be obtained through higher-intensity modes of market participation, involving investments in local executives, distribution, and marketing programs.

*Breakfast cereal, a relatively new introduction to the Bulgarian market, is the fastest growing sector in the Bulgarian bakery products market. According to a research study (Euromonitor, 2006), ready-to-eat breakfast cereals grew by 90 percent in value terms during 2000-2005 and the market grew by approximately 14 percent just in 2005. Despite this impressive growth, cereal consumption in Bulgaria is low compared to other countries, which illustrates the immaturity of the market and its potential for the future. Besides the "novelty" of breakfast cereals, a key reason for the success of breakfast cereals in Bulgaria is their healthy image, which manufacturers have carefully created by illustrating that their products are part of a balanced diet. Although the concept of health and wellness is growing in popularity in Bulgaria, consumers still need additional education on the subject. The foreign cereal manufacturing companies like Nestle, Kraft, Kellogg and General Mills etc. have therefore invested heavily in radio and television advertising to promote a healthy image for their products and attract health conscious consumers. These companies have also set up demonstrations in supermarkets that are designed to educate consumers on the health benefits of breakfast cereals. By using samples and other promotional materials, manufacturers have tried to inspire trials and eventually repeat purchases of their products. These campaigns mainly targeted the bigger cities, where consumers are generally more willing to try new products. The entry of foreign brands in the breakfast cereals in Bulgaria is further moved ahead by the fast expansion of supermarkets and the development of this distribution channel over the next several years will play a crucial role in making breakfast cereals more widely available (Euromonitor, 2006).*

Many companies begin their internationalization opportunistically through a variety of arrangements that may be described as "piggybacking," because they all involve taking advantage of a channel to an international market rather than selecting the country-market in a more conventional manner. Piggybacking is an interesting development. The method means that organizations with little exporting skill may use the services of one that has. Another form is the consolidation of orders by a number of companies in order to take advantage of bulk buying. Normally these would be geographically adjacent or able to be served, say, on an air route. The fertilizer manufacturers of Zimbabwe, for example, could piggyback with the South Africans who both import potassium from outside their respective countries. Such practices may be noticed as American breakfast cereal products like Post from the owners of the leading US brand, which entered in the Mexican market via their subsidiary Kraft rather than direct from USA, thus leading to the rather bizarre situation of packs of breakfast cereals with English language packaging covered with stickers in Spanish. The most common form of piggybacking is to internationalize by serving a customer who is more international than the vendor firm.

Thus, a customer requests an order, delivery, or service in more than one country, and the supplier starts selling internationally in order to retain the customer and increases its penetration of the account. This is particularly common in the case of business-to-business companies and technology-oriented start-ups (Arnold, 2003). The innovative concept of market entry strategy is based on moving with *consumer space* which indicates that foreign firms enter the destination market by developing adequate consumer awareness on the products and services prior to launch. This strategy is followed largely by the fast moving consumer goods manufacturing companies and such practice is termed as go-to-market strategy. Go-to-market planning enables the firm to achieve higher margins, accelerated revenue growth and increased customer satisfaction through existing sales channels. An effective go-to-market strategy aligns products & services, processes, and partners with customers and markets to deliver brand promise, the desired customer experience, and tangible value. Go-to-market strategy services help technology suppliers overcome market challenges.

*Anti-ageing products are driving growth in Hong Kong's skin care market, on the back of increasing consumer interest in premium products and the development of consumer-focused cosmetics retailing. Consumer interest in premium products has been spurred, in part, by recent media reports on the safety of chemicals present in some skin care products. Catching on to this consumer trend, manufacturers have been introducing more premium anti-ageing products containing rare ingredients, and products benefiting from more advanced technology, to the market. This has generated greater consumer interest in premium quality products and has provided a further boost to the market. Guerlain, for example, is expected to launch a new skin care cream in 2006, which is based on a rare orchid extract and is expected to retail for more than US$350. Further, a recent entrant to Hong Kong's skin care market, Sulwhasoo which is a premium herbal based brand from Amore Pacific of Korea that draws on Oriental medicine by using a unique compound of five herbs to deliver a range of products targeted at women over 35. The value driver of growth in the anti-ageing products market in Hong Kong is the trend towards concept stores and beauty boutiques, which are retail outlets designed to emphasize the experiential aspects of premium cosmetic products. Developed to attract new customers and gain their loyalty in Hong Kong's increasingly competitive market, these brand-specific beauty salons and spas, not only engage in a highly personalized product sales process, but also provide make-up and skin care services. Since 2004, major players, such as Kose, L'Oréal, H2O and cult brand Aesop, have set up concept stores around the city, in the hopes of developing a loyal customer base (Hofmann, 2006). Such retail strategy where concept of the product is delivered with practical experience on it establishes the go-to-market strategy on consumer space.*

Some firms who are aggressive have clearly defined plans and strategy, including product, price, promotion, and distribution and research elements. Passiveness versus aggressiveness depends on the motivation to export. In countries like Tanzania and Zambia, which have embarked on structural adjustment programs, organizations are being encouraged to export, motivated by foreign exchange earnings potential, saturated domestic markets, growth and expansion objectives, and the need to re-pay debts incurred by the borrowings to finance the programs. The type of export response is dependent on how the pressures are perceived by the decision maker. The degree of involvement in foreign operations depends on "endogenous versus exogenous" motivating factors, that is, whether the motivations were a result of active or aggressive behavior based on the firm's internal situation (endogenous) or a result of reactive environmental(exogenous) changes (Piercy, 1982). There is certainly no single strategy that fits all firms, products and markets. The competitive strategy for an established firm to start a new venture and launch a new product must be shaped by the characteristics of the firm, the market, and other environmental factors. Market entry through expansion of the company draws many challenges to firms considering new business options. Capitalizing on overseas markets often opens doors to new levels of top and bottom line growth. Moreover, introducing a new product or service into a new market is an even bigger strategic challenge. A Successful Entry strategy may conceptualize and implement well structured entry processes to drive future growth, explore diversified stream of revenues and augment profit margins. It also addresses new competitors, customers, partners, suppliers and other market dynamics. However, there are five major modes which a foreign firm may apply to enter in the international markets. These modes of entry include exporting, contractual agreement, joint venture, strategic alliance and wholly owned subsidiaries.

## EXPORTING

A firm may organize indirect export through the intermediaries or export agents of the parent country. On the contrary, in direct exporting foreign markets are reached by exporters through agents located outside their parent markets. Exporting is a low risk-low investment strategy wherein a company may minimize the risk of dealing internationally by exporting domestically manufactured products either by minimal response to inquiries or by systematic development of demand in foreign markets. Exporting activity requires small capital for quick start. Exporting is also a good way to gain international experience. A major part of the overseas involvement of large firms is through export trade managed by the various channels involved in

*Table 13.1 Export Channels*

| ***Indirect Exporting*** | Direct Exporting |
|---|---|
| Broker | Representative |
| Manufacturer's Export Agent | Merchant Middlemen |
| Combination Export Manager | Company Sales Manager |
| Group Export Forum | Own Distribution Network |
| Domestic Middlemen | |
| Company Based Managers | |

the process. The channels involved in direct and indirect exporting are listed in Table 13.1.

Some companies, which occasionally carry out export activities typically, use the services of the broker. Brokers are the middlemen who bring buyers and sellers in contact for a negotiated commission or brokerage. They are just the trade facilitators and do not take the ownership of the product. These brokers operate in international markets independently and do not belong to any firm. The manufacturer's export agent (MEA) may be an exclusive agent engaged by the firm to offer services as desired by the firm. The MEA's are vested with the right to take marketing decisions on behalf of the firm, arrange negotiations and trade agreements and the delivery of the consignment to the buyer.

The Combination Export Manager (CEM) provides services over and above the broker and the MEA by way of taking over the entire export operations of a firm on a commission basis. The export operations involve a variety of activities like identifying the country, markets, analyzing consumer behavior, product designing, technological improvements, competitive pricing, distribution, promotion, negotiations with the governments of countries, public relations and collecting marketing information. The group export forums are associations of exporters who collectively manage to export activities. These forums are recognized by the government of the parent country and provide admissible concessions on export activities like licensing, taxes and duties infrastructure, etc. Middlemen who have base in the parent country of the exporting firm also function as one of the channels for indirect exports. The company based managers are the salaried personnel of the exporting firm and possess the responsibility of total export management. In direct exporting activities, the firm appoints its own export representatives for conducting the export operations in the respective markets or countries. The Merchant Middlemen are a type of intermediary based in foreign markets that buy products on their own and resell these to the identified countries functioning with substantial operational managers. They may also take up export activities without involving any indirect channel. Such offices may also be networked as an effective distribution channel for a region in order to cater to identify countries thereof.

*Li & Fung, Hong Kong's largest export trading company, has been an innovator in supply-chain management. It performs the higher-value-added tasks such as design and quality control in Hong Kong, and outsources the lower-value-added tasks to the best possible locations around the world. To produce a garment, for example, the company might purchase yarn from Korea that will be woven and dyed in Taiwan, then shipped to Thailand for final assembly, where it will be matched with zippers from a Japanese company. The corporate philosophy of Li & Fung envisages that for every order, the goal is to customize the value chain to meet the customer's specific needs. The organizational approaches that keep the company towards growth in profits and size largely set around small customer-focused units, competitive incentives and compensation structure and it's leaning towards of venture capital strategy as a vehicle for business development (Fung and Margaretta, 1998). The company operates in partnership with customers to cater to their needs of competitive pricing, quality, on-time delivery, as well as ethical sourcing. The company manages the logistics of producing and exporting private label consumer goods across many producers and countries*[1].

The firms choosing to enter the international markets through exporting activities may choose to engage the goods listed under open general license which does not involve heavy documentation process. However the goods that are not controlled, regulated or prohibited by other government departments need to be reported to customs prior to export by means of export declaration. On the contrary regardless of their value, export of all goods that are controlled, regulated, or prohibited need to be supported by valid permits, licenses, or certificates required by the government departments or agencies that regulate the export of these goods. A firm also opts for direct exporting as a platform to enter into the destination country. This approach is the most ambitious and difficult as the exporting firm handles every aspect of the exporting process independently from market research and planning to foreign distribution and collections. Consequently, a significant commitment of management time and attention is required to achieve good results. However, this approach may lead to maximum profits, higher control and long-term growth.

## CONTRACTUAL AGREEMENT

There are several types of contractual agreements including patent licensing agreement, turnkey operation, co-production agreement, management contract, and licensing. The patent licensing agreement is based on either a fixed fee or a royalty-based agreement and delivering managerial training on manufacturing and quality control process. The plant construction, personnel training, and initial production runs on a fixed-fee or cost-plus arrangement are be covered under turn-key operation agreement. The co-production agreement was one of the popular practices among the Soviet-bloc countries, where plants were built and then paid for with part of the output. In the Middle East, the management contract requires that an MNC provide key personnel to operate the foreign enterprise for a fee until local people acquire the ability to manage the business independently.

## LICENSING

This is one of the common tools of franchising a firm to set quality and operational control standards. In the past, multinational companies used licensing for many reasons. One of the major reasons may be towards the use of a trade mark of the company. Licensing may be understood as one of the varieties of contractual agreements whereby a multinational firm makes available intangible assets such as patents, trade secrets, know-how, trademarks, and company name to foreign companies in return for royalties or other forms of payment. Transfer of these assets is usually accompanied by technical services to ensure their proper use. It also helps in regulating the import and export operations of firms in such countries or regions where trade restrictions prohibit the movement of products. Some of the advantages of licensing are as follows:

- Licensing is a quick and easy entry tool with little capital investment in the foreign markets
- Some countries offer licensing as the only means of tapping the market.
- Licensing is also considered to be an effective tool for life extension of products during their stage of maturity in order of their life cycle.
- Licensing is a good alternative to start foreign production and marketing activity in a destination country which has economic inflation, shortages of skilled-labor, increasing domestic and foreign governmental regulation and restriction, and severe international competition.
- In the licensing arrangement periodic royalties are guaranteed, whereas shared income from investment fluctuates and stays risky.
- The company which has strong domestic base can benefit through licensing arrangement in developing customized products without expensive research.
- Licensing provides an alternative when exports are no longer profitable because of intense competition.

- Licensing can reduce transportation costs and help promoting exports in non-competitive markets.
- One of the major advantages of licensing is the immunity over stringent political intervention as expropriation.

On the contrary, the economic liberalization policy envisages the de-licensing of goods and services (notified) for mutual business growth. Under contract manufacturing, a firm gets its products manufactured by an independent local firm as per the agreement. Such export mechanism is chosen by the firms typically where the marketing potential seems to be low with tariff walls that are too high. Assembling involves the import of raw material and mechanical parts for manufacturing any product. Such an operation is usually labor intensive, despite high capital investment in business. This mode of entry into international marketing would be advantageous in countries which do not impose heavy import duties and which encourage free exports. Assembling firms take the benefit of low wage rates by shifting labor intensive operations to the foreign market that results in a lower final price of the product. Largely, local laws of a country play a big role in the decision-making for setting up an assembling unit in foreign country.

*Procter & Gamble offered most of its exceptional growth through continuous innovation and building global research facilities. The company lagged behind in achieving its growth objectives by spending greater and greater amounts on research and development for smaller and smaller payoffs during 2000. This situation revolutionized the strategic management process of the company to dispense with the company's age-old invent it ourselves approach and reorient to innovation following connect and develop model. Now, the company collaborates with suppliers, competitors, scientists, entrepreneurs, and others, systematically scouring the world for proven technologies, packages, and products that P&G can improve, scale up, and market, either on its own or in partnership with other companies. Connect and develop approach, brought P&G an increase of about 60 percent productivity through research and development. In the past two years, P&G launched many new products for which some aspect of development came from outside the company (Hustom and Sakkab, 2006). Among most successful connect-and-develop products of the company include Oil of Olay, Tide, Crest dental products and Mr. Clean Magic Eraser. The success of this strategy further revealed in launching a unique portfolio in the US Market. The company that revolutionized the laundry industry with the launch of Tide(R) in 1946 has begun offering an on-premise laundry (OPL) and daily cleaners program to hotels in select markets across the United States. Marketed under the P&G Pro Line(TM) brand name, the Lodging Program aims to leverage reputation of the company as a leader in home and commercial cleaning products to help hotel housekeeping staffs discover how the company's top- performing brands maximize productivity and increase guest satisfaction. The program is built around popular household-name laundry brands including Tide, Downy(R), and Clorox(R) Bleach, as well as daily cleaners including Spic and Span(R) 3-in-1 Disinfecting All-Purpose Spray and Glass Cleaner and Comet(R) Disinfecting Bathroom Cleaner. The Lodging Program presents an alternative to the housekeeping departments of lodging establishments (Proctor and Gamble, 2005).*

Technology licensing is a contractual arrangement in which the licensor's patents, trademarks, service marks, copyrights, trade secrets, or other intellectual property may be sold or made available to a licensee for compensation that is negotiated in advance between the parties. A technology licensing agreement usually enables a firm to enter a foreign market quickly, and poses fewer financial and legal risks than owning and operating a foreign manufacturing facility or participating in an overseas joint venture. In considering the licensing of technology, it is important to remember that foreign licensees may attempt to use the licensed technology to manufacture products in direct competition with the licensor or its other licensees.

## FRANCHISING

Franchising is not a business itself, but a way of doing business. It is essentially a marketing concept introducing an innovative method of manufacturing and distributing goods and services. Franchising is a business relationship in which the franchisor (the owner of the business providing the product or service) assigns to independent entrepreneur (the franchisee) the legal right to manufacture, market and distribute the franchisor's goods or service using the brand name for an agreed period of time. The International Franchise Association defines franchising as a continuing relationship in which the franchisor provides a licensed privilege to do business, plus assistance in organizing training, merchandising and management in return for a consideration from the franchisee. Franchising has become popular because it allows a much greater degree of control over the marketing efforts in the foreign country. In franchising, product lines and customer service are standardized, two important features from a marketing perspective though cultural differences might require adaptation. Franchising can offer people looking at self-employment a greater chance of success than starting their own businesses, but it is a path that many people are not aware is open to them. A franchisor's main ongoing commitment to his franchisees is to provide support. A support program should be well defined prior to joining a given franchise group and is likely to cover areas such as staff issues, marketing and system compliance. There are four possible models of franchising as discussed below:

- **Manufacturer-Retailer:** Where the retailer as franchisee sells the franchisor's product directly to the public. (e.g. Automobile dealerships).
- **Manufacturer-Wholesaler:** Where the franchisee under license manufactures and distributes the franchisor's product (e.g. Soft drink bottling arrangements).
- **Wholesaler-Retailer:** Where the retailer as franchisee purchases products for retail sale from a franchisor wholesaler. (e.g. Hardware equipments and automotive product stores)
- **Retailer-Retailer:** Where the franchisor markets a service, or a product, under a common name and standardized system, through a network of franchisees.

The first two categories cited above are often referred to as product and trade name franchises. These include arrangements in which franchisees are granted the right to distribute a manufacturer's product within a specified territory or at a specific location, generally with the use of the manufacturer's identifying name or trademark, in exchange for fees or royalties. The business format franchise, however, differs from product and trade name franchises through the use of a format, or a comprehensive system for the conduct of the business, including such elements as business planning, management system, location, appearance and image, and quality of goods.

*Papa John's has recently expanded its business in Edinburgh and Glasgow (UK). Its new-look stores compete with more established names like Pizza Hut and Domino's Pizza. The competition in the fast food market is fierce and challenging for potential franchisees. Papa John's operates a comprehensive marketing and public relation campaign for all stores. Launch events typically include a 'grand opening' day with entertainment, free pizzas and visits from local dignitaries. It also runs national marketing campaigns and special offers, backed up by a marketing team to help franchisees promote their stores at a local level. Franchisees can expect to pay extra for those services. The prospective franchisees need to undergo three stages interview process which include an initial telephone interview to ascertain suitability and solvency of applicants, an informal meeting and presentation of factual details including an outline of potential working hours and staffing requirements and a more formal gathering to discuss site positioning and to release paperwork, including a legal/franchise agreement and a business plan template to present to the bank. The company has proposed a 5 percent royalty fee on the store's weekly net sales figures, and a 4 percent marketing fee is also charged on its weekly net sales*[2].

There are many benefits of becoming a franchisee of which major ones are listed as under:

- The franchisor provides detailed consultation and training in operating the business as well as choosing locations for the business
- The franchisee benefits from operating under the established brand image and reputation of the franchisor
- The franchisees usually need less capital than they would if they were setting up a business independently because the franchisors, through their pilot operations and buying power, will have eliminated unnecessary expenses.
- The franchisor helps the franchisee obtain occupation rights to the trading location, comply with planning (zoning) laws, prepare plans for layouts, plans ergonomics and refurbishment, and provide general assistance in calculating the correct level and mix of stock for the opening launch of the business.
- The franchisee taps into the bulk purchasing power and negotiating capacity made available by the franchisor by reason of the size of the franchised network.
- The franchisee has access to use of the franchisor's patents, trade marks, copyrights, trade secrets, and any secret processes or formulae.
- The franchisee has the benefit of the franchisor's continuous research and development programs, which are designed to improve the business and keep it up-to-date and competitive.

One of the drawbacks of franchising is the need for careful and continuous quality control. Such close supervision of the various aspects of distant operations requires well-developed global management systems and labor-intensive monitoring. Inevitably, the relationship between the franchisor and franchisee must involve the imposition of controls. These controls will regulate the quality of the service or products to be provided or sold by the franchisee to the consumer. As the effective managerial skills are required, international franchising has become successful largely among those enterprises which have long experience with franchising at home before venturing out in international markets.

## JOINT VENTURES

A joint venture involves partnership between two or more business firms interested in pooling their resources and expertise to achieve a common goal. The risks and rewards of the enterprise are also shared. The reasons for forming a joint venture may include business expansion, development of new products or moving into new markets, particularly overseas. The joint venture may offer more resources, increased capacity of production, enhanced technical expertise and established markets and distribution channels. Entry into an international market would be possible either as a wholly owned subsidiary of any firm or as a joint venture. Joint ventures provide the best partner-like manner of obtaining foreign trade income the firm chooses to begin a business relationship with a firm in the host country. These two partners could agree upon a contract setting out the terms and conditions of how this will work. Alternatively, joint ventures may be set up as a separate joint venture business, possibly a new company. A joint venture company can be a very flexible option wherein partners own substantial resources in the company, and agree on a managing strategy. Firms of any size can use joint ventures to strengthen long-term relationships or to collaborate on short-term projects. A successful joint venture can offer:

- Access to new markets and distribution networks
- Increase in production capacity
- Risk sharing and control process policies among business partners
- Working with specialized staff and technology

However, partnering in business may also be complex. It may consume time and effort to build the right relationship while operational problems may grow with the following ideological and functional discrepancies:

- The objectives of the venture are not clear and communicated among the partnering firms
- There exists an imbalance in levels of expertise, investment or assets set into the venture by the different business partners
- Coordination problems of cross- cultural issues and management styles affecting the functional integration and workplace co-operation
- Lack of sufficient leadership and support in the early stages

Success in a joint venture depends on thorough research and analysis of aims and objectives. This should be followed up with effective communication of the business plan to everyone involved. International joint ventures are used in a wide variety of manufacturing, mining, and service industries and frequently involve technology licensing. The company looking for a joint venture invites foreign firms by issuing by a regional or global invitation to share stock ownership in the new unit. However, the control of the unit will rest with the companies accepting either a minority or a majority position. Largely, multi-national companies prefer wholly owned subsidiaries for effective control. A major potential drawback of joint ventures, especially in countries that limit foreign companies to minority participation, is the loss of effective managerial control. This can result in reduced profits, increased operating costs, inferior product quality, exposure to product liability, and environmental litigation and fines. When firms decide to create a joint venture, the terms and conditions need to set out in a written agreement. This will help prevent any misunderstandings once the joint venture is up and running. A written agreement should cover:

- The structure of the joint venture
- The objectives of the joint venture
- Financial contributions, liabilities, distribution of profit, and other matters related to corporate finance and accounts
- Protocol on transfer assets or employees in or out of the joint venture
- Ownership of intellectual property created by the joint venture
- Management and control of operational issues
- Responsibilities, tasks and processes to be followed in production and operations activities
- Protocol on managing liabilities, sharing of profits and losses
- Policy and process of disputes settlement between the partnering firms in the joint venture, and
- Exit policies to being the joint venture to an end and cause and effect management at post-closure.

*Ranbaxy Laboratories Limited (Ranbaxy) has raised its equity stake in Nihon Pharmaceutical Industry Co., Ltd. (NPI), a Joint Venture between Ranbaxy and Nippon Chemiphar Co. Ltd. (NC), from the present 10% to 50%. With this enhancement, NPI will become a 50:50 Joint Venture between Ranbaxy and NC. Ranbaxy and NC have signed the agreement on November 11, 2005. The increasing financial stakes of Ranbaxy in the shareholding of the joint venture reinforces the Company's strong commitment to the Japanese market. Further, the new structure recognizes the equal commitment of both partners and their intent to grow the generics business in Japan, in a collaborative manner. Ranbaxy and NPI have had a successful relationship. This logical move by Ranbaxy to enhance its stake flows from the increased comfort level of both partners and take the business to higher levels of performance. The 50:50 JV exemplifies the synergy and the strengths, which the respective companies bring to the Joint Venture. In Japanese ethical pharmaceutical industry, NC is one of the first companies to recognize the importance of generics and to make the generic business a pillar of the company's business. NC intends to be a leading company in Japan's generics market. Both partners have a complementary role to play. NC provides the regulatory know how and in-depth knowledge of the Japanese market, while Ranbaxy brings to the table, its diversified and rich generics product pipeline along with its astute understanding of the global generics business*[3].

Smaller firms often want to access a larger partner's resources such as a strong distribution network, specialist employees, and financial resources. The larger company might benefit from working with a more flexible, innovative partner or simply from access to new products or intellectual property (IP). Joint ventures offer mutual advantages for domestic and foreign firms to operate in a global competitive business environment sharing both capital and risk and by making use of mutual technical potentials. Japanese companies, for example, prefer entering into joint ventures with American firms as such arrangements help them to ensure against possible trade barriers. American firms, on the other hand like to venture with Japanese firms to explore product innovation at low-cost Japanese manufacturing technology, and make pace to enter a wide Asian market. The joint venture in this ways helps both the international firms to utilize established channels and to out-perform potentially tough competitors in respective countries. House Foods and Takeda Pharmaceutical have signed a joint venture agreement on their beverage and food businesses. Under the terms of the agreement, the two companies will establish a new company, House Wellness Foods Corporation, with a capital of 100 million yen ($840,000), on April 2006. House Foods will have a 66% stake in the new company while Takeda Pharmaceutical will retain the remaining 34%. After the initial 18-month joint venture period, the new company will become a wholly owned House Foods subsidiary (Tsukioka, 2006). A joint venture serves as a center of resource appropriation and making a foreign firm's entry into a new terrain easier than other modes. It should not be viewed as a handy vehicle to reap money without effort, interest, or additional resources. In view of the above benefits, the joint ventures stand as a popular mode to seek entry in a foreign country.

## STRATEGIC ALLIANCE

A strategic alliance for international marketing is developed by pooling resources directly in collaboration. This strategy is more advantageous than joint venture. In this process the business partners bring together the specific skills of production, marketing and control in order to maximize their profit and have a major stake in the international business scenario. Many organizations have come to rely on alliances with key players in the marketplace as strategic ventures for maintaining a competitive advantage. These key relationships can help foster organizational learning, thus giving an edge over the competition. This serves as a primary motivation for alliance formation. A new trend of collaborative strategy in international business has gained popularity based on strategic alliance through which leading firms, particularly in high-tech industries gain mutual benefit. Strategic alliances are partial merger, but have comprehensive impact on the performance of the firm. They involve mutual dependence and shared decision making between two or more separate firms. Strategic alliances differ from joint ventures as they encompass selected activities within time limits. Strategic goals pursued through strategic alliances are product exchange or supply alliances, learning alliances in research and development and market positioning alliances (Schoenmakers and Duysters, 2006). There are some important types of alliance that can be set-up for optimizing the business. They are:

- Technology based alliances
- Production based alliances
- Distribution based alliances
- Resource based alliances

One way for a firm to enter into a foreign market is to create a strategic alliance. A global strategic alliance is an agreement among two or more independent firms to cooperate for the purpose of achieving common goals such as a competitive advantage or customer value creation. Strategic partnerships may emerge in many forms including research and development consortium, co-production alliance, co-marketing partnerships, cross-licensing and cross-equity arrangements. Such alliances do not result in formation of a separate corporate entity but equity joint ventures form new strategic allies as legal entities to do specified business. The emergence of strategic alliances in Canada and other industrialized countries are related to economies of scale or scope, resource pooling, and risk and cost sharing among alliance partners. They include globalization of the world economy, systemic technological change, and the growing acceptance of the view that competition, by itself, does not necessarily ensure optimum, innovation-led growth. While international alliances provide firms with strategic flexibility, enabling them to respond to changing market conditions, they can also be effective paths for achieving global scale in enterprise operations along with mergers and acquisitions and green field investment. The driving forces behind international strategic alliances include cost economizing in production and research and development, strengthening market presence, and accessing intangible assets (Nam-Hoon and Kentaro, 2005). In the recent trends of globalization, the practice of entering the international market through such alliances seems to be gearing up along with political support from developing countries. However, the companies having a larger share in the international market still reserve the right to entertain or not, any such alliances. Strategic alliances offer many advantages in business, of which some significant ones are as indicated below:

- The organizational efficiency will be improved with the flexibility and informality in strategic alliances
- Alliances developed strategically offer access to new markets and technologies
- The risk and expenses are shared among the allies reducing the impact of risk on the participating members
- The alliance would help the partners build their independent brand and manage retailing of goods and services
- Alliances can take various forms, from simple research and development deals to heavy budget projects.

Strategic alliances are especially useful for seeking entry into emerging markets. Foreign firms in emerging markets seek to optimize the market performance in global economy and strategic alliances appear to be the obvious solution for mutual benefit. Given this pattern of benefit, the strategic alliances of US and European manufacturing firms account for over half of the market entries into Latin America and Asia.

*ING is one of the largest financial services companies among the prominent global firms, offering banking, insurance and asset management in over 50 countries. It has spread over its business to 60 million private, corporate and institutional clients in 60 countries with a workforce of over 115,000 people as in 2003. ING was founded in 1991 by a merger between Nationale-Nederlanden and NMB Postbank Group to become the first bancassurer of Netherlands. During the past 15 years ING has become multinational with very diverse international activities. The company holds insurance operations and asset-management activities in the Americas. It is well-established in the United States with retirement services, annuities and life insurances and has leading positions in non-life insurance in Canada and Mexico. Furthermore, the company is active in Chile, Brazil and Peru. The operating profits for the company in Americas have been increasing in €1310 million in 2003 to €1669 in 2004 before tax. In 2004, ING successfully repositioned itself in the wholesale banking market. The insurance business of the company in the Netherlands introduced a far-reaching plan to improve its customer service, with positive results so far. The business lines of the company further sharpened their focus on profitable top line growth, managing costs and risks and showing good bottom-line results. These four pillars are all equally important to generate above-average returns for shareholders. ING has diversified business activities in developing markets which offer a broad range of services in the fields of banking, insurance and asset management and has made its identity obvious in Asia/Pacific, Latin America and Central Europe amidst the competing local and multinational companies. In Latin America, ING is the largest insurer in Mexico and has important businesses in Chile and Brazil* (Rajagopal, 2005).

The convergence of business practices of the partnering firms often emerges as a major challenge to perform the alliance task as in international business arena partnering firms belong to different socio-cultural environments. Alliance managers must make difficult decisions about when to partner and with whom, as well as how to structure and manage the partnership. Managers who can leverage information and knowledge across each stage of the alliance process will find that a knowledge-based approach is critical to the success of any partnership. In U.S.-Japanese alliances in the past, for example, Japanese companies saw these partnerships as a way to learn from their partner, while their U.S. counterparts used these alliances as a substitute for more competitive skills, ultimately resulting in an erosion of their own internal skills. Therefore, with companies that look on alliances as a way of learning from their partners, practices that enable knowledge sharing, creation, dissemination and internalization become critical (Parise Salvatore and Sasson, 2002). Cisco Systems and Polycom Inc. have a strategic agreement for joint development, licensing, and sales of Internet protocol (IP) telephony solutions. The objective of the alliance is to deliver enhanced IP telephones to enterprise customers; this agreement combines Polycom's leadership in audio conferencing technologies and Cisco's industry-leading expertise in IP networking and IP telephony. Based on this agreement, Polycom and Cisco have brought a Voice over IP (VoIP) conference phone to market that provides customers with industry-leading group conferencing capabilities within the Cisco IP Telephony environment[4].

## WHOLLY-OWNED SUBSIDIARIES

The multi-national companies also plan to enter into a new international market establishing themselves in overseas markets by direct investment in a manufacturing or assembly subsidiary company. In view of the frequently changing economic, social and political conditions globally, these wholly-owned subsidiaries are highly risk averse. A wholly owned subsidiary in manufacturing can involve investment in a new manufacturing or assembly plant or the acquisition of an existing plant (such as Coca-Cola Company purchases local bottling plants in developing countries). The presence of actual manufacturing operations helps support marketing activities. As manufacturing is established abroad through direct investment, parts and components are often exported from the home country. Besides manufacturing subsidiaries, establishing a sales subsidiary requires relatively low levels of capital investment which leads to low risk. HP Financial Services has emerged in 2002 as the parent company Hewlett Packard's (HP) new leasing and financial services subsidiary. HP Financial Services (HPFS) is designed to enhance the worldwide sales efforts of the parent company by delivering a broad range of financial services and asset management capabilities that can positively impact the customer and partner relationships and shareowner value of the parent company . The HPFS represents approximately 4 percent of total revenue of parent company. This new subsidiary brings a centralized business model for the financial services offered to customers as part of a total HP solution[5].

*Cadbury has played an excellent strategic move by acquiring Green & Black's (G&B), organic food products, which has been leading with 90 percent market share in organic chocolates. In the global marketplace for organic products, the organic chocolate market in United Kingdom was worth £24 million in 2004 and growing on an average by a phenomenal 30% each year since 2002. With this acquisition G &B has enabled Cadbury to enter both the organic and premium chocolate markets, which are growing faster than chocolate confectionery overall, with a well-established brand that already enjoys significantly wider distribution than many other organic products. G & B is the fastest growing chocolate confectionery brand in the UK and will also benefit from Cadbury's strong presence in impulse channels such as newsagents, where distribution of their products is still relatively weak. Nonetheless the company's sales have more than quadrupled between 2001 and 2004 thanks to a combination of other factors, including good distribution across various channels from foodservice to supermarkets, the premium image of the brand and the company's fair trade policies* (Benkouider, 2005).

The parent ventures, which are managed by wholly-owned subsidiaries, are more successful than shared management ventures, where both companies-parent and subsidiary-contribute on operational strategies. Problems often arise in shared situations because managers of international ventures have communication problems and different attitudes regarding time, job performance and the desirability of change (Killing, 1982). Firms become multinational companies by setting up manufacturing or marketing subsidiaries overseas and transferring knowledge, which embodies its advantage, from one country to another. That is, knowledge flows from headquarters to overseas subsidiaries. Venturing is serious business, requiring skill, patience, and entrepreneurial flair. Most new ventures involve entering unfamiliar markets, employing unfamiliar technology, and implementing an unfamiliar organizational structure. An approach of particular promise is the new-style joint venture, in which a small company with vigor, flexibility, and advanced technology joins forces with a large company with capital, marketing strength, and distribution channels (Rajagopal, 2006). In order to determine the fit between the parent company and its subsidiaries, corporate strategists should evaluate the operational areas which includes the critical success factors of the business, the parenting opportunities in the business, organizational attributes of the parent company, and the financial results (Campbell *et al*, 1995).

## DEVELOPING ENTRY PLAN

An international marketing plan is prepared considering various factors that determine marketing functions across various countries. However, the marketing plan primarily needs to be designed considering the principal business components as stated below:

- Commitment on decisions taken by the marketing firm
- Selection of country or cluster of countries (trade region)
- Mode of entry in the market
- Appropriate marketing strategy in tune to the marketing environment of the identified country or region.
- Building effective marketing organization

The selection of a country is a critical exercise that involves the examination of all the above variables besides undertaking the demand analysis and financial estimates. The commitment of the firm to its trading decisions in the selected country, cost-benefit ratio study, and market operational methods largely determine the mode of entry of the firm into the international marketing avenue. The marketing strategy needs to be evolved assessing the objectives of the firm in the local markets in order to acquire differential advantage. Once the marketing-mix is critically analyzed, an implementation strategy can be formulated by the marketing firm. However, to ensure effective implementation of marketing policies, the marketing organization needs to be strengthened first. The decentralized organizational structure at regional levels (like Central Asia, South-East Asia, Middle-East, Far-East, etc.) would be appropriate for a marketing firm when planning for international marketing in more than one country. Such an organizational set-up would facilitate monitoring of demand, supply, price trend and political interventions more comprehensively. The centralized set-up would be of greater cost but less effective in exercising the marketing implementation and control measures.

A two stage selection process is required for the firm in identifying the product, market and services for international marketing. In this process, first, potential international markets need to be explored. Secondly, comparison of the domestic market of the firm with those abroad needs to be carried out in order to ensure that marketing at the international level has cooperative advantages over the domestic market (Rajagopal, 2004). Identifying a marketing region is always better than restricting to an individual country for the purpose of cost effective distribution networking. In addition, the tariff walls at the border countries need to be studied carefully. The firm involved in the international marketing should also make efforts to develop export markets in the initial stage. This would help in product specialization. International business firms have found that exporting is cheaper than manufacturing in overseas markets. There still remain some basic issues to be examined by the firm engaged in international marketing. These are:

- Size and growth
- Marketing potential of a country or region
- Similarities in host countries
- Free trade area, customs, common market
- Economic and political unions
- Appropriate economies of scale in managing business
- Accessibility, infrastructure and its cost
- Possibilities of decentralizing business activities
- Geographical boundaries of the markets
- Long run market segmentation

Exporting firms should understand that the export operations are subordinate to the domestic market policies and that the policy of the business firm to market the surplus home produce in the international market, would largely be determined by the opportunities offered by the host country or regional markets. However, the considerations on —(i) the firm's extent of awareness on varying requirements of consumers (ii) market response to the design and packaging of the product (iii) the impact of the pre-launch promotion among the focus groups and (iv) the size of the market which influences the adaptation process of goods and services at the international markets level.

*Roche is a pharmaceutical research, technology and market-driven company, whose unique portfolio of products and services creates superior value for the customers. The products of the company are delivered through its affiliates located all over the world. Affiliates or regional representations are direct link to the customers and local markets of the company. Roche Diagnostics integrates its own know-how with that of selected partners from a wide range of specialized areas. With this objective in mind, Roche Diagnostic's strategic alliances and collaborative partnerships are aimed at combining potential with an innovative and ambitious approach. Best known examples of successful and long lasting partnerships are the global alliances with Hitachi (since 1978) for clinical chemistry and immunoassay systems, with Sysmex (since 1998) for hematology systems and with Stago (since 1973) in selected countries for coagulation systems. Roche Centralized Diagnostics (formerly Roche Laboratory Systems) directs its products and services at private labs, laboratory associations and central hospital laboratories, offering high-performance analysis systems to measure hundreds of different parameters in clinical specimens as well as programs to optimize lab processes, from sample down to result management. In cooperation with its partners Hitachi, Sysmex and Stago, Roche Centralized Diagnostics offers a full line of solutions for laboratories of all workloads. Roche Centralized Diagnostics' ultimate goal is to improve patients' health through the application of modern laboratory diagnostics as an integrated part of health management systems. In another alliance Roche-Syntex Mexico is engaged in selling the diagnostic reagents and equipments to the government and private clinics. The company also provides the diagnostic equipments to these health institutions and hospitals on lease. The business environment of the diagnostic market in Mexico is highly competitive and distributor oriented. The laboratory diagnostics supplier base in Mexico is confined to the selected suppliers dominating 80% of the total market* (Rajagopal, 2003).

The firms preparing for international marketing should also keep track of the international subsidies provided to the developing countries. A strong political and economic information system would help the firms in preparing international marketing plans more effectively. The synthesis of these inputs for planning is essential in pursuing global strategies. Thus integration of this information with the border-country profiles is a pre-requisite for sound plans. The selection of a market place at international level is a critical process and is required to be filtered at many intermediate levels to select the core business country.

## CONTROL MANAGEMENT

A control feedback system is one of the core components of international marketing management and it serves to assess performance. Monitoring is one of the tools to measure the degree of the success of international marketing and needs to be incorporated in the plan itself. The marketing plans need to specify the periodicity of the control exercises and its prime objective. The monitoring calendar for international marketing firms may be designed keeping the following checks in mind:

- Budgetary control
- Plan implementation
- Performance of marketing functions (11Ps) which include product, price, place, promotion, packaging, pace, people, performance, psychodynamics, posture and proliferation
- Periodical appraisals of marketing information
- Social, cultural and political changes

The overall objective of these checks and controls is to determine the achievement of targeted results on time. These points need to be administered from the corporate office of the business firm in a centralized manner in order to enable effective planning and execution process. The standardization of marketing-mix is usually centralized to ensure the quality of all the components of the mix across the markets in the operational region. Besides, it is important to provide a common business language across markets which would help in understanding local markets more analytically. The checks need to be exercised at different levels of the marketing plan execution and to build-up a strong communication and information system. A consolidated document of the target group index (TGI) may be an appropriate tool for information processing and analysis. The variables which need to be covered in the TGI include consumer goods, industrial goods, services, spatial and temporal trend of demand and price, distribution patterns, marketing budgets, response to advertising, communication services and the like. International marketing research needs to be conducted on specific issues of interest and inferences may be tagged along with the Monitoring and Evaluation (M&E) process. Nevertheless, M&E should be conducted periodically as a tool of control.

## EXIT POLICY

It is essential that the firm entering into the international market needs to analyze the level of profitability, asset-production ratio, production costs, sales projections, and the risk factors in the short and long run. Further, it is very important that the firm should make all possible arrangements for a smooth ejection from the international business in case of an unavoidable loss to property, brand or functional markets. The firm usually faces exit barriers after entry. A firm will be reluctant to commit on non-recoverable investments that have been made, people hired, contracts signed if there is likelihood of a forced exit. Another consideration for the marketer is the potential loss of goodwill accompanying withdrawal from an important and visible market. The French automaker Peugeot probably lost a great deal of brand equity and money in the U.S. market before finally exiting in 1992. The specific exit reasons for international firms to leave the operational stream are listed below:

- Shut down of specific operations
- Labor scarcity and high wage rates
- Market speculation and its impact
- Employees' demand, labor problems and threats
- Changing government regulations
- International trade policies
- Total mismanagement

Hence, exiting strategy should also be carefully designed together with the approaches for entering the international market. Enough capital cushions are to be built or insured against risks in the world markets and against abrupt exits. In the era of global marketing, the company needs sufficient resources and capability to nurture and sustain its products and brands, thus surmounting exit barriers by never having to face them.

## MARKET UNCERTAINTIES AND ENTRY DECISIONS

In turbulent markets the competitive strategy provides the conceptual magnitude that integrates various functional activities and marketing programs for sustaining the competitive threats. The effective competitive strategies have a direct bearing on possessing the relative market share and growth of the business organization. The strategies are the directional statements and need to be converted into the step-by-step plan of action for effective plan implementation. The strategic directions have four options that can be expressed by 4As - arena, advantage, access and activities. The arena may be defined as serving the targeted market segment through an appropriate scale of operations and scope of activities to be performed for competitive advantage. The advantages in the process consist of positioning the products theme that differentiates the business from competitors. The access may be referred to the communication and distribution channels used to reach the market in the uncertain business conditions. These activities are interdependent and are affected by the change in any of the factors. The arena of the market largely dictates the customers to be served by the company, the competitors to by-passes and the key success factors to be considered upon. Each market has distinctive profile of key success factors developed by the attributes of the market. The recent development of corporate strategies shows that many multi-national companies are considering their choice of the market arena based on the following factors:

- There is an increasing trend of market fragmentation. New segments with specific needs are emerging and are being served by the specialist competitors by offering tailor made goods and services.
- The traditional market boundaries are disappearing as a consequence of the rush of substitutes emerging due to the technological growth.
- The transformation of existing self-contained regional and national markets into global markets.

In the above discussed situations the challenge for the corporate sector management may be observed as to find the right balance of global reach and standardization of the activities versus the traditional strategies or local adaptation. The companies need to find out the competitive advantages within the chosen arena of business. The core issue associated with the competitive advantage is positioning of the theme that sets a business apart from the rivals in the way that is meaningful to target the customers. It is necessary for the companies to move aggressively against the competitors to retain their market territories and build a strong defense. Thus Kodak asserted itself in the film market against the strategies of Fuji in American market. The supply gluts also put pressure on advantages. The markets for the pharmaceuticals, electronics and automobiles suffer chronic global overcapacity to the extent of 15-40 percent. Such problem situation demands the companies to develop the strategies of competitive advantage to hold the key success factors and become the market leader. Such strategies are required as there are too many firms competing and the customers may back integrate by their marketing requirement rather than buying them. This situation reduces the volume of market demand relative to supply and the customers may sell their excess capacity on competition with their one-time supplier. The need for the competitively advantageous strategies may further be justified as a large number of firms are increasingly productive in reference to the rapid diffusion of the technologies. The customers' bargaining power also works out to be an instrument to either broaden or narrow the differences between the competitors. The companies that use intermediaries are often encountered with balancing the power of distribution and delivery of services. In consumer markets the retail trade is forcing major concessions on the multi-national brands. Such strategies hold the access to the retail network through a long chain of channels. Conventionally the choice of appropriate scale in business and scope thereof were guided by the concepts of *the bigger is better* and *umbrella control of activities*. In the current era of globalization the decentralization of activities and production sharing have become more effective tools in marketing. The profit centre approach (PCA), control circles and total quality management practices has endorsed the success of small integrated units operating in a well defined market. In view to promote the PCA concepts and maintain the control circles, the large companies are increasingly creating the autonomous, small and entrepreneurial units to find responsive solutions to the customer problems in the well defined market niches (Webster, 1989). Corporate structures are changing in order to accommodate the concept of PCA and control circles and are exploring for the long term advantages by way of heavy investment to develop the core competencies.

*BMW, Honda, and Toyota, among other companies, begin with a strong brand that imparts sales momentum to each model. Brands that are weak—because their products have acquired a reputation for shoddy workmanship, their designs are not evocative, or their models bear little relationship to one another—cannot pursue this top-down approach. But a company stands a good chance of selling more cars and, step by step, of rehabilitating the brand if managers take pains to match each model to the consumer segments most likely to be interested in it, identify and overcome the obstacles that keep browsers from becoming purchasers, and emphasize both the functional and the process and relationship benefits of the model in question. BMW Direct is an initiative of BMW (GB) to help selected company car fleet buyers streamline their service for employees. BMW Direct is a web based fully personalized, car configuration and ordering system for the purchase of new BMWs. This highly efficient rules based web application delivers a level of information previously unavailable outside of a showroom. The BMW Direct solution provides users with the ability to view details on all eligible cars online and then go on to configure them against a full menu of accessories. BMW Direct is truly 'CRM' compliant, providing two-way communication via automated alerts and e-mails and incorporating a Contact Centre to ensure immediate access to trained product advisors. Users can track online the status of their individual orders whether by web, phone, fax or email. The call centre functionality includes phone and e-campaign generation, customer enquiry handling and profiling to customized promotions (Rajagopal, 2003a). Post-sales support is delivered using a thin client solution, (using Citrix) to BMWs contact centre in Croydon and order management centre in Bracknell in UK.*

The technological changes are the main impetus behind new market opportunities. The extent of such change may be explained from super technologies to the appropriate and intermediate technologies. The strategic choices have wide ranging ripple effects through the organization that determine the key success factors and growth performance. Some companies would be making right strategic choices by improving the implementation process of competitive advantages. These companies are guided by the shared strategic vision and are driven by the responsive attitude towards the market requirements. They emphasize the continuous strive to satisfy the customers. A strategic vision in managing markets may be understood as the guiding theme that explains the nature of business and the future projections thereof. These projections or business intentions depend on the collective analysis of the environment that determines the need for the new developments or diversifications. The vision should be commissioned on a concrete understanding of the business and the ability to foresee the impact of market forces on the growth of business. The vision will motivate the organization for collaborative business planning and implementation. The powerful visions are also the statements of intent that create on obsession with winning thorough out the organization (Day, 1990). The business strategy broadly incorporates the following dimensions:

- Customer needs
- Consumer segments
- Technology and resources
- Activities in the value added chain

The strategic thrust has a significant magnitude and direction in sailing the business though the turbulent situation. The factors associated with the competitive advantage and business investments uphold the strategic thrust to achieve the business objectives though the positive channel efforts. The competitive advantage may be assessed in reference to the superior customer value and lowest delivered cost. Such combination of the strategies may be termed as competitive superiority that explains cost effective delivery strategy to enhance the customer value. An overall edge is gained by performing most of the activities at a lower cost than competitors. This would enable the company to optimize its cost of delivery of the new products and simultaneously enhance the value of customer value to up-hold the strategic thrust of the company.

*Canon delivers innovative digital business solutions to ensure that its customers achieve and maintain the information edge. The increasingly competitive global marketplace, and the fact that the organizations must store, process and share immense volumes of information with both speed and accuracy have been the key areas of the company to penetrate in the territorial gateways like Mexico for Latin American market. The company functions with four key areas in Mexican market that include marketing, logistics, sales and services operations. The marketing activities of the company consist of planning and budgeting, pricing, forecasting, purchases, marketing research and developing promotional strategies. The company is also engaged in developing attractive media –mix and advertising campaigns and launches the loyalty programs for its major brands. The virtual shopping network is also a major part of the marketing functions performed by the company in the country. The company feels that the loyal, ongoing customers are the backbone of every business and in the prevailing highly competitive environment, these shoppers cannot be ignored or else they may be won over by competitors. The consumers might have bought such products many times in their life or some might have purchased at least once in life time. There is no single way to segment a market. The most important factors influencing a consumer's involvement level are their perceived risks. The purchase of any product involves a certain amount of risk, which may include product failure, financial, operational, social, personal and psychological. The repeat customers are more apt to buy a full range of merchandise, not merely items that are under promotional programs. This means that the dealers and retailers of the company can reach profit margin goals. The logistics functions of the company is largely international trade oriented as the Canon Mexico is a part of Canon USA and many products of the company are acquired from its USA counterpart as inbound logistics. The import process has been one of the major activities of the company in Mexico. The logistics of the company further involves the key activities of transport, inventory management and developing appropriate overseas trade and information strategies* (Rajagopal, 2003b).

There are major types of strategies catalogued and given various names by different authors. Often these strategies and tactics are so bold and innovative that they "change the rules of the game." Leaders are increasingly being advised to seek that objective in planning and executing their strategies. The pace of change today is dizzying with new technological breakthroughs occurring at shorter intervals and global competition putting the heat on. Mergers and acquisitions change the competitive landscape unexpectedly, and strategic alliances develop even among the companies that were, or still are, competitors. The concept of "*Hyper-competition* explains the highly aggressive form of competition that characterizes hi-tech industries today. Hyper-competition is said to be increasingly making its way into other industries as well. They speak in terms of surprise, speed and mobility, terms suggestive of the military approach. Not that aggressive action is new in business so much so as the level, intent and severity of business "combat" have changed dramatically. It is necessary to build the strategic business mindset to outwit the competitors and gain competitive advantages over the segmented markets. The following factors need to be considered for achieving the strategic business leadership:

- A clear sense of desired outcomes before acting. Develop a plan capable of delivering outcomes that will add significant value to a state of affairs.

- Explore possibilities outwards to capture the larger context, to see how the pieces fit together.
- Adaptive to realities and flexible in choice of tactics. Recognize that once action begins the "game board" is fluid offering both new threats and new opportunities.
- Wherever possible, attempt to achieve multiple objectives through singular actions.
- Plan a couple of steps ahead of competition.
- Anticipate the actions of business rival and strategically rehearse next responses should those contingencies arise.
- Core discipline to observe the market moves and rival reactions.
- Capitalize on business crises or behavioural change in the markets in order to turn them to advantage.
- Stay future-focused.
- Plan the business strategy implementation in both sequential and parallel direction to accomplish goals and sustain the impact thereof.
- Develop negotiations with the business intermediaries on win-win platform at an acceptable cost.
- Supplement actions with those of others (allies, partners, joint ventures.)
- Be patient, with a good sense of timing.
- Be able to scrap or alter plans when information indicates actions are not attaining their intended results.
- Develop alternate strategies for contingencies
- Use speed and surprise to gain advantage.
- Form alliances with opponents of his opponents in business.
- Learn the strengths and weaknesses of rivals.
- Be aggressive in pursuing goals, cordon the moves and ready to take on to the next.
- Assure that everyone in the company knows one's role and is equipped with the resources to contribute.
- Monitor activities in the operating environment.
- Use "what if" speculation to stretch thinking in the direction of opportunities and possibilities.

– Study the logic of the opponent's tactics with an eye toward determining what their ultimate end purposes may be.

These are some tested aspects of thinking employed by leaders to gain and hold strategic advantage. They can serve as a checklist when responsibilities include thinking strategically. Customers want more of everything they value. If they value low cost they want it lower. If they value convenience they want it easier and faster. If they look for state of the art they want it first and want to push the envelope. If they need expert advice they want more time and dedicated effort and investment. By raising the level of value that customers can expect from everyone, leading companies are driving the market and driving their competitors out of business, or at least into a malaise of mediocrity. Here are a few options for managerial consideration:

- Alter the industry structure to change the basis of competition. Reconfigure the value chain - retailers become wholesalers and suppliers, insurers takeover brokerages, banks move into insurance, etc.
- Improve the position of the business within the industry by way of acquisitions and market share. Alter the playing field to achieve an enhanced scale of operations and competitive positioning.
- Innovate and create new opportunities - new products, services, and markets.
- Employ barriers to entry in terms of significant capital investment, proprietary technology, or in the magnitude of resources required to compete effectively.
- Increase the dependence of customers for products and services in terms of the total value for customers or higher costs of switching to alternates.
- Change and enhance supplier relationships to obtain cost and quality improvements, reduced cycle times, and integrated processes.
- Change the basis of competition by creating a service relationship and differentiation. Move away from price to service, software, and customer relationships.
- Centralize into high volume, low cost, automated, 'focused factories', to achieve the lowest cost operations in support of customer value.
- Decentralize into custom, low volume, flexible factories, quick to market, responsive, and able to customize products to specific customer requirements.

Controls may be considered as checkpoints used to verify performance progress by comparison with some standard in a given competitive environment. Generally the business standards are established by top management in the planning process. The control and analysis process need to be revised with the growing size of the firm and its business operations. Controls must go along with the expansion process and tight control should ensure consistency in product and marketing performance. Since multinational companies typically have several foreign subsidiaries in different parts of the world, a good control system is important to ensure that these subsidiaries move together toward a common goal, spelled out by the corporate strategic plan to meet any market uncertainties. These issues need to be considered in anticipation by the international firms while deciding the entry strategies in foreign markets.

## DRIVERS OF GLOBALIZATION

There are over 200 countries in the world and it is difficult for the marketer to determine a critical path of success across the countries or regions. Exceptionally, couple of companies like Fuji, Kodak and Coca-cola that have spread their business in over 100 countries developed gradually. The characteristics of the global market place are diverse and international marketing approaches are different. The companies need to adapt a strong rationale for grouping the countries into segments. The multinational and the global corporation are different as the former operates in a number of countries and carries adjustment in the production and marketing practices in each country at a highly relative costs (Levitt, 1998). The global corporation operates with the stanch loyalty at relatively low costs with standardization. Coca-cola and Pepsi-Cola companies have standardized their products globally according to the regional and ethnic preferences of consumers. The most effective world competitors integrate quality and trust attributes into their cost structure. Such companies compete on the basis of appropriate value of price, quality, trust and delivery systems. These values are considered by the companies in reference to the product design, function and changing consumer preferences like fashion. The multi-national corporations know a lot about the business environment in a country, put their efforts on adapting to the given environment and sets gradual penetration process in the country. On the contrary, the global corporations recognize the absolute need to be competitive and drive through the lower prices by standardizing its marketing operations. The global corporations treat the world as composed of a few networked and standardized markets than many independent and customized markets.

There are five major categories of drivers that propel companies towards globalization. These drivers include market, competition, cost, technology and government. Of these, the market driver has been considered as one of the strongest forces that push the process of global marketing.

*The major driver of change for General Motors today is the same as for most companies; it's globalization. Advances in technology and communication are making the 'small world' a reality, and the world will only get smaller and smaller in coming years... This trend towards global integration should be- viewed as an opportunity—not a problem.* -John F. Smith, Jr., CEO of General Motors

The **market drivers** comprise the needs of common customers, global customers, global channels and transferable marketing. The common customers needs become a compelling factor for the multinational companies when customers of the different countries have the same needs in a product category. The free trade and unrestricted travel has created homogenous groups of customers across the countries in reference to specific industries. However, some markets that typically deal with the culture bound products like food and beverages, apparel and entertainment strongly resist the shift towards globalization and remain multi-domestic serving to the different customer preferences and differentiated products across the countries. On the contrary the global customers need the same products or services in many countries like the case of Kodak films or Hilton Hotels. The global channels, distribution and logistics companies offer seamless transport, storage and delivery services. The companies can expand internationally provided the channel infrastructure is met with the distribution needs of the company. Hence their integrated networks thrive to bring the multinational companies close to the global distributors, retail stores like super markets and departmental stores in order to generate systems effect. Transferable marketing is applied to the same marketing ideas on brand names, packaging, advertising and other components of marketing-mix in the different countries. Nike's campaign anchoring the basketball champion Michael Jordan pulled-up the brand in many countries. This is how the good ideas of multinationals get leveraged world over.

The **competitive drivers** support the companies for matching their strategies appropriately with their moves in the market. The existence of many global competitors indicates that an industry is mature for international business operations. The global competitors operate on cost advantages over the local competitors. The emergence of strong global competitors has served to develop the market infrastructure for the local companies and also help in transfer of technological skills enabling the domestic company to explore the scope of expansion. The competitive efforts put pressure on companies to globalize their marketing activities to derive optimum performance by interpreting appropriately the competitor signals. When Kodak backed out from sponsoring the 1984 Los Angeles Olympics, the Fuji Film entered into the sponsorship issue immediately at the prescribed price and was one of the official sponsors of the Olympics. By the time Kodak reconsidered to participate in this international event, the time overran. However, for the Olympics of 1988 and ABC-TV Kodak become sport program sponsor (Finnerty, 2000).

The **cost drivers** are largely based on the scale of economies that involve the cost of production functions in large and complex industries, cost of outsourcing, diffusion and adaptation of technology, tariffs and taxes and costs associated with the basic and advanced marketing functions. The macro economic factors of the neighboring countries also govern the cost drivers. When a new automobile plant is set-up, it aims at designing, manufacturing or assembling and delivering a particular model by penetrating into the neighboring markets to gain the advantages of economies of scale. The automobile plant of Toyota at Kentucky manufacture the Camry model for catering to the markets of NAFTA group of countries. The high market share multi-domestic companies derive gains from spreading their production activities across multiple product lines or diversified business lines to achieve advantage through the scope of economies. The manufacturing and marketing activities of Proctor and Gamble, Unilever, Colgate-Palmolive may illustrate this global attribute that is explained by the cost drivers. The other cost drivers include global sourcing advantages, low global communications and automation processes. The location of strategic resources to the production plants, cost differences across the countries and transport costs are also some important considerations of the cost drivers.

The lowering of trade barriers made globalization of markets and production a theoretical possibility, and technological change has made it a tangible reality. Since the end of World War II, the world has seen major advances in communications, information processing, and transportation technology including, most recently, the explosive emergence of the Internet and World Wide Web. The **technology drivers** play a significant role in global business. Global expansion of the multinational companies has been highly stimulated by the technological advancements in the designing, manufacturing and marketing of consumer and industrial products. The services were also improved by many technological breakthroughs. The internet revolution has triggered the e-commerce as open access channel with a strong driving force for the global business in the consumer and industry segments. Improved transport and communication now makes it possible to be in continuous contact with producers anywhere in the world. This makes it easier for companies to split production of a single good over any distance. Storage and preservation techniques have revolutionized the food industry for example, so that the idea of seasonal vegetables is no longer relevant today as anything can be exported all year round from anywhere.

In addition, the IT revolution has made the movement of investment capital around the globe an almost immediate process ensuring that financing opportunities across the developed and developing world have both expanded and become more flexible. However, non-economic drivers of global integration, from travel to telephone traffic maintained their forward momentum, making the world more integrated at the end of 2002 than ever before. Technological upgrading, in the form of introduction of new machinery and improvement of technological capabilities, provides a firm with the means to be successful in competition. In the process of introducing better technologies, new lower-cost methods become available, which allow the firm to increase labor productivity, i.e., the efficiency with which it converts resources into value. Firms will adopt these newer methods of production if they are more profitable than the older ones. The ability of a firm to take advantage of technical progress is also enhanced if the firm improves its entrepreneurial and technological capabilities through two competitiveness strategies, namely (i) learning and adaptation, and (ii) innovation. The latter is a process of searching for, finding, developing, imitating, adapting, and adopting new products, new processes, and new organizational arrangements. Because rivals do not stand still, the firm's capacity to develop these capabilities, as well as its ability to compete, depends on the firm's maintaining a steady pace of innovation (Asian Development Bank, 2003). Containerization has revolutionized the transportation business, significantly lowering the costs of shipping goods over long distances. Before the advent of containerization, moving goods from one mode of transport to another was very labor intensive, lengthy, and costly. It could take days to unload a ship and reload goods onto trucks and trains. The efficiency gains associated with containerization, transportation costs have plummeted, making it much more economical to ship goods around the world, thereby helping to drive the globalization of markets and production.

The **government drivers** for the globalization include diplomatic trade relations, customs unions or common markets. The government drivers add favorable trade policies, foreign investment regulations, bilateral or regional trade treaties and common market regulations. The introduction of global standard norms like ISO certifications by the respective countries may be one of the effective measures to promote the globalization through uniform quality perspectives. In the past the government barriers to foreign market entry protected the domestic markets and made the global marketing an uphill task. WTO has been instrumental in promoting government drivers for improving trade in the developing countries.

*At the Fourth World Trade Organization Ministerial Meeting held in Doha in November 2001, Ministers launched a comprehensive set of multilateral trade negotiations and a work program. This mandate is sometimes referred to as the Doha Development Agenda, reflecting a shared desire to ensure that the trading system is relevant and responsive to the needs of developing countries. Among the areas covered by the negotiations or the work program are market access in manufactures, agriculture and services, certain rules (including anti-dumping, subsidies and countervailing measures, and regional arrangements), trade and environment, trade-related intellectual property rights, the relationship between trade and investment, the interaction between trade and competition policy, transparency in government procurement, trade facilitation, and dispute settlement. Developing countries were particularly instrumental in putting certain issues on the agenda, including trade and technology transfer, trade, debt and finance, small economies, implementation issues (mostly pending from the Uruguay Round) and special and differential treatment. Between*

*1990 and 2001, South-South trade grew faster than world trade with the share of intra-developing country trade in world merchandise exports rising from 6.5 per cent to 10.6 per cent. Over this period, developing country economies grew much faster than those of the developed and transition countries. The liberalization of the trade and investment regimes of a large number of these countries has played a significant role in this expansion. Much of this expansion in South-South trade took place in developing Asia (which accounts for more than two-thirds of intra-developing country trade). Manufactures, in particular office and telecom equipment, played a leading role in the growth of intra-developing country trade. This strong performance can be attributed in part to open trade and investment policies in the major developing economies of Asia. Trade liberalization in Asia took various forms in the 1990s: some of it was undertaken on a unilateral basis, some arose from multilateral efforts* (World Trade Organization, 2003).

Integrating a worldwide strategy involves five key dimensions: selecting markets for their global strategic importance; standardizing products; locating value-adding activities in a global network; using uniform marketing techniques; and integrating competitive moves across countries. Industry globalization drivers that are defined as the industry conditions that determine industry globalization potential and organization and management factors largely determine the use of global strategy. Such drivers have the strongest influence in global trade. The application of global strategy in industries with high globalization potential improves business performance. The global companies constantly search for opportunities to achieve the benefits of globalization; take a zero-based view of existing activities; flout conventional wisdom and established practices; systematically analyze industry, strategy, and organizational linkages; and make multiple reinforcing changes in strategy and organization. They assume that strategy should be global unless proven otherwise, and they think globally and act locally.

Besides, the five drivers discussed above, there exists other reasons to market products and services globally. The major factors that influence the drivers of globalization may be illustrated as under:

- Market Saturation
- Trade Deficit
- Foreign Competition
- Emergence of New Markets
- Globalization of Markets
- Opportunities via Foreign Aid Programs
- Other Reasons

The most evident reason to drive the companies go global is the market potential in the developing countries that constitute as major players in the world market. The companies such as *Nintendo, Disney* and the Japanese Motorcycle industries (Honda, Kawasaki, Suzuki etc.) have been greatly benefited from exploiting the markets of the developing countries and reassuring their growth in the world market to harness the promising market potential. The emerging scope of spatial diversification has also been one of the drivers for enhancing the global business utilizing the additional production capacity at the economies of scale and low-cost outsourcing. The production sharing of *Volvo* industries in India (Bangalore) where the company manufacture engines for its heavy transport vehicles may be cited as one of the examples. The thrust of Japanese motorcycle industry in the US markets is aided significantly by its low-cost position. The saturation of the demand for the products and services of a company in domestic market may also be an effective driver to globalization wherein the company looks for building the value for its brand across the boundaries. When a product that is near to the end of its life cycle in the domestic market while beginning to generate growth abroad. *Dickson Poon's* export of high brand value luxury goods from America to the Far-east may be cited as an example of gaining advantage of general rise in the conspicuous consumption that is regarded as a sign of prosperity. Sometimes the cross-culture attributes of overseas markets that become the source of new product ideation, also may be considered as one of the potential drivers for globalization of business and explore the strategic alliances with prominent regional or multinational brands thereof. The tested market entry approaches may be implemented in the emerging markets such as South-east Asia as shown by the Revlon in cosmetics though risk of international currency prevails, legal issues and business protocols. However the most difficult task for the global companies to develop products with a universal appeal as illustrated by *Gillette* with its fragrances. On the contrary *Lego* is facing hardship in the Far-east markets to popularize its concept of *do it yourself* (DIY) for creative learning against the head-on competition of video games industries attracting the same segment of buyers ( age group 5- 14).

## REFERENCES

Arnold, D. (2003). *The Mirage of Global Marketing: How Globalizing Companies can Succeed as Markets Localize*. Financial Times Prentice Hall, Upper Saddle River, NJ, (pp. 24-65).

Asian Development Bank (2003). Drivers of change: Globalization, technology and competition. section III, competitiveness in developing Asia, Asian development Outlook.

Benkouider, C. (2005). Going Organic: Cadbury Acquires Green and Black's. *Euromonitor*, 20 May (Online edition) www.euromonitor.com.

Campbell, A., Goold, M., Alexander, M. (1995). Corporate Strategy-The Quest for Parenting Advantage. *Harvard Business Review, 73*(2), 120-132.

Day, G. S. (1990). *Market Driven Strategy: Process for Creating Value*. New York: The Free Press, (pp. 10-18).

Euromonitor (2006). Breakfast Cereals Boom in Bulgaria. *Euromonitor online*. January www.euromonitor.com.

Finnerty, T. C. (2000). Kodak Vs. Fuji – The Battle for Global Market Share, Institute of Global Business Strategy. Lubin School of Business, Pace University, New York, (pp. 1-23).

Fung, V., & Magretta, V. (1998). Fast Global and Entrepreneurial: Supply Chain Management- Hong Kong Style. *Harvard Business Review, 76*(5), 103-114.

Hofmann, O. (2006). Anti-ageing Skin Cream Booms in Hong Kong. *Euromonitor*, May (online edition).

Hustom, L., & Sakkab, N. (2006). Connect and Develop: Inside Proctor and Gamble's New Model for Innovation. *Harvard Business Review, 84*(3), 58-66.

Killing, P. J. (1982). How to make a Global Joint Venture Work. *Harvard Business Review, 60*(3), 120-127.

Levitt, T. (1998). The globalization of markets. In M. W. Taylor & G. L. John (Ed.), *International and Global Marketing-Concept and Cases*. Irwin McGraw Hill, Boston, (pp. 13-23, 1998).

Nam-Hoon, K., & Kentaro, S. (2005). International Strategic Alliances: Their Role in Industrial Globalization. OECD, STI Working Paper # 2000/5.

Parise, S., & Sasson, L. (2002). Leveraging Knowledge Management across Strategic Alliances. IBM Institute for Business Value Study, Cambridge, Massachusetts. USA.

Piercy, N. (1982). Company Internationalization: Active and Reactive Exporting. *European Journal of Marketing, 15*(3), 26-40.

Proctor & Gamble (2005). P & G Launches Loading Program in Selected US Markets. Corporate web site, News, November 14, 2005 http://www.pg.com.

Rajagopal (2003). *Sales Force Re-organization for Maintaining Profitable Growth: A Case of Roche Diagnostics Mexico (A),* Discussion case, ITESM, Mexico City Campus, (pp. 1-19).

Rajagopal (2003a). *Building Customer Loyalty through Relationship Networking: A Case of BMW Mexico. Discussion Case*, ITESM, Mexico City Campus, (pp. 1-16).

Rajagopal (2003b). *Striving with Competition in Global Imaging Market: Canon in Mexican Business Environment* ITESM, Mexico City Campus, (pp. 1-22).

Rajagopal (2004). Conceptual Analysis of Brand Architecture and Relationships within Product Category. *Journal of Brand Management, 11*(3), 233-247.

Rajagopal (2005). Virtual Sales Offices for Insurance Services in Mexico: A Case of ING Comercial America, Discussion Case, ITESM, Mexico, (pp. 1-21).

Rajagopal (2006). Innovation and Business Growth through Corporate Venturing in Latin America: Analysis of Strategic Fit. *Management Decision, 44*(5), 703-718.

Schoenmakers, W., & Duysters, G. (2006). Learning in Strategic Technological Alliances. *Technology Analysis and Strategic Management, 18*(2), 245-264.

Tsukioka, A. (2006). Joint venture agreement on food and beverages. Japan Corporate News Network, Feb. 27, 2006.

Webster Jr., F. E. (1989). It's 1990- Do you know where your marketing is? Mass Marketing Science Institute, Cambridge MA.

World Trade Organization (2003). World Trade Report, Executive Summary, WTO, Geneva, (pp. 14-15).

## ENDNOTES

1. Corporate website, Li & Fung http://www.lifung.com
2. For details on the case study please see Case Study :Papa John's, New Business.Com http://www.newbusiness.co.uk/cgi-bin/showArticle.pl?id=3562
3. Ranbaxy Laboratorios Ltd. : Ranbaxy Consolidates Relationship with Japan JV Partner Nippon Chemiphar, Rainbaxy Press Release, November 11, 2005 http://www.ranbaxy.com/newsroom
4. For details see Polycom Corporate Website: Information on strategic ally partners, http://www.polycom.com

[5] Hewlett Packard Development Company: HP Financial Services as Wholly Owned Subsidiary, News Release, Corporate Office, Aug 13, 2002 http://www.hp.com/hpinfo/newsroom/press/2002/020813a.html

# Chapter XIV
# Profit Impact on Marketing Strategy and Brand Management: Methodological Perspectives

**Rajagopal**
*Monterrey Institute of Technology and Higher Education, ITESM, Mexico*

**Amritanshu Rajagopal**
*Dentalia, Mexico*

In developing strategy, both corporate and business unit management need to be able to realistically appraise the level of performance that should be expected for a given business, and to be clear as to what factors explain variations in performance between businesses, and within a business over time. Important guidelines that help address these questions have been developed from the Profit Impact of Market Strategy (PIMS) program[1].

## BACKGROUND TO THE PIMS METHODOLOGY

At the heart of the PIMS program is a business unit research database that captures the real-life experiences of over 5,000 businesses. Each business is a division, product line, or profit centre within its parent company, selling a distinct set of products and/or services to an identifiable group of customers, in competition with a well defined set of competitors, for which meaningful separation can be made of revenue, operating costs, investment, and strategic plans. The business's served market is defined as the segment of the total potential market that it is seriously targeting by offering suitable products and/or services and toward which it is making specific marketing efforts. On this basis each business reports, in standardized format, over 300 items of data, much of it for at least four years of operations. ROI is defined as follows: pre-tax after deduction of corporate expenses but prior to interest charges divided by average investment where this is equivalent to the historic net book value of plant and equipment plus working capital (i.e., total assets less current liabilities). Note that four year averages are used for all figures. The information

*Table 1. Key- determinants of ROI in the PIMS database*

| **Category of factor** | **Impact on ROI as factor increases** |
|---|---|
| Marketplace standing | Positive |
| Market share | Positive |
| Relative market share | Positive |
| Served market concentration | |
| Market environment | Positive |
| Real market growth | Positive |
| Selling price inflation | Positive |
| Market differentiation | Negative |
| Purchase amount immediate customers | Negative |
| Importance of purchase to end user | |
| Differentiation from competitors | Positive |
| Relative product quality | Positive |
| Relative price | Negative |
| Relative direct cost | Negative |
| % Sales new products | Negative |
| Marketing/sales revenueb | Negative |
| R&D/sales revenue | |
| Capital and production structure | Negative |
| Investment/ sales revenue | Negative |
| Investment/ value added | Negative |
| Receivables/ investment | Positive |
| Fixed capital /investment | Negative |
| Capacity utilization | Positive |
| Unionization | Negative |
| Labor effectiveness* | Positive |

collected covers, *inter alia*, the market environment, competitive situation, internal cost and asset structure, and profit performance of the business. A full listing of the information captured by the PIMS database is given by The Strategic Planning, Institute's PIMS data manual[2].

The businesses in the database have been drawn from some 500 corporations, spanning a wide variety of industry settings. These corporations are based for the most part in North America and Europe. An understanding of why one business should be loss making while another achieves premium returns lies at the heart of strategy formulation. To explain this variance, cross-sectional analysis is carried out on the database to uncover the general patterns or relationships that account for these profit differentials. The fundamental proposition that underpins this approach is that the name of a business has no bearing on its level of performance. Research on the database has identified some 30 factors that are statistically significant at the 95 percent probability level or better in explaining the variance in profitability across businesses. These factors, which operate in a highly interactive way, collectively explain nearly 80 percent of the variance in ROI across the database. The more powerful factors are listed in Table 1 under four categories: marketplace standing, market environment, and differentiation production structure. It should be noted at the outset that part of the explanation of variance is definitional. This comes about because some of the profit-explaining variables, such as investment/sales revenue, contain elements, which are also present in the construction of the dependent variable, ROL However; the emphasis is on behavioral relationships. Definitional elements are included in the independent variables only when it is impossible to separate out the behavioral and definitional effects of a particular factor.

## MARKETPLACE STANDING

There are several measures of a business's marketplace standing: market share (the business's sales expressed as a percentage of total sales made within the served market), market share rank., and relative market share (,the business's market share divided by the sum of the shares of its three leading competitors). Whichever measure is adopted, a strong positive correlation between marketplace strength and profitability is observed. It should be remembered that market share in and of itself is not important: it is an output measure which reflects a business's historic and potential ability to gain substantive competitive advantages within its activities and in the marketplace[3]. Factors, which explain the underlying reasons why share may help profitability, are shown in Table 2

*Table 2.*

| *Potential benefits of strong market standing* |
|---|
| * Experience curve" and "learning curve" benefits<br><br>Widely publicized by the Boston Consulting Group, the experience curve effect sees cost per unit come down in a fairly predictable manner as cumulative volume doubles.<br><br>* Economics of scale and scope<br><br>Can drive down cost per unit throughout the cost structure of a business as well as benefiting balance sheet productivity. Key areas for potential benefit are seen to be:<br><br>- Purchases: stronger negotiating stance with suppliers leads to preferential terms<br>- Manufacturing: plant scale and run length<br>- Distribution: drop size and drop density<br>- Marketing/R&D: spreading fixed cost component over a larger number of units<br>- Investment productivity<br><br>• Improved asset utilization<br><br>• Improved ability to control all current asset components and extend current liabilities<br><br>* Relative perceived quality<br><br>Higher market visibility offering the "low-risk" option for buyers in many instances. Scale benefits should give ability to establish stronger brand and better control distribution.<br><br>* Competitive ability<br><br>- Potential to act as "Industry statesman"<br>- Opportunities to set and administer prices<br>- Size may deter competitive attack<br>- Size will heighten ability to control the chain from supplier to customers<br>- Better ability to spread risk and explore more competitive avenues |

Powerful as these factors are, the fact remains there is nothing inevitable about the relationship between share and profitability. Over 30 percent of the businesses in the database with market shares above 40 percent have R01's below the average of 22 percent. These businesses have often become victims of their own success, wedded to historic investment decisions and burdened with complexity costs.

What the PIMS data highlight is the danger of low market share in an environment that is either marketing- or R&D-intensive. This is because both marketing and R&D have many of the characteristics of a fixed cost. Businesses with small market shares often find that they have to spend as much as their larger competitors on these activities, but do not have the same volume over which to spread the costs. The result is that they are trapped in the low-profit cells. The value-for-money in a business is a critical determinant of gaining competitive advantage. PIMS assesses this position by judging a business's relative competitive standing in terms of quality and price. It then examines how that offer is supported by new product activity, marketing, and R&D expenditure and the extent to which price is underpinned by the relative direct cost position of the business. "Relative perceived quality" is seen as the key driver of business performance under this category of factor. Quality in the MIS database is defined from the perspective of the external marketplace. Customers evaluate the total benefit bundle of products and services offered by the business and rank it relative to leading competitors as being superior, equivalent, or inferior. The "relative perceived quality" measure used by PIMS is then computed by subtracting the percentage of product and service attributes that are judged as being superior to competitors from the percentage which is judged as inferior. Relative perceived quality has a major positive impact on profitability. Businesses whose offer is judged as clearly superior to that of competitors on average achieve more than twice the ROI of businesses whose offer is judged as inferior. Not only is the relationship between quality and return one of the key determinants of performance in the database, but it is extremely robust in all types of business and marketplace situations. Businesses that achieve a significant quality advantage relative to their competitors can choose to benefit in one of two ways: either they can charge premium prices or grow market share at competitive pricing levels, or some combination of both. Relative perceived quality is closely related to profitability. The implications appear to be that high-share businesses that offer poor quality weaken in position, while weak-share businesses that offer high quality strengthen in position - both extremes may be transitory in nature.

## Capital and Production Structure

Within this category of factor, the most powerful of the PIMS findings relates to investment intensity. The definition of investment in this context is fixed capital, measured on an historic basis as the net book value of plant and equipment, plus working capital, defined as current assets less current liabilities. Investment intensity itself is measured in two ways: first, investment is rationed to sales revenue in the conventional manner; and, second, investment is rationed to the value added actually generated by the business (where value added is defined as net sales revenue less all outside suppliers' inputs). Both measures are simultaneously employed to assess investment intensity, as many businesses have low levels of investment to sales (turn their asset base frequently) but because of a high bought-in component have high levels of investment to value added, Having cautioned that a balanced view on the overall investment intensity of a business is only achieved by using both measures in combination, on an individual basis each measure is similarly related to profit performance in the PIMS data base, and here the more familiar investment/ sales revenue ratio is employed to illustrate the investment intensity effect.

As the investment intensity in a business rises, so the ROI that it achieves falls dramatically. This finding is the most powerful negative relationship in the database, with R0I's averaging only 8 percent for investment intensive businesses, compared to 38 percent for low investment intensity businesses. The finding is consistent with the experiences of many businesses in sectors such is airlines, shipbuilding, base chemicals, low alloy steel, refining, smelting, and commodity pulp and paper, which in large degree achieve at best modest rates of return. Part of the reason for the relationship is definitional. As the investment level in a business increases, it simultaneously increases the denominator of the R01 ratio, hence dragging down the value of the ratio. That there is a behavioural element to the investment intensity effect is vividly illustrated if the return on sales (ROS) achieved at different levels of investment is considered. If a business is to hold ROI as investment intensity increases, ROS should increase smoothly. In practice, ROS is at best flat, and in fact starts to tail off at higher levels of investment intensity. Moreover, it should be remembered that return has been taken pre-tax and pre-interest, with no financial charge made on the amount of investment used in the business. If even a modest capital charge rate is applied to a business's returns to reflect its investment, the relationship would start to turn sharply down. If businesses were sufficient to offset the level of investment that they need to sustain their sales, there is indeed a powerful behavioural element to the ROI/investment intensity finding.

At the start, it was observed that profit performance varies enormously from business to business and within a business over time. Several of the key research findings arising from the PIMS database that help to explain this variance in performance have been discussed. Care must be cautioned in interpretation. Comprehensive insight is not obtained by examining one or two factors at a time: it requires a multifactor approach in order to start to capture the complexities and tradeoffs in business. To this end, PIMS researchers have developed several models that help assess the level of ROI, cash flow, productivity, and so forth that should be expected for a business, given its structural make-up. Once these benchmarks have been established, attention can be focused on the next stage of strategy formulation; that of managing change. It can be extremely misleading to use the general findings presented for this purpose. That market share is generally closely related to profitability is observable; but that is not to argue, of course, that a business should try to grow share in all instances - the feasibility and cost-benefit trade-off of such a move needs close examination. To this end, other modelling techniques and the database itself, via matched sample, analysis, provide important empirical vehicles for the identification and evaluation of particular strategy moves by researchers and practitioners alike.

## MARKET UNCERTAINTIES AND ENTRY DECISIONS

In turbulent markets the competitive strategy provides the conceptual magnitude that integrates various functional activities and marketing programs for sustaining the competitive threats. The effective competitive strategies have a direct bearing on possessing the relative market share and growth of the business organization. The strategies are the directional statements and need to be converted into the step-by-step plan of action for effective plan implementation. The strategic directions have four options that can be expressed by 4As - arena, advantage, access and activities. The arena may be defined as serving the targeted market segment through an appropriate scale of operations and scope of activities to be performed for competitive advantage. The advantages in the process consist of positioning the products theme that differentiates the business from competitors. The access may be referred to the communication and distribution channels used to reach the market in the uncertain business conditions. These activities are interdependent and are affected by the change in any of the factors. The arena of the market largely dictates the customers to be served by the company, the competitors to by-passes and the key success factors to be considered upon. Each market has distinctive profile of key success factors developed by the attributes of the market. The recent development of corporate strategies shows that many multi-national companies are considering their choice of the market arena based on the following factors:

- There is an increasing trend of market fragmentation. New segments with specific needs are emerging and are being served by the specialist competitors by offering tailor made goods and services.
- The traditional market boundaries are disappearing as a consequence of the rush of substitutes emerging due to the technological growth..
- The transformation of existing self-contained regional and national markets into global markets.

In the above discussed situations the challenge for the corporate sector management may be observed as to find the right balance of global reach and standardization of the activities versus the traditional strategies or local adaptation. The companies need to find out the competitive advantages within the chosen arena of business. The core issue associated with the competitive advantage is positioning of the theme that sets a business apart from the rivals in the way that is meaningful to target the customers. It is necessary for the companies to move aggressively against the competitors to retain their market territories and build a strong defense. Thus Kodak asserted itself in the film market against the strategies of Fuji in American market. The supply gluts also put pressure on advantages. The markets for the pharmaceuticals, electronics and automobiles suffer chronic global overcapacity to the extent of 15-40 percent. Such problem situation demands the companies to develop the strategies of competitive advantage to hold the key success factors and become the market leader. Such strategies are required as there are too many firms competing and the customers may back integrate by their marketing requirement rather than buying them. This situation reduces the volume of market demand relative to supply and the customers may sell their excess capacity on competition with their one-time supplier.

Need for the competitively advantageous strategies may further be justified as a large number of firms are increasingly productive in reference to the rapid diffusion of the technologies. The customers' bargaining power also works out to be an instrument to either broaden or narrow the differences between the competitors. The companies that use intermediaries are often encountered with balancing the power of distribution and delivery of services. In consumer markets the retail trade is forcing major concessions on the multi-national brands. Such strategies hold the access to the retail network through a long chain of channels. Conventionally the choice of appropriate scale in business and scope thereof were guided by the concepts of *the bigger is better* and *umbrella control of activities*. In the current era of globalization the decentralization of activities and production sharing have become more effective tools in marketing. The profit centre approach (PCA), control circles and total quality management practices has endorsed the success of small integrated units operating in a well defined market. In view to promote the PCA concepts and maintain the control circles, the large companies are increasingly creating the autonomous, small and entrepreneurial units to find responsive solutions to the customer problems in the well defined market niches[4]. Corporate structures are changing in order to accommodate the concept of PCA and control circles and are exploring for the long term advantages by way of heavy investment to develop the core competencies.

*BMW, Honda, and Toyota, among other companies, begin with a strong brand that imparts sales momentum to each model. Brands that are weak—because their products have acquired a reputation for shoddy workmanship, their designs are not evocative, or their models bear little relationship to one another—cannot pursue this top-down approach. But a company stands a good chance of selling more cars and, step by step, of rehabilitating the brand if managers take pains to match each model to the consumer segments most likely to be interested in it, identify and overcome the obstacles that keep browsers from becoming purchasers, and emphasize both the functional and the process and relationship benefits of the model in question. BMW Direct is an initiative of BMW (GB) to help selected company car fleet buyers streamline their service for employees. BMW Direct is a web based, fully personalized, car configuration and ordering system for the purchase of new BMWs. This highly efficient rules based web application delivers a level of information previously unavailable outside of a showroom. The BMW Direct solution provides users with the ability to view details on all eligible cars online and then go on to configure them against a full menu of accessories. BMW Direct is truly 'CRM' compliant, providing two-way communication via automated alerts and e-mails and incorporating a Contact Centre to ensure immediate access to trained product advisors. Users can track online the status of their individual orders whether by web, phone, fax or email. The call centre functionality includes phone and e-campaign generation, customer enquiry handling and profiling to customised promotions[5]. Post-sales support is delivered using a thin client solution, (using Citrix) to BMWs contact centre in Croydon and order management centre in Bracknell in UK.*

The technological changes are the main impetus behind new market opportunities. The extent of such change may be explained from super technologies to the appropriate and intermediate technologies. The strategic choices have wide ranging ripple effects through the organization that determine the key success factors and growth performance. Some companies would be making right strategic choices by improving the implementation process of competitive advantages. These companies are guided by the shared strategic vision and are driven by the responsive attitude towards the market requirements. They emphasize the continuous strive to satisfy the customers. A strategic vision in managing markets may be understood as the guiding theme that explains the nature of business and the future projections thereof. These projections or business intentions depend on the collective analysis of the environment that determines the need for the new developments or diversifications. The vision should be commissioned on a concrete understanding of the business and the ability to foresee the impact of market forces on the growth of business. The vision will motivate the organization for collaborative business planning and implementation. The powerful visions are also the statements of intent that create on obsession with winning thorough out the organization[6]. The business strategy broadly incorporates the following dimensions:

- Customer needs
- Consumer segments
- Technology and resources
- Activities in the value added chain

The strategic thrust has a significant magnitude and direction in sailing the business though the turbulent situation. The factors associated with the competitive advantage and business investments uphold the strategic thrust to achieve the business objectives though the positive channel efforts. The competitive advantage may be assessed in reference to the superior customer value and lowest delivered cost. Such combination of the strategies may be termed as competitive superiority that explains cost effective delivery strategy to enhance the customer value. An overall edge is gained by performing most of the activities at a lower cost than competitors. This would enable the company to optimize its cost of delivery of the new products and simultaneously enhance the value of customer value to up-hold the strategic thrust of the company.

*Canon delivers innovative digital business solutions to ensure that its customers achieve and maintain the information edge. The increasingly competitive global marketplace, and the fact that the organizations must store, process and share immense volumes of information with both speed and accuracy have been the key areas of the company to penetrate in the territorial gateways like Mexico for Latin American market. The company functions with four key areas in Mexican market that include marketing, logistics, sales and services operations. The marketing activities of the company consist of planning and budgeting, pricing, forecasting, purchases, marketing research and developing promotional strategies. The company is also engaged in developing attractive media –mix and advertising campaigns and launches the loyalty programs for its major brands. The virtual shopping network is also a major part of the marketing functions performed by the company in the country. The company feels that the loyal, ongoing customers are the backbone of every business and in the prevailing highly competitive environment, these shoppers cannot be ignored or else they may be won over by competitors. The consumers might have bought such products many times in their life or some might have purchased at least once in life time. There is no single way to segment a market. The most important factors influencing a consumer's involvement level are their perceived risks. The purchase of any product involves a certain amount of risk, which may include product failure, financial, operational, social, personal and psychological. The repeat customers are more apt to buy a full range of merchandise, not merely items that are under promotional programs. This means that the dealers and retailers of the company can reach profit margin goals. The logistics functions of the company is largely international trade oriented as the Canon Mexico is a part of Canon USA and many products of the company are acquired from its USA counterpart as inbound logistics. The import process has been one of the major activities of the company in Mexico. The logistics of the company further involves the key activities of transport, inventory management and developing appropriate overseas trade and information strategies*[7].

There are major types of strategies catalogued and given various names by different authors. Often these strategies and tactics are so bold and innovative that they "change the rules of the game." Leaders are increasingly being advised to seek that objective in planning and executing their strategies. The pace of change today is dizzying with new technological breakthroughs occurring at shorter intervals and global competition putting the heat on. Mergers and acquisitions change the competitive landscape unexpectedly, and strategic alliances develop even among the companies that were, or still are, competitors. The concept of "*Hyper-competition* explains the highly aggressive form of competition that characterizes hi-tech industries today. Hyper-competition is said to be increasingly making its way into other industries as well. They speak in terms of surprise, speed and mobility, terms suggestive of the military approach. Not that aggressive action is new in business so much so as the level, intent and severity of business "combat" have changed dramatically. It is necessary to build the strategic business mindset to outwit the competitors and gain competitive advantages over the segmented markets. The following factors need to be considered for achieving the strategic business leadership:

- A clear sense of desired outcomes before acting. Develop a plan capable of delivering outcomes that will add significant value to a state of affairs.
- Explore possibilities outwards to capture the larger context, to see how the pieces fit together.
- Adaptive to realities and flexible in choice of tactics. Recognize that once action begins the "game board" is fluid offering both new threats and new opportunities.
- Wherever possible, attempt to achieve multiple objectives through singular actions.
- Plan a couple of steps ahead of competition.
- Anticipate the actions of business rival and strategically rehearse next responses should those contingencies arise.
- Core discipline to observe the market moves and rival reactions.
- Capitalize on business crises or behavioural change in the markets in order to turn them to advantage.
- Stay future-focused.
- Plan the business strategy implementation in both sequential and parallel direction to accomplish goals and sustain the impact thereof.
- Develop negotiations with the business intermediaries on win-win platform at an acceptable cost.

- Supplement actions with those of others (allies, partners, joint ventures.)
- Be patient, with a good sense of timing.
- Be able to scrap or alter plans when information indicates actions are not attaining their intended results.
- Develop alternate strategies for contingencies
- Use speed and surprise to gain advantage.
- Form alliances with opponents of his opponents in business.
- Learn the strengths and weaknesses of rivals.
- Be aggressive in pursuing goals, cordon the moves and ready to take on to the next.
- Assure that everyone in the company knows one's role and is equipped with the resources to contribute.
- Monitor activities in the operating environment.
- Use "what if" speculation to stretch thinking in the direction of opportunities and possibilities.
- Study the logic of the opponent's tactics with an eye toward determining what their ultimate end purposes may be.

These are some tested aspects of thinking employed by leaders to gain and hold strategic advantage. They can serve as a checklist when responsibilities include thinking strategically. Customers want more of everything they value. If they value low cost they want it lower. If they value convenience they want it easier and faster. If they look for state of the art they want it first and want to push the envelope. If they need expert advice they want more time and dedicated effort and investment. By raising the level of value that customers can expect from everyone, leading companies are driving the market and driving their competitors out of business, or at least into a malaise of mediocrity. Here are a few options for managerial consideration:

- Alter the industry structure to change the basis of competition. Reconfigure the value chain - retailers become wholesalers and suppliers, insurers takeover brokerages, banks move into insurance, etc.
- Improve the position of the business within the industry by way of acquisitions and market share. Alter the playing field to achieve an enhanced scale of operations and competitive positioning.
- Innovate and create new opportunities - new products, services, and markets.
- Employ barriers to entry in terms of significant capital investment, proprietary technology, or in the magnitude of resources required to compete effectively.

- Increase the dependence of customers for products and services in terms of the total value for customers or higher costs of switching to alternates.
- Change and enhance supplier relationships to obtain cost and quality improvements, reduced cycle times, and integrated processes.
- Change the basis of competition by creating a service relationship and differentiation. Move away from price to service, software, and customer relationships.
- Centralize into high volume, low cost, automated, 'focused factories', to achieve the lowest cost operations in support of customer value.
- Decentralize into custom, low volume, flexible factories, quick to market, responsive, and able to customize products to specific customer requirements.

Controls may be considered as checkpoints used to verify performance progress by comparison with some standard in a given competitive environment. Generally the business standards are established by top management in the planning process. The control and analysis process need to be revised with the growing size of the firm and its business operations. Controls must go along with the expansion process and tight control should ensure consistency in product and marketing performance. Since multinational companies typically have several foreign subsidiaries in different parts of the world, a good control system is important to ensure that these subsidiaries move together toward a common goal, spelled out by the corporate strategic plan to meet any market uncertainties. These issues need to be considered in anticipation by the international firms while deciding the entry strategies in foreign markets.

## COMPREHENSIVE BRANDING

Comprehensive branding (CB) may be defined as the management of both the manufacturing and marketing process chain for ensuring the customer perceptions of the products of a company. In other words the company chooses to establish the brand image that is as close as possible to the opinion of the customer that The gathers from the available resources and actually experiences with the product with lowest variation. The concept of comprehensive branding encompasses two components of *total quality management* and *integrated marketing communications*. There is a parallel process to these two programs driven by the creation of delivery of references that the consumer uses in making purchase decisions and utilizing the key tools of benchmarking, specifications and process control. The inputs fro the specifications are provided to the company for design manufacturing process for product and message image by the consultants and suppliers. In turn the message is passed to the agencies by the consultants and suppliers do the same to their employees. The message is carried by the media from the agencies and distributors act as the carriers of product. Both media and distributors deliver the message and products to the customers for setting specifications for the products and message. The actions processed through the consultants, agencies and media constitute the *integrated marketing communication (IMC)* which communicates a consistent message to consumers through alignment of the agencies and media with vision of the company and he image of the brand. The component of *total quality management (TQM)t* is experienced in the comprehensive branding process through the inputs delivered by the suppliers, employees and distributors about the product and services. The TQM helps in communicating the corporate vision to ensure that every step of the product path, form manufacturing to the consumer delivery, maintains the integrity of the brand image. The synergy of IMC and TQM make the company to present the comprehensive branding strategy in the market. In this process the company ensures that all communications and the product paths have total compatibility with the specifications and perceptions of the brand image of the company that has been chosen to portray and as perceived by the customers.

A company's advertising, promotion, changes in name, new logo design or other activities will not successfully build a brand unless there are certain well-defined values which are consistently communicated and demonstrated by the company which are recognised and appreciated by customers. Once brand values have been identified, they should drive all other activities impacting on customers and be used to achieve consistency, which is so meaningful to consumers. All aspects of marketing and communications should reflect the brand values, as should company employees in demonstrating those values in their behaviour to customers .Building a brand is a corporate strategic issue and not a short-term tactical activity. For companies wanting to satisfy the needs of consumers and beat the competition, then building a brand provides an opportunity which, if realised, could do not only this but also defy the test of time - for brands have no limit to their life expectancy. Many brands established in the 1930s are still the top brands in the late '90s. From Coca-Cola to Colgate, Kelloggs to Kodak, we see many examples of the big brands successfully having defended their number one position in their chosen markets and they, along with other famous names, have become synonymous with their industries.

Brand loyalty also means that companies achieve a greater consistency of demand through customer retention. Over time, good brand strategies generate the production volume which gives the economies of scale necessary to have a favourable impact in unit costs. In turn, this allows companies to achieve higher margins, putting them in a winning situation. Brand resilience can help companies ride out stormy weather, as with Mercedes in 1982, when other car manufacturers around the world suffered disastrous sales, apart from Mercedes which continued to sell well: often up to 50 per cent more than other European competitors. And, because of the magnetic influence they have over purchasing behaviour, successful brands allow companies to charge premium prices for their products and services, which of course generate higher profits. Surveys indicate that brand leaders can return a margin four to six times that of the closest competitors. Brands can even assist moves across industries to penetrate new markets. Dunhill is an excellent example of this. Formerly based in the declining-image industry of tobacco, Dunhill is now firmly established internationally in upmarket clothing, toiletries and fashion accessories.

A firm, which would like to involve itself in the international business, may look for its entry into international marketing in many possible ways including exporting, licensing, franchising, or as a production firm with multi-national plant locations. However, at any level of market entry the managerial trade-off lies between extent of risk and operational control. The low intensity modes of entry minimize risk *e.g.* contracting with a local distributor requires no investment in the destination country market as the local distributors may own offices, distribution facilities, sales personnel, or marketing campaigns. Under the normal arrangement, whereby the distributor takes title to the goods or purchases them as they leave the production facility of the international company, there is not even a credit risk, assuming that the distributor has offered a letter of credit from his bank. At the same time such arrangement to enter a destination country may minimize control along with the risk factor. In many cases, low-intensity modes of market participation cut off the international firm with information network while operational controls can only be obtained through higher-intensity modes of market participation, involving investments in local executives, distribution, and marketing programs.

*Breakfast cereal, a relatively new introduction to the Bulgarian market, is the fastest growing sector in the Bulgarian bakery products market. According to a research study*[8]*, ready-to-eat breakfast cereals grew by 90 percent in value terms during 2000-2005 and the market grew by approximately 14 percent just in 2005. Despite this impressive growth, cereal consumption in Bulgaria is low compared to other countries, which illustrates the immaturity of the market and its potential for the future. Besides the "novelty" of breakfast cereals, a key reason for the success of breakfast cereals in Bulgaria is their healthy image, which manufacturers have carefully created by illustrating that their products are part of a balanced diet. Although the concept of health and wellness is growing in popularity in Bulgaria, consumers still need additional education on the subject. The foreign cereal manufacturing companies like Nestle, Kraft, Kellogg and General Mills etc. have therefore invested heavily in radio and television advertising to promote a healthy* *image for their products and attract health conscious consumers. These companies have also set up demonstrations in supermarkets that are designed to educate consumers on the health benefits of breakfast cereals. By using samples and other promotional materials, manufacturers have tried to inspire trials and eventually repeat purchases of their products. These campaigns mainly targeted the bigger cities, where consumers are generally more willing to try new products. The entry of foreign brands in the breakfast cereals in Bulgaria is further moved ahead by the fast expansion of supermarkets and the development of this distribution channel over the next several years will play a crucial role in making breakfast cereals more widely available*[9].

Many companies begin their internationalization opportunistically through a variety of arrangements that may be described as "piggybacking," because they all involve taking advantage of a channel to an international market rather than selecting the country-market in a more conventional manner. Piggybacking is an interesting development. The method means that organizations with little exporting skill may use the services of one that has. Another form is the consolidation of orders by a number of companies in order to take advantage of bulk buying. Normally these would be geographically adjacent or able to be served, say, on an air route. The fertilizer manufacturers of Zimbabwe, for example, could piggyback with the South Africans who both import potassium from outside their respective countries. Such practices may be noticed as American breakfast cereal products like Post from the owners of the leading US brand, which entered in the Mexican market via their subsidiary Kraft rather than direct from USA, thus leading to the rather bizarre situation of packs of breakfast cereals with English language packaging covered with stickers in Spanish. The most common form of piggybacking is to internationalize by serving a customer who is more international than the vendor firm. Thus, a customer requests an order, delivery, or service in more than one country, and the supplier starts selling internationally in order to retain the customer and increases its penetration of the account. This is particularly common in the case of business-to-business companies and technology-oriented start-ups[10]. The innovative concept of market entry strategy is based on moving with *consumer space* which indicates that foreign firms enter the destination market by developing adequate consumer awareness on the products and services prior to launch. This strategy is followed largely by the fast moving consumer goods manufacturing companies and such practice is termed as go-to-market strategy. Go-to-market planning enables the firm to achieve higher margins, accelerated revenue growth and increased customer satisfaction through existing sales channels. An effective go-to-market strategy aligns products & services, processes, and partners with customers and markets to deliver brand promise, the desired customer experience, and tangible value. Go-to-market strategy services help technology suppliers overcome market challenges.

*Anti-ageing products are driving growth in Hong Kong's skin care market, on the back of increasing consumer interest in premium products and the development of consumer-focused cosmetics retailing. Consumer interest in premium products has been spurred, in part, by recent media reports on the safety of chemicals present in some skin care products. Catching on to this consumer trend, manufacturers have been introducing more premium anti-ageing products containing rare ingredients, and products benefiting from more advanced technology, to the market. This has generated greater consumer interest in premium quality products and has provided a further boost to the market. Guerlain, for example, is expected to launch a new skin care cream in 2006, which is based on a rare orchid extract and is expected to retail for more than US$350. Further, a recent entrant to Hong Kong's skin care market, Sulwhasoo which is a premium herbal based brand from Amore Pacific of Korea that draws on Oriental medicine by using a unique compound of five herbs to deliver a range of products targeted at women over 35. The value driver of growth in the anti-ageing products market in Hong Kong is the trend towards concept stores and beauty boutiques, which are retail outlets designed to emphasize the experiential aspects of premium cosmetic products. Developed to attract new customers and gain their loyalty in Hong Kong's increasingly competitive market, these brand-specific beauty salons and spas, not only engage in a highly personalized product sales process, but also provide make-up and skin care services. Since 2004, major players, such as Kose, L'Oréal, H2O and cult brand Aesop, have set up concept stores around the city, in the hopes of developing a loyal customer base[11]. Such retail strategy where concept of the product is delivered with practical experience on it establishes the go-to-market strategy on consumer space.*

Some firms who are aggressive have clearly defined plans and strategy, including product, price, promotion, and distribution and research elements. Passiveness versus aggressiveness depends on the motivation to export. In countries like Tanzania and Zambia, which have embarked on structural adjustment programs, organizations are being encouraged to export, motivated by foreign exchange earnings potential, saturated domestic markets, growth and expansion objectives, and the need to re-pay debts incurred by the borrowings to finance the programs. The type of export response is dependent on how the pressures are perceived by the decision maker. The degree of involvement in foreign operations depends on "endogenous versus exogenous" motivating factors, that is, whether the motivations were a result of active or aggressive behavior based on the firm's internal situation (endogenous) or a result of reactive environmental changes (exogenous)[12]. There is certainly no single strategy that fits all firms, products and markets. The competitive strategy for an established firm to start a new venture and launch a new product must be shaped by the characteristics of the firm, the market, and other environmental factors. Market entry through expansion of the company draws many challenges to firms considering new business options. Capitalizing on overseas markets often opens doors to new levels of top and bottom line growth. Moreover, introducing a new product or service into a new market is an even bigger strategic challenge. A Successful Entry strategy may conceptualize and implement well structured entry processes to drive future growth, explore diversified stream of revenues and augment profit margins. It also addresses new competitors, customers, partners, suppliers and other market dynamics. However, there are five major modes which a foreign firm may apply to enter in the international markets. These modes of entry include exporting, contractual agreement, joint venture, strategic alliance

## REFERENCES

Albrinck, J., Hornery, J., Kletter, D., & Neilson, G. (2001). Adventures in corporate venturing. *Strategy and Business, 22*, 119-129.

Biggadyke, R. (1979). The risky business diversification. *Harvard Business Review, 57*, 103-111.

Frost, P. J., & Egri, C. P. (1990). Influence of political action on innovation: Part I: *Leadership and Organization Development Journal, 11*(1), 17-25.

Ghemawat, P. (1991). *Commitment: The dynamics of strategy.* New York: Free Press.

Ligos, M., Cohen, A., & Gilbert, J. (2004, May). Extreme makeovers. *Sales and Marketing*

*Management, 156*(5), 36-43.

Suarez, F. F., & Lanzolla, G. (2005, April). The half yruth of first mover advantage. *Harvard Business Review*, 1-8 (Ref R 0504J).

Tushman, M., & Nadler, D. (1986). Organizing for innovation. *California Management Review, 3*(1), 73-84.

Zahra, S. A. (1993). Environment, corporate entrepreneurship and financial performance: A taxonomic approach. *Journal of Business Venturing, 8*(4), 319-340.

Zahra, S. A. (1996). Governance, ownership and corporate entrepreneurship: The moderating impact of industry's technological opportunities. *Academy of Management Journal, 39*(6), 1713-1735.

Zimmerman, E. (2004, January). Motivation on any budget, *Sales & Marketing Management, 156*(1), 37-44.

## ENDNOTES

1 Schoeffier S, Buzzell, R D and Heany D F (1974), Impact of strategic planning on profit performance, Harvard Business Review, 52 (2), 137-45

2 Buzzell R D and Gale B T (1987), The PIMS principles, New York, The Free Press

3 Buzzell R D, Gale B T and Sultan R G M (1975), Market share - a key to profitability, Harvard Business Review, 53 (1), 97-106

4 Frederick E Webster Jr.: It's 1990- Do you know where your marketing is?, Mass Marketing Science Institute, Cambridge 1989.

5 Rajagopal (2003), Building Customer Loyalty Through Relationship Networking : A Case of BMW Mexico, Discussion Case, ITESM, Mexico City Campus, 1-16

6 Day Geogr. S (1990), Market Driven Strategy: Process for Creating Value, The Free Press, New Cork, 10-18

7 Rajagopal (2003), Striving with Competition in Global Imaging Market : Canon in Mexican Business Environment, ITESM, Mexico City Campus, 1-22

8 Euromonitor (2006): Breakfast Cereals Boom in Bulgaria, January

9 Ibid

10 David Arnold (2003): The Mirage of Global Marketing: How Globalizing Companies can Succeed as Markets Localize, Financial Times Prentice Hall, Upper Saddle River, NJ, 24-65

11 Olivier Hofmann (2006), Anti-ageing Skin Cream Booms in Hong Kong, Euromonitor, May (online edition)

12 Piercy, N (1982), Company Internationalization: Active and Reactive Exporting". European Journal of Marketing, 15 (3), 26-40.

# Chapter XV
# Technology and Retailing Firms:
## Challenges Ahead

**Rajagopal**
*Monterrey Institute of Technology and Higher Education, ITESM, Mexico*

Technology is associated as one of the principal factors of production and economic growth of a country or development sector as an agent of growth and prosperity. However, retailing sector which is part of the distribution side of the economy has also contributed significantly to advances in technology, economic growth and the betterment of society. Technology and retailing have been inextricably linked both in terms of their development and their ability to deliver unique benefits to consumers (Tamilia and Reid, 2007). Increasing globalization and competitiveness in the retail environment is thrusting retail firms to reach high levels of consistent experimentation of new technology in store management, product information, and customer services. Technology management can be used to help retailers test new ideas and implement the most successful ones. However, human behavior is particularly important in the retail setting, where projects are generally focused on testing new concepts, increasing collaboration, and implementing new technologies (Thomas *et al,* 2008).

In the scenario of growing competition, retailer firms can also establish how a customer relationship management and monitoring system ensures the buying decision making process through the use of joint project teams and facilitating technology. Development and innovative applications of e-commerce transactions, as well as the integration of available technology, can provide an organization with a unique opportunity to remain competitive within today's global business environment. Although technology plays an important role in gaining a competitive advantage for organizations worldwide, information technology professionals, consumers and e-retailers ensure proper security measures to overcome harmful impact of the misuse of these same technologies (Medlin and Romaniello, 2008).

## TECHNOLOGY SHIFTS IN RETAILING

The history of retailing also dates back with a history of the role of technology in society. A bird's eye view at the evolution of retailing reveals that technology has played a role as the primary enabler of change. As technology grows sophisticated, the consumer's expectations also swell exponentially. In fact the convergence of a few key technologies is enabling that change. Smart cards payment technology has driven new revolution in retailing as this technology has not only helped in increase the quick buying decisions of consumers but also attracted large mass of potential customers into retail gamut. Smart cards have offered a wide variety of applications that could revolutionize payment transactions, reduce costs, and spur online purchasing. Despite the benefits these electronic purses offer, a number of issues inhibit their widespread use, especially in open systems. A tested technology, smart cards can store various types of encrypted information as well as cash balances and digital signatures. A secret key can be used to secure e-commerce transactions as well as protect the card contents. These keys are vulnerable to attack, however, and the stored-value feature is attractive to international money launderers. Despite some risk factors the smart cards are globally accepted by the retailers (Kearns and Loy, 2003).

There has been a significant change in retail trading over the years. Modernization, systematization, and consolidation are the catch phrases and keys to understanding retail. The present age is that of rocket science retailing which is an act of blending the traditional forecasting systems with the prowess of information technology. It fuses data and instinct with computer models to create a high-tech forecasting system supported by a flexible supply chain. The need is to evaluate not what the retailer sold but what it could not sell and what it could have sold had the inventory been available. Merchandise decisions have become more complex and the penalties for errors even steeper. To reduce the fallouts and to increase the customer satisfaction, merchandise planning has become all the more important. A new set of software tools and sophisticated techniques have emerged, which promise to revolutionize the entire merchandising chain, from buying to stocking to pricing. The latest techniques used for efficient inventory management include vendor managed inventory, forecasting techniques, inventory classification, computer assisted ordering, distribution centers and direct store delivery (Kumar and Banga, 2007).

The technology impact on the various functions in retailing has been increasing. As the number of channels for a retailer increases, managing the dynamics of customer behaviour in the rapidly emerging multi-channel environment becomes complex. Building and retaining a long-term association with customers require that relationship management applications should be able to accommodate the various channels. Multi-channel customers are the most valuable customers and hence multi-channel integration would improve customer loyalty and retention (Ganesh, 2004). Besides self service retail stores and grocery stores, the technology has enormously supported the buying process of consumers for capital goods like automobiles. The purchase of a car is a highly involved process when compared with other retail experiences. Despite the range of purchase channels available and the increased level of accessible information, the majority of customers still choose to buy a car through a traditional dealer network. However, since the end of twentieth century the computer assisted buying process was well received by customers (Reed and Sekar, 2004).

E-shopping is influenced by time and attractiveness of virtual sales offers and effectiveness of customer relations. These factors vary widely in reference to consumer segments and markets attractiveness and induce compulsive buying behavior among customers, which is judged by the satisfaction in spending and perceiving pleasure of buying occasionally exercising choice and passing time in knowing new products, services, technologies and understanding fellow customers (Watkins and Bond, 2007, Rajagopal 2007). Retailers using a "store as the brand" strategy invest in creating a specific, unique shopping experience for their target customer and encourage leisure and group buying behavior where delivery of customer satisfaction seems to be an effective source of differentiation (Carpenter *et al*, 2005). Change-of-season sales are most frequently introduced with attractive sales promotions in reference to price discounts or two for one price basis and linked with objectives of moving a volume of stock. Retail promotional sales also include general sales, and these are linked with other promotional objectives and activities such as increasing profit and inventory management (Fam, 2003). A company's information technology (IT) structure and its brand architecture are intended to minimize transaction costs both within the organization and between the organization and its customers. Business-to-consumer (B-to-C) e-commerce fundamentally alters the structure of those transaction costs relevant to the IT structure and the brand architecture. Manufacturing companies typically implement contemporary changes in the IT structure and the brand architecture to support consumers in retail buying as B-to-C e-commerce is highly important to them and that these changes result in a stronger integration within and between the IT structure and the brand architecture (Treiblmaier and Strebinger, 2008).

## TECHNOLOGY FOR STORE MANAGEMENT AND PAYMENTS

Information and Internet-based technologies have fostered new supply chain initiatives in food retailing which have significantly contributed towards enhancing the efficiency of store format, membership in a chain, unionization, and adoption of variety of information diffusion tools. The major breakthrough has emerged in supply chain management in the fields of data sharing, decision sharing, and technologies that support product assortment, pricing, and merchandising decisions (Timothy and Robert, 2007). Among many innovative technological processes, radio frequency identification (RFID) is gaining popularity among retail firms for managing the inventory and just-in-time supplies. RFID tag has the potential to significantly reduce costs in retailing. Although this technology is still not cost effective for all manufacturers, it may soon become mainstreamed as its advantages outweigh its initial investment. With many manufacturers and vendors becoming early adopters, the cost barrier for RFID will quickly be eliminated. It is unlikely, however, that RFID tags will replace bar codes in the near future because of the start-up cost to retailers and suppliers (Pate *et al*, 2007). RFID tags enhance the operational efficiency as the retailers can store much more information about products than bar codes can, and unlike bar codes they don't have to be seen by a scanner to be recorded. In fact, RFID tags can signal their presence to scanners a few yards away even when obscured by packaging, so the contents of a closed container can be quickly scanned and recorded. It is observed in many research studies that logistics and information technology strategies are developed and implemented in a parallel way by both manufacturers and multiple retailers. Applying improved technology suggests that multinational firms possess greater operational efficiency at both secondary and in-store distribution operations as compared to firms using conventional practices, which is largely attributed to their integration of logistics and information technology operations (Bourlakis and Bourlakis, 2006).

There other technology based innovative payments systems were developed in emerging economies. China views the development of a low-cost, noncash payment network in rural areas as critical to increasing rural spending and closing the wealth gap with urban areas. A payment-settlement system among merchants, banks, and mobile-phone network providers has been a major revolution in the application the technology with low rate of investment which can quickly be recouped through transaction commission fees and mobile-phone usage charges. An SMS-based payment system, closely fits into the personal, economic and operational requirements to make payments as users simply send an SMS message specifying the mobile-phone number of the payee and the amount to transfer, along with a personal identification number. Within seconds, the payee receives both a confirmation message by SMS and the money in the designated account. The payer receives a confirmation message. Consumers can also make retail purchases or pay services, use the system to receive payments like salaries and wages, or transfer money to friends and relatives. Large migrant labor pool of China and India also have access to such technology benefit which has proved to be convenient, inexpensive, and secure system for sending money home. The experience of the Philippines shows that SMS-based payment systems have been widely followed and further rapidly catching on to new "mobile-wallet" systems. Advances in technologies have allowed service providers to incorporate many different technologies into the delivery of their services. These technologies have been implemented in the service encounter for the customer to use with varying degrees of success. The factors influencing consumer attitudes towards and adoption of self-service technologies (SSTs) across three different technologies used in the banking industry reveals that service attributes related to trust, quality and time are major attributes influence attitudes toward each of these technologies and offers an explanation of the varying degrees of acceptance found among consumers (Curren and Mueter, 2005). Online retailing and the digitization of merchandizing has changed the commercial landscape where virtual shelf space is infinite and consumers can search through innumerable options. Traditional marketing research methods such as test markets, focus groups and controlled field experiments observe certain limitations. Some are vulnerable to observation and manipulation by competitors while the virtual store not only addresses those limitations and broadens the horizons of marketing research (Raymond, 1996).

## DRIVING THROUGH E-COMMERCE

The rapid development of electronic commerce (e-commerce) has seen emerging electronic service retailers attracting the interest of, and gaining the patronage of, both service providers and customers. However, there is consensus that the e-commerce industry in general has not been able to cope with all the challenges of, and to realize the true potential of, the technology-based marketplace. Some research studies argue that although the Internet marketplace possesses unique characteristics, there are certain traditional values that remain central to business success in all markets (La and Kandampully, 2002). In an increasingly competitive market there is a keen interest among retailers to understand as much as possible about consumer behavior. Advances in technology have presented retail marketers with many new research tools with which to monitor such behavior. Video monitoring technology offers an objective and accurate research tool for retailers to keep a watch on consumer behavior (Kirkup and Carrigan, 2000). However it is a wrong notion for those managers, who believe that filling their websites with a broad array of information, diverts attention from their company's core offerings. A new global study, however, has revealed that such information increases customer attractiveness and using consumers' desire for providing better value is the strongest predictor of superior shareholder value for e-commerce companies (Eisingerich and Kretschmer, 2008).

It has been recognized that enhancing the role of technology in a service organization would serve to reduce costs and improve service reliability. The new information technology is becoming an important factor in the future development of financial **services** industry, and especially **banking** industry. However, it is argued that there remains an important role for customized relationships in the delivery of any service proposition (Durkin *et al*, 2008). A large number of customers use the Internet, as a medium of business (electronic-commerce). Association of self service technologies with customers indicate that six attributes common to the diffusion model including perceived convenience and financial benefits, risk, previous use of the telephone for a similar purpose, self-efficacy, and Internet use, play a significant role in the performance of retail banking operations (Eastin, 2002). It can be state that banks adopting information technology based capital-intensive techniques are more efficient as both cost and profit frontier gain competitive advantage in the financial markets (Casolaro and Gobby, 2007).

The most important electronic commerce design goal was developed to address electronic commerce as a whole, securing the essential steps of each e-commerce transaction including the offer, the order and the payment. Globe-ID(R) is a system based on an intermediation server which acts as a trusted third party for merchants and consumers. It contributes directly to the security and notarization of the transactions, manages the e-commerce player accounts, and acts as a gateway to the private networks of traditional financial instruments (Pays and de Comarmond, 1996). In order to get along with increasing competition, retailing firms need to encourage usage of advanced technology. However, adoption of new technology may require substantive cognitive efforts from both retailers and consumers. Therefore, firms should be able to influence their consumer's knowledge base and diffuse successful concept for high-tech marketing. This process has so far been used only marginally means that the most prominent high-technology marketers are likely, little by little, to dominate their market (Hanninen and Sandberg, 2006). The use of e-commerce is basically unaffected by the size of the city where the household lives. Geographically remote consumers are discouraged from purchasing goods by the fact that they cannot inspect them beforehand. Leisure activities and cultural items (i.e., books, CDs, and tickets for museums and theaters) are the only goods and services for which e-commerce is used more in isolated areas (de Blasio, 2008).

In increasing global competition, the retailers whether running a physical store, a catalog business, an e-commerce site, or a combination of the three, need to offer customers superior solutions to their needs, treat them with respect, and connect with them on an emotional level. Retailers also have to set prices fairly and make it easy for people to find what they need, pay for it quickly, and then move on. Hence, e-commerce is shifting--from making purchases online to going shopping online, a social experience in which people interact in a 3-D Web space. Moving ahead with the growing technology in the days to come in all sorts of markets, customers will use choice-boards, an interactive buying platform and manufacturing companies and retailers would be able to use on-line systems that let people develop design of their own products by choosing from a menu of attributes, prices, and delivery options. It is found that self service technologies which can be customized by the users build higher sense of belongingness and safety with the banking industry. The association with the self service technologies in a financial operations lead to three forms of positive attachment, based on three different foundations, which include the credibility of the organization, compatibility between the values of the organization and those of the consumer, and interpersonal or relational considerations (Aldlaigan and Buttle *et al*, 2005).

## TECHNOLOGY AND GLOBALIZATION

It has been observed that the technology has homogenized the world markets for variety of customer and industrial needs. The reduction in the tariff barriers, duties and liberalization process worldwide has further given a stimulus to the international marketing across the regional boundaries. Markets today not only provide the multiple goods and services to the customers but also expose their behavior to the cross-cultural differences and innovations. The specialization of the production process has also brought such cultural changes by business penetrations in the low production skills regions across the countries. The apparel from Asian countries like Indonesia, Korea and all types of consumer goods from China, electronics from Japan and perfumery from France may be some good examples to explain the specialization and cross-cultural sharing of consumer behavior. Conducting business is a creative enterprise and doing it out of one's own country is more demanding. The industry structure varies dramatically across the countries in the world and a global enterprise to strive against odds requires strong adaptation behavior. In the international business, a company needs to best prepare itself to achieve competitive advantage in the marketplace. The international partnering in reference to production technology, co-branding, distribution and retailing may bring a high success to the companies of home country in increasing the market share in the region as well as augmenting the customer value for mutual benefit.

The emergence of virtual shopping and liberalization of economic policies in the developing countries all over the world competition has become like a traditional derby in which many companies participate for neck to neck race. In this business game the rules are subject to change without notice, the prize money may change in short notice, the route and finish line is also likely to change after the race begins, new entrants may join at any time during the race, the racers may form strong alliances, all creative strategies are allowed in the game and the state legislation may change without notice and sometimes with retrospective effect. Hence, to win the race any company should acquire the strategies of outwitting, outmaneuvering and outperforming the competitors. In this process, a company must understand thoroughly all the moves of the rival firms from various sources. The locales of the business rivalry have to be spotted to assess their strengths. Under the given situation it may be necessary for a firm to hold the shoulder of a strong brand to swim across the competitive safely enhancing the reach to the markets. To do so, international partnering may prove to be one of the most popular and low risk strategies.

The companies of developing countries may look into this concept not only for growing their market share in the region, also to acquire long-term sustainability in the international business by using new technologies in financial and marketing operations. There may also be possibility of engaging the strategic international relationship with two or more companies to cooperate out of mutual need and to share the risk in achieving common objectives. The star alliance in aviation industry and multiple alliances in e-commerce *e.g.* Microsoft, Telmex-Podigy in Mexico as Internet service provider company, may be described as the success agents of multiple international partnering strategy. Such alliances would offer opportunities for rapid expansion into new markets, access to new technology and the scope of profit optimization.

## REFERENCES

Aldlaigan, A., & Buttle, F. (2005). Beyond satisfaction: customer attachment to retail banks. *The International Journal of Bank Marketing*, *23*(4), 349-359.

Bourlakis, M., & Bourlakis, C. (2006). Integrating logistics and information technology strategies for sustainable competitive advantage. *Journal of Enterprise Information Management*, *19*(4), 389-402.

Casolaro, L., & Gobbi, G. (2007). Information Technology and Productivity Changes in the Banking Industry. *Economic Notes*, *36*(1), 43-76.

Curran, J. M., & Meuter, M. L. (2005). Self-service technology adoption: comparing three technologies. *Journal of Services Marketing*, *19*(2), 103-113.

de Blasio, G. (2008). Urban-Rural Differences in Internet Usage, e-Commerce, and e-Banking: Evidence from Italy. *Growth and Change*, *39*(2), 341-367.

Durkin, M. (2007). Understanding registration influences for electronic banking. *The International Review of Retail, Distribution and Consumer Research*, *17*(3), 219-231.

Eisingerich, A. B., & Kretschmer, T. (2008). In E-commerce more is more. *Harvard Business Review*, *86*(3), 20-21.

Ganesh, J. (2004). Managing customer preferences in a multi-channel environment using Web services. *International Journal of Retail & Distribution Management*, *32*(3), 140-146.

Hanninen, S., & Sandberg, B. (2006). Consumer learning roadmap: a necessary tool for new products. *International Journal of Knowledge and Learning*, *2*(3), 298-307.

Kearns, G. S., & Loy, S. (2003). Global acceptance of stored-value smart cards: Analysis of inhibitors and facilitators. *International Journal of Services Technology and Management*, *3*(4), 417-428.

Kirkup, M., & Carrigan, M. (2000). Video surveillance research in retailing: Ethical issues. *International Journal of Retail & Distribution Management*, *28*(11), 470-480.

Kumar, B., & Banga, G. (2007). Merchandise planning: An indispensable component of retailing. *The Icfaian Journal of Management Research*, *6*(11), 7-19.

La, K. V., & Kandampully, J. (2002). Electronic retailing and distribution of services: Cyber intermediaries that serve customers and service providers. *Managing Service Quality*, *12*(2), 100-116.

Medlin, B. D., & Romaniello, A. (2008). The cost of electronic retailing: Prevalent security threats and their results. *International Journal of Electronic Marketing and Retailing*, *2*(1), 80-96.

Pate, S. S., Blaylock, K., & Southward, L. (2007). RFID: An interface survey between students and retailers. *The Marketing Review*, *7*(3), 273-281.

Pays, P. A., & de Comarmond, F. (1996). An intermediation and payment system technology. *Computer Networks and ISDN Systems*, *28*(7), 1197-1206.

*Rajagopal (2007). Influence of Brand Name in Variety Seeking Behavior of Consumers: An Empirical Study. International Journal of Management Practice, 2(4), 306-323.*

Raymond, B. R. (1996). Virtual Shopping: Breakthrough in Marketing Research. *Harvard Business Review, 74*(2), 120-131.

Reed, G., Story, V., & Saker, J. (2004). Information technology: changing the face of automotive retailing? *International Journal of Retail & Distribution Management, 32*(1), 19-32

Tamilia, R. D., & Reid, S. E. (2007). Technological innovation and the rise of the department store in the 19th century. *International Journal of Technology Marketing, 2*(2), 119-139.

Thomas, R., Tillmann, W., & Fawcett, S. (2008). Project management in retailing: integrating the behavioral dimension. *The International Review of Retail, Distribution and Consumer Research, 18*(3), 325-341.

Timothy, P., & Robert, K. (2007). Evaluating food retailing efficiency: the role of information technology. *Journal of Productivity Analysis, 27*(2), 101-113.

Treiblmaier, H., Strebinger, A. (2008). The effect of e-commerce on the integration of IT structure and brand architecture. *Information Systems Journal, 18*(5), 479-498.

Watkins, M., & Bond, C. (2007). Ways of experiencing leisure. *Leisure Sciences, 29*(3), 287-307.

# About the Authors

**Dr. Rajagopal** is Professor of Marketing at Monterrey Institute of Technology and Higher Education (ITESM), Mexico City Campus and Fellow of the Royal Society for Encouragement of Arts, Manufacture and Commerce, London. He is also conferred as Fellow of the Institute of Operations Management, UK in 2009. He has been listed with biography in various international directories including Who's Who in the World, 2008 and 2009, and 2000 Outstanding Intellectual of the 21st Century published in 2008 by International Biographical Center, Cambridge UK. He teaches Competitor Analysis, Marketing Strategy, Advance Selling Systems, International Marketing, Services Marketing, New Product Development and other subjects of contemporary interest to the students of undergraduate, graduate and doctoral programs. Dr. Rajagopal holds masters and doctoral degrees in Economics and Marketing respectively from Ravishankar University in India. His specialization is in the fields of Marketing Management, Rural Economic Linkages and Development Economics. He has to his credit 27 books on marketing and rural development themes and over 300 research contributions that include published research papers in national and international refereed journals. He has imparted training to senior executives and has conducted 55 management development programs. His research contributions have been recognized by the Government of Mexico and he has been awarded the status of National Researcher (SNI-level II) since 2004.

* * *

**Ananya Rajagopal** has obtained Bachelor's degree in Industrial and Systems Engineering form Monterrey Institute of Technology and Higher Education (ITESM), Mexico City Campus and also earned Bachelor's degree in International Business Administration from Alliant International University, San Diego, USA. She has been associated with various research projects during her studies and published couple of research papers in international refereed journals. She has worked extensively on retail banking and currently affiliated to HSBC Mexico at the corporate office as Project Leader- Latin America in Human Resources division.

**Amritanshu Rajagopal** is an Industrial and Systems Engineering at Monterrey Institute of Technology and Higher Education (ITESM), Mexico City Campus and is actively involved in marketing research projects. He has published couple of papers in refereed international journals and presented research works in international conferences. Currently he is serving as Zonal Coordinator in Dentalia, Mexico.

**Dr. Jesus Enrique Potillo Pizaña** has obtained Born Bachelor's degree in Marketing and Master's degree on Business Administration from Monterrey Institute of Technology and Higher Education (ITESM). Dr. Jesus Enrique has also earned Master's degree from the American Graduate School of International Management (Thunderbird). He got doctoral degree in Business Administration with specialization in marketing, from ITESM and the University on North Carolina in Chapel Hill. He has been professor and Director of different departments at ITESM since 1993 and currently serving as Dean of Undergraduate Programs, and Research and Technological Development at the same institution. He has participated in several research and consultancy projects. Dr. Jesus Enrique has also conducted several marketing and research Seminars at national and international levels.

**Preeta Vyas** is a Research Associate in the marketing area at Indian Institute of Management, Ahmedabad. A Ph.D. from Gujarat University, she teaches basic marketing course and advertising and sales promotion course at IIMA and other leading management institutes in India. She has done extensive research in the area of sales promotion and related fields and written cases and working papers. She presented a paper at the International Conference on E-Commerce Research at Dallas, US, in October 2003. She was invited to present a paper at the International Conference on Economics and Business Research in December 2005 at Miami, US and at IAMB conference at Singapore in March 2007. She has visited business schools in Paris, Scotland, and University of North Florida in 2002-2003.

**Ankush Sharma** has obtained Bachelor's degree in Engineering with specialization in industrial and production engineering stream. He has also acquired Post-graduate Diploma in Management with specialization in marketing from the Institute of Technology and Management, Mumbai (India). Mr. Sharma has been working in the field of consumer durable products and market research in corporate firms. He has done research in the areas of retailing and consumer durable as well as packaging in grocery vertical network. Currently he is Faculty in the Institute for Technology Management in Navi Mumbai, India.

**Ernesto Fierros** is an Electronic and Telecommunications Engineer from Monterrey Institute of Technology and Higher Education (ITESM), Mexico City Campus since 2005. He achieved his Masters degree from the same Institute in Telecommunication Management in 2007. He is currently working with his own enterprise engaged in providing solar and wind renewable energy solutions, developed in association with Solherco SA de CV, a Mexican Company.

# Index

## C



## D

## U



## V



## W